Praise for *Character M*

"In a world where the hole in the moral ozone continues to widen, *Character Matters* is an absolute must read. With Lickona's brilliant new manual, parents and teachers have what they need to do what matters most: help their children become people of solid character."

—Michele Borba, Ed.D., author of *Building Moral Intelligence* and *Don't Give Me That Attitude!*

"One of our nation's foremost authorities on character education, Tom Lickona has made another major contribution to the character education movement. Whether you are a parent, teacher, student, or concerned member of the school community, *Character Matters* will be an invaluable resource for implementing quality character education."

—Sanford McDonnell, chairman of the board of the Character Education Partnership and chairman emeritus of McDonnell Douglas Corporation

"Tom Lickona has done it again. This outstanding book is the ideal blend of theory and practice. It is a wonderful resource for parents, teachers, and all those concerned with our young."

—Kevin Ryan, founder and director emeritus of the Boston University Center for the Advancement of Ethics and Character

"*Character Matters* is an extremely useful book for all—whether they be parents, teachers, or counselors—who work with young people. Down-to-earth, pithy, accessible, the book is full of sound advice and practical help. We should all be deeply grateful to its author, Tom Lickona, for sharing his considerable wisdom with us."

—F. Washington Jarvis, headmaster, The Roxbury Latin School, Boston

"*Character Matters* is both a tour de force and an excellent guide for parents and teachers who want to help young people toward strong character development. It will be useful both in public schools and in programs where religious values are recognized as part of character formation. If you are really concerned about the character development of young people in our culture, you may find yourself buying several copies!"

—Fr. Benedict J. Groeschel, C.F.R., psychologist and
author of *Spiritual Passages*

"*Character Matters* offers a comprehensive set of hands-on strategies for helping children develop the strong moral character they need to navigate the challenges of adolescence and adulthood. Imbued with a clear vision of the potential and promise of young people and punctuated with illustrations and anecdotes, this book makes character education eminently accessible, enormously creative, and a highly collaborative undertaking. Lucid, engaging, and rich in practical wisdom, *Character Matters* is a must read for parents and educators who care about the kinds of *persons* our children will become."

—Karen E. Bohlin, head of school, Montrose School, Natick,
Massachusetts, a National School of Character;
senior scholar, Boston University's Center
for the Advancement of Ethics and Character

CHARACTER MATTERS

How to Help Our
Children Develop Good
Judgment, Integrity, and
Other Essential Virtues

Thomas Lickona

A TOUCHSTONE BOOK
Published by Simon & Schuster
New York   London   Toronto   Sydney

TOUCHSTONE
Rockefeller Center
1230 Avenue of the Americas
New York, NY 10020

TOUCHSTONE and colophon are registered
trademarks of Simon & Schuster, Inc.

For information regarding special discounts for bulk purchases,
please contact Simon & Schuster Special Sales at 1-800-456-6798
or business@simonandschuster.com

Designed by Christine Weathersbee

Manufactured in the United States of America

13 15 17 19 20 18 16 14 12

Library of Congress Cataloging-in-Publication Data
Lickona, Thomas.
Character matters : how to help our children develop good judgment,
integrity, and other essential virtues / Thomas Lickona.
p. cm.
Includes bibliographical references and index.
1. Moral education—United States. 2. Home and school—United States.
3. Education—Parent participation—United States. I. Title.
LC311.L52   2004
370.11'4—dc22   2003059191
ISBN-13: 978-0-7432-4507-4
ISBN-10:   0-7432-4507-5

to Mary,
with gratitude for
her constant care

ACKNOWLEDGMENTS

I would like to express my heartfelt thanks:

To all the parents, teachers, principals, and other educators whose work to raise and educate children of character I have gratefully drawn upon in the pages of this book.

To my wife, Judith, for her steadfast support; for being, as always, my first editor; and for helpful suggestions on every chapter, especially the introduction.

To my whole family, especially my eighty-six-year-old mother, for their constant love.

To Caroline Sutton, my editor at Simon and Schuster, for invaluable counsel on both organization and content that made this a far better book than it would otherwise have been and for cheering me on each step of the way.

To Robin Straus, my agent, for her warm friendship and for finding me such a good editor and publisher.

To Peg Haller, the copy editor, for her thoughtful and meticulous work on the manuscript.

To Cherylynne Li for the cover design and Christine Weathersbee and Joy O'Meara Battista for the interior design.

To my colleague Marvin Berkowitz for his helpful comments on chapters 10 and 12.

To all my colleagues in character education—too numerous to name—who labor diligently to make education for character part of every school in the nation.

To the Character Education Partnership for its national leadership in character education and in particular its National Schools of Character recognition program (www.character.org) that has identified many of the models of excellence cited here.

To the State University of New York at Cortland, for its strong support of our Center for the 4th and 5th Rs (respect and responsibility), which through its nine years of work with schools and communities has been the source of much of the book's material.

To the John Templeton Foundation, the Humanitas Trust, the Surdna Foundation, the Sanford and Priscilla McDonnell Foundation, the Casillas Foundation, the New Hampton School, and the many individuals who have generously supported our center's work over the years.

To Marthe Seales, my administrative assistant, for all the dedicated work she does to make it possible for us to operate a character education center.

And, finally, to God, who makes all things possible.

Cortland, New York
July, 2003

A child is a person who is going to carry on what you have started. He is going to sit where you are sitting and, when you are gone, attend to those things which you think are important. You may adopt all the policies you please, but how they are carried out depends on him. He will assume control of your cities, states, and nations. He is going to move in and take over your churches, schools, universities, corporations. The fate of humanity is in his hands.

—ABRAHAM LINCOLN

Fame is fleeting; popularity an accident; riches take wings. Only one thing endures: character.

—HORACE GREELEY

The aim of education is to guide students in the process through which they shape themselves as human persons—armed with knowledge, strength of judgment, and moral virtues—while at the same time conveying to them the spiritual heritage of the nation and the civilization in which they are involved.

—JACQUES MARITAIN

Intelligence plus character—that is the goal of true education.

—MARTIN LUTHER KING, JR.

A general dissolution of principles and manners will more surely overthrow the liberties of America more than the whole force of the common enemy.

—JOHN ADAMS

Morals are the foundation upon which a country rises to great heights. Take away morals, and individuals, leaders, and countries fall.

—OLD SPIRITUAL WISDOM

Children develop character by what they see, what they hear, and what they are repeatedly led to do.

—JAMES STENSON

CONTENTS

INTRODUCTION

Portraits of character touch something deep in the human heart. In the award-winning Civil War documentary by Ken Burns, one of the most commented on and moving moments was the reading of a letter written by a Union soldier, Major Sullivan Ballou, to his wife, Sarah, a week before his death at the Battle of Bull Run:

> My very dear Sarah,
>
> The indications are very strong that we shall move in a few days—perhaps tomorrow. Lest I should not be able to write again, I feel impelled to write a few lines that may fall under your eye when I shall be no more.
>
> I have no misgivings about, or lack of confidence in, the cause in which I am engaged, and my courage does not halt or falter. I know how strongly American Civilization now leans on the triumph of the Government, and how great a debt we owe to those who went before us through the blood and sufferings of the Revolution. And I am willing—perfectly willing—to lay down all my joys in this life to help maintain this Government, and to pay that debt. . . .
>
> Sarah, my love for you is deathless . . . and yet my love of Country comes over me like a strong wind and bears me irresistibly on to the battle field.
>
> The memories of the blissful moments I have spent with you come creeping over me, and I feel most gratified to God and to you that I have enjoyed them so long. . . . I have, I know, but few and small claims upon Divine Providence, but something whis-

pers to me—perhaps it is the wafted prayer of my
little Edgar, that I shall return to my loved ones un-
harmed. If I do not, my dear Sarah, never forget how
much I love you, and when my last breath escapes me
on the battle field, it will whisper your name.

Here was a humble man, a courageous man, who loved his family and loved his country and, spurred on by high ideals, did his duty
as he saw it without complaining. Tom Brokaw, interviewing veterans
of World War II in his best-selling book *The Greatest Generation,* was
struck by many of the same qualities. September 11 produced abun-
dant examples of unassuming heroism and sacrificial generosity.

We are moved by these stories of character because they show
us human beings at their best. They reveal our capacity for goodness. They challenge us to be more than we might otherwise be.
And they renew our faith in every child's potential to grow into a
person of character.

As we begin a new century, we have a sharper sense of how
much character matters. We need good character to lead purposeful,
productive, and fulfilling lives. We need character to have strong and
stable families. We need character to have safe, caring, and effective
schools. We need character to build a civil, decent, and just society.

We are troubled, however, by the unraveling of the moral fabric
of our society. In a recent national poll, nearly three of four American adults said that they believe that people in general lead less
honest and moral lives than they used to.[1] Says a high school
teacher, "Kids today are more cynical than ever about the lack of
honesty they see in the adult world."

We're troubled by all the ways societal moral decline is reflected,
as it inevitably is, in the attitudes and behavior of our children. We're
troubled by the precocious sexual behavior of the young. We're troubled by the bad language that comes out of the mouths of even elementary school children. We're troubled by the breakdown of the
family and the growing numbers of parents who seem to let their
children do and watch what they please. We're troubled by a ubiquitous media culture that grows more violent and vulgar by the day.

How can we renew our moral culture?

Children are 25 percent of the population but 100 percent of the future. If we wish to renew society, we must raise up a generation of children who have strong moral character. And if we wish to do that, we have two responsibilities: first, to model good character in our own lives, and second, to intentionally foster character development in our young.

Happily, an effort to do this is under way. For more than a decade, there has been a resurgence of character education in our nation's schools. It can be seen in a spate of character education books and curricular materials; in federal funding for character education and character education mandates in more than two-thirds of the states; in the emergence of national advocacy groups such as the Character Education Partnership and the Character Counts! Coalition; in the new *Journal of Research in Character Education,* the National Schools of Character awards competition, and reports on how to prepare future teachers to be character educators; and in an explosion of grassroots character education initiatives.

Character education is welcomed by parents who need support for the hard work of raising good children in a hostile moral environment; welcomed by teachers who went into teaching hoping to make a difference in the kind of person a child becomes and are demoralized to be in a school that gives up teaching right from wrong; and welcomed by all of us who are saddened by the decline in values as basic as common courtesy that we once took for granted. Effective character education in our schools is something all of us have a stake in, not just educators and parents, but everyone who cares about a decent society.

The premise of the character education movement is that the disturbing behaviors that bombard us daily—violence, greed, corruption, incivility, drug abuse, sexual immorality, and a poor work ethic—have a common core: the absence of good character. Educating for character, unlike piecemeal reforms, goes beneath the symptoms to the root of these problems. It therefore offers the best hope of improvement in all these areas.

Character education, of course, is not only the responsibility of schools. It is the shared duty of all those who touch the values and lives of the young, starting with families and extending to faith communities, youth organizations, business, government, and even the media. The hope for the future is that we can come together in common cause: to elevate the character of our children, our own character as adults, and ultimately the character of our culture.

At the heart of effective character education is a strong partnership between parents and schools. The family is the first school of virtue. It is where we learn about love. It is where we learn about commitment, sacrifice, and faith in something larger than ourselves. The family lays down the moral foundation on which all other social institutions build.

Parents, if they make the effort, can remain formative influences even during the challenging adolescent years. *Building a Better Teenager,* a 2002 research report based on hundreds of studies, concludes that the most academically motivated and morally responsible teens—and the ones least likely to engage in risky behaviors—are those who enjoy warm and involved relationships with their parents and whose parents set clear expectations and monitor their activities in age-appropriate ways.[2]

For the past nine years, our Center for the 4th and 5th Rs (respect and responsibility) at the State University of New York at Cortland has worked with schools and parents to promote the development of good character. We publish a *Fourth and Fifth Rs* newsletter (www.cortland.edu/c4n5rs) spotlighting character education success stories and run the Summer Institute in Character Education, which trains teachers, counselors, administrators, and other educators from across the country.

Character education, we always emphasize, is not a new idea. Down through history, all over the world, education has had two great goals: to help students become smart and to help them become good. They need character for both. They need character strengths such as a strong work ethic, self-discipline, and perseverance in order to succeed in school and succeed in life. They need character qualities such as respect and responsibility in order to have positive interpersonal relationships and live in community. At the beginning of our republic, the Founders argued that a democracy—government by the people—could not thrive without virtuous citizens, ones who understood and honored democracy's moral underpinnings: respect for individual rights, voluntary compliance with the law, participation in public life, and concern for the common good. For most of our nation's history, character education was at the center of the school's mission.

Unlike the nondirective and often relativistic values education of the recent past—which encouraged students to "make your own decision" without grounding them in the content of character— character education is the deliberate effort to cultivate virtue. The school *stands for* qualities of character such as hard work, respect, and responsibility. It promotes these through every phase of school life, from the example of adults to the handling of discipline to the content of the curriculum.

What is the content of character that we should try to model and teach in school, at home, and in our communities? In this book, I set forth ten essential virtues that are affirmed by nearly all philosophical, cultural, and religious traditions: wisdom, justice, fortitude, self-control, love, a positive attitude, hard work, integrity, gratitude, and humility. Part 1 explains these ten essential virtues and the way character profoundly affects the quality of our individual and collective lives.

Part 2 shows how parents can raise children of character and how schools can help parents fulfill their primary role as children's first and most powerful moral teachers.

Part 3 shows how all classroom teachers, regardless of subject matter, can create a learning community that fosters responsible work and moral behavior.

Part 4 shows how any school can become a school of character. Here and throughout the book, I report on exemplary elementary, middle, and high schools, many of which have won national recognition for excellence in character education. These schools have reaped the rewards of fewer discipline problems and higher academic performance by putting character first.

Part 5 shows how to involve an entire community in promoting good character.

Character education, to be sure, can be done ineffectively, as little more than slogans, banners, and adults' urging kids to be good. But schools that do character education well—in a way that transforms the school culture, the daily experience of students and staff—create an environment in which diligent effort, mutual respect, and service to others are the rule rather than the exception. A growing body of character education research (see, for example, *What Works in Character Education,* www.character.org) documents these positive outcomes. Hal Urban, an award-winning high school history teacher, a character education speaker, and the author of *Life's Greatest Lessons,* shares his firsthand observations:

> I've had the good fortune to visit schools all over the country that have character education programs in place. The first word that pops into my mind when I visit them is "clean." I seen clean campuses and buildings, hear clean language, and see kids dressed cleanly and neatly. I also see courtesy being practiced by everyone—students, teachers, administrators, custodians, and cafeteria workers. Most important, I see teaching and learning going on in an atmosphere that is caring, positive, and productive.

At the end of a unit on slavery, a fifth-grade boy in New Hampshire said, "*We* think slavery was bad, but what are people going to say about *us* in a hundred years?" Most of us would be likely to agree that our contemporary society faces serious social-moral problems and that these problems have deep roots and require systemic solutions. Many of us are also now coming to recognize the link between public life and private character—that it is not possible to develop a virtuous society unless we develop virtue in the hearts, minds, and souls of individual human beings. Families, schools, and communities can and must each do their part in creating a culture of character by raising children of character. Indeed, the health of our nation in the century ahead depends on how seriously all of us commit to this calling.

PART ONE

Why Character Matters

CHAPTER 1

Why Character Matters

*I was a punk before I came to this school. I used to make
little kids cry. When I met Mrs. Brown, I changed. I'm
not a punk anymore, because Mrs. Brown taught me
character.*

—DREW, A SIXTH GRADER

*Nothing is more important for the public weal than to
train up youth in wisdom and virtue.*

—BEN FRANKLIN

Why does character matter?

A headmaster remembers that above the door to the main
classroom building where he went to school as a boy, the following
words were engraved:

Be careful of your thoughts,
   for your thoughts become your words.
Be careful of your words,
   for your words become your deeds.
Be careful of your deeds,
   for your deeds become your habits.

Be careful of your habits,
   for your habits become your character.
Be careful of your character,
   for your character becomes your destiny.

The Greek philosopher Heraclitus said it simply: "Character is destiny." Character shapes the destiny of an individual person. It shapes the destiny of a whole society. "Within the character of the citizen," Cicero said, "lies the welfare of the nation."

"Transmitting values," as the essayist Lance Morrow points out, "is the work of civilization." A glance at history reminds us that civilizations do not flourish forever. They rise, and they fall. They fall when the moral core deteriorates—when a society fails to pass on its core virtues, its strengths of character, to the next generation. The historian Arnold Toynbee observed, "Out of twenty-one notable civilizations, nineteen perished not by conquest from without but by moral decay from within."

More than a century ago in a lecture at Harvard University, Ralph Waldo Emerson asserted, "Character is higher than intellect." Writes the psychiatrist Frank Pittman, "The stability of our lives depends on our character. It is character, not passion, that keeps marriages together long enough to do their work of raising children into mature, responsible, productive citizens. In this imperfect world, it is character that enables people to survive, to endure, and to transcend their misfortunes." "To do well," Stephen Covey says, "you must do good. And to do good, you must first *be* good."

All of us who are parents naturally want our children to be successful. But we know in our bones that success without *character*—qualities such as honesty, a sense of responsibility, kindness, and determination in the face of difficulty—doesn't count for much. The novelist Walker Percy once said, "Some people get all A's but flunk life." In living a life well, as a proverb puts it, "An ounce of character is worth a pound of intelligence."

As a society, we are beginning to recover this age-old wisdom. Schools are taking up the work of character education. We have a renewed concern about the character of our government and corporate leaders, having learned painfully that expertise without ethics is a menace to society. Best-selling books such as *Emotional Intelligence,*[1] *The 7 Habits of Highly Effective People,*[2] and *The Book of Virtues*[3] are essentially reflections on character and its importance in our individual and collective lives. Life, such writings remind us, is a moral and spiritual journey for which we need a reliable inner compass.

THE RIGHT STUFF

Character is having "the right stuff." As parents and educators, we labor to teach kids this—that it's what's inside that counts.

We know good character when we see it. At age nineteen, Bob Wieland landed a contract with the Pittsburgh Pirates but was drafted to serve in Vietnam. There he lost both of his legs in a mine explosion. In the hospital, he sank into a deep depression and wasted away to eighty-seven pounds. Then one morning he woke up and said to himself, "What *can* I do? It won't help me to focus on what I *can't* do." He began to lift weights, then to lift competitively, and went on to set a world record by bench-pressing five hundred pounds. He also learned to walk on his hands. On September 8, 1982, with pads on his knuckles, he left his California home and set out to walk across America on his hands. He got thousands of people to sponsor his trip, with the proceeds going to alleviate hunger in this country and around the world. It took him three years, eight months, and nearly 5 million hand steps to reach his destination of Washington, D.C. When he got there, he said, "I wanted to show that through faith in God and dedication, there's nothing a person can't achieve."

For the past two decades, images of character have come in abundance from the Giraffe Project (www.giraffe.org), based in Langley, Washington. This project is dedicated to finding and honoring "human giraffes"—people sticking out their necks for the common good. Codirectors Ann Medlock and John Graham have created a character education curriculum around these everyday heroes. Students read giraffe stories, find and tell stories about giraffes in their own school or community, and then are challenged to become giraffes themselves by sticking their necks out to make a difference. Over the past twenty years, the Giraffe Project has built a bank of more than a thousand stories of giraffes of all ages. Here are just three:

Every payday for more than a quarter of a century, the late Michael Greenburg bought three pairs of gloves. On the coldest days of winter, he headed for the toughest parts of town and talked street people into accepting them. He helped the homeless by doing what he could—over and over again.

Twelve-year-old Craig Kielburger in Toronto read about the murder of a Pakistani child who had spoken out against child slavery in his country. Craig started Free the Children, a movement dedicated to ending slavery worldwide. He raised money, spoke out, and even went on a global fact-finding trip. After the media picked up his story, several major companies pledged not to buy products made by child labor.

British doctor Alice Stewart has quietly done a lifetime of painstaking research on the effects of radiation. One of her many discoveries was that a single X-ray of a fetus could double the risk of childhood cancer. Thanks to her, thousands of children's lives have been spared. She has ruffled a lot of feathers in medicine and industry but continues her research on public health hazards.[4]

These human giraffes have compassion and courage, but they also have another quality: They find fulfillment and even joy in their work. It feels good to do good. Some years ago, the PBS talk show host Dennis Wholey edited a book titled *Are You Happy?*—a question he put to forty people, half famous, half not.[5] In every case, people cited as the source of their greatest happiness the times they made a positive contribution to the lives of others. The world tells our children that happiness is to be found in sexual pleasure, beauty, popularity, wealth, power, or unending good health. They need to learn what Aristotle taught ages ago: A fulfilling life is a life of virtue. You can't be happy unless you're good.

THE CONTENT OF
OUR CHARACTER

In his famous "I Have a Dream" speech, Martin Luther King, Jr., said he dreamed of the day when all Americans "will be judged not by the color of their skin but by the content of their character."

What is the content of character? The content of good character is virtue. Virtues—such as honesty, justice, courage, and compassion—are dispositions to behave in a morally good way. They are objectively good human qualities, good for us whether we know it or not. They are affirmed by societies and religions around the world. Because they are intrinsically good, they have a claim on our conscience. Virtues transcend time and culture (although their cultural expression may vary); justice and kindness, for example, will always and everywhere be virtues, regardless of how many people exhibit them.

We can assert that virtues are objectively good—not subjective preferences like taste in music or clothes—because they meet certain ethical criteria:

- They define what it means to be human. We are more fully human when we act virtuously—generously rather than selfishly, justly rather than unjustly, honestly rather than deceitfully.
- Virtues promote the happiness and well-being of the individual person.
- They serve the common good, making it possible for us to live and work in community.
- They meet the classical ethical tests of reversibility (would you like to be treated this way?) and universalizability (would you want all persons to act this way in a similar situation?).

TEN ESSENTIAL VIRTUES

What virtues are most important for strong character?

The ancient Greeks named four. They considered *wisdom* to be the master virtue, the one that directs all the others. Wisdom is good judgment. It enables us to make reasoned decisions that are both good for us and good for others. Wisdom tells us how to put the other virtues into practice—when to act, how to act, and how to balance different virtues when they conflict (as they do, for example, when telling the honest truth might hurt someone's feelings). Wisdom enables us to discern correctly, to see what is truly important in life, and to set priorities. As the ethicist Richard Gula points out, "We cannot do right unless we first see correctly."

The second virtue named by the Greeks is *justice*. Justice means respecting the rights of all persons. The Golden Rule, which directs us to treat other persons as we wish to be treated, is a principle of justice that can be found in cultures and religions around the world. Since we are persons ourselves, justice also includes self-respect, a proper regard for our own rights and dignity. Schools, in their character education efforts, often center on justice because it includes so many of the interpersonal virtues—civility, honesty, respect, responsibility, and tolerance (correctly understood not as approval of other people's beliefs or behaviors but as respect for their freedom of conscience as long as they do not violate the rights of others). A concern for justice—and the capacity for moral indignation in the face of injustice—inspires us to work as citizens to build a more just society and world.

A third, much-neglected virtue is *fortitude*. Fortitude enables us to do what is right in the face of difficulty. The right decision in life is often the hard one. One high school captures that truth in its motto: "Do the hard right instead of the easy wrong." A familiar maxim says, "When the going gets tough, the tough get going." Fortitude, as the educator James Stenson observes, is the inner toughness that enables us to overcome or withstand hardship, defeats, inconvenience, and pain. Courage, resilience, patience, perseverance, endurance, and a healthy self-confidence are all aspects of fortitude. Teen suicide has risen sharply in the past three decades;

one reason may be that many young people are unprepared to deal with life's inevitable disappointments. We need to teach our children that we develop our character more through our sufferings than our successes, that setbacks can make us stronger if we don't give in to feeling sorry for ourselves.

The fourth virtue named by the Greeks is *self-control* (which they called "temperance"). Self-control is the ability to govern ourselves. It enables us to control our temper, regulate our sensual appetites and passions, and pursue even legitimate pleasures in moderation. It's the power to resist temptation. It enables us to wait and to delay gratification in the service of higher and distant goals. An old saying recognizes the importance of self-control in the moral life: "Either we rule our desires, or our desires rule us." Reckless and criminal behaviors flourish in the absence of self-control.

The Greeks covered a lot of the moral territory but by no means all of it. A fifth essential virtue is *love*. Love goes beyond justice; it gives more than fairness requires. Love is the willingness to sacrifice for the sake of another. A whole cluster of important human virtues—empathy, compassion, kindness, generosity, service, loyalty, patriotism (love of what is noble in one's country), and forgiveness— make up the virtue of love. In his book *With Love and Prayers*, F. Washington Jarvis writes, "Love—selfless love that expects nothing back—is the most powerful force in the universe. Its impact on both the giver and the receiver is incalculable." Love is a demanding virtue. If we really took seriously the familiar injunction to "love your neighbor as yourself," says an essay on this virtue, would we not make every effort to avoid gossiping about others and calling attention to their faults, given how sensitive we are to such things said about us?

A *positive attitude* is a sixth essential virtue. If you have a negative attitude in life, you're a burden to yourself and others. If you have a positive attitude, you're an asset to yourself and others. The character strengths of hope, enthusiasm, flexibility, and a sense of humor are all part of a positive attitude. All of us, young and old, need to be reminded that our attitude is something we *choose*. "Most people," Abraham Lincoln said, "are about as happy as they make up their minds to be." Said Martha Washington, "I have learned from experience that the greater part of our happiness or misery depends on our dispositions and not on our circumstances. We carry the seeds of the one or the other with us in our minds wherever we go." A 1998 book by Michael Loehrer, *How to Change a Rotten Attitude: A Manual for Building Virtue and Character in Middle and High School Students* (order@corwin.sagepub.com), recognizes the great importance of attitude in educating for character.

Old-fashioned *hard work* is a seventh indispensable virtue. There is no substitute in life for work. "I challenge you," says the great basketball coach John Wooden, "to show me one single solitary individual who achieved his or her own personal greatness without lots of hard work."[6] Hard work includes initiative, diligence, goal-setting, and resourcefulness.

An eighth essential virtue is *integrity*. Integrity is adhering to moral principle, being faithful to moral conscience, keeping our word, and standing up for what we believe. To have integrity is to be "whole," so that what we say and do in different situations is consistent rather than contradictory. Integrity is different from honesty, which tells the truth to others. Integrity is telling the truth to one-self.[7] "The most dangerous form of deception," says author Josh Billings, "is self-deception." Self-deception enables us to do whatever we wish, even great evil, and find a reason to justify our actions.

Gratitude is a ninth essential virtue. "Gratitude, like love, is not a feeling but an act of the will," observes writer Anne Husted Burleigh. "We choose to be thankful, just as we choose to love." Gratitude is often described as the secret of a happy life. It reminds us that we all drink from wells we did not dig. It moves us to count our everyday blessings. Asked what was the biggest lesson he learned from drifting twenty-one days in a life raft lost in the Pacific, the war hero Eddie Rickenbacker answered, "That if you have all the fresh water you want to drink and all the food you want to eat, you ought never to complain about anything."

Humility, the final essential virtue, can be considered the foundation of the whole moral life. Humility is necessary for the acquisition of the other virtues because it makes us aware of our imperfections and leads us to try to become better people. "Humility," writes the educator David Isaacs, "is recognizing both our inadequacies and abilities and pressing our abilities into service without attracting attention or expecting applause." "Half the harm that is done in the world," said T. S. Eliot, "is due to people who want to feel important." "Every virtue turns worthless," writes the philosopher Dietrich von Hildebrand, "if pride creeps into it—which happens whenever we glory in our goodness." Without humility, observes another writer, we keep all our defects; they are only crusted over with pride, which conceals them from ourselves. Humility enables us to take responsibility for our faults and failings (rather than blaming someone else), apologize for them, and seek to make amends. The psychiatrist Louis Tartaglia, in his book *Flawless! The Ten Most Common Character Flaws and What You Can Do about Them,* says that in more than twenty years as a therapist he has found the most common character flaw to be "addiction to being right."[8] ("Do you find yourself discussing disagreements," he asks, "long after they are finished, just to prove you were right?") The key to character growth in therapy and life, he says, is simply the humble willingness to change.

The life of virtue is obviously difficult. Nearly everyone falls short in the practice of these ten virtues at least some of the time. And yet most of us also possess these character strengths at least to some degree. It helps, I believe, to think of each of the essential virtues as a continuum and to focus on making progress in practicing that virtue more consistently. We can also take heart from knowing, as the educator James Coughlin points out, that the virtues are linked; a decision to work seriously on even one virtue will be likely to pull all the other virtues up (just as a serious weakness in one of the virtues tends to pull the others down).

THE TWO SIDES
OF CHARACTER

The ten essential virtues can be thought of as constituting what Aristotle called the life of right conduct. This life of character has two sides: right conduct in relation to other persons and right conduct in relation to oneself. The virtuous life includes other-oriented

virtues such as fairness, honesty, gratitude, and love, but it also includes self-oriented virtues such as fortitude, self-control, humility,
and putting forth our best effort rather than giving in to laziness.

These two kinds of virtue are connected. For example, we need
to be in control of ourselves in order to do right by others. A man
with an alcohol or gambling problem often finds his marriage and
family life suffering. In a book of personal accounts of sexual addiction, a pastor told of once being in a hotel alone with time on his
hands and deciding out of curiosity to visit one of the local strip
joints—something he had never done before. He rationalized that
he was doing it as a kind of sociological study. The next time he traveled, he went to another strip joint. Over time, it became an obsession and nearly wrecked his ministry and marriage.

WHAT IS THE CURRENT CONDITION
OF OUR CHARACTER?

Without the virtues that make up good character, no individual can
live happily and no society can function effectively. Without good
character, the human race does not make progress toward a world
that respects the dignity and value of every person.

If this is true, we have no greater responsibility than to try to
raise up people of character. How are we doing as a nation in fulfilling that responsibility?

The evidence is not encouraging.

The country got its first hard look in the mirror nearly a decade
ago with the publication of *The Index of Leading Cultural Indicators*.[9]
This index used sobering statistics to measure societal changes between 1960 and the early '90s. During that thirty-year period, the population grew 41 percent, the gross domestic product tripled, and total
spending by government at all levels increased more than fivefold.

During that same period, however, nearly every indicator of social stability and moral health shifted dramatically in a negative direction. Violent crime increased more than 500 percent. Teen
suicide tripled. The divorce rate more than doubled—becoming the
highest in the world. About 40 percent of children now go to sleep

in homes where their fathers do not live; most divorced fathers pay no child support. Fatherlessness is now the leading predictor of nearly every childhood pathology.[10]

Between 1960 and 1991, births to unmarried mothers increased more than 400 percent. They continue to rise; one of three babies is now born out of wedlock, compared to one of twenty in 1960. The percentage of children living in poverty declined briefly during the 1960s but between 1970 and the early '90s increased 40 percent. More than one in five children now live in poverty. Since the Supreme Court's 1973 legalization of abortion, there have been more than 40 million abortions in the U.S.—one about every twenty seconds. U.S. teens have the highest abortion rate in the developed world.

Average television viewing per household rose from five hours in 1960 to more than seven hours in 1992 and continues to climb. The average teen now spends less than two hours a week reading and more than twenty hours a week watching TV. Between 1960 and 1993, average test scores for all students on the Scholastic Aptitude Test (SAT) dropped 73 points.

2002 REPORT CARD ON AMERICAN YOUTH ETHICS

More recent data, equally troubling, come from other sources. One is the "2002 Report Card on the Ethics of American Youth," issued by the California-based Josephson Institute for Ethics (www.josephsoninstitute.org). Published every other year since 1992, this report card is based on a national survey of thousands of high school students (more than twelve thousand in the 2002 sample). Here are some of the 2002 findings:

- Three out of four students admitted to cheating on an exam in school during the past year.
- Nearly four in ten students said they had stolen something from a store during the past year.
- Nearly four in ten said they "would lie to get a good job."

In the 2000 edition of *Who's Who Among American High School Students,* 80 percent of the students selected—considered the best and the brightest of the nation's youth—admitted to cheating in school, the highest percentage in the twenty-nine-year history of the survey. Most said they considered it no big deal. Research reported by Duke University's Center for Academic Integrity (www.academicintegrity.org) indicates that on most college campuses, over 75 percent of students admit to some cheating.[11] More than a third of college students told a 1999 *U.S. News & World Report* survey that they would steal from an employer (only 6 percent of those over forty-five said they would do so).

Paradoxically, despite high levels of self-reported dishonesty, 76 percent of all students in the 2002 Josephson survey had high "ethical self-esteem"—agreeing with the statement, "When it comes to doing what is right, I am better than most people I know." Nearly eight in ten agreed that "it's not worth it to lie or cheat because it hurts your character." If character is defined as moral values in action, it is clearly not measured by self-opinion or mere espousal of high ideals.

CHARACTER IN THE FACE OF TEMPTATION: THE LOST WALLET EXPERIMENT

Our character determines how we act when we think we're invisible to others. Or as an old saying has it, "Character is what you do when nobody's looking."

A few years ago, a simple experiment gave people in countries around the world a chance to reveal their character when they thought no one was watching.[12] Researchers conducting the experiment "lost" more than 1,100 wallets to see how many would be returned. Each wallet contained $50 in local currency and the name and phone number of the owner. The wallets were left on sidewalks and in phone booths; in front of office buildings, discount stores, and churches; and in parking lots and restaurants. Then the wallet droppers sat back and watched.

All told, 56 percent of the wallets were returned; 44 percent were whisked away. But from one country to another, the results varied greatly. First prize for honesty went to Norway and Denmark, where fully 100 percent of the wallets were returned. Finishing in the bottom four spots were Italy (35 percent returned), Switzerland (35 percent), Hong Kong (30 percent), and Mexico (21 percent). The United States placed in the middle range with 67 percent returned.

If these data are any indication, honesty is more a part of the national character in some countries than in others. But cities and towns within the same country also varied widely. Within the United States, the four most honest communities out of ten chosen for the experiment were Seattle (90 percent returned); Concord, New Hampshire (80 percent); Cheyenne, Wyoming (80 percent); and Meadville, Pennsylvania (80 percent). Tied for worst place to lose your wallet were Atlanta, Las Vegas, and Dayton, Ohio—where half the wallets were never seen again.

The moral of the story? Culture matters. The character of a community or country—in this case its social norms regarding honesty—influences the character of its citizens. (It doesn't *determine* their character, since even in the least honest places, some persons scrupulously returned wallets.) There's hope in this: If you can raise the norms of a group (a school, a neighborhood, a community), you can raise the operative character of the group's members.

WHAT MOTIVATES HONESTY?

What accounted for the differences in honesty across and within communities and cultures?

Clues come from interviews in the lost wallet experiment. Most of the returners, young and old, said their parents had instilled in them the desire to do the right thing.

Some people cited their religious faith as the reason for their honesty. In Malaysia, a twenty-year-old woman running a fruit stand said, "Being a Muslim, I'm aware of how to overcome temptation." Lena Kruchinina, a governess in the Russian city of Vladimir, explained, "Several years ago, I could have taken it, but now I am completely changed. As they say, 'Thou shalt not covet thy neighbor's goods.'"

For others, empathy appeared to play a key role. The world over, people who looked as if they could really use the $50 turned it in, while those who looked as if they didn't need it took the money and ran. Canadian Brian Toothill was typical of honest individuals of meager means who expressed concern for the wallet's owner. He found a wallet in a Saskatoon telephone booth and told the interviewer, "The wallet was down low in the booth, so I thought it might belong to a handicapped person in a wheelchair. They'd need the money more than I do, wouldn't they?" In truth, Brian himself was out of work and just minutes before had been searching for bottles and cans he could sell. But his values were stronger than his need for cash.

CHARACTER IN THE FACE OF EVIL: THE RESCUERS STUDY

Character determines how we respond when someone loses a wallet. It also determines how we respond when a civilization loses its soul.

The Third Reich of Nazi Germany systematically and ruthlessly murdered 11 million civilians, including 6 million Jews. Many of those who perpetrated this horror enjoyed their work. Adolf Eichmann confessed that going over the death lists from the concentration camps was his favorite bedtime reading.[13] Rudolph Hess, commandant at Auschwitz, had a window installed in a gas chamber so he could watch the victims die.[14] Nazi guards would sometimes kick prisoners to death or turn loose police dogs trained to eat live human flesh.

When the ghastly machinery of the death camps was revealed after World War II, a glimmer of redemption emerged in the stories of persons who had stood against this tide of evil and risked their lives to rescue Jews. What led them to do it? Why did they disobey the Nazi authorities when most of their fellow citizens did not? What kind of families did they come from?

Eva Fogelman, author of *Conscience and Courage*, writes that "a rescuer's life was intricate and terrifying. A careless word or one wrong move could lead to death."[15] Estimates of the number of people who rescued range between fifty thousand and a million, the lower figure considered more likely. But even if the highest estimate were true, it would represent less than one-half of 1 percent of the total population under Nazi occupation.

In 1988, researchers Samuel and Pearl Oliner published *The Altruistic Personality,* the most extensive study ever conducted of persons who rescued Jews from the Holocaust.[16] The Oliners and their research team interviewed 406 rescuers who had lived in Nazi-occupied Europe. For purposes of comparison, they also interviewed 126 nonrescuers, persons who had lived in the same occupied countries at the same time as the rescuers but did not get involved in helping Jews.

Rescuers did not consider themselves moral heroes. Again and again, they spoke of simply doing "what had to be done." Most of them hardly deliberated before acting. Asked how long it took them to make their first helping decision, more than 70 percent said "minutes."

WHAT MOTIVATED RESCUE?

The Oliners' study found three kinds of "moral catalysts," sometimes operating in combination, that moved people to rescue. For the majority of rescuers (52 percent), a *norm-centered motive*—allegiance to the moral code of one's social group—led to their first helping act. Such persons often began rescue work at the request of a person who was an authority figure within their group. For example, Ilse, the wife of a German Lutheran minister, initially took Jews into her home because her husband and church asked her to do so.

A sub-group (19 percent) of these norm-centered rescuers had so strongly internalized a social norm that their helping action appeared to be independent of any authority. For example, a Danish man, part of a rescue group that smuggled more than seven thousand Jews out of Denmark by ferry to Sweden, explained:

The basic morality in this little homogeneous country is to

be nice to your neighbor and to treat people well. Denmark is a very lawful society. People would stop others from doing illegal things. Even during blackouts, there was no theft. The main reason I helped the Jews is that I didn't want anybody to hurt my neighbors, my fellow countrymen, without cause. It was based on good morals and good traditions.

For more than a third of the rescuers (37 percent), an *empathic orientation*—a response of the heart to people in pain—motivated their first helping act. For some of these individuals, merely knowing that others were suffering was enough to motivate action; for others, a direct encounter with a person in distress led to helping. A Polish woman recounted:

In 1942, I was on my way home from town when M. came out of the bushes. I looked at him in striped camp clothing, his head bare, shod in clogs. And he begged me, his hands joined like for a prayer—could I help him? It still makes me cry. How could one not have helped such a man?

For a small minority of rescuers (11 percent), their first helping act was motivated by a *belief in universal ethical principles of justice or caring*. For example, Suzanne, a high school mathematics teacher born in Paris, was deeply involved in saving children, hiding them in various schools. While she did not consider herself religious, she saw herself as "a very moral person," which she attributed largely to her Protestant upbringing. She had not directly witnessed the mistreatment of Jews. Asked why she helped them, she responded simply, "All men are born free and equal by right."

Other principled rescuers emphasized an ethic of care—a feeling of obligation to help all people out of a spirit of generosity and concern for their welfare. For example, Louisa and her husband joined the Dutch underground in 1940 and for the next five years hid Jews in their home. She said, "These were people in need, and we helped them." She described herself as very influenced by her Christian religion in her childhood.

These three moral orientations—norm-centered (acting in accord with the values of one's group), empathic (moved by another's distress), and principled (committed to a universal ethic of justice or care)—were three different paths to the virtuous act of rescuing. What they have in common, the Oliners believe, is the *capacity for extensive relationships*—a feeling of responsibility for the welfare of others, including those outside one's immediate family and community circle. This extensive disposition stands in sharp contrast to the "constrictedness" that tended to characterize nonrescuers in the study. Constricted people were more centered on themselves and their own needs, reserving their sense of obligation to a small circle of others.

THE ROOTS OF CARING

What kind of developmental histories gave rise to rescuers' capacity for extensive caring?

Rescuers were much more likely than nonrescuers to describe close family relationships in which parents modeled and taught caring values. Said one woman, "My mother always said to remember to do some good for someone at least once a day." By contrast, parents of nonrescuers were more likely to emphasize economic values ("Get a good job," "Be thrifty") than moral concerns.

Nonrescuers more often described their parents as using physical punishment to discipline—typically experienced by the child as a cathartic release of aggression on the parent's part rather than anything related to the child's behavior. Rescuers, by contrast, remembered their parents as only occasionally punishing and more often "explaining things," telling the child that he or she had made "mistakes" or hadn't understood the other person's point of view.

Rescuers' parents were also much more likely to explicitly teach a positive attitude toward different cultures and religions and the obligation to help others generously without concern for rewards or reciprocity. Said one rescuer, "My father taught me to love God and my neighbor, regardless of race or religion. At my grandfather's house, when they read the Bible, he invited everybody in. If a Jew happened to drop in, he would ask him to take a seat. Jews and Catholics were received in our place like everybody else." Another rescuer asserted, "When you see a need, you have to help. We are our brother's keeper."

As rescuers grew up, distinctions of class and religion were far less important to them than to nonrescuers in choosing friends. Rescuers also developed a greater "internal locus of control" than nonrescuers—a stronger feeling that they could shape events and a greater willingness to risk failure.

It was no accident, this study concludes, that when the lives of outsiders were threatened, persons who had been developing an extensive orientation from childhood responded by reaching out. Saving others from the Holocaust grew out of the ways in which they ordinarily related to other people. When the war was over, they were likely to continue this pattern. In postwar life, significantly larger percentages of rescuers than nonrescuers participated in community service. Their most common activity was attending to the sick or aged.

The research on rescuers has important implications for both families and schools. Families need to nurture an inclusive caring that reaches beyond the home. Schools must foster that same spirit of inclusiveness and the actual experience of caring community through day-to-day relationships.

CHARACTER AS TRANSFORMATION OF MORAL SELF

The rescuer study sheds important light on the nature and roots of character, but it's not the whole story.

As psychologists Anne Colby and William Damon point out in their book *Some Do Care: Contemporary Lives of Moral Commitment,* not everyone in Nazi-occupied Europe who had the rescuers' personality characteristics (empathy, a sense of internal control, feelings of responsibility for others) and family backgrounds (parents who taught tolerance and caring) took the life-endangering step to rescue Jews.[17] Most, in fact, did not. Early experience, like culture, may influence but does not determine adult moral behavior. What other factors help to explain why a particular person chooses to act compassionately and courageously without counting the cost?

To try to answer that question, Colby and Damon asked a group of "expert nominators"—theologians, philosophers, and historians of varying political ideology, religious beliefs, and sociocultural backgrounds—to define criteria for a "moral exemplar" and then to suggest persons who fit those criteria. There was a surprisingly high degree of consensus on five criteria for exemplars: (1) a sustained commitment to moral ideals; (2) a consistency between one's ideals and means of achieving them; (3) a willingness to sacrifice self-interest; (4) a capacity to inspire others; and (5) a humility about one's own importance.

Using these five criteria, Colby and Damon proceeded to identify and interview twenty-three moral exemplars. Educationally, the exemplars ranged from having completed eighth grade to having earned medical, doctorate, and law degrees. They included religious leaders of different faiths, businessmen, physicians, teachers, charity workers, an innkeeper, a journalist, lawyers, heads of nonprofit organizations, and leaders of social movements. Ten were men; thirteen were women. Their contributions spanned civil rights, the fight against poverty, medical care, education, philanthropy, the environment, peace, and religious freedom.

In the course of their lives, each of these remarkable individuals, Colby and Damon found, developed a personal goal that involved a moral transformation. In most cases, mentors and colleagues played an influential role in the development of this defining goal. In all cases, the goal involved a commitment to a cause or principle that led to a life of uncompromising integrity and service.

As a striking example of this goal-driven transformation, these researchers cite the Russian scientist Andrei Sakharov. Until he was thirty-six, Sakharov was a pillar of the Soviet Union's Communist establishment. He invented the Russian H-bomb. He was considered both a brilliant scientist and a patriot. He had never rocked the boat.

Then, in 1957, he became concerned about radioactive contamination following Soviet nuclear weapons tests and wrote memos urging caution. A few years later he personally contacted Nikita Khrushchev to try to persuade him to halt further testing—and was told to cease meddling in affairs of state. By 1966 he was dissenting publicly, warning against the reintroduction of Stalinism. In 1967 he pleaded the case of two Soviet dissidents sentenced harshly under Soviet law. A year later he lost his clearance for scientific work. In 1970, with two close colleagues, he founded the Moscow Human Rights Committee to advocate publicly for persecuted people throughout the Soviet Union. In 1973 he appealed to the United Nations to intervene on behalf of Soviet dissenters sent to psychiatric hospitals. In 1986, having become the target of intense attacks from the state media, he was exiled from Moscow to the city of Gorki.

Here, then, is a journey of moral growth in adulthood—from a secure, establishment scientist to a principled defender of human rights willing to risk all. This journey confronted Sakharov with repeated opportunities to decide whether to move forward on the path he had chosen or to withdraw. Each time, supported and challenged by like-minded colleagues committed to human freedom, he chose to move forward. His ethical pilgrimage illustrates how the course of character development may continue over a lifetime, propelled not by determining factors from childhood, personality, or culture, but by freely chosen acts in service of a compelling ideal.

The lessons for us as teachers and parents? First, to provide young people with opportunities to think about and set worthwhile goals that will develop their character and give them the sense of purpose that every young person needs. Second, to model that process ourselves, so that young people have adults in their lives who are visibly committed to high ideals and engaged in actualizing them more fully.

THE CHARACTER OF
OUR DEMOCRACY

Character affects every area of society. On a trip in November 1999, I had a conversation with a woman who was making a transition to university personnel work after more than thirty years in the business world. She had worked for five different companies. When I told her of my work in character education, she spoke of how, in her experience, character profoundly affects business:

> If you don't have character in business, then you won't have team spirit. Character affects how you treat your colleagues and how you treat your customers. When there is no character, you get corruption. People look out for themselves only.

Two years later, with the country awash in corporate scandals, her words seemed prophetic. The cooked books, stock manipulations, and insider trading that constituted the corruption within Enron, WorldCom, and other corporate giants emerged as another measure of the moral ground we've lost. The runaway greed that gave rise to these scandals reflected changes in corporate culture, aided by government policies that removed many of the regulatory checks on the lust for money. The result has been a fast-growing gap between the rich and the rest of the country—a gap that weakens families and is altering the very character of our democratic society.

This transformation is documented in detail in Kevin Phillips's 2002 book, *Wealth and Democracy.*[18] Phillips does not write from the left; he is, in fact, a lifelong Republican. The growing concentration of wealth in the hands of a small number of Americans, he says, far exceeds anything that has happened in our history. It has profound political as well as economic consequences because money continues to buy political influence and therefore shapes public policy.

- In 1999, the average income (after taxes) of the middle 60 percent of Americans was *lower* than in 1977. Meanwhile, between 1982 and 1999, the four hundred richest Americans increased their average net worth from $230 million to $2.6 *billion.* Among the Western nations, the United States has the highest level of income inequality.
- In 1990, CEOs made 85 times what the average worker made. By 2000 they made 531 *times* the average worker's pay. In 1981, America's ten most highly paid CEOs received an average salary of $3.5 million; by 2000 that figure had soared to $154 million.

- From 1980 to 1999, the five hundred largest corporations tripled their assets and profits. During that period those same corporations eliminated approximately 5 million American jobs.
- Fewer than half of all Americans have any pension plan other than Social Security. American workers work the longest hours—350 hours more per year than the average European worker—yet have the least health coverage, maternity leave, vacation time, and notice of job termination of any Western nation.
- The Internal Revenue Service, during the past two decades, has spent more of its time and budget auditing working-class people, including the working poor, than it has auditing millionaires and billionaires.
- By the early 1990s, nearly 22 percent of children in the United States lived in poverty, compared to 10 percent in Great Britain and 4 percent in Belgium.

In short, as Phillips and other economic and political analysts have pointed out, our economy is rapidly redistributing national wealth into the pockets of the already affluent and powerful. It hasn't always been this way. In the 1940s and '50s, the middle 60 percent of Americans got the largest share of growth in the economic pie. But our present economy has reversed this. A democratic society, Phillips says, cannot long endure such an imbalance of wealth and its corrupting effects on politics and social policy—and remain a democracy that is responsive to the public interest.

How does the character of the economy affect the character of citizens? For one thing, as the French writer Alexis de Tocqueville observed nearly two centuries ago, greed and corruption at the top tend to foster greed and corruption at all levels. People think, "If those guys are just out for themselves and break the rules to grab what they can get, then I'd be a fool not to do the same."

What's more, close to 30 percent of the population are poor or near-poor. The chief cause of poverty and near-poverty in America is not the lack of available work, nor the inadequacy of welfare, nor the female-headed family, although all of those are contributing factors. The chief cause of poverty is that millions of workers are not paid a living wage.

This puts tremendous stress on families. A few years ago, in our small upstate New York city of 18,000, the newspaper ran a five-part series on the working poor, including families that were working two or three low-paying jobs and couldn't pay their bills, couldn't buy shoes for their kids, couldn't afford to take their kids to the dentist, and so on. Not only does this mean real suffering for parents and children and a lower overall quality of life, it also means less family time. A speaker at a Boston conference on economic justice spoke to this issue when he said, "Raising wages is the most family-friendly thing you could do."

It isn't just low-income families that are stressed by an unjust economy. Many middle-class parents would like to spend more time with their children but can't because of economic pressures. Says a Chicago editor, "My brother and his wife live very modestly but have been so severely downsized at their jobs that they must work extra and odd hours to make ends meet." As a society, we *say* we value family (in policy statements, political campaigns, and the like), but then we adopt or maintain social policies that undermine families. If we are serious about building the character of our youth, we will need to get serious about closing the gap between rhetoric and reality when it comes to the family.

SEX AND CHARACTER

If we are serious about the character of our children, we will also need to take an honest look at the moral condition of our sexual culture.

Most Americans would be likely to applaud the fact that people in general, including parents and kids, are much more comfortable talking about sex than they were prior to the 1960s. Couples having sexual problems in their marriages are more likely to try to do something about it. These are healthy changes. But along with this greater openness have come a sexualizing of popular culture and a sexualizing of children that is disturbing to parents and others across the ideological spectrum.

As one reflection of this concern, TV talk show hosts Oprah Winfrey and Dr. Phil have both recently devoted a program to the problem of oral sex—on the rise, according to at least one national survey[19]—among thirteen- and fourteen-year-olds and sometimes even younger kids. Some boys are reportedly demanding oral sex from their girlfriends the way they used to expect a good-night kiss. Some girls say they have performed oral sex on many boys. There are also stories of oral sex parties and oral sex going on in school hallways, at dances, and at football games.

In April 2000, the *New York Times* ran an article titled "The Face of Teenage Sex Grows Younger." It quoted psychotherapists counseling children, usually girls, who were emotional wrecks because of early sexual activity. Dr. Allen Waltzman, a Brooklyn psychiatrist, commented, "I see girls, 7th- and 8th-graders, even 6th-graders who tell me they're virgins . . . but they've had oral sex 50 or 60 times."[20] On Dr. Phil's show, a young girl looked into the camera, tears streaming down her face, and said to other kids who might be viewing: "Don't do this . . . please don't do this. You will lose all your self-respect. Things will get worse for you, much worse."

At a skating rink in a southern city, a father stopped to pick up his eleven-year-old daughter. In the center of the darkened rink were forty or fifty children, all about his daughter's age or younger, forming a circle. As the father drew closer, he could see that in the center of the circle were several boys and girls acting out positions of simulated sex. Several boys made sandwiches of little girls. One boy stood behind a girl, his arms around her and his hands on her genital area. The surrounding circle of kids watched in fascination. The father says that when they saw him approaching, a few straggled away, but most showed no embarrassment. When he reported all this to the rink manager, the manager said that no one else had complained, that "dirty dancing" was not allowed in his rink, and that in the future he would increase the lighting. Then he added, "But it's a different world."[21]

Kids can't entirely be blamed for such behavior. But the rest of us can be. We have created the world they have to grow up in.

The breakdown of sexual morality has spawned a plague of problems—promiscuity, sexual addictions, infidelity, unwed pregnancies, fatherless children, STDs, abortions, sexual harassment, the sexual abuse of children, children acting out sexually, an ever more eroticized media, a huge pornography industry (next to gambling, the most lucrative Internet business), and the damage done to marriages and families by many of these problems. To a large extent, we are still in cultural denial about the cost of sex without social controls. Benedict Groeschel, a Franciscan priest-psychologist-author who works with the poor and lectures worldwide on moral and spiritual matters, challenges us to face the hard truth:

> Americans in leadership positions should be aware that much of the world is scandalized by our moral behavior. We export pornography by the ton—literature, electronic pornography, disks, movies. The public media in our country are a septic tank of toxic waste. People have been very anxious that terrorists will poison the reservoirs. They are already poisoned—not by foreign terrorists but by our fellow Americans who bring into our living rooms poisons that destroy the moral lives of children and lead them into sexual relationships that are the furthest thing from a faithful marriage. TV and the Internet have been used to corrupt moral values to such an extent that many of our young people have practically none at all. This has been going on for many years. Why is it that a class action suit is not brought against the media for the corruption of the morals of minors?[22]

Everywhere I travel around the world, people resent the corruption of their young by American media. In Japan, traditional sexual morality is fast crumbling as teens adopt the latest fashion of their Western peers, "friends with (sexual) privileges" instead of emotional attachments to boyfriends or girlfriends. In Latin America, educators complain of the same trend. Much is written about the AIDS epidemic now ravaging southern Africa—the number of AIDS orphans is predicted to reach 40 million in the next ten years—but far less about the moral roots of the crisis. One exception was a speech at the November 1999 World Congress on Families by Dr.

Margaret Ogola, who heads a hospice for HIV-positive orphans in Kenya. She said that for generations in black Africa, religious taboos had been largely effective in suppressing sexual activity outside marriage. But those tribal norms of sexual morality were, she said, "shattered by Western influences"—both the mass marketing of contraceptives and the hedonistic messages of what she called "Planet Hollywood."[23] Significantly, Uganda, where an emphasis on premarital abstinence and marital fidelity is now national policy, is the only country in the world to succeed in lowering the rate of HIV/AIDS (from 21 percent in 1991 to 6 percent in 2003).

Unrestrained sexual freedom has also led to the widespread use of abortion as backup birth control. Abortion is a wrenchingly difficult social issue; none is more divisive. But even those who defend abortion as a woman's legal right say it should be rare. Can our country credibly claim that "we respect life and terrorists don't," and can we credibly teach respect for life to our children, while we continue to end a developing human life four thousand times a day? In his book *Making Abortion Rare: A Healing Strategy for a Divided Nation,* David Reardon observes that postabortion syndrome (depression, guilt, nightmares, loss of self-worth), which half of women who abort say they experience to some degree, can be attributed to the fact that most women who have an abortion are conflicted over its morality.[24] More than 70 percent say they think it is wrong—the taking of a human life—but they are choosing *against* their conscience because they feel as if they have no other choice. Even if, strictly speaking, there is always an alternative to the choice of abortion, women clearly need support systems that reduce the felt pressure to abort: prenatal care for themselves and their unborn child; adequate postnatal health care; help with adoption if they choose that; parental work leave; affordable day care; and adequate housing and employment opportunities. As we work to meet the needs of women, organizations such as American Feminists for Life (www.feministsforlife.org) challenge us—in language reminiscent of the rescuer study—to simultaneously adopt an inclusive social ethic and enlarge our circle of caring to encompass the most vulnerable members of the human family, babies in the womb.

Not all the social indicators, of course, are negative. During the

1990s, teenage sexual intercourse and pregnancy both declined significantly. After September 11, volunteerism rose; Habitat for Humanity, for example, reported a fourfold increase in volunteers in the following year. Violent youth crime is coming down, as is overall violence. Says Karol DeFalco, a middle school administrator with the New Haven, Connecticut, schools, "The number of kids who are carrying guns has dropped. The number of kids suspended from school is down. Kids' attitudes toward fighting have also changed dramatically."

We can be encouraged by these positive trends, while still coming to grips with the fact that absolute levels of most character-related problems remain high, far higher than they were a few decades ago.

THE NATIONAL CHARACTER
EDUCATION MOVEMENT

If humility is a virtue in a person, it is also a virtue in a people. It is a tribute to the American national character that we retain the capacity to examine our collective conscience and be galvanized by our moral failures. The renewal of character education in our schools—in some cases, in whole communities—is at least in part a recognition that we stand at a cultural crossroads. Either we will come together to try to solve our cultural problems or we will see social and moral regression proceed with gathering speed.

To be sure, people perceive our moral and spiritual troubles differently. Those on the ideological right are less likely to recognize the corruption of our democracy, and the damage to families, by economic injustices and the accelerating concentration of wealth in the hands of a few. Those on the ideological left are less likely to recognize the corruption of both adult and child character by a decadent sexual culture. Most in the vast middle tend not to recognize how much in recent decades family life has deteriorated—at a heavy cost to the young—as electronic media replace family interactions and more than a million children a year see their parents go their separate ways.

We are only beginning to address these problems. However, the fact that we are more aware of the problems and beginning to confront them is cause for hope.

When schools return to their historical mission of developing character, they are often pleasantly surprised by the fruit of their efforts. Hilltop Elementary School in Lynnwood, Washington (http://staff.edmonds.wednet.edu/hte/), undertook character education in the early 1990s because of the increasingly rude and disrespectful behavior of its students; it went on to become a National School of Character. (See Appendix for the Hilltop story.) A Hilltop teacher who was initially skeptical about character education comments on her school's turnaround:

> I was opposed to doing character education at first. I said, "We have too much to teach already. This is the job of the home." But then I saw the change in the kids. I saw the change in how staff related to each other. We're a different school now. I look forward to coming to work.

Our society's social and moral problems have been many years in the making and will not be easily reversed. They will require solutions supported at all levels, from local communities to the federal government. It is not yet clear whether we have the national will to do what is truly needed to build a more just, caring, and decent society.

Nevertheless, character education is a good thing, an essential thing, for us to do. Focusing on character in our families, schools, and communities will make a difference—has already made a difference—for those involved. If the effort becomes widespread enough, it will make a difference for our whole country and perhaps, to the extent that we become a better people, for the rest of the world.

PART TWO

Create Families of Character

CHAPTER 2

Raise Children of Character

What used to happen to tenth graders is now routine among eighth graders. Trouble with the law. Promiscuity. Pregnancy. Parties with alcohol and without adults in attendance. Drugs.

—A MIDDLE SCHOOL COUNSELOR[1]

Parents are powerful people. The worst mistake they can make is to underestimate their influence.

—A RABBI

A mother whose daughter attends a private high school recounted a conversation she had with another mother whose daughter attends a different private school. The second mother said, "We're so relieved about the prom. The dance is at the hotel, the parties afterwards are at the hotel, and the kids all have rooms at the hotel for the night."

The first mother swallowed hard and said, "But don't you realize the signal that sends to kids—what it gives them permission to do?"

The second mother sighed and said, "Well, at least they're not drinking and driving."

In reporting this exchange, the first mother commented, "We draw a line, and then we cross that. We draw another line, and then we cross that. Pretty soon we've compromised our standards to the point of disappearing."

Our parenting, including the standards we teach and uphold, has a profound impact on our children's moral development and behavior. When we do not set high standards, we abandon our children to their own immature desires and the negative pressures of the peer group and culture.

Our parenting also greatly affects our children's ability to learn and do the disciplined work of school. The psychologist Robert Evans reminds us that in their 1992 book *America's Smallest School: The Family,* educators Paul Barton and Richard Coley predicted the failure of school reform if it ignored a basic fact: The family is the cradle of learning. They pointed out that student achievement improves when there are two parents in the home; when children are well cared for and feel secure; when the family environment is intellectually stimulating; when parents encourage self-regulation and perseverance; and when they limit TV, monitor homework, and ensure regular school attendance.[2]

In these vital areas, however, growing numbers of families are not meeting children's needs. As Evans observes, most children today arrive at school less ready to learn. At the very time that teachers face mounting pressures to increase student achievement, they have to cope with the decline of things they used to take for granted: students' attention, respect for authority, rudimentary social skills, and willingness to work.[3]

The sources of these problems, as Evans and others note, are well known. Millions of children are growing up in single-parent households (some of which, through lots of parental love and monitoring, manage to help their children thrive, but the odds are tougher than for two-parent homes). Many of these children are essentially fatherless; many are poor. In all kinds of families, including affluent and intact families, parents are spending less time with their children, providing less guidance, and setting fewer limits. Despite the fact that heavy television viewing increases children's aggression and lowers academic performance, parents allow their children to devote more time to television than to school and homework combined. Three-quarters of sixth graders have TVs in their bedrooms.[4]

To be fair, even the most competent and conscientious parents often struggle to get through the week and are beset by feelings of failure. Parenting is inherently hard work. We get our training on the job. The job is harder than ever because the family has fewer allies (such as the extended family and cohesive neighborhoods) and more enemies (such as a toxic media culture, other parents who are overpermissive, and an economy that doesn't pay a living wage). Because families are more stressed than ever, and because there are many more negative forces in our children's lives, parents need to be much more intentional than in past generations about creating a family life and more vigilant about raising a moral child. Good character will not be absorbed from our current moral environment.

To all families, whatever their strengths and struggles, the school's message must be: Make your children your first priority. Because the family is the foundation of both intellectual and moral development, *helping parents to be good parents is the single most important thing a school can do to help students develop strong character and succeed academically.*

Without pretending to have all the answers—parenting is a complex art and every child unique—schools can recommend to parents some practical principles of bringing up children. The following are eleven such principles, grounded in research and the wisdom of the ages, that can guide us in the demanding but rewarding work of raising children of character. (This chapter may be copied for a school's parents.)

1. Make Character Development a High Priority

In the graduate course I teach on character education, I ask my students to write about their own character development. One young woman wrote, "I was an only child, and my parents let me have my own way most of the time. I know they wanted to show how much they loved me. But I have struggled with selfishness my whole life."

The educator James Stenson, author of *Compass: A Handbook on Parent Leadership*, observes, "Successful parents see themselves as raising adults. They view their children as adults in the making."[5]

This means we need to take the long view. How will what we do as parents now affect our child's character in the future? What kind of character do we want our children to possess when they are grown men and women? Will they be hardworking, generous, and responsible adults? Will they make loving husbands and wives and capable mothers and fathers? How is our approach to parenting likely to affect these outcomes?

Many parents today attach a great deal of importance to their children's getting good grades and having high self-esteem. In fact, however, a child's character—the kind of person he or she is becoming—is much more relevant to leading a good and fulfilling life.

Our character consists of our habits. The habits we form as children and adolescents often persist into adulthood. Parents can affect, for good or ill, their children's habit formation. Imagine that your children will be asked someday, "How did your parents influence your character development?" What do you hope they will say?

2. Be an Authoritative Parent

Parents must have a strong sense of their moral authority, of having the right to be respected and obeyed.

In the 1960s, a great many adults lost confidence in their moral authority. During this same period, Diana Baumrind, a psychology professor at the University of California at Berkeley, began to do research showing that adult authority, properly exercised, is vital to children's and teenagers' moral development.

By observing families firsthand, Baumrind identified three styles of parenting: *authoritative, authoritarian,* and *permissive.* Authoritarian parents used a lot of commands and threats but little reasoning. Permissive parents were high on affection but low on authority. By contrast, authoritative parents combined confident authority with reasoning, fairness, and love:

> The child is directed firmly, consistently, and rationally; the parent both explains reasons behind demands and encourages give and take; the parent uses power [to enforce rules and commands] when necessary; the parent values both obedience to adult requirements and independence in the child; the parent sets standards and enforces them firmly but does not regard self as infallible; the parent listens to the child but does not base decisions solely on the child's desires.[6]

Baumrind initially studied preschoolers and followed them until they were nine. Her central finding was that the most self-confident and socially responsible children had authoritative parents.[7]

Subsequent studies documented the effectiveness of authoritative parenting with teens. Temple University psychologist Laurence Steinberg and colleagues studied twenty thousand adolescents and their families in nine different communities across America. They found that teens with authoritative parents were the most confident, persevering, and successful in school and the least likely to abuse drugs or alcohol.[8]

To establish an authoritative parenting style—and it's never too late to start—we should aim to have *a zero tolerance policy for disrespectful speech and behavior*. Nearly all children will slip into disrespect now and then, but when they do, they need immediate corrective feedback ("What is your tone of voice?" "You are not allowed to speak to me in that way, even if you're upset"). If we do not firmly and consistently correct such behavior, we will find our tolerance zone for disrespect getting wider and wider—and our children's disrespectful attitudes getting steadily worse. If we allow kids of any age to get away with being disrespectful, they will quickly lose respect for our moral authority. And if they don't respect our moral authority, they won't respect our rules, examples, or moral teachings. They are also likely to be less teachable by other adults.

3. Love Children

Stacks of studies show the importance of parental love for children's healthy development.[9] Love makes children feel secure, significant, and valuable. When they feel loved, they become emotionally attached to us. That attachment makes them more responsive to our authority and receptive to our values.

Love means spending time with kids. One-on-one time is especially important. We need emotionally intimate time and shared activity to keep any relationship—between spouses, between parents and kids—strong and growing.

To protect one-on-one time, we need to plan it. I know a school superintendent, a father of four, who can show you in his appointment book which child he'll be spending the coming Saturday afternoon with. "If I didn't schedule that time," he says, "it wouldn't happen." "To make sure we have family time," a mother says, "we have a rule. On two days a week, there are no outside activities."

The time we spend with our children will be among their most treasured memories. The late Christiaan Barnard, originator of the heart transplant, remembered the times with his father:

> Whenever we were ill, my father got up late at night to doctor us. I suffered from festering toenails that pained so much I would cry in bed. My father used to draw out the fester with a poultice made of milk and bread crumbs or Sunlight soap and sugar. And when I had a cold, he would rub my chest with Vicks and cover it with a red flannel cloth. Sunday afternoons we walked together to the top of the hill by the dam. Once there, he would sit on a rock and look down at the town below us. Then I would tell my problems to my father, and he would speak of his to me.

Quantity of time is as important as quality. Says a father of three, "It's very important to be with your kids in everyday situations. That's when you see how they're behaving, what attitudes they're picking up. That's when you get to monitor behavior: 'Don't talk to your mother like that,' 'Is that any way to treat your little brother?'"

Love as Communication

The quality of our love often comes down to the quality of our communication. Good communication doesn't happen automatically simply because we make the time for it. We often need to do something deliberate to bring about a meaningful exchange of thoughts and experiences.

When our older son, Mark, was thirteen, I became frustrated with the fact that our exchanges typically consisted of my asking questions and his giving monosyllabic answers. ("How was school?" "Fine." "How'd the game go?" "Great.") One day, in exasperation, I said, "You know, someday I'd like to have a real conversation. I ask all the questions. It would be great if, for a change, you asked *me* a question."

He said, "Okay, Dad, how are your courses going this semester?" It was the first time I ever talked to him about my teaching. After that, even if we had only five minutes in the car, we'd do "back-and-forth questions": I'd ask him one (for example, "What was the best part and the worst part of your day?"), he'd ask me one (often the same question), and so on. It became a family tradition.

How can we make time for the family meal and develop its potential for meaningful communication? John and Kathy Colligan of Endwell, New York, had five children, and they and their kids all had the usual out-of-home commitments (games, lessons, meetings, etc.). But they made a decision to have a daily family meal. Kathy explains:

> We had to vary the time between 4:30 and 8:30 depending on the season, sports, and so on. We asked the kids to make this commitment. We took the phone off the hook. The TV was off. We made a rule that only positive conversation would be allowed—no criticism, carping, or tattling. We be-

gan with grace, asking Jesus to be present at the table with us. We pointed out the specialness of each person—which got us looking at the goodness in each other. At first, the kids complained fiercely. But now they are all parents themselves, and we have asked each of them independently, "What are the things we did as a family that you want to do with your own children?" All have said, "The family meal."

To make the family meal a time for good discussion, it helps to have a "topic." Sample topics: "What's something you did today that you feel good about?" "What was something that happened today that never happened before?" "What is something you're looking forward to?" "Who has a problem the rest of the family might be able to help with?"

In our family, we'd sometimes clip out a letter to an advice columnist and read it aloud—but not the answer. For example: "I'm 15, I'm pregnant, and I'm scared to death to tell my folks. What should I do?" We'd go around the table and each say what advice we thought the columnist should give, and only then would we read the answer. These discussions gave us a good vehicle for sharing our deepest beliefs and values.

Love as Sacrifice

To love one's children is to be willing to make sacrifices for their sake. A wise person once said, "Being a responsible parent means putting yourself second for a quarter of a century." There is often no greater sacrifice, no greater act of love for one's children, than to endure the inevitable trials of marriage. Said one mother, "The most important thing parents can do for their children is to love each other and stay together."

About a million children see their parents divorce each year. In a major shift from a generation ago, however, both secular and religious marriage counselors are now urging married couples having problems to do everything possible to work out their difficulties and save their marriage. That advice is based on the experience of many couples who vastly underestimated the pain of divorce for both adults and children.

In *The Unexpected Legacy of Divorce: A 25-Year Landmark Study,* researcher Judith Wallerstein documents in detail the often lasting psychological repercussions of marital and family breakdown. There are exceptions: Some children eventually emerge from the suffering of divorce stronger persons; some, as adults, are determined to make their own marriages last. But for a great many, time does not heal the wounds.

In his book *Endangered: Your Child in a Hostile World,* Johann Christoph Arnold quotes Cindy, a youth counselor living in Boston. She was five when her parents told her and her brothers and sisters that they would be getting a divorce.

> Later that night I saw Dad walking out with a suitcase in hand, and his alarm clock with the cord wrapped around it. He looked at me and said, "Honey, remember, Daddy loves you." And then he walked out. That memory is so vivid. What does it mean when a father tells his little girl, "I love you," but then walks out on you? It's even hard to trust that my husband really loves me. It's like I'm still waiting for my father to come home.[10]

Marriages fail for many reasons, including child abuse, spousal violence, and infidelity. But we need to remember: Kids do better when they have two parents under the same roof. Parents parent better when there are two of them to support each other. The love between a mother and a father contributes greatly to a child's sense of security and overall well-being.[11] And by staying together through good times and bad, we teach our children a vital life lesson about the meaning of commitment.

4. Teach by Example

Teaching by example includes treating our children with love and respect, but it goes beyond that. It has to do with how we treat each other as spouses—something that children have countless opportunities to observe. When we fight, do we fight fair? What kind of language do we use? Do we reconcile soon or stay angry? Healthy families, research shows, have reconciliation rituals that enable them to forgive and make up quickly.[12]

Our example also has to do with how we treat and talk about others outside the family—relatives, friends, neighbors, and teachers. The mother who says in front of her child, "This is a dumb assignment," about homework a teacher has given, is modeling a disrespect that will not be lost on the child. "Disrespect," says one parent educator, "usually begins in low-level ways. Kids become desensitized to it."

These days, the most important example we set may be the stands we take—especially stands that are unpopular with our children or at odds with what other parents are permitting. What do we prohibit? Violent video games? TV shows and movies that contain sex, violence, or foul language? All forms of pornography? Music with lyrics that denigrate particular groups? Immodest dress? Parties where there's drinking? Prom overnights? Said a father, "Our daughter is the only one among her friends who is not going to the overnight beach party after the senior prom. She is very unhappy with us right now, but that's our decision."

Do our kids know where we stand on the moral issues of the day—respect for life, war and peace, threats to the environment, the plight of the poor? If we've ever taken a stand in the workplace or public arena or even in a conversation with one other person, have we shared that, and our reasoning, with our children? Stands like these define our values. They let our children know what we care deeply about. That's essential if we hope to pass on our values and the importance of integrity in a life of character. If our kids never see *us* standing up for what we believe, never going against the tide, how can we expect them to have the courage to stand up to pressure from *their* peers?

5. Manage the Moral Environment

In previous generations, the family existed within a larger societal context that generally supported the values parents were trying to teach their children.

No longer. Today, combating the social environment—in large

part the creation of the media and a marketplace culture—is a never-ending battle. The journalist Amy Welborn comments on how the marketplace increasingly seeks to sexualize children: "You see it in the racks of clothes for girls from seven on—the difficulty of finding an outfit that doesn't scream 'slut.'"[13]

The sexual corruption of children is arguably the most insidious attack on their innocence and character, but the media culture warps their values in other ways as well. Many parents are distressed by how materialistic their children are, never content with what they have. Increasingly, youth seek their self-esteem and identity in clothes or cars.

In chapter 3, I recommend specific guidelines parents can use to try to manage the media environment—to control TV, movies, music, video games, and the Internet. The basic rule: Kids must ask permission for any given television show, video game, item to be downloaded from the Internet, etc. Children's use of such media is a privilege, not a right.

Equally important, however, is taking an educational approach—*explaining* our moral objections to something rather than simply forbidding it. If we merely prohibit a TV program, movie, or CD without making clear our moral reasons for doing so, we're likely to produce just resentment in our children rather than the development of conscience and internal controls.

Taking an educational approach is illustrated by a mother whose fourteen-year-old daughter, Kylene, kept bugging her to be able to watch the popular TV comedy *Friends,* whose hip characters all sleep around. Kylene said all of her friends at school watched it, and she felt "totally out of it" because she didn't. Her mother said sorry, but she didn't approve of the values in the show.

Kylene wouldn't quit. Finally, her mother said, "Okay, let's watch one episode together." A few minutes into the show, the mother said, "Let me tell you why I have a problem with what *she* just said to *him.*" A minute later, she said, "Let me tell you why I have a problem with what *he* just said to *her.*" At the end of the show, Kylene said, "Okay, Mom, I get it!" and that was the end of her nagging about *Friends.* The moral standard had been conveyed, concretely.

Managing the moral environment today also means a higher degree of supervision than it did in the past. A mother of eleven- and six-year-old girls, not knowing other parents she could trust, said: "My children's friends come over to our house nearly every day. They feel safe here. But I don't allow my girls to go to other kids' houses, strict as that may sound. I don't know what the language will be there, what will be on the TV or VCR, whether there'll be pornography on the coffee table, or whether Mom will have a boyfriend in the home."

Said a mother to her sixteen-year-old daughter, who was leaving for a party (which the host parents were going to supervise): "I'll call to see if you're there. If you're not, I'll notify the police and report you as a missing person." Her daughter said, "You wouldn't." The mother said, "I would."

Parents who take pains to supervise their children can take heart from what the research shows: "hands-on" parents—those who set rules and expectations; know about their children's activities, friends, and behaviors; and monitor them in age-appropriate ways—have teens with lower rates of sexual activity as well as lower rates of drug, alcohol, and tobacco use than their peers.[14]

At the same time that we're working hard to protect our children from dangers, we should make an equal effort to expose them to what is uplifting, noble, and heroic. Somewhere in the evening paper there's at least one example of integrity, courage, or compassion. Teach With Movies (www.TeachWithMovies.com) is a source of dozens of good movies featuring inspiring role models and strong character development themes. And there are hundreds of good books whose admirable characters will live in a child's heart and imagination. *Books That Build Character* by William Kilpatrick provides an annotated bibliography of more than three hundred books appropriate for different levels—early childhood, childhood, and adolescence.

6. Use Direct Teaching to Form Conscience and Habits

We need to practice what we preach, but we also need to preach what we practice. Direct moral teaching helps to form a child's conscience and habits of behavior.

"Say please and thank you." "Don't interrupt." "Look at a person who's speaking to you." "Pick up your toys and clothes." "Cover your mouth when you cough." "Clear your dishes." "Remember your telephone manners." "Write or call to say thank you when you receive a gift." Literally hundreds of teachings like these communicate to children, "This is how we behave," "This is how we live." "Raising a civilized child," quips columnist Judith Martin, "takes twenty years of constant teaching and another ten of review."

Direct teaching includes explaining why some things are right and others wrong. Why is it wrong to lie? Because lying destroys trust, and trust is the basis of any relationship. Why is it wrong to cheat? Because cheating is a lie—it deceives another person—and it's unfair to all the people who aren't cheating. This kind of moral reasoning helps children develop a conscience so that they'll be able to give themselves reasons why they should or shouldn't do something. The inner voice of conscience becomes crucial when they're tempted to do something wrong and we're not around.

Our efforts to form a child's conscience should be proactive. We shouldn't wait for something to go wrong before teaching what's right. The great basketball coach John Wooden tells how his father instructed him and his brothers:

> Dad had "two sets of threes." These were direct and simple rules aimed at how he felt we should conduct ourselves in life. The first set was about honesty: "Never lie. Never cheat. Never steal." My brothers and I knew what this meant and that Dad expected us to abide by it. The second set of threes was about dealing with adversity: "Don't whine. Don't complain. Don't make excuses." Dad's two sets of threes were a compass for me in trying to do the right thing and behaving in a proper manner.[15]

Direct moral instruction also includes teaching a child positive alternatives to the behavior we're trying to correct. When our first granddaughter, Monica, was an exuberant three-year-old, she would interrupt an adult conversation—at the table or anywhere else—by saying, "Excuse me!" If that didn't gain her the floor, she'd repeat in rising volume, "Excuse me! *Excuse* me! *EXCUSE* me!" Her parents would then chide her for this behavior, but it would happen again the next time. The solution was to teach her an alternative behavior: to silently touch the nearest adult's arm as a signal that she wished to speak. That adult would then nod to acknowledge her, and when the adult speaking was done, Monica would take her turn. This, of course, took patient reminders and practice, as establishing new behaviors always does.

Direct teaching can also take the form of guiding our children to another source of wisdom—giving them a good book, a pamphlet, or another helpful resource that speaks to the issue at hand. Teens, especially, may be more likely to see the validity of a parent's perspective when it's confirmed by another source. A Canadian mother told me she was stunned and at a loss for words when her sixteen-year-old daughter, Lisa, disclosed that she and her boyfriend were thinking of having sex. When the mother said, "But sex is meant for love," Lisa replied, "But we *do* love each other, and this is how we want to express it." To help her daughter reflect on the meaning of love, I suggested she give her a pamphlet titled *Love Waits.* It reads:

> *Love is patient; love is kind. Love wants what is best for another person. Love will never cross the line between what's right and wrong. It's wrong to put one another in danger of having to deal with hard choices, choices that could change your lives forever.*
>
> *Having sex before marriage may feel right for the moment. But the possible costs of an unexpected pregnancy, abortion, and sexually transmitted disease—as well as the deep hurts that can come from a broken relationship—outweigh the feelings of the moment. The feelings are temporary; their consequences are long-lasting.*
>
> *All good things are worth waiting for. Waiting until marriage to have sex is a mature decision to control your desires. If you are getting to know someone—or are in a relationship— remember: If it's love, love waits.*[16]

7. Teach Good Judgment

Good judgment is a big part of good character. Helping our children become thoughtful decision makers goes beyond conscience formation (directly teaching what's right and wrong and why). Developing our kids' decision-making skills means teaching them certain questions or "tests" they can use to evaluate any given behavior. Should I let this person copy my homework? Go to a party that I know my parents wouldn't approve of? Tell less than the whole truth if they ask where I've been? Participate in gossiping about a kid at school that my friends don't like?

Here are nine ethical tests we can teach our children to apply:

1. **The Golden Rule (reversibility) test:** Would I want people to do this to me?
2. **The fairness test:** Is this fair to everybody who might be affected by what I say or do? Who might be affected, and how?
3. **The what-if-everybody-did-this test:** Would I like it if everyone else did this? Would I want to live in that kind of world?
4. **The truth test:** Does this action represent the whole truth and nothing but the truth?
5. **The parents test:** How would my parents feel if they found out I did this? What advice would they give me if I asked them if I should do it?
6. **The religion test:** Does this go against my religion?
7. **The conscience test:** Does this go against my conscience? Will I feel guilty afterward?
8. **The consequences test:** Might this have bad consequences, such as damage to relationships or loss of self-respect, now or in the future? Might I come to regret doing this?
9. **The front-page test:** How would I feel if my action were reported on the front page of my hometown paper?

Kids won't, of course, apply all these tests to every moral decision they make. But even if they apply some of them, they'll make better decisions than if they act on impulse or without considered judgment. Even asking *one* of the above questions—about consequences, for example—could deter a behavior that brings harm to self and others. Interviewing Monica Lewinsky about her affair with President Clinton, Barbara Walters asked, "At any time, did you consider the possible consequences your actions might have for yourself, for the president, for his family, or for the country?" Lewinsky replied, "No, I did not."

In addition to the nine ethical tests, there's a problem-solving process we can teach our children to use when they're faced with a moral dilemma where the best course of action isn't immediately clear. For example, some kids at school are picking on another kid, but you're afraid that if you tell an adult, it might just get worse for the kid and maybe they'll turn on you. Or you've been accepted into the popular crowd at school, but they don't like the girl you've been best friends with and make it clear you have to choose between them and her. With these or any other difficult moral challenges, the following steps can guide decision making:

1. **Consider alternatives:** What are the different ways I could try to solve this problem?

2. **Weigh consequences:** What are the likely good and bad results of the different alternatives for the people who would be affected, including myself?

3. **Identify values:** What moral values are involved? Which are most important?

4. **Seek advice:** What person(s), such as parents, teachers, or an older sibling, could I ask for help in deciding what to do in this situation?

5. **Make a decision:** Which course of action does the best job of respecting the important values and achieving the greatest good and least harm for those affected?

Advice seeking is especially important to stress with our children. They should know that even adults, if they are wise, don't make important decisions—especially about tough problems—without seeking counsel from at least one person whose judgment they respect.

Finally, we should teach kids that important decisions require a clear mind and a calm emotional state. Decisions shouldn't be made when we're tired, stressed, angry, or upset in any way. And they shouldn't be made in a hurry. We will almost never regret taking more time to make an important decision. We may very well regret not taking enough time.

8. Discipline Wisely

A mother I once counseled said that dinners with her two-and-a-half-year-old son had become a nightmare. Jonathan would start out by refusing to come to the table. His parents would coax him to come. If they got him there, he would often refuse to eat. They would then promise him a nice dessert. He'd eat a little food and scream for dessert. They would bring out the dessert, sometimes trying to get him to alternate between spoons of dinner and spoons of dessert.

I suggested that they take charge of the situation by saying in a matter-of-fact way, "Jonathan, it's dinnertime. You can eat with us or play in your room. But if you don't eat now, there's no food later. No dinner, no bedtime snack. Do you understand? The rule is: *Put your dinner in your tummy, and you will get a snack that's yummy.* Now, you tell us the rule."

When Jonathan tested this rule, as I was sure he would, his parents had to be prepared to follow through, calmly and lovingly put him to bed without snack and with a minimum of words, and let him cry himself to sleep if necessary. That's exactly what happened the first night. The second night, and thereafter, Jonathan came to dinner without a fuss.

Although only two, Jonathan had learned an important character lesson: In life there are rules and consequences. In his parents' initial handling of the dinner situation, they didn't convey either. Once they did—offering him a clear choice ("Eat dinner with us or go to bed hungry")—he complied. He took a significant step toward fitting into the social world.

In many families, discipline is the area where moral training breaks down. Disciplining wisely means setting expectations, holding kids accountable to them, and responding to their lapses in a way that both *teaches what's right* and *motivates the child to do what's right*. This means discipline should be clear and firm but not harsh. If we're always barking and booming, yelling and screaming, our kids will be afraid of our anger rather than focused on what they did wrong and how to correct it. Discipline should convey our confidence that our children can do better and should nurture their capacity and will to be good, even when we're not around to scold them.

Often a disciplinary consequence is needed to help children realize the seriousness of what they've done and motivate them not to do it again. In imposing consequences, however, many parents come down too hard in a moment of anger ("You're grounded for a week!"), later feel like a "meanie," especially when kids play the suffering victim, and end up going back on what they said—which undercuts their authority. A better approach is to ask a child, "What do *you* think is a fair consequence for what you did?" Most of the time, kids won't let themselves off easily. And if *they* come up with a fair consequence, they've served as their own judge and jury, which is better for their character development because they're taking responsibility for their actions. It's also a good idea, whenever possible, to *anticipate* a problem and establish an agreed-upon consequence in advance. ("What's a fair consequence for not picking up your toys the next time I ask?" "That we lose them for the next day.")

In many situations, restitution is a fitting moral consequence and teaches kids the important lesson that when you do something bad, you should do something good to make up for it. Restitution has the greatest value for children's moral development when we require them to take responsibility for making things right by asking themselves, "What can I do to make up for what I did?"

Whenever possible, discipline should also teach empathy. The failure to empathize—to put yourself in the other person's shoes—underlies many, if not most, hurtful actions. We can help kids develop empathy by asking questions that require them to take perspective: "How could you be helpful in this situation?" "Why am I upset with you?" "How does that make your sister feel?" "What could you do to make her feel better?"

Our children will remember how we responded to their moral transgressions. Catherine, now twenty-nine, says, "My dad was a strict but tender father. In tenth-grade, I had adopted the ungracious habit of referring to certain classmates as 'losers.' Dad took me aside and pointed out that it wasn't right to dismiss anyone like that, as if they weren't persons, as if they didn't have a soul. That habit ended that day."

A story that illustrates all the elements of disciplining wisely—teaching respect, fostering empathy, taking transgressions seriously, and requiring children to figure out how to make restitution—comes from Helena Zapletalova, my neighbor of many years who died this summer at the age of ninety-two. One of seven children, Helena grew up in Moravia, Czechoslovakia. She said that when she was seven years old, after the death of her grandmother, her grandfather came to live with them.

> My grandfather taught himself to carve, and made toy horses for my four brothers. I said to him, "Please make something for me." And so he spent a long time carving a doll for me. But when he gave it to me, I cried, "That's an ugly doll! I don't want that doll!"
>
> My mother heard this and said to me, "Go to your room. I will come and talk with you."
>
> When my mother sat down with me, I said, "It *is* an ugly doll! Why are you angry at me for telling the truth?"
>
> She answered, "You think that is the truth because you are not seeing with the eyes of the heart. If you use your heart's eyes, you will see that your grandfather worked hard for weeks trying to please you. With every stroke of the knife, he was thinking of you. This doll is full of love. I'm surprised you don't have eyes that can see that."

I said, "But it doesn't look like the dolls in the shops."

My mother said, "Anyone can buy those dolls. All you need is money. This doll was made for you, not for anyone else."

I felt ashamed and began to cry. My mother continued, "You have hurt your grandfather, and you have hurt me, because I love my father and I can see the love in his gift."

I said, "How can I make it right?" My mother said, "You didn't ask me before you insulted him, so don't ask me to tell you how to make it right. You will have to find the answer inside yourself."

She left me sitting on the edge of the bed. I thought and thought. It was a very hard problem for a little girl.

Finally, I went to my grandfather and said, "Grandfather, don't you think this doll would look nice if we painted on a face and some clothes and shoes?" He said, "What a good idea! Why didn't I think of that? Go and get your father's paints."

We painted the doll together, and it became my favorite toy.[17]

Helena said that when she went to the university, she took the doll with her. Sometimes she would talk to the doll and say, "Why didn't I think more before I spoke out and hurt my friend's feelings?" And whenever she faced a hard problem, the doll would remind her to look inside herself to find the answer.

What did Helena's mother do that succeeded in turning Helena's ungrateful reaction to her grandfather's gift into a character lesson for life? First, she helped her understand all the love her grandfather had put into the doll—a love she could see if she looked at the doll "with the eyes of the heart." She developed Helena's empathy by making it clear that she had hurt her grandfather and, in hurting him, hurt her mother as well. Finally, she insisted that Helena take the responsibility for finding a way to make things right and thereby gave her confidence that she had the resources within herself to solve life's problems. (Encouraging our children to have this confidence in their own ability to solve problems, of course, can and should be combined with encouraging them to seek helpful advice from parents and others when they face a difficult decision.)

9. Solve Conflicts Fairly

Conflicts go with the territory of family life. They can create anger and other bad feelings that eat away at relationships. Handled well, however, they can provide important opportunities for families to grow stronger and to foster children's character development.

One of the ways we can turn family conflicts to good is to use a fairness approach to solving them. A fairness approach has three parts: (1) achieving mutual understanding; (2) arriving at a fair, agreed-upon solution to the problem; and (3) holding a follow-up meeting to evaluate how the solution is working.

The fairness approach can be used with teens and even with young children. The sooner, the better. As an example of starting early, consider the experience of the mother of Phillip, seven, and Ben, five. She used the fairness approach with her sons to address the chief source of upset in their home, the kids acting badly when she was on the phone. She began by stating the purpose of the meeting and trying to get mutual understanding of the problem:

Mom: In a fairness meeting, the three of us will work
           together to solve the problem.
Ben: I don't get it.
Phillip: If you keep your big mouth shut, you might
           understand, dummy!
Ben: You shut up yourself!

The fairness meeting was off to a rocky start. But the mother persisted:

Mom: I want *both* of you to be quiet and listen. Now,
           the problem is it upsets me when you guys get
           wild when I'm on the phone and I can't carry on a
           conversation. What are your feelings about this?

Phillip: Are you going to tell Daddy about this?
Ben: Are you?
Phillip: I haven't been so bad.

The mother comments, "This type of reasoning on the part of the kids went on for what seemed like an endless time. It was very hard to get the idea of the meeting across to them. I was astonished to see how punishment-oriented they were." But she persevered: "We need to come to an agreement that is fair to all of us. I want to understand your feelings about this problem." Finally, there was a breakthrough:

Phillip: Mom, I really don't like it when you get on the phone and talk so long.
Ben: Yeah, the other night you talked on the phone when you said you would play a game with us, and then there wasn't time.
Mom: You feel I spend too much time on the phone?
Ben: You're not home that much, Mommy, and when you are, you should want to be with me.

"The more we talked," the mother says, "the more I understood their feelings of rejection when I'm on the phone for a long time. I explained that I often do get carried away, but that with working and going to school and taking care of our home, I hardly have time to see my friends, and this is often my only way of keeping in touch with them."

Once they understood each other's feelings, the mother, Phillip, and Ben were able to brainstorm solutions to the problem. They eventually worked out the following Fairness Agreement, which they all signed and posted:

1. If Mom has promised to do something with us, she will tell the person she is busy and will call back later.
2. We will make a list of things to do while Mom is on the phone.

3. Mom will try to make her calls shorter.
4. If Mom has to be on the phone for a longer time,
   she will tell us, and we will behave.

Two days later, Mom and the boys held a follow-up meeting, the final step in the fairness process. The mother reports, "We agreed we had stuck to our plan. The kids played together or did things independently when I was on the phone, and I made calls shorter. We agreed there has been less arguing and hassling about this problem."

The fairness approach promotes children's moral growth in three ways: (1) it respects them by listening to their feelings; (2) it requires them to take the perspective of others; and (3) it involves them in helping to solve family problems and maintain family harmony. One study found that when parents took a fairness approach to conflicts, their teenagers became more cooperative and more oriented to the needs of others.[18]

10. Provide Opportunities to Practice the Virtues

All of the virtues develop through practice. We don't develop goodness in children simply by talking about it. As educator John Agresto puts it, "Character development is not a spectator sport."

There are many ways we can provide our children with opportunities to practice the virtues. For starters, we can give them real responsibilities in family life: housework, yard work, helping to prepare meals and clean up, taking care of younger siblings, and so on. A mother of three sons (ages two, four, and six) says, "The rule in our house is that you get a chore for each year of your age. Our boys are all very proud of what they do." Kids should not be paid for these regular chores; such jobs are the way they contribute to the family. When they get to be school age, they can be given an allowance—a separate matter—as one of the benefits of family life and taught how to spend it wisely.

Another of our children's important responsibilities is to do their best work in school and make the most of their education.

Homework is part of that responsibility. Children should see homework not only as a means of getting good grades but as an opportunity to develop habits of good character such as self-discipline and putting duty before pleasure. They should understand that to do homework shoddily or not at all shows poor self-discipline and a lack of respect for the teacher, who typically has designed the homework to extend or reinforce school learning. Parents can help kids form good homework habits by establishing (1) a system, such as a daily planner, for keeping track of homework assignments; (2) a homework study time—ideally, the same time each day; and (3) a homework study area where they can work without distraction.

Helping children learn to set and work toward goals develops the virtues of planning, organization, and perseverance. My colleague Michele Borba interviewed a California father of seven whose children were known to be likable, courteous, and hardworking. He was asked what he did that might explain why his children turned out so well:

> Well, there's one thing I remember doing since my kids were young. Once a month I'd ask each child, "What goal do you have for yourself this month?" I'd try to help them think of something they wanted to achieve. Then we'd talk for a few minutes about what they could do to attain that goal. Every few days I'd check in and ask, "How are you doing? Do you need any help?" As they got older, they started to come to me to tell me their goals. I think these little talks helped my kids stay focused on what they wanted to achieve, and usually they were successful. I guess it really helped them to become self-motivated.

11. Foster Spiritual Development

One night, at the end of the graduate course I teach on character education, a student stayed to talk. He said he lifted weights competitively but that it was increasingly difficult to compete because so many people in the sport use steroids. I asked how athletes could continue to use steroids when everything you read says that steroids can make you sterile, cause cancer, and do other terrible things to your body.

He said, "People know all that, but they don't care." The professor in one of his physical education courses had recently shown a videotape which reported the results of a survey of amateur weight lifters, collegiate and postcollegiate. The survey posed this question: "If you could take a drug that would guarantee you'd win every competition for five years, but at the end of five years the drug would be certain to kill you, would you take that drug?" A majority of the weight lifters said yes.

If we ask ourselves how it is that a significant number of young people in our society would trade their very lives for five years of drug-dependent success, the answer comes back: They are spiritually adrift. As one mother said, upon hearing the results of that survey, "Those young men don't know why they're here."

Historically, religion has, for most people, offered a vision of life that tells us why we're here and where we're going. Religion can be a controversial subject. It is certainly possible to be an ethical person without being religious, and having religious faith by no means guarantees that a person will be good. But for a great many persons, religion gives life a higher meaning and an ultimate reason for leading a moral life: God expects it.

For young people who do not have faith in God, there is, I believe, a greater temptation especially in today's culture to make a god of something else: money, sexual pleasure, power, prestige, or, as in the case of the weight lifters, success at any price.

Research shows that young people who frequently attend religious services, who say that religion is important to them, and who belong to religious denominations that explicitly prohibit drug use are more likely to avoid drug involvement than their less religiously engaged peers. Likewise for teen sexual activity, single parenthood, and delinquent behavior; those teens who most often attend church have the lowest rates of these problems. One of the ways religion deters adolescents' involvement in self-injurious or antisocial behaviors is by influencing them to choose friends who do not engage in those activities.[19]

Studies of adults produce similar findings. Dr. Martin Seligman, former president of the American Psychological Association, reports, "Religious Americans are clearly less likely to abuse drugs, commit crimes, divorce, and kill themselves. They are also physically healthier and live longer. . . . Religions instill hope for the future and create meaning in life."[20]

What do religious parents do to try to foster faith—the kind of faith that is not just professed but lived out in everyday life? A Catholic mother comments:

If you see God as the center of things, it affects everything. There is a standard of behavior. It comes partly from people who have tried to discern the mind of God over the ages. We also have our own hearts to listen to. There is someone who has created us to behave in a certain way, so much so that if we don't behave in that way, we are unhappy. We are called to goodness, to live our lives according to a very high standard.

The psychologist Edward Hoffman describes the strong family life experienced by Lubavitcher Jews and their children's remarkable freedom from the drugs, sex, and violence that plague other urban children. Religious rituals such as the weekly lighting of Sabbath candles on Friday evening are a focal point for the whole family. After every meal, all family members take part in singing the traditional thanksgiving prayers. Lubavitcher children are expected to make a small contribution every Friday to the "charity box" displayed in the home. Says one Hasidic rabbi, "It's not so much that children 'take orders' from parents as that all family members 'take orders from God.'"[21]

Such practices ground morality in a meaning system, a view and experience of life in which being a good person is a central moral imperative.

At a talk I gave to parents, one mother asked, "What if you're not sure what you believe about God? I'm not. But I'm at the point of thinking I should expose my children to church. They won't be able to make an informed decision about this if they've never been exposed to it, but I don't know what to tell them about what I believe." I said she should tell them the truth: that she's not sure what she believes but wants them to have an experience of going to church that will help them someday decide for themselves.

In the spiritual domain, as in all areas, our personal example makes a difference. Mary, a young mother who is devout in her own faith, recalls her father:

> Dad always closes his letters with, "Work hard and pray a lot." This never sounds phony because it's what he does. He has worked hard all his life. He built the two homes we lived in and did all the repairs. And he prays throughout the day. My most powerful image of my father is of catching him kneeling at the foot of his bed, late at night before he retired, saying his personal prayers.

A caveat: Even parents who do all the right things—make character development a high priority, love their children, set a good example, discipline wisely, foster spiritual development—will still find raising children the toughest job on earth. Our children will make mistakes growing up, just as we did.

When our sons were teenagers, I took them to see a live performance of Bill Cosby at the Landmark Theater in nearby Syracuse, New York. In one routine, Cosby acted out the scene in Genesis in which God gives his first children, Adam and Eve, just one rule—"Don't eat the apples on that tree"—and they promptly disobey it. "All you parents out there," Cosby said with a chuckle, "if you have trouble getting your kids to obey, don't get discouraged. Remember that God had a hard time, too."

That said, it's our job as parents to make the most of the many opportunities we have to help our children grow to be strong and good people. For the process of developing character begins, like everything else, in the home.

CHAPTER 3

Build a Strong Home-School Partnership

Much has to be asked of schools, but much must also be asked of parents.

— HAROLD LEVY, FORMER CHANCELLOR,
NEW YORK CITY SCHOOLS

Parent involvement is the leading indicator of school success.[1] Parents' income level and educational background, the research finds, are less important for student success than parental interest and encouragement. And when schools and parents present a united front concerning character matters—respect for rules and authority, responsibility toward homework, honesty on tests and term papers, and sportsmanship at athletic events—students get a clear and consistent message and are more likely to take it seriously.

Yet in many communities across America, the essential alliance between home and school has eroded. Says the principal of an Oakland, California, middle school:

> We had a parent calling this week to complain that her child's grade on a Spanish assignment was lowered because she didn't put a heading on the paper. The Spanish teacher

had explained the requirement, but no matter. We have a lot of kids who are very good at getting their parents to believe that the teacher was mean or unfair. The problem we have with these parents is that they don't see their task as *supporting* the school.

In being aggressive advocates for their children, such parents seem not to realize that their constant interventions are likely to hurt rather than help their children—by leading them to be manipulative, less respectful of all authority, and unwilling to take responsibility for their actions.

Schools, for their part, also often act in ways that damage the home-school partnership. When the school fails to set high standards for learning and conduct and allows the children entrusted to it to get away with shoddy work and bad behavior, it damages the partnership. When a student is the victim of peer cruelty and the school does nothing to respond to a parent's complaints, it damages the partnership. When the school conveys a "We're the experts" attitude about sex education and fails to take seriously parental objections concerning material that violates a family's moral or religious beliefs, it damages the partnership.

Fortunately, a great many schools, especially those committed to character education, are making an effort to build a strong home-school partnership. Such schools reach out to parents in a spirit of humility, asking, "What can the school do to help us work together to provide the best possible education for your child? How can we improve?" In such partnerships, the school and parents promote a shared set of expectations concerning children's learning and behavior. Let's look at twenty ways schools and families are working together to help young people grow in knowledge and virtue.

1. Affirm the Family as the *Primary* Character Educator

The first step is for the school to be very clear about how it sees the complementary responsibilities of home and school regarding character development. Those responsibilities can be expressed in two simple statements:

1. The family is the first and most important influence on a child's character.
2. The school's job is to *reinforce* the positive character values (work ethic, respect, responsibility, honesty, etc.) being taught at home.

The reality, of course, is often otherwise: Many parents today aren't fulfilling their primary role in character formation. Regardless of the reality, however, the school should set forth—and work toward—the home-school relationship as it should be: The family lays down the foundation, and the school builds on that base.

2. *Expect* Parents to Participate

One way to increase parent involvement is simply to expect it.

Under its new principal, Vera White, Jefferson Junior High in Washington, D.C., dramatically raised its expectations of parents, 90 percent of whom are single parents, by asking each to give at least twenty hours a year in volunteer service to the school. The great majority met or exceeded that expectation. In the mid-nineties, Hilltop Elementary School in Lynnwood, Washington, began to ask each of its families to volunteer in a classroom for two hours a week. Seventy-five percent now do.

In Eugene, Oregon, at the Kennedy Middle School, winner of a 1999 National School of Character award, there are now so many parent volunteers that one parent serves almost full-time as the volunteer coordinator. Principal Kay Mehas describes parent involvement:

I have been an elementary and a middle school principal. During the first week of school, I tell my parents you need to be *more* involved in middle school than you were in elementary school. Students are figuring out where they fit in society. When they see you at school, it sends them a message about your priorities. We also encourage parents to drop in and eat lunch with their students whenever they can. For example, one father arranged his work schedule so he could eat lunch here every Thursday.[2]

3. Provide Incentives for Parent Participation

Along with raising expectations, some schools have provided incentives to motivate parental participation. New York City schools, for example, found that participation in parent-teacher conferences improved dramatically after a policy was instituted whereby only parents who came to a conference could receive their child's report card.

Scheduling parent conferences sooner in the school year provides another incentive for parents to come. Many schools now hold the first parent conference sometime in September rather than in October or November. Instead of "Here's how your child is doing this year (well in this subject, not so well in that)," the agenda becomes "What goals would you like your child to work on this year? How can we work together to make that happen?" Many schools also involve students in this early conference in order to help them take responsibility for goal setting.

4. Provide Programs on Parenting—and Work to Increase the Turnout

Most schools—usually through their PTA or PTO—offer programs on parenting, sometimes a whole course. The perennial problem: How to get more parents to take advantage of these programs?

Here are some ways schools have increased their turnouts:

1. Feed the family. (One school, for three consecutive weeks, offered a Thursday dinner at 5 P.M. for families, followed by a parenting class.)

2. Schedule a performance by the children, followed by the speaker for parents.

3. Provide baby-sitting or some kind of supervised activity for the kids (a film, games, activities in the gym) while the parents are listening to the parenting talk. (Variation: Have a mother-child activity one time while the dads go to the parenting talk, and reverse it the next time.)

4. Have a talk (for example, on solving conflicts in family life, dealing with peer pressure, or making wise sexual choices in the teens) that addresses parents and kids together.

5. Provide transportation. Send home a questionnaire in advance to see who needs a ride.

6. Schedule the presentation twice, at two different afterschool times (such as late afternoon and early evening) to accommodate differences in parents' schedules.

7. Hold a breakfast meeting. (One district got four hundred fathers to turn out for its October "Character Education Breakfast for Dads.")

8. Offer incentives to kids to get their parents to come (such as a "no-homework pass" for the weekend if your parent attends the event).

9. Have a catchy title (for example, "Raging Hormones," "Steering Your Teenage Driver," and "I Can't Hear You When I'm Yelling").

10. Match topics to the time of the year (for example, "Unplugging the Holiday Machine").

11. Survey parents to see what times are best for them and what topics they most want to hear about.

12. Offer the presentation over lunch at parents' work sites.

13. Offer a high-quality video series on parenting.

14. Require a ticket for attendance. (The ticket is free, but having to request or pick up a ticket gets parents to put the event on their calendars.)

15. Get the word out more than once: Post the event on the school website, mail postcard invitations, send e-mail reminders, and use an automated message machine to call every parent.

5. Get the Program to the Parents

No matter how effectively the school promotes its parenting programs, only a minority of parents will typically show up for any given offering. The main strategy for helping parents to parent effectively must therefore be home-based, not school-based. *If you can't get the parents to the program, get the program to the parents.*

For example, at the end of each month, Benjamin Franklin Classical Charter School (Franklin, Massachusetts), a 1998 National School of Character, sends parents the upcoming month's character education curriculum outline, which provides information on six things:

1. **The monthly character theme** (for example, fortitude, explained)
2. **The weekly virtues** (supporting the monthly theme, for example, patience, perseverance, and courage, each defined)
3. **Family service suggestions** (for practicing the weekly virtues in family and community life)
4. **Family reading suggestions** (titles of books that support that month's focus virtues)
5. **Curriculum connections** (how the monthly theme is being taught by your child's teacher through literature and history)
6. **Student goals** (suggestions for specific, virtue-related goals that your child can write with your guidance and then work on over the course of the month).[3]

6. Assign "Family Homework"

Many teachers also design "family homework"—character-related assignments that students take home to do with their parents. If a parent is not available to work with, students are encouraged to do the assignment with another older family member or adult. In this approach, the child serves as the bridge between school and home.

Deb Brown, author of *Growing Character: 99 Successful Strategies for the Elementary Classroom* (www.CharacterEducation.com) and a sixth-grade teacher in rural Saint Albans, West Virginia, gives family homework every week. One of her assignments is to interview one's parents about video games: What do they approve of and disapprove of? Why? Do they think violent video games influence kids' behavior? How? Another family assignment, focused on heroes, looks like this:

Who is a hero for you?	*Why is this person a hero for you?*
1.	1.
2.	2.
3.	3.
4.	4.

She gives each student two copies of this page, with the instructions: "Ask a parent to fill out one copy, listing their heroes and why those persons are heroes. Separately, do the same thing yourself on the other page. Then sit down together and compare and discuss what you each wrote." Parents are often delighted to find that they made their child's list. Valuable conversations occur about the persons the parent and child each listed and the character virtues represented by their choice of heroes. Students then bring the completed sheets to class, where they serve as the basis for a rich discussion of what a hero is.

An eighth-grade health education teacher has her students interview their parents about the following questions: "What qualities would you like me to look for in a boyfriend (or girlfriend) if that becomes an interest in my life? What qualities would you like me to look for someday in a husband (or wife)?" This assignment is the occasion for a very meaningful conversation that most parents would not otherwise have, touching on an area of their children's lives where parental guidance is very much needed.

Family character-related activities, whether student-initiated or parent-initiated, are most effective if they are a project and priority of the whole school rather than left to the initiative of individual teachers. For example, at Pearson Elementary School in Modesto, California, teachers Janie Hamilton and Marla Loew have developed a *Character Connection* (www.characterconnectionprogram.com) binder of weekly "values-based discussion homework" that is used at various grade levels. An extensive reading list recommends children's books by character trait. An excellent collection of family homework ideas is *Homeside Activities,* a grade-by-grade series available from the Developmental Studies Center, one of the nation's leading character education organizations (www.devstu.org).

7. Form Parent Peer Support Groups

Parents who won't turn out for a PTA talk may walk around the block to a parent support group where they can talk informally about parenting issues with other parents they've gotten to know.

The school should take steps to set up these parent support groups. Says Katie Moffett, a former Virginia counselor, "In our middle school, we called parents to ask them to be part of our parent support groups. We trained mothers to be facilitators. They all started support groups in their neighborhoods. Sometimes we invited speakers to come in from the community. When a gang moved into our area a year later, the parents were able to help their kids resist involvement. They already had a relationship with the police, who had come to some of the support group meetings. The gang never got a toehold."

Here are some guidelines for parent support group meetings:

1. Train parent facilitators to run the meetings,
   or provide clear guidelines if the groups will
   be choosing their own facilitators.

2. Keep the groups small, no bigger than ten parents.

3. Let the groups decide how often to meet (perhaps monthly at first, then less often later on).

4. Conduct the meetings in a circle to allow for good eye contact and equal participation.

5. Begin with a round-robin, with parents introducing themselves, telling the ages of their children, and stating what issues (TV, chores, homework, boy-girl concerns, etc.) they'd like to discuss.

6. Review the list of proposed topics and have the group choose one, with a backup, that they'd like to discuss in that meeting.

7. Encourage parents to speak personally and anecdotally (What did you go through as a kid? How do you think things are different today? What have you tried in your family that seems to work? What do you have trouble with?)

8. Do a common reading (such as a good book, booklet, or article on parenting). Early on, invite an older, more experienced couple to join a meeting and ask them to address, "If we had it to do all over again, this is what we'd do . . ." and "A couple of things we did that worked out well for us were . . ."

9. If the group wishes, have someone at each meeting make a list of the ideas that are mentioned, with a copy for all.[4]

Schools can also facilitate parent connections through a buddy system. Just as new kids in a school are assigned a buddy, new parents are paired with veteran families. Buddy parents contact new parents, get together, answer questions, and in general help the new parents learn about the school and community.

8. Involve Parents in Planning the Character Education Program

Parents must be partners in planning a school's character education initiative. Their involvement is essential for building trust.

The first way to make parents partners is to give everybody a chance to have input. Bill Parsons, when he was principal at West Point Elementary School (706-812-7973) in Georgia, sent home a letter that asked parents, "What character qualities would you like our school to model and teach?" It provided a list of thirty qualities and asked parents to check their top ten. It also gave parents places to check if they did not support teaching character in the school or if they had questions they wished to discuss with the principal.

If the school is already doing character education, a good way to give all parents a voice is to provide a list of the school's current target virtues, with the request, "Mark three that you think the school should be emphasizing more, rank them in order of importance, and give your reasons if you wish."

I spoke at a middle school parents' night where the school distributed and collected this kind of questionnaire on the spot, immediately scanned and reported the results to the audience, and then used the findings as the springboard for a stimulating discussion. Overwhelmingly, the several hundred parents present said they wanted the middle school to put more emphasis on teaching respect. The facilitator then called on parents—there were hands all over the room—who gave reasons and examples of why they felt more attention to respect was needed.

A third way to involve parents in shaping the character effort is to have parent representatives on the school's character education leadership committee(s). This gives parents a chance to interact with teachers, administrators, and others in developing the program, guiding its implementation, and making changes to improve it.

A fourth way is to have a monthly letter from the principal on the school's character education program, keeping all parents abreast of the program, encouraging their participation in school-based events, asking them to promote the virtues at home, and inviting feedback and questions.

9. Establish an Ongoing Forum for Parents

An open forum gives parents an ongoing opportunity for input—not only about the character education program but about anything else that might be a concern. Such a forum contributes to a climate of openness, mutual listening, and trust that benefits the character education effort and all other aspects of home-school relations.

For the past eleven years, principal Nancy Robb of Palatine High School in Palatine, Illinois, has held monthly meetings with parents, one in English that draws about a hundred people each time and one in Spanish that draws between forty and eighty. She calls these open meetings her "advisory board."

At these sessions Principal Robb presents issues she wants input on, and parents can bring up issues they want to discuss. Parents turn out for these meetings and take them seriously because they can see she acts on their concerns. The meetings have also created a telephone network that makes it possible for the school and parents to work together to see that student parties are alcohol-free.[5]

10. Form a Parents' Character Education Committee

The school should also give parents a leadership role in the character effort. One effective way to do that is to create a parents' character education committee made up mostly or entirely of parents and chaired by a parent. Its mission is to keep parents informed about and involved in the character education effort.

Part of this group's job is to help organize special, school-based, character-related events—such as an assembly, a Grandparents Day, a family film night, a parenting talk, a community service activity, or a common book project. In a Detroit middle school, for example, the parents' committee got more than three-quarters of parents and students to read *To Kill a Mockingbird* and come out for an April evening during which small groups of parents and kids spent an hour discussing the character themes and lessons of this novel.

The most important responsibility of the parents' committee, however, is motivating and helping parents to model and teach character at home.

For example, at Brookside Elementary School (Binghamton, New York), a 1998 National School of Character, the parents' committee wrote and sent home a monthly "Character Corner" column (front and back of one page). It suggested specific ways parents might foster the monthly virtue in family life (for example, "You can teach your children courtesy by showing them how to hold the door for someone coming behind them"). It also listed books for bedtime reading and family videos that could be used to foster the monthly virtue. When this kind of communication is coming *from* parents *to* parents, and not just from the school administration, it gets a more receptive response.

Finally, the parents' character committee can put parenting tools (books, videos, etc.) in the hands of families by developing a Parents' Corner—in the school's media center, for example.⁶ Three resources with helpful bibliographies for early childhood through adolescence are Michele Borba's *Building Moral Intelligence,* William Kilpatrick's *Books That Build Character,* and my own *Raising Good Children.* A very helpful book on discipline is Borba's *No More Misbehavin'.*

How do you get busy parents to serve on a parents' character education committee? Have the principal invite them, personally.

11. Make a Moral Compact with Parents

Nothing is more destructive of teacher morale and the school-home partnership than parents' rushing to the defense of their children when they've gotten in trouble at school. To avoid this pattern, and to get a critical mass of parents on board in support of the school's character education goals, parents must be asked to *sign on*. What's missing in most schools is an explicit moral compact between home and school to work together to achieve the school's character aims.

Cheating, for example, has become a serious problem in most secondary schools. When students are caught cheating, parents commonly criticize the teacher (for failing to make the assignment clear, making the penalty too harsh, etc.) rather than holding their child responsible. To try to promote academic honesty, some schools have an honor code whereby students pledge "not to lie, cheat, or steal or tolerate such behavior in my presence." But to make such a code work, the school should send it home to parents and ask them for a commitment of support: "I have read the Honor Code and discussed it with my child. I support the school's efforts to promote academic integrity and to hold students accountable to that standard."

What should a school do if, despite its proactive efforts to form a moral compact, a parent whose child has violated a rule persists in defending the child and attacking the school? One principal shares what she does:

> At that point I stop and ask, in a calm and sincere voice, one or both of the following questions: "How would you like the school to handle this?" and "What lesson would you like your child to learn from this experience?" These questions almost always give parents pause. They force them to be more responsible and reflective: How *do* they want the school to handle it? Do they really want the school to have separate rules for their child? Do they really want their child to walk away thinking, "My actions have no consequences. I can break rules and get away with it"?

12. Renew the Compact

Parents' commitment to character and the school-home partnership will grow stronger if it's regularly renewed.

Brookridge Elementary School in Brooklyn, Ohio, renews its moral compact with parents every month. In February, for example, the virtue of the month is honesty. A letter from school counselor Jerry Wolf goes home to families explaining the school's focus for that month and encouraging parents to discuss honesty at home and to set and post "family goals for honest actions" ("I will be honest by _____"). Parents are also invited to show support for the school's character effort by returning the monthly "Parents' Pledge," in this case the pledge for honesty:

PARENTS' PLEDGE FOR HONESTY

- I will demonstrate to my child that my word is my bond.
- I will encourage my child to be honest, understanding that everyone makes mistakes.
- I will stress to my child the importance of having a good reputation.

        Parent's signature _____
        Student's name _____

The fastest way to lose our good character is to lose our honesty.
—AESOP

13. Extend the Compact to Discipline

Discipline, more than any other area, is where parents and schools butt heads. When that happens, everybody loses—especially kids, who develop the attitude that if they get in trouble at school, it's no big deal, because their parents will take their part.

Parents should be asked—at a parents' orientation, through a letter from the principal, in the school handbook, and in the school's character education literature—to work *with* the school in matters of discipline. The school should help parents understand that this is in their child's best interest. Just as it's not good at home if a child plays one parent against another, it's not good if a student plays the parent against the school.

If parents have reason to believe that a teacher, coach, or some other school staff member has not been fair to their child, or if they are just not sure what happened, they should approach the school quietly, without telling the child. The school should ask parents to do this.

Parents are more likely to support the teacher's discipline if they know the policy from the outset. At the elementary and middle school levels, the principal should encourage all teachers to send parents their academic and behavioral expectations, with a copy of their rules and consequences if they have a formal plan, including at what point parents will be asked to help solve a problem.

14. Extend the Compact to Sports and Other Co-curricular Activities

In a school committed to character, extracurricular activities must be governed by the same high character expectations that apply to every other phase of school life.

Of all the school's extracurricular activities, sports typically have the greatest impact on the school's moral culture, for good or for ill. Deliberate strategies are needed to make sports a character-building rather than character-eroding experience. Partnering with parents is a good place to start, especially since many parents are part of the problem (demonstrating egregious sportsmanship at athletic events, for example).

As an example of how to extend the home-school moral compact to sports, consider the approach taken by Catholic Central High School (CCHS) in Troy, New York. (Some public schools have equally strict policies.) In order to play on a sports team at CCHS, the student and at least one parent must attend the mandatory athletes' meeting at the start of the season. If they can't make this session, they must come to school sometime during the next day to view a video of the meeting. The meeting opens with a ten-to-fifteen-minute character-focused talk, "Life Lessons I Learned from Athletics," by one of the school's successful graduates and former athletes.

The principal, the affable but no-nonsense Sister Kate Arseneau, then gives a brief talk about the "three A's" that the school expects of all its students: attendance, academic performance, and attitude. The athletic director goes over the Student Pledge and the Parent Pledge, which must be signed for an athlete to be eligible to play. The pledges commit students and their parents to honoring the team training rules; to respecting their coach, their teammates (all hazing is forbidden), and opposing teams; and to observing good sportsmanship not only at their own games but at all school athletic events. Following the meeting for parents and students, the principal meets with the coaches to go over the expectations for them as role models and character educators. (See also *PLUS: Positive Learning Using Sports,* by Jeffrey Pratt Beedy, jbeedy@newhampton.org; *Winning with Character,* a character and leadership curriculum for high school and college student athletes and coaches developed by University of Idaho's Dr. Sharon Stoll and University of Georgia's coach Bobby Lankford, bobbylankford@sports.uga.edu; and PositiveCoaching Alliance, www.positivecoach.org.)

15. Extend the Compact to Combating the Effects of the Media

If we hope to win the battle for the hearts, minds, and character of our children, schools and parents must work diligently together to protect kids from the cultural poisons of media sex, violence, vulgarity, and materialism.

Step one in the plan should be a letter from the principal at the start of the year that raises parental consciousness concerning the media's effects on kids and suggests limits parents can put in place.

Parents typically don't have a clue, unless the school tells them, about the media's negative effects on the school environment. The media's sexualizing of children shows up at school in all sorts of ways: in children's speech, their actions, and their dress.

Nor do most parents know what the research shows. Schools should tell them. In March 2002, *Science* magazine reported that teenage boys and girls who watch more than three hours of TV a day are *four times* more likely as adults to fight or assault another person, compared to teens who watch less than an hour a day. This difference held regardless of whether the teens came from stable, middle-class homes or from low-income families with a history of childhood neglect. Other research shows that the more TV kids watch, the lower their level of enthusiasm for learning.

The school can also bring this issue home to parents by conducting a media survey of its own students. Here are some of the survey questions used by Emma Tinoco, principal of the Campus Chihuahua junior high school in Chihuahua, Mexico: "What are your favorite TV programs? What video games do you play? Do you have a TV in your own room? About how much time each day do you watch television? Do you watch TV while doing homework (sometimes, never, always)? Do you watch TV while eating dinner (sometimes, never, always)? Are there any TV shows (list them) that your family does not permit you to watch?"

Principal Tinoco scheduled a meeting of parents at which the results of the media survey were revealed. *Friends* was the favorite TV show of these middle schoolers. Tinoco then showed clips from several episodes of *Friends* and asked parents to discuss in small groups: "What kind of messages and values are these shows presenting?" and "Are these the values we want our children to absorb?"

Schools should also point out that the problem with television isn't just *what* kids are watching; it's also *that* they are watching. Time spent watching TV is almost always better spent doing something else—something that contributes to relationships, learning, and our growth as persons. Television steals precious family time, often displacing dinner conversation and bedtime reading.

To help families get control of the media, schools should offer specific suggestions and guidelines. The following are some starting points that individual families can modify to suit their needs:

1. We use media to promote family life and good values. We don't allow media in our home that go against our values or undermine family life.
2. No TV before school, before homework is done, or during dinner.

3. You must ask permission to turn on the TV and may watch only approved programs.

4. Watching television is a special event, not a regular routine. In general, it is also a family event, not a private pastime.

5. Certain nights are "quiet nights"; the TV stays off so that we can focus on family activities and doing other things we need to do. (Choose these nights together as a family.)

6. All video games must be previewed by a parent.

7. Pornographic and hate websites are off limits (and blocked by an Internet screen installed by the family).

8. Internet rules: No use of the Internet—no e-mails, accessing websites, chat rooms, or instant messaging—without a parent's prior approval and presence at home. You must have parental permission to download anything.

9. No R-rated movies and no PG-13 or PG movies without parental permission. (Parents can check out the content of current films by consulting www.screenit.com.)

Schools should suggest that parents sit kids down for a family meeting to explain these policies, for instance by saying, "The things you take into your minds can stay there for a very long time. Parents who care about their kids care enough to set limits on TV, the Internet, and other media."

Parents should also be encouraged to let networks and advertisers know when they are happy or unhappy with the content of particular programs. One way to do that is to join Parents Television Council (www.ParentsTV.org) and participate in their e-mail feedback to networks and sponsors.

Schools, I believe, should also strongly encourage parents to consider having no TV (just a VCR for playing good videos). Adults raised in families without TV almost always look back with gratitude. Among the benefits, they usually learned to love to read.

16. Be Responsive to Parental Complaints

The moral compact between school and parents obviously goes both ways: Parents have a responsibility to support the school's character-building efforts, but schools have an equal responsibility to be respectful of and responsive to parents' concerns.

Nothing erodes parental trust faster than a school's stonewalling in the face of a parent's complaint. "Our district," says a mother, "has had a 'blame the victim' attitude, has ignored due process rights, and has been hostile toward parents who come forward on behalf of mistreated students." For example, a middle school African-American student, who had lost her hair because of leukemia treatments, was repeatedly harassed by a group of other girls. "Ashley is a bald bitch" was scrawled on the girls' bathroom mirror. Her younger brother was repeatedly called "nigger" on the school bus by another boy. The parents' appeals to the school administration produced no action. In another district, high school administrators were unresponsive to parents' complaints that a group of boys were circulating a list, "The Top 10 Kids to Beat Up On."

To demonstrate its commitment to taking parental concerns and complaints seriously, a school administration should establish a complaints procedure and send a letter home (with a copy to school staff) at the start of the school year:

> If your child is experiencing *any kind of problem at school,* especially unfair, unkind, or disrespectful treatment, *we want to know.* Your child's safety, well-being, and success at school are our highest priority. We are committed to creating a safe and welcoming learning environment for all students. Please use our complaint procedure to let us know about any concern you may have so that we can take appropriate steps to address it.

In addition, the school is wise to conduct periodic surveys of all parents, asking questions such as "How safe does your child feel at school?" and "Describe any experience your child has had causing

him or her to feel unsafe or unwelcome at school." Such a survey
will bring problems to light and provide objective data on how widespread they are.

The school must then prove its sincerity by quickly and genuinely *acting upon* parents' expressed concerns. It takes strong
moral leadership at the top—with the virtues of justice, honesty,
and humility—to rise above institutional defensiveness and establish a track record of responding promptly and conscientiously to
parental complaints.

17. Respect the Primacy of Parental Rights Regarding Sex Education

It's especially crucial to respect parents' rights—and to take their
complaints seriously—when the issue is as sensitive as sex education.

Parents have the primary moral authority over anything as personal, intimate, and value-laden as their child's education about sex.
A school's failure to respect the primacy of parents' rights regarding
the formation of their child's sexual conscience and the sexual information their child is exposed to in the classroom does grave damage
to the trust necessary for a successful school-parent partnership.

With regard to sex education, parents have a right to (1) have input into the selection of a sexuality curriculum through a process
that all parties consider to be open, balanced, and fair; (2) have sex
education that is character education, that sets high expectations
and guides students toward right decisions, ones truly in their best
interests and the interests of society (see chapter 4 for recommendations regarding character-based sex education); and (3) know *in
advance* about any potentially controversial material (for example,
on contraception, abortion, or homosexuality) that will be presented
to their child, whether in a class or school assembly, and have their
child excused from material they find objectionable.

Twenty-five years ago, the public schools of Pittsfield, Massachusetts, adopted an elementary school human sexuality program
called LAMO (Learning about Myself and Others) that is a model
of a school-home partnership. Parents and children voluntarily at-

tend classes together at the school (one per year in grades one and two, four sessions per year in grades five and six). When the teacher poses a question, each child works on it with his or her parent. Parents give their views and help their children clear up misunderstandings. Following each session, parents are given take-home materials for further discussion with their child.

Parents report that the LAMO program has helped them create a relationship of trust in the home that enables them to communicate openly with their children as they move through the secondary school years. The pregnancy rate for students who have participated with their parents in the LAMO elementary program has remained near zero throughout their middle school and high school years.[7]

18. Increase the Flow of All Positive Communication between School and Home

The school should strive to increase the general flow of communication between school and home. The more communication there is, the more parents will feel like partners in their child's education and the more they will invest in their child's learning and character development.

Jennie Carnahan, a fourth-grade teacher at Burton Street Elementary School in Cazenovia, New York, sends a parent questionnaire home at the start of the year. Sample items: "List five words that describe your child's character (e.g., competitive, cheerful, friendly, generous, perfectionist)." "What motivates your child?" "What upsets your child?" "What are your child's out-of-school interests?" "What academic subject is your child's strongest? Weakest?" "What academic area(s) would you like to see stressed this year?" "What social skills would you like to see developed?"

Marilyn Lance, teacher of the year for New York State in 2000, has as her motto: "Never give up on a kid—or a parent." Besides calling all parents personally to invite them to Open House night, she makes one-to-two-minute calls throughout the year, often leaving a brief message on an answering machine letting parents hear something positive about their child. She finds that when she's made a good-news call first, she gets a much more positive response when she has to call home about a problem.

Cindy Christopher, a third-grade teacher in Tully, New York, sends home a monthly calendar so parents can see at a glance what's coming up (a spelling bee on Monday, a guest speaker on pets on Wednesday, a field trip to a dairy farm on Friday). Knowing what's happening at school also enables parents to have more fruitful conversations with their kids about school. Instead of asking, "What did you do at school today?" (to which kids invariably answer, "Nothing"), parents can say, "Tell me one thing you learned today from the man who spoke about pets." (See Christopher's book *Building Parent-Teacher Communication*[8] for many other good ideas.)

19. Let Parents Know What Work Is Expected and Send Home Regular Reports

It's an act of respect and caring on the teacher's part to let parents know exactly what work is expected and to send home regular reports. Being informed helps parents to encourage their child's responsibility toward schoolwork.

Some teachers leave the homework for the week on their school's Parent Link answering service. Paul Cornell, a middle school social studies teacher in Lowville, New York, has developed a web page that posts all of his homework assignments for the quarter. He says that many parents access it to see what's expected of their child. Students who work more slowly have the chance to get started on assignments well before the due date. Cornell also uses a software program called Gradequick that prints out reports to parents on students' missing work. (In Provo, Utah, the school district uses a web service that enables parents to get monthly and even weekly updates on their child's grades.)

20. Provide Family Support Centers and Community Schools

Sweet Home School District in Amherst, New York, is one of a growing number of districts that have established an in-school Family Support Center (contact Anne Nowak, anowak@shs.k12.ny.us). Staffed by two professionals and partnered with seventeen area organizations, Sweet Home's center provides "one-stop" shopping for needed services (help with an academic or behavior problem, marriage counseling, drug or alcohol counseling) or referral to community agencies that can assist in other areas of need (health matters, financial counseling). In Montgomery County, Maryland, Linkages to Learning (www.montgomerycountymd.gov/content/linkages) has found school-based family support centers to improve student learning and family functioning. (See also UCLA's Center for Mental Health in Schools, www. smhp.psych.ucla.edu.)

A traditional school can become a "community school," a year-round community center offering a wide range of educational and recreational services to students, parents, extended family members, and other community members. In many places, community schools have helped restore a badly needed sense of community around the school. Research carried out by Yale University finds that students at community schools have higher math and reading scores and the schools have less vandalism, increased parent involvement, and a better community image. For additional resources on school, family, and community partnerships, visit the website of the National Network of Partnership Schools (www.csos.jhu.edu/p2000/index.htm) and the website of the Coalition of Community Schools (www.communityschools.org).

* * *

Historically, the school and the family have been two of the major formative institutions shaping the values and character of the young. Working at cross-purposes, they put children at risk. Working together, in the many ways that have been shown to be possible, they have great potential to set our children on the path to school success and a virtuous life.

CHAPTER 4

Talk to Kids About Sex, Love, and Character

I lost my virginity when I was fifteen. My boyfriend and I thought we loved each other. But once we began having sex, it completely destroyed any love we had. I felt he was no longer interested in spending time with me—he was interested in spending time with my body.

—A TWENTY-TWO-YEAR-OLD WOMAN

I wish someone had been preaching abstinence in my ear when I was in high school. That was when my sexual activity started. I don't even want to think about my college years. I wish I had saved this for my wife.

—A TWENTY-SIX-YEAR-OLD HUSBAND

Sandy, a bright and pretty girl, asked to see her ninth-grade health teacher, Mr. Bartlett, during lunch period. She explained that she had never had a boyfriend, so she had been excited when a senior had asked her out.

After they dated for several weeks, he asked her to have sex with him. She was reluctant, but he persisted. She was afraid of appearing immature and losing him, so she consented.

83

"Did it work?" Mr. Bartlett gently asked. "Did you keep him?"

Sandy replied, "For another week. We had sex again, and then he dropped me. He said I wasn't good enough. There was no spark."

She continued, "I know what you're going to say. I take your class. I know now that he didn't really love me. I feel so stupid."[1]

Brian, a college senior, recounts his first sexual experience:

I first had intercourse with my girlfriend when we were fifteen. I'd been going with her for almost a year, and I loved her very much. She was friendly, outgoing, charismatic. We'd done everything but have intercourse, and then one night she asked if we could go all the way.

A few days later, we broke up. It was the most painful time of my life. I had opened myself up to her more than I had to anybody, even my parents. I was depressed, moody, and nervous. My friends dropped me because I was so bummed out. I felt like a failure. I dropped out of sports. My grades weren't terrific.

I didn't go out again until I got to college. I've had mostly one-night stands. I'm afraid of falling in love.[2]

As parents and educators, we worry about many areas of our children's decision making—sex, drugs, drinking, and drinking and driving—where the wrong choices can carry a high cost. But we sense that they are most vulnerable, most at risk emotionally as well as physically, in the sexual area of their lives. The damage to our children's health, heart, and character from premature sexual involvement may go deeper, and last longer, than the effects of any other mistakes they might make.

"I'm forty-two years old," a high school teacher said to me after a workshop on this topic, "and I'm still dealing with emotional issues stemming from sexual relationships when I was young." Because sexual decisions have such important life consequences, a strong home-school partnership—committed to helping our children make wise choices—is nowhere more important than it is in this domain.

Sex, however, is delicate territory. The potential for controversy is higher here than in any other area of education. But four decades after the sexual revolution, there is emerging common ground. Abstinence is now recognized to be the wisest choice for many reasons. More than a half million unmarried teens get pregnant each year. Having a baby when you are an unmarried teenager is the surest route to poverty for you and your child. One in three sexually active singles gets an STD by age twenty-four. Until the mid-1970s, there were only two common STDs—syphilis and gonorrhea; now there are more than twenty.

Condoms haven't solved these problems. The typical annual failure rate for adult couples using condoms to prevent pregnancy is 14 percent; the failure rate for teens can go as high as 30 percent because alcohol or drug use often reduces their ability to use condoms correctly or at all. Over the past twenty years, teens have shown the greatest increase in the use of condoms but simultaneously the greatest increase in STDs. A 2001 National Institutes of Health report, summarizing hundreds of studies, concluded that condoms reduce sexual transmission of HIV/AIDS by 87 percent (*if* used 100 percent of the time), provide about 50 percent protection against gonorrhea, but *provide no proven protection against six of the leading eight STDs,* including human papilloma virus (the cause of virtually all cervical cancer), chlamydia (the fastest-growing cause of infertility), and herpes.[3] One reason condoms don't provide better protection against STDs is that the germs can be passed on by skin-to-skin contact in the whole genital region, only part of which is covered by the condom. (For a summary of the NIH results and related research, see the publication *Sex, Condoms, and STDs: What We Now Know,* www.medinstitute.org.[4])

SEX AND THE HUMAN HEART

For human beings, of course, sex is about much more than the body. Our entire person is involved. That's why sex has uniquely powerful emotional and spiritual consequences. And there is no condom for the heart.

To educate adequately about human sexuality, both schools and parents must therefore address the emotional hurts and regrets that commonly follow temporary sexual relationships. According to a

2000 survey conducted by the National Campaign to Prevent Teen Pregnancy, 72 percent of teenage girls and 55 percent of boys who have had sexual intercourse say they wish they had waited.

Many adults also express sexual regrets. A young married woman confided to her counselor, "I had a lot of partners before marriage. I know it's affected my ability to bond with my husband." Says John Diggs, M.D., a physician–abstinence educator who talks to students about human relationships: "You can have many friends, but it just doesn't work to have many sexual partners." Research finds that couples who were not sexually involved before marriage and are faithful to their spouses during marriage are more satisfied with their current sex life than those involved sexually before marriage or engaged in extramarital affairs.[5]

Although the emotional fallout from uncommitted sex is only recently getting attention, we've known about it for a long time. At a 1999 "Beyond Relativism" conference at George Washington University, Dr. Armand Nicholi, clinical professor of psychiatry at Harvard Medical School, commented:

> Not long after the sexual revolution was under way, clinicians—even orthodox Freudians—observed that the new sexual freedom was creating a psychological disaster. We began to study Harvard students who complained of emptiness and despondency.
>
> There was a gap between their social conscience and the morality of their personal lives. The new sexual permissiveness was leading to empty relationships and feelings of self-contempt. Many of these students were preoccupied with the passing of time and with death. They yearned for meaning, for a moral framework. When some of them moved away from moral relativism to a system of clear values— typically embracing a drug-free lifestyle and strict sexual code—they reported that their relationships with the opposite sex improved, as did their relations with peers in general, their relationship with their parents, and their academic performance.

Because sex has profound personal and social consequences, ethical sexuality[6]—acting with respect for oneself and others—must be considered part of good character. Sex education must therefore be character education. It must, as Boston educator Kevin Ryan points out, teach students that bringing self-discipline to their sexuality is a means of developing their character and preparing themselves for a deep, loving relationship as an adult.

A SEXUALLY TOXIC ENVIRONMENT

For both schools and families, the task of teaching sexual self-control is made much more difficult by the fact that young people today are growing up in a world that pushes sex at them constantly. A mother of an eighth grader picked up a copy of *Teen People* magazine for the first time and was "amazed . . . it was page after page of young teens dressed in very provocative ways and in very provocative poses."[7]

An eighth-grade boy quoted in the *New York Times* said his interest in sex began in third grade when he started watching *Beverly Hills 90210*. "The people were cool," he said. "I wanted to try what they were doing on the show."

James Coughlin, creator of the Facing Reality sexuality curriculum, comments, "We socialize kids to have sex. No culture in human history has ever done this to its children."

Faced with this moral environment, what strategies can we use to teach our children to make good sexual choices, ones that will build their character and protect their heart, health, and happiness?

1. Be Clear About What Kids Need In Order to Avoid Premature Sex

To exercise sexual wisdom in today's world, young people need (1) internally held convictions about why it makes sense to save sexual intimacy for a truly committed relationship; (2) strengths of character, such as good judgment, self-control, modesty, genuine respect for

self and others, and the courage to resist sexual pressure and temptation; and (3) support systems for living out this commitment, including, ideally, support from their families, faith communities, schools,
and at least one good friend who has made the decision to wait.

2. Point Out the Positive Trends

We can take heart from the fact—and should certainly point out to
our children—that despite all the pressures, growing numbers of
young people are not getting sexually involved.

A December 2002 *Newsweek* cover story titled "The New Virginity" reported the Centers for Disease Control's latest data: high school
students who have *not* had sexual intercourse are now in a majority
(52 percent) for the first time in twenty-five years. Moreover, only one-
third of students say they are "currently sexually active."[8] Most of this
change is accounted for by an increase in the virginity rate—up more
than 10 percent in the 1990s—among high school boys.[9]

3. Help Kids Understand Why Some Young People Get Sexually Involved

Kids are less likely to be pulled into sexual activity themselves if
they have insight into why some of their peers do get sexually involved. Knowledge is power. As parents and educators, we can help
young people step back from the scene and understand the many
factors that can lead to sexual activity.

1. Sexual attraction. Human beings are sexual creatures; we are
sexually interested in and attracted to others. Sexual desire doesn't
compel anyone to have sex, but in the absence of inhibiting counter-
influences it can easily lead to sexual activity.

2. No good reason not to. "I got sexually involved," says a college
senior, "because I couldn't answer the question, 'Why *shouldn't* I
have sex?'"

3. *Partner pressure.* Pressure from a partner—a boyfriend or girlfriend they wanted to keep—is the reason teens most often cite for their initial decision to have sex.[10]

4. *Desire to express love.* Many young people think sex is simply a natural way to express the love they feel for each other.

5. *Desire to be normal.* Says a high school health teacher, "In recent years, many kids have gotten it into their heads that there is something wrong with them if they haven't had sexual intercourse by the time they're sixteen."

6. *Early dating.* A study in the *Journal of Adolescent Research* found that of those who began single dating when they were seventh graders, 71 percent of boys and 90 percent of girls had intercourse by the time they graduated from high school.[11] Of those who did not begin single dating until age sixteen, only 16 percent of boys and 18 percent of girls had sexual intercourse by high school graduation.

7. *Steady dating.* The same study found that steady dating, which typically increases the time a couple spends alone, significantly increased the likelihood of sexual intercourse.

8. *Need for intimacy.* Many young people, especially girls, turn to sex to try to meet the need for intimacy. "If Dad isn't there giving nonsexual attention," says one psychologist, "a girl will often go after sexual attention from boys."

9. *Low self-worth.* Says a girl who got pregnant at fifteen, "My brothers and their girlfriends said if you didn't do it, you were a nerd. I had always been sort of an outcast, and I didn't want to be called a nerd."

10. *The search for identity.* Says Cheryl Jones, an adolescent therapist, "I see girls who up until now have been the perfect kids— straight A's, followed all the rules. Then they turn fifteen or sixteen, and they think, 'I don't want to be just what my parents want me to be.' They know what they *don't* want to be, but they don't know what *to* be, so they become the opposite, a kind of antipersonality." (Becoming one's own person as a teenager is less likely to involve this kind of rebellion if parents, from childhood on, have been helping their children to define their own interests and sense of self.)

11. A change in environment. For some young people, sexual activity starts when they enter a new environment such as college, where there is the potential to live much more freely.

12. Parental permissiveness. Fourteen-year-old Courtney complained that her parents "let me go over to my boyfriend's house when they know his parents aren't home. That is weird." Eventually, she and her boyfriend had sex.

13. Parents' example. Says a high school boy who lives with his divorced father, "What's the big deal about sex? A lot of my dad's girlfriends spend the night."

14. Nothing better to do. In the South Bronx, New York, where the teen pregnancy rate is nearly twice the national norm, a community agency sponsored an essay contest for adolescents on the question, "How Can the Problem of Teenage Pregnancy Be Solved?" One of the winning essays argued that many teens have sex "because they are bored—they have nothing better to do." One pregnancy prevention program found that when teens got involved in community service, the pregnancy rate dropped.

15. Sex education that doesn't send a clear abstinence message. Says a high school boy in Los Angeles, "They pass out condoms, teach pregnancy-this and STD-that, but they never really say it's wrong."

16. Sexual abuse. One in four girls and one in six boys are sexually abused by age eighteen. Sexually abused youth, often because of their low self-worth, are more likely to become sexually active, often with older partners.

17. *Drugs and alcohol.* Drugs and alcohol impair moral judgment and weaken inhibitions. Teens who say they have used drugs or been drunk in the past month, for example, are much more likely to have had sex than teens who have never been drunk or used drugs.[12]

18. *A highly sexualized environment.* A sexually stimulating media culture sends the unrelenting message that sex is the center of the universe. Add to this the sexualized peer environment created by young people themselves, including increasingly provocative dress.

4. Talk about What Counts as "Sex"

Given the fact that many young people are having oral and even anal sex and still think they're "virgins," we want to be sure to talk about what counts as "sex." Here, for example, are some things we can say about oral sex:

1. Oral sex is definitely a sexual act. That's why they call it oral *sex.*
2. It's usually something boys ask girls to perform on them.
3. No boy who truly cares about or respects a girl would ever ask her to do this.
4. *All* of the sexually transmitted diseases can be passed on through oral sex. Doctors, for example, report seeing more and more teens with oral herpes.
5. If you engage in oral sex, especially if you're a girl, you are in danger of experiencing the same emotional hurts—low self-esteem, feeling used, feeling degraded—that can follow uncommitted sexual intercourse.
6. If you're a boy and are getting girls to do this, even if they seem willing, you are abusing the girl (Would you want somebody doing this to your sister?) and abusing your own sexuality (Is this

something you would want your future wife to
know?).

7. If you engage in this behavior, you're not treating
your body with reverence for the sacred gift that
it is.

Most parents and educators will also want to give guidance
about "how far is too far." Not everyone will agree on where to
draw the line, but I think it's best to draw it conservatively—
for example, at "brief hugs and light kissing." We can explain,
"Sex is progressive. If you're strict with yourself, you won't find
yourself struggling with the temptation to go a little bit farther
the next time." A high school counselor put it this way: "If you
don't want to drive over a cliff, don't pull up to the edge and race
the engine."

5. Teach Kids Nonsexual
Ways to Be Intimate

Since many kids are looking for love when they get involved in sex,
both parents and schools need to talk to them about what real intimacy is and how to achieve it.

True human intimacy means knowing another person—his or
her thoughts, feelings, hopes, and dreams—and being known in return. We have to *learn* how to attain this kind of intellectual, emotional, and spiritual intimacy. If we don't learn this, we'll be
handicapped in our adult relationships—in our marriages and our
relationships with our children.

By having them practice at school and at home, we can teach
young people the skills of intimacy, such as the art of asking questions that draw out the inside of another person and create meaningful and enjoyable conversation. Questions such as:

- What are two things you really like doing?
- What are two things you're good at?
- Who is someone you admire? Why?

- What's one of your greatest achievements in life
  so far?
- What is a way you've helped another person?
  A way another person has helped you in your life?
- What's one way you've changed as a person?
- What was a disappointment or hurt that was tough to
  deal with when it happened but helped you become a
  stronger and wiser person?
- How do you make decisions about important things?
- What do you worry about?
- What is something you have strong beliefs about?
- What is something in your life that you're grateful for?
- What are two of your most important goals in life?
- What is your concept of God, if you believe there is a
  God? When do you feel closest to God?

6. Offer a Vision

Young persons are thinking human beings, and they need a way to think about sex that will ground them and make their decisions solid. It's clearly not enough just to encourage them to "wait." They want to know what they're waiting *for*. To get to college? To turn a certain age? Until they feel "ready"? Or until they're in a mature, committed relationship where sex makes sense because it expresses and deepens that genuine commitment?

Historically, of course, we've called such a commitment marriage. In schools, saving sex for the committed relationship of marriage is increasingly being presented to students as a decision that has many benefits—for them, the children they may bring into the world (whose chances of school and life success are dramatically better with two parents), and society as a whole. To be effective, however, a "save sex for marriage" message can't be delivered in soapbox fashion with preachy moralizing. It has to be offered as a vision with persuasive power, expressed in rational terms that appeal to young people's intelligence.

Different teachers and parents will choose different ways of articulating this vision. Here is one approach:

Sex is so special, it deserves a special home. It's most meaningful, most fulfilling, when it's part of something bigger—a continuing, loving relationship between two human beings. When you're married, your sexual intimacy expresses your total commitment to each other. You're saying with your body, "I give myself to you, completely." Not being totally committed changes the meaning of the sex act. Then it's not part of the complete giving of yourself. Even if you're engaged, you can always get disengaged. Half of the couples who are engaged have been engaged before.

From this perspective, you join your bodies when you join your lives. The ultimate intimacy belongs within the ultimate commitment. Of course, saving sex for marriage, by itself, doesn't guarantee a successful marriage; that requires hard work and sacrificial love from both spouses. But marriage is the best place for sex because it's the most serious, total, and public commitment between two people that human society has ever been able to devise.

Here's a second approach, a little more philosophical but one that adolescents can still get their minds around:

We're all made in such a way that certain choices or ways of acting "work" and make us happy, and others don't. There's a law that governs human nature and human relationships, just as there's a law that governs physical nature. Toss a ball up, and it comes down. Treat people badly, and you lose their respect and eventually your self-respect. Actions have consequences.

What are the natural consequences of having sex? Bonding and babies. If you have sex with someone, you're very likely to create an attachment, a bond. If you have sex, you may also create a new human life, even if you're trying to avoid that.

Both of these consequences—an emotional attachment and a new life—can be the source of great happiness in a relationship where two people have made a real commitment to stay together. But if a binding commitment doesn't exist, the emotional attachment created by sex will, in most cases, be broken, causing emotional pain. And if a secure commitment doesn't exist, then a child brought into the world won't have two parents to love and raise him or her. A child born out of wedlock who grows up without a father, for example, is more likely to have problems in school, problems in peer relationships, and problems later in life.

And here's a third approach that brings religion into the picture. If you have religious faith as a parent, you'll want to integrate that into the moral upbringing of your child. Even public school teachers can objectively describe religious worldviews, in the spirit of teaching *about* religion, something that the Supreme Court's 1963 decision (which banned school-sponsored prayer) actually *urged* schools to do as part of their responsibility to educate students about their cultural heritage. A teacher can introduce a religious vision of sexuality by saying, for example, "A public school can't constitutionally promote religion, but it has an obligation, as a matter of fairness, to include religious perspectives along with other views." For example:

> Rabbinic teaching for at least 2,500 years has consistently opposed premarital sex. Judaism enshrines sexual intercourse as a sanctified element in the most intimate and meaningful relationship between two human beings: the sacred marriage bond.
>
> *—Rabbi Isaac Frank*

> The promise of two people to belong always to each other makes it possible for lovemaking to mean total giving and total receiving. It's the totality of married life that makes sexual intercourse meaningful.
>
> *—Father Richard McCormick*

Islam views sexual love as a gift from God. It is a sign of God's love and mercy. It is permitted only to those couples who have joined themselves in a lawful marriage.

—Muzammil Siddiqi, *Islamic teacher*

7. Talk about the Emotional Dangers of Uncommitted Sex

What are the various emotional dangers of uncommitted sex that we should be aware of as adults and help young people name and understand? Here are ten:

1. *Worry about pregnancy and disease.* Becky, thirteen, first had sex with her fifteen-year-old boyfriend. She knew her parents and other family members would be hurt if they found out. When she missed her period, she went into a panic. She even had thoughts of committing suicide. Finally, she confided in her grandmother, who took her to get a pregnancy test. To Becky's great relief, it was negative. With her grandmother's support, she decided she didn't want to go though that again and broke up with her boyfriend.

Says Russell Henke, health education coordinator in the Montgomery, Alabama, public schools, "I see kids going to the nurse in schools, crying a day after their first sexual experience, and wanting to be tested for AIDS. For some, it's enough to cause them to stay away from further sexual involvement."

2. *Regret and self-recrimination.* Both guys and girls can suffer sharp regret following a sexual relationship, but girls are usually more vulnerable. A girl who sees sex as a way to "show you care" may feel cheated and used when the boy doesn't show a greater romantic interest after the sexual experience. Says a fifteen-year-old girl, "I didn't expect the guy to marry me, but I never expected him to avoid me in school."

Sometimes the regret goes in the other direction; a person feels trapped after a relationship turns sexual. Says a sixteen-year-old girl, "I truly regret that my first time was with a guy that I didn't care that much about. Since that first night, he expects sex on every date. I'd like to end this relationship and date others, but after being so intimate, it's awfully tough."

Guys who get emotionally as well as sexually involved with a girl can also suffer deep regrets. Here's one who did:

> A year ago, I started dating a girl two years younger. We fell head over heels in love. When I would go to her house, her folks would go to bed early so we could be alone.
>
> We started necking a little, and then all the time. I started getting a little fresh, and she resisted, but she finally gave in for fear of losing me. Before we knew it, we had gone too far.
>
> We started feeling guilty about what we were doing, but we consoled ourselves that we were in love and that as soon as she was out of school, we'd be married. Then one night we had a terrible argument, and although it had nothing to do with sex, I know it would never have happened if we had been behaving ourselves.
>
> Anyway, she hit me, and I hit her back. I have never forgiven myself for that. She went running home and told her mother *everything* that happened between us. You can imagine what happened after that.
>
> I was going to college at the time. I couldn't keep my mind on my studies. Finally, I knew I was flunking out, so I quit college and joined the Navy. I saw her on the street just once before I left for basic training. She cried and told me she still felt the same about me, but it was too late then.
>
> I'd give anything in the world if she had stuck by her guns and I hadn't been so persistent. Any girl who thinks she has to put out to keep a guy is crazy. I would have stayed with her if she had only let me hold her hand. But I was selfish.[13]

3. Guilt. Guilt is a special form of regret, a strong sense of having done something morally wrong. A sixteen-year-old boy in California said he stopped having sex with girls when he saw and felt guilty about the pain he was causing. "You see them crying and confused. They say they love you, but you don't love them."

Guilt after sex may stem from one's religious convictions. Lucian Shulte, a Roman Catholic, says his parents taught him the importance of chastity, and he had always planned to wait until he was married to have sex. But then one warm summer night, he found himself with a girl who was very willing, and they had intercourse. It was over in a hurry and lacked any intimacy:

> In the movies, when people have sex, it's always romantic. Physically, it felt good, but emotionally it felt really awkward. I was worried that our relationship was now going to be a lot more serious than it was before. It was like, "Now what is she going to expect from me?"[14]

He felt guilty about what he had done and also worried about pregnancy and disease. He promised himself, never again.

Now, as a college student, he's still faithful to that decision. Lucian's story is an example of "renewed" or "emotional" virginity. It shows that regardless of past mistakes, a young person can start over. We need to emphasize that point with our students and children: You can't change the past, but you can choose the future.

Many teens—more than 300,000 a year—turn to abortion when they find themselves facing a pregnancy. As both sides of the abortion debate now acknowledge, abortion ends a developing life (there's a beating heart at eighteen days, measurable brain waves at six weeks). Many women experience guilt and other emotional repercussions after abortion, sometimes right away, sometimes years later. Here, for example, a young mother, now in her early thirties, writes about the abortion she had when she was in college:

> It was my sophomore year. I came back from winter break sick as a dog. The doctor in the campus infirmary took a urine test and told me in a nonjudgmental way that I was pregnant. "What would you like to do?" he asked. "I want to get rid of it," I said. He quietly wrote

down the phone number and address of the local Planned Parenthood.

The "procedure" was surprisingly simple. There was strong cramping, but I could handle that. If someone had asked me right then how I felt about what I had just done, I would have said, "Wow, this is great! I have my health back, I have my life back!"

Go ahead, ask me now. I am, at this moment, crying.

How callous I was. Just a kid, really. Self-centered and shallow. There were, and are now, so many other alternatives.

I am humbled by my two amazing living children. Most of all, I am humbled by my friend, Amy. She felt so strongly for her miscarried unborn child that she gave the child a name and a funeral. I didn't give mine a second thought—until I grew up.[15]

Guys, too, can suffer from the emotional aftershocks of abortion. Bottom line: Abortion is not a quick fix. Our children need to know that.

4. Loss of self-esteem and self-respect. Many persons suffer a loss of self-esteem after they find out that they have a sexually transmitted disease. John had not heard of human papilloma virus (HPV) before he had sex with his girlfriend. Soon after, he noticed some small bumps on his penis. His physician told him he had genital warts caused by HPV. The warts did not respond well to acid treatment, laser techniques, and excisional surgery. After protracted unsuccessful treatments, he began to worry that the warts might prevent his ever being able to marry.[16]

Sometimes the loss of self-esteem after uncommitted sex leads a person into further sexual relationships of a demeaning nature. Says a college senior who works as a residence hall director:

There are girls in our dorm who have had multiple pregnancies and multiple abortions. Because they have so little self-esteem, they will settle for any kind of attention from guys.

So they keep going back to the same kind of destructive situations and relationships that got them into trouble in the first place.

On both sides of dehumanized sex, there is a loss of dignity and self-worth. A twenty-year-old college guy confides, "You feel pretty crummy when you get drunk at a party and have sex with some girl, and then the next morning, you can't even remember who she was."

5. *The corruption of character.* When people treat others as sexual objects, they not only lose self-respect, they corrupt their character in the process.

Frequently, sex corrupts character by leading people into lying to get sex. Common lies include "I love you" and "I've never had an STD." In one study, three-fourths of men who knew they had a sexually transmitted disease said they had sex without telling their partners about their infection.

The Rhode Island Rape Crisis Center, in a 1988 survey of 1,700 students grades six to nine, asked, "Is it acceptable for a man to force sex on a woman if they've been dating for more than six months?" Sixty-five percent of the boys said yes. So did 49 percent of the girls.[17]

Sex that isn't tied to love and commitment undermines character by subverting self-respect, self-control, and responsibility. Unchecked by a moral code, sexual desires and impulses easily run amok and lead to habits of exploiting others.

6. *Shaken trust.* Young people of both sexes who feel used or betrayed after the breakup of a sexual relationship may experience, in future relationships, difficulty trusting. They don't want to be burned again.

7. *Rage over betrayal.* Every so often, the media carry a story about a person who had a rage reaction following a ruptured sexual relationship. Not long ago, our local paper carried a story about a twenty-seven-year-old guy named Scott who had been living for a year and a half with his girlfriend, Linda. They had made plans to marry. Then, with no warning or explanation, she moved out of their apartment.

Scott said, "I couldn't eat, I couldn't sleep." When he found that Linda was dating another guy, he lost it, went into a jealous rage, and stabbed her new boyfriend to death.

It's true that people often feel angry when somebody breaks up with them, even if sex hasn't been involved. But the sense of betrayal is usually much greater if sex has been part of the relationship.

8. Depression and suicide. Given what we know about the emotional aftermath of broken sexual relationships, it is reasonable to think that the pain from such breakups is a factor in the suicide deaths of some young people. According to a 1991 study in the journal *Pediatrics,* the attempted suicide rate for sexually experienced girls between the ages of twelve and sixteen is six times higher than it is for girls that age who are virgins.[18] Dr. Kirk Johnson reports 2003 data from the National Longitudinal Study of Adolescent Health showing that boys between fourteen and seventeen who are sexually active are significantly more likely to feel depressed and attempt suicide than boys who are not sexually active.

9. Ruined relationships. Sex can turn a good relationship bad. Says twenty-four-year-old Karen:

> With each date, my boyfriend's requests for sex became more convincing. After all, we did love each other. Within two months, I gave in. Over the next six months, sex became the center of our relationship. At the same time, new things entered—anger, impatience, jealousy, and selfishness. We just couldn't talk anymore. We grew very bored with each other. I desperately wanted a change.[19]

10. Negative effects on marriage. Most teens say they dream of being happily married someday. As parents and teachers, we can help them orient toward this goal by asking: "If you have this dream, what sexual decisions at this point in your life will help you attain it? What problems might be caused by being sexually intimate before marriage?" Here are four such problems:

- **Comparisons.** Says one young husband, "When I make love with my wife, I think, 'This girl could kiss better,' or 'This girl could do that better.' I can't get rid of the comparisons."
- **Infidelity.** Studies reported in the *Journal of Marriage and the Family* find that persons who are sexually active before marriage are more likely to be unfaithful to their spouses after marriage.
- **Infertility.** One in five newly married American couples cannot conceive a baby. Infertility is a tremendous stress on a marriage. If it was caused by a sexually transmitted disease such as chlamydia, the stress is even greater.
- **A greater chance of divorce.** Sex can also fool you into marrying the wrong person. John and Kathy Colligan, experienced counselors of couples preparing for marriage, comment, "We see many engaged couples who are living together. We find out by talking with them that they have little in common. They haven't discussed their values and goals. We can see that this is a marriage likely to fail, and time after time, it does."

Seven different studies, summarized in David Myers's book *The Pursuit of Happiness,* all find that couples who lived together before their marriage are significantly more likely to divorce than couples who did not live together.[20] If you really want to get to know somebody and find out whether you want to spend your life with that person, sex can make that harder, not easier, to do.

8. Discuss the Rewards of Waiting

As important as it is to discuss the dangers of uncommitted sex, it's also important to help young people identify, in positive terms, the benefits of saving sex for the truly committed relationship of marriage. Here are nine rewards of waiting[21]:

1. Waiting will make your dating relationships

better. You'll spend more time getting to know
each other.

2. Waiting will help you find the right mate,
someone who values you for the person
you are.

3. Waiting will increase your self-respect.

4. Waiting will gain the respect of others.

5. Waiting teaches you to respect others.
You'll never tempt or pressure anyone.

6. Waiting takes the pressure off you.

7. Waiting means a clear conscience (no guilt)
and peace of mind (no conflicts, no regrets).

8. Waiting means a better sexual relationship in
marriage, free of comparisons and based on trust.
By waiting, you're being faithful to your spouse
even before you meet him or her.

9. By practicing the virtues involved in waiting—
such as faithfulness, good judgment, self-control,
modesty, and genuine respect for self and others—
you're developing the kind of character that will
make you a good marriage partner and that will
attract a person of character, the kind of person
you'd like to marry and have as the father or
mother of your children.[22]

9. Talk about Tough Issues

We need to address three other sexual issues, ones that adults often
find hard to talk about but that young people need guidance on, especially in today's sexual culture.

Pornography. The Internet has made pornography more accessible to youth of all ages. According to one survey, kids under the age
of seventeen spend 65 percent more time on Internet pornography
sites than they do on game sites.[23]

We can say to young people, "Pornography debases sex. It violates the dignity of the human person and the dignity of the human

body. It treats people as sex objects. It also puts images in our minds that we may not be able to forget, even when we want to."

Pornography is also addictive. Like other addictions, it brings short-term pleasure but then starts to run your life. It will lower your self-respect.[24]

Later on, the habit of pornography can cause marital problems. Wives whose husbands are involved with pornography often feel demeaned, betrayed, and isolated from their husbands, victims of a kind of spiritual adultery.

For males, the use of pornography is also usually accompanied by masturbation. These two habits then reinforce each other, making it harder to break either one.

Masturbation. "Expert" advice regarding masturbation has swung between extremes, from warnings by doctors in the nineteenth century attributing various diseases and even insanity to this habit, to recommendations by some twentieth-century sex educators encouraging the young to masturbate as a healthy way to "explore their sexuality" and as a safe alternative to intercourse. Many parents, however, without resorting to scare tactics, wish to gently but firmly help their children resist this temptation. For some parents, the reason may be religious, their belief that sex is meant by God to be relational, an expression of love between two persons. "The problem with masturbation," as one father explained to his thirteen-year-old son, "is that it's having sex with yourself." There are also psychological considerations: Once masturbation becomes a habit, it is hard to stop and is likely to lessen a young person's feelings of self-respect. Many teens use masturbation as a way to escape emotions of anxiety or depression, and end up feeling worse because the problems are still there. Carried into marriage, the habit of masturbation can weaken the attraction between husband and wife and cause problems in their sexual relationship.

Homosexuality. There is no scientific consensus about the factors influencing sexual orientation. Columbia University researchers William Byne and Bruce Parsons reviewed 135 studies on sexual orientation and concluded, "There is no evidence at present to substantiate a biological [genetic] theory, just as there is no evidence to support any single psychological explanation."[25]

Some young people are unsure of their sexual orientation in their early teens. By adulthood, however, only about 2 percent of the population self-identify as homosexual.[26]

Several studies have found a significantly higher risk of attempted suicide among teens who identify themselves as homosexual or bisexual. For each year's delay in bisexual or homosexual self-identification, however, the odds of a suicide attempt diminish significantly.[27] Higher rates of depression, anxiety, and other psychological problems have been found among adults who report "some homosexual experience in the past twelve months" even in a country such as the Netherlands, where social attitudes are more accepting of homosexual relationships and same-sex couples have the legal right to marry.[28] In February 2003, the *Journal of Consulting and Clinical Psychology* reported a study of 103 pairs of twins, one of whom was homosexually active and the other not; the twin who was homosexually active was more than five times more likely to experience suicidal symptoms.

If your child thinks he or she may have a homosexual orientation, above all you want to maintain a loving relationship. You can do this, however, without approving of homosexual activity. Parents who for moral or religious reasons do not approve of homosexual sex can stress the distinction between having an attraction to the same sex and acting on it sexually. All young persons should be strongly encouraged to practice abstinence to avoid the physical and psychological dangers of uncommitted sexual activity. The risks of homosexual activity are even greater than those of heterosexual activity. Homosexually active males have been found to be at greater risk for HIV, hepatitis, gonorrhea, anal cancer, and gastrointestinal infections. Homosexually active females (the great majority of whom, at some point, also have sex with males) have been found to be at greater risk for bacterial vaginosis, hepatitis B and C, and having sex with men who are high risk for HIV.[29] If your child experiences a homosexual attraction, it's wise to seek competent professional counseling from someone whose values and beliefs are consistent with your own. (A psychiatrist who is a help-ful source of referrals in this area is Richard P. Fitzgibbons, M.D., R82488@aol.com.)

All parents and teachers, as a matter of moral principle, should also teach young people to treat every person, regardless of sexual orientation, with love, justice, and respect.

10. Implement Character-Based Sex Education in Schools

Schools, for their part, must do all they can to support parents in helping young people make sexual decisions that are truly in their best interest and the best interest of society. The best way to do so is to implement character-based sex education. Increasingly taught as part of a course on marriage and parenting (the best context), char-acter-based sex education teaches five key ideas:

1. Abstinence is the *only* medically safe, emotionally healthy, and morally responsible choice for unmar-ried teens. Abstinence means avoiding not only sex-ual intercourse but also other forms of genital contact and sexual intimacy that may lead to inter-course and that in themselves violate true respect for self, others, and the special meaning of sex.
2. Condoms don't make sex physically safe (you can still get pregnant or catch a disease), emotionally safe (you can still get hurt), or ethically loving (you can't claim to love someone if you're gambling with their health and happiness).
3. Abstinence is the best marriage preparation, not just best "for me" but also best for my future spouse, my future children, and my community and country.[30]
4. Waiting until marriage to have sex is an excellent way to develop self-discipline, respect for others, caring, courage, and other important qualities of character.

5. If you haven't waited in the past, you can make a
    different choice in the future.

One of the most promising ways to implement character-based
sex education is to recruit and train high school students to teach
the curriculum to their younger peers. For example, schools and
youth organizations in more than six states now participate in *Peers
Educating Peers* (www.peersproject.org), a federally funded abstinence education project that trains high school juniors and seniors
to teach a curriculum for grades six through ten. Says eighteen-year-
old Savannah Smith, who graduated from the program: "It really
helped to hear it from the high school students. They were close to
our age and were encouraging role models."

A. C. Green's Game Plan (www.ProjectReality.org) is an abstinence curriculum that stresses making a "game plan" for avoiding
and handling pressures and temptations.[31] For teachers and parents
of high school students, *Sex and Character* (www.fteinfo.com) is a
highly readable resource that deals intelligently with sex, love,
dating, and marriage. A small book for teens that presents the medical, moral, emotional, and spiritual reasons to save sex for marriage
is *Sex, Love & You: Making the Right Decision* (Tom and Judy Lickona, with William Boudreau, M.D.; www.avemariapress.org). The
Institute for Youth Development (www.youthdevelopment.com) is
developing a primer on marriage that can be easily integrated into
any abstinence education course. For a comprehensive directory of
abstinence curricula, books, and speakers, contact the National Abstinence Clearinghouse (www.abstinence.net).

In teaching abstinence, one can't emphasize too strongly to
young people that in the sexual area of their lives, as in any area of behavior, they can always choose to make a fresh start. Says a sixteen-
year-old girl, "I've had sex with a lot of guys, but I was always drunk
so I didn't think it mattered. Now I realize that I gave each of those
guys a part of myself. I don't want all that pain anymore. I'm going to
make a new beginning and not have sex again until I'm married."[32]

If we truly care about kids, of course, we will do everything we
can in our classrooms and families to help them avoid the pain of
premature sex in the first place. As we prepare to educate our chil-

dren about this crucial area of their lives, we would do well to keep in mind the words of the writer Lance Morrow: "You cannot light a candle in a high wind. What is needed for adolescent development to occur is shelter, safety. A context of abstinence is the beginning of such shelter."[33]

Finally, if we want to call forth the best in our children, the case for waiting should go beyond appealing to their self-interest. We should also appeal to their sense of moral responsibility. We should ask them to consider, What kind of life do I want for a child that I might bring into the world? Do I want to give my child every chance to grow up healthy and happy with two committed parents? And how do I wish to affect the life of a person I am involved with? Do I want to have it on my conscience that I caused someone to get a sexually transmitted disease, lose the ability to have a baby, or suffer emotional problems?

In the current culture, sex may often seem like a casual thing. But sex is an act that is full of consequences. Sex, as a philosopher observed, is essentially deep. That's a very good reason to save it for marriage, the deepest and most loving commitment two people can make to each other.

PART THREE

Create Classrooms of Character

CHAPTER 5

Build Bonds and Model Character

Many students have grown up in a world of drive-through relationships. Adults have to gain their trust. They have to see that you're real.

— JEFFREY PRATT BEEDY,
NEW HAMPTON SCHOOL,
2002 NATIONAL SCHOOL OF CHARACTER

If you want students to be respectful, you have to model respect. You cannot teach where you do not go.

— BARBARA LUTHER,
ELEANOR ROOSEVELT HIGH SCHOOL,
2002 NATIONAL SCHOOL OF CHARACTER

Gloria Shields has been teaching ninth-grade English in Virginia high schools for more than twenty years. On the first day of the school year, she tells her students, "I'm going to empower you to make a difference in the world—to be a success in whatever way you choose to contribute. We have just a short time together here, but we're going to be working on long-term goals."

She then explains her "attitude box," which sits on a table next to the door:

> If you're going to do your best work here, you don't want to come in with an "attitude." If you do arrive with an attitude—"I'm mad at my boyfriend because we just had an argument," "I'm upset with a teacher because I just got a bad grade on a test I studied hard for"—I'd like you to write it on one of these slips of paper before class starts and drop it in the attitude box. If you'd like to talk with me about it, write that at the bottom, and we'll make an appointment.

She also tells her students, "I will treat you with the greatest dignity and respect."

"I wasn't always this kind of teacher," Gloria Shields told me, and she explained:

> I used a lot of sarcasm in my early years. Then in my seventh year of teaching, I had a boy named Alvin. He was a twenty-year-old senior and was repeating senior English, having failed my class by twelve points the year before. I didn't see him as a person; I just saw him as a problem—a poor student. Because he was a failure, he made *me* feel like a failure.
>
> Alvin had a job after school at the local Texaco gas station. One afternoon after I bought gas there, I got a flat tire pulling away. I had never changed a tire before, and I couldn't do it—couldn't get the lug nuts off.

As she struggled with the tire, she noticed Alvin leaning back in his chair against the gas station wall.

> I saw him watching me the whole time. I got madder and madder—"Why that little creep, why doesn't he come over here and help me?" But he didn't make a move.

Finally, he got up and sauntered over to where I was. He flicked away the cigarette he'd been smoking and said in his Virginia drawl, "Havin' trouble changin' that tire, huh, Miss Shields?"

"That's right," I said.

"You don't know how to do it, do you?"

"That's right," I said.

"How's that make you feel?"

"Like a failure," I said.

"Now you know how I feel in your English class." He paused. "Tell you what, Miss Shields. I'll help you change that tire, if you help me pass senior English."

"It's a deal," I said.

That was a life-changing moment. From that point forward, I was a different teacher and a different person. I took all the sarcasm out of my voice.

I asked her what she did differently with Alvin after the tire episode.

I would often work with him after school, before he went to his job. I said to him, "Look, you've got to help me. When you don't understand something, I need you to tell me what part of it you don't understand."

I still get Christmas cards from Alvin. Each year, I tell all my classes the story about Alvin and the flat tire. I say to them, "If you're not doing well in this class, you need to help me understand what's going on." I tell them I'm still learning and that teaching is the hardest thing I've ever done—even harder than parenting teenagers. I tell them there's a lot I don't know, more than they'd ever guess. I try to create an atmosphere where it's okay to make mistakes. I tell them I've made every mistake a teacher can make. My main message is that we have to work together.

I haven't had to make a discipline referral in six years.

When I share Gloria Shields's story with teachers in workshops, I ask, "What change occurred in her character as a result of the experience with Alvin, and how did it make her a better teacher and a better character educator?"

People say things such as, "She became more humble," "She developed empathy with her students," "She made herself human by saying that she's still learning and makes mistakes," "She made it clear to her students that she wants them to succeed and believes that they can." These changes, teachers say, gave her a *relationship* with her students.

1. Teach as if Relationships Matter

The story of Gloria Shields confirms what good teachers have always known: The teacher-student relationship is the foundation of effective instruction. A good teacher-student relationship

1. helps students to feel loved and capable.
2. motivates them to do and be their best, because they care about what the teacher thinks of them.
3. makes it easier for the teacher and student to communicate and work together to overcome obstacles to learning.
4. leads students to identify with their teacher and thereby opens them to the positive influence of the teacher's character expectations and personal example.

This last process—a student's identification with and emulation of a caring, nurturing adult—is a central part of socialization. It often occurs without a young person's even being aware of it. This identification happens in the home between kids and loving parents, and it happens outside the home between kids and other adults with whom they form emotional attachments. We tend to become like the people with whom we bond. When children do not bond with moral adults, the development of conscience and character is retarded.

2. Use the Power of a Handshake

Bonding can begin with something as simple as a handshake.

Charlie Abourjilie is a former high school history teacher in High Point, North Carolina, current coordinator of character education for the state of North Carolina, and author of the book, *Developing Character for Classroom Success* (www.CharacterEducation.com). He explains the power of a handshake:

> Every day, I stood at the door and shook the hands of all my students as they entered the classroom. In the half a second it took to shake a hand, I made a direct, meaningful, and personal connection with that student.
>
> I also talked to my classes about the power of a handshake. I pointed out that it has ended wars and created powerful alliances. We discussed the value of a good handshake in the business world, on job interviews, in meeting a date's father—what a positive human resource it can be.

3. Get to Know Students as Individuals

Good teachers build the relationship in both directions; they and their students learn about each other. Sean Reber, who teaches second grade in Windsor, New York, uses his "teacher's corner" to facilitate this reciprocal interaction:

> I want my students to know that I am not just their teacher but also a husband, a father, and a person with various interests. In my teacher's corner, I display pictures of my wife, daughter, and dog; my college diplomas; trophies from high school; photos of classes I taught when I lived in California; some of my favorite books; and hobby items. During the first few weeks of school, while the rest of the class is doing seatwork, I meet with each of my students in the teacher's corner for about ten minutes. They come with an "All about Me" book they've made. In these conversations, I

get to know them on a more personal level, and they get to know me. It gives me a closer relationship with each child.

A first-grade teacher gives every child a laminated 3" x 3" card to keep in the upper right corner of the desk. On one side is a smiley face; on the other, a frown. The teacher explains to the class: "If you're feeling okay when you come in here, put your face smile side up. If you're upset about something, put it frown side up. The first chance I get, I'll come over, and you can tell me what the trouble is." With kids who have the frown side up, she has a brief conversation that helps her key in on a problem that needs solving or at least a sympathetic ear.

4. Use Bonding to Improve Behavior

When teachers bond with their students, they increase academic learning and their moral influence on students. Frank Bibbo, a tenth-grade biology teacher in Roxbury, New York, speaks of both of these benefits:

> I greet students in the hall and make eye contact with each of them when they come into my room. My students tend to hate the New York State Regents [the mandated final exam]. I tell them I hate it too, but we're in this together. That creates a feeling of being on the same side. Last year one hundred percent of my students passed the biology Regents.
>
> Because many of our students have racist or anti-Semitic attitudes, I tell stories from my life about people of different races and religions that I've known, worked with, and respected. They respond to this personal approach.
>
> This year I had a boy who was using the f-word in class, mostly when they were working in groups. I spoke to him after class and said in a calm way, "Mike, I can't let you use that language in here. It's just not respectful. Could you try to work on that for me?" After that, he caught himself when

he slipped. I thanked him for making that effort. By the end
of the quarter, it was no longer a problem.

Sometimes a student's general behavior shows a remarkable improvement once the teacher establishes a rapport with that student.
An example of this kind of turnaround comes from Velma Decker,
who taught second grade at Ralph R. Smith Elementary School in
Hyde Park, New York, for twenty-five years. Kids loved her; parents
would regularly ask if their child could be placed in her classroom.
She remembers one child, however, who initially presented a real
challenge.

> This little girl came from a very poor family. She was always
> upset about something. The least little thing would set her
> off; she'd cry and carry on. At first, I thought speaking
> sharply to her might work, so I said, "Now listen here, I
> want you to settle down and stop this." Well, that didn't
> help.
>
> Then one day, I just took her by the hand, brought her up
> to my desk, and sat her on my knee. I talked to her quietly.
> She calmed down and leaned her head on my shoulder. Af-
> ter that, I never had a problem with her. All she needed was
> a little bit of love.

5. Use the Power of Example

If we want to teach character, we have to display character. Says a
middle school teacher, "Some of our staff think character education
is just for the kids. They don't see that this is as much about *us* as it
is about them. If *we* aren't persons of character ourselves, how can
we possibly expect *them* to be?"

Often a teacher's lapses from good character are the most
salient thing about that teacher. A mother says her sixth-grade
daughter came home very upset one day because the teacher said to
another girl, in front of the whole class, "What, are you stupid?"

Research confirms that the humanity of the teacher is the most important moral lesson in the character curriculum. Dr. Leslie Laud, in her study *How Good Teachers Nurture Character*, observed elementary school teachers known for how well they foster character development in their students:

> I had expected to see a lot of use of activities, programs, and curricular innovations—practices that could be clearly described and replicated. Instead, my research found that the most salient influences on students' character appeared to be the qualities individual teachers embodied and modeled in the presence of children.
>
> Over several weeks of observation, I identified 627 "moral moments" that could arguably build character. Of these, 602 reflected personal qualities embodied by the teacher such as warmth, responsibility, respect, and compassion.[1]

One teacher, for example, taught her students how to solve peer conflicts by taking the other person's perspective. Her students, Laud says, were amazingly adept at this skill. During an interview, this teacher explained that perspective taking is a skill she constantly works on in her personal life with her husband and children.

"The most exacting, humbling, and rewarding task in character education," Laud concluded, "is nurturing our own character." Her insight echoes a famous quote from Gandhi: "You must be the change you want to see in the world."

6. Use a Self-Inventory to Focus on Role Modeling

To examine their role modeling on a regular basis, some schools use a self-inventory with questions that teachers agree to reflect on periodically. Answers are "for your eyes only" rather than for any evaluation by others. Here are some sample questions:

1. Do I greet students by name and make eye contact with them?
2. Do I come to class on time?
3. Am I well prepared?
4. Do I return work promptly?
5. Do I treat students impartially and not show any kind of favoritism?
6. Do I maintain civility and graciousness even under stress?
7. Do I model patience?
8. Do I refrain from talking negatively about students in the faculty room and elsewhere?
9. Do I refrain from talking negatively about colleagues?
10. Do I hold out high expectations that challenge all my students to do their personal best?

7. Invite Guest Speakers Who Are Positive Role Models

If we want to maximize the power of good example, we'll take steps to expose students to many positive role models, not just those within the school. Rich Parisi, former principal of a 2000 National School of Character, the Morgan Road Elementary School in Liverpool, New York, describes one instance:

We had Kim Black, a former Morgan School student who won an Olympic Gold Medal at Sydney, give an assembly for our students. She talked about how hard she had trained and how she made the track and field team by only one one-hundredth of a second before going on to win the gold. We gave every student an index card. After Kim Black's speech, they wrote down on one side of the card a dream they have, and on the other side three things they could do to achieve their dream.

WHAT THE RESEARCH SHOWS

When students feel connected with significant people in their lives, they are less likely to engage in behaviors that jeopardize their future.

That was the conclusion of the 1997 National Longitudinal Study of Adolescent Health, which interviewed more than 12,000 seventh- to twelfth-grade students from eighty high schools across the country and their feeder middle schools. The researchers looked at four categories of unhealthy risk behavior: delinquency, violence, sexual intercourse, and substance abuse. The study identified two "protective factors" that tended to keep teens from becoming involved in these risk behaviors. Most important was *family connect-edness,* a feeling of closeness to parents. Next in importance was *school connectedness,* a feeling of closeness to people at school.[2]

Observes education writer Jay Matthews, "In school, there is no greater motivation for students than the knowledge that at least one adult knows them well and cares about what happens to them."

Research on resilience has produced similar findings. Resilient kids manage to beat the odds. They face, and are able to overcome, all kinds of adversity: parental neglect, abuse; physical handicaps; war; or a parent's mental illness, alcoholism, or criminality. Resilient children, studies show, usually possess four strengths: social competence, problem-solving skills, a sense of identity, and hope for the future.[3] Such children, in explaining how they have overcome obstacles in life, often cite a "special teacher" who was not just an academic instructor but also a confidant and an inspiring role model.

As Henry Adams said long ago, "A teacher affects eternity." Caring, dedicated teachers have always been a significant influence on the values and character of a child. Today, the school often takes on even more importance as a refuge from the moral chaos of many students' homes and neighborhoods. For these children, a teacher, coach, or counselor may very well be *the* most positive moral influence in their lives. We owe it to those students, and to all of our students, to make that influence count for good.

CHAPTER 6

Teach Academics and Character at the Same Time

Schools have long had three core tasks: to prepare young people for the world of work; to prepare them to use their minds well, to think deeply; and to prepare them to be thoughtful citizens and decent human beings.

—THEODORE AND NANCY SIZER[1]

School records of character-based schools show consistent improvement in student achievement and behavior.

—JULEA POSEY AND MATTHEW DAVIDSON,
Character Education Evaluation Toolkit[2]

Whatever you are, be a good one.

—ABRAHAM LINCOLN

Becoming a person of character means becoming the best person we can be. It follows that growing in character means developing *both* our ethical potential and our intellectual potential.

Human maturity includes the capacity to love and the capacity to work. Virtues such as empathy, compassion, sacrifice, loyalty, and forgiveness constitute our capacity to love. Virtues such as effort,

121

initiative, diligence, self-discipline, and perseverance constitute our capacity to work and to become competent at the tasks of life.

Understood this way, our work ethic and competence aren't something separate from our character; rather, they are part of it. In fact, how well we do our work, how capably and conscientiously we perform jobs large and small, is one of the primary ways we affect the quality of other people's lives. It takes hard work to develop our talents so that we can use them to make a positive difference in the world.

Once schools have this basic understanding—that good character is needed for both interpersonal relationships *and* personal achievement, for social responsibility *and* academic responsibility—the false dichotomy between character education and academics disappears. Virtue is human excellence. To be a school of character, a community of virtue, is to be equally committed to two great goals: intellectual excellence and moral excellence.

When people see character development in this way, as the foundation for both academic achievement and moral growth, they're less likely to say, "We'd like to do more character education, but with all the pressures from learning standards and testing, there's just not time."

"IF WE DO CHARACTER EDUCATION, WILL ACADEMIC LEARNING IMPROVE?"

Educators often ask, "If we invest time and energy in developing a character education program, will student learning improve?"

We can confidently answer yes, academic learning will improve, *if* (1) the school's character education program improves the quality of human relationships between adults and kids and kids and each other, thereby improving the environment for teaching and learning; *and* (2) the character education effort includes a strong academic program that teaches students the skills and habits of working hard and making the most of their education.

Is there evidence to support this prediction? Yes, from two sources. The first is data from individual schools, which often began character education because of low student achievement and frequent discipline problems, and saw test scores rise and discipline problems decline after implementing a quality character education program. (The Character Education Partnership's annual *National Schools of Character* publication is a source of many such success stories; www.character.org.) Evidence also comes from controlled research studies that have found that students in a school implementing a quality character education program outperform students in a school that is comparable in makeup but has not implemented such a program. (For the most comprehensive analysis of these studies, see the 2004 report *What Works in Character Education?*, a review of character education research conducted for the Character Education Partnership by University of Missouri at Saint Louis psychologists Marvin Berkowitz and Mindy Bier. See CEP's website for how to get a copy of this report.)

To cite an example from the scientific research, a national study by California's Developmental Studies Center compared, over a period of three years, twelve elementary schools implementing *The Child Development Project* (a comprehensive character education program combining values-rich children's literature, collaborative learning, developmental discipline, a caring community in the classroom and school, and strong parental involvement) with twelve matched schools not implementing the program. Students in program schools were significantly superior in classroom behavior, achievement motivation, and reading comprehension. Moreover, when program students went on to middle school (when the character program was no longer in effect), they continued to show superiority on character measures such as conflict resolution and on academic superiority as measured by grade-point averages and standardized test performance.[3] (For further educational research, see "The Relationship Between Character Education and Academic Achievement" by Jacques Benninga and Marvin Berkowitz in the fall, 2003, maiden issue of the *Journal of Research in Character Education,* www.infoagepub.com or e-mail editor, Andrew_Milson@baylor.edu.)

To cite an example from the experience of schools: In the late nineties, then superintendent Dr. John O'Connell implemented a "3

Rs" character program in Allegany County, Maryland, focused on "respect, responsibility, and the right to learn." Discipline referrals declined steadily during the first and second years. Academic gains began to appear during year one, then grew significantly during year two, especially at the high school level (a 41-point jump in SAT scores), even as the county's poverty rate rose from 46.5 to 50 percent. O'Connell comments, "Creating a safe and orderly environment that honors respectful and responsible behavior is the foundation on which sustainable academic success gets built."

If intellectual development and moral development are the two goals of character education, what are the practical strategies by which schools can achieve both of these aims simultaneously?

1. Name the Virtues Needed to Be a Good Student

"Academic expectations teach virtues," says Holly Salls, author of the forthcoming book, *A New Vision of Character Education*, and a high school philosophy and theology teacher at Chicago's Willows Academy. "But it's important to name them in order to bring them into the consciousness of both the teacher and the students." Here are the character virtues that she believes a strong academic program teaches and that she challenges her students to work on:

- responsibility for your work
- thoroughness
- organization and neatness
- punctuality
- self-control and willpower
- honesty
- working quietly out of respect for others
- time management
- being prepared
- giving your best effort
- concentration

- perseverance
- accepting disappointments
- enduring things you don't want to do

"The classroom," Salls says, "is a place to learn and practice all of these habits." Parents of Willows students provide support on the home front. A mother of two girls comments, "When my daughters say they don't 'feel like' doing their best work on a particular homework assignment, I say, 'Anybody can do what they *feel* like doing. But if you can do things you *don't* feel like doing, you can do anything.'"

2. Teach as if Purpose Matters

Mose Durst cofounded a small private K–8 school in San Leandro, California, called The Principled Academy (www.principled academy.org). He wrote a book, *Principled Education,* in which he argues that educators must ask themselves—and engage students in asking—questions about "first things." Questions such as, What makes life worth living? What is a life that is honorable and virtuous? To what should we give our efforts? What is the purpose of learning?

When Durst teaches writing to 7th- and 8th-graders at The Principled Academy, he begins by talking to them about its purpose:

> I explain that first of all, we should have a love of the truth. We should see writing as a way of communicating truth. We should want to be able to express to others—in a beautiful way—the truth about our own lives or about life as we learn about it from a work of literature. I find that if I can get students to connect with the purpose of writing, they are more motivated to take up the challenge.

3. Teach as if Excellence Matters

Motivated by a sense of purpose, students are more likely to engage in the quest for excellence.

The next step is to engage them in the diligent effort needed to pursue excellence. In Mose Durst's junior high school class, learning to write means learning to rewrite. He makes a copy of each student's first draft for every student in the class. Together, the class identifies the strengths of each paper and areas for improvement. He works with students not only on getting their grammar and punctuation right but also on style—on varying their sentence structure so as to produce syntactically pleasing sentences.

When we encounter instruction of this quality, we can see why teaching and learning can be considered moral acts. There is a dedication of self to something inherently worthwhile. One learns to be obedient to the demands of the process. One learns that there are no shortcuts to quality. All of these lessons build character.

4. Teach as if Integrity Matters

Laura Brewer-Heileg is chair of the math department at Eleanor Roosevelt High School, a Community of Caring 2002 school and National School of Character in Greenbelt, Maryland. (Contact Barbara Luther, character education chairperson, bluther@pgcps.org.) With nearly three thousand students (56 percent African-American, 10 percent Asian, 30 percent Caucasian, 4 percent Hispanic), it is the largest high school in the state of Maryland. It also has a distinguished academic record; as its percentage of minority students has risen, so has its scores on the SAT (Scholastic Aptitude Test).

Laura Brewer-Heileg is typical of the school's faculty: absolutely serious about learning, completely committed to character in both its work-related and moral dimensions. She says, "I see the teacher-student relationship as the basis for everything. I want my students to know that if they do something wrong, it's bad for our relationship."

This belief frames how she addresses such issues as academic honesty.

> I use a little bit of humor—for example, I act out all the ways I know students sometimes cheat, including using their PalmPilots to e-mail test answers to another student.

They laugh. But I want them to know why cheating really bothers me. I tell them, "You can recover fairly quickly from a zero on a test if you're caught cheating. But it takes a long time to recover from an act of dishonesty. It creates a lack of trust between us. It damages our relationship."

"I feel I don't just teach math," she said to me. "I teach whole-person development."

5. Teach as if Students Can Take Responsibility for Their Learning

Columbine Elementary School in Woodland Park, Colorado, is a 2000 National School of Character (columbineelementary@ myschool mail.com). Its mission statement commits the school to helping "every child become competent in academic skills, responsible for their actions, confident in their abilities, and enthusiastic, lifelong learners." To make these goals a reality, Columbine has seven "personal and social responsibility standards"—viewed as "habits of mind"—that are integrated into classroom instruction and students' report cards:

1. Practices organizational skills
2. Supports and interacts positively with others
3. Is enthusiastic about learning
4. Takes risks and accepts challenges
5. Accepts responsibility for own behavior
6. Listens attentively, follows directions, stays on task
7. Evaluates own learning

Each standard is broken down into four or five specific skills. For each skill there are four levels of competence: in progress, basic, proficient, and advanced. Charts posted all around the school help students understand what these standards or good habits look like in practice. For example, the first item under "practices organizational skills" has to do with "completing and turning in work." The four levels of competence in this particular skill are:

- **In progress:** I rarely complete my work and turn it in on time.
- **Basic:** I sometimes remember to hand in my completed work, but I need a lot of reminding.
- **Proficient:** I usually remember to hand in my completed work with few reminders.
- **Advanced:** I consistently hand in my work with no reminders.

Teachers teach students the seven standards and use them to evaluate students' progress. Students use them to self-assess. In assemblies, the fifth graders (the highest grade in the school) do humorous skits showing what kind of behavior meets a particular standard and what doesn't. "It's a hoot," says Principal Michael Galvin. Before parent-teacher conferences, teachers sit down with all students individually to rate where they are on the standards and help them set goals.

"Our students are really hooked on the idea of being aware of their own learning," Galvin comments. "Once you achieve that, you can let go of extrinsic incentives. You won't see many pizza parties at our school."[4]

6. Use an Instructional Process That Makes Character-Building Part of Every Lesson

The psychologist-educator Spencer Kagan points out that in character education *how* we teach may be even more important than *what* we teach. If we want character education to transfer to real-life performance situations beyond the classroom, then we must use classroom "learning structures" that enable students to *practice* the virtues.

One way to make these learning structures an integral part of everyday academic instruction is illustrated by Maureen Mulderig, principal of Walberta Park Primary School in Syracuse, New York.

In any subject area, the teacher can use a learning structure called "numbered heads together." The kids count off (one, two, three), and then the teacher poses a question such as, "How do you spell zebra?" or "What causes snow?" Students first write down responses individually, then huddle in their groups to compare and discuss ideas and come up with an agreed-upon answer—making sure that each group member knows the answer. The teacher then calls a number, and students with that number must show or explain their answer to the class.

This learning structure gives children practice in several character skills: attentive and respectful listening, helping each other understand a concept, arriving at a consensus, and taking the responsibility of being prepared to report the group's answer to the rest of the class.

At Mulderig's school, a teacher support group called SAM (Structure a Month) meets to share ways teachers have used that month's focus structure, to troubleshoot challenges, and to learn a new structure for the next month. This constant sharing of ideas helps teachers to feel supported, to refine their practice, and to deepen their commitment to effective teaching. (For more ways to use learning structures, see Kagan's article in our center's spring 2002 newsletter; www.cortland.edu/c4n5rs.)

7. Manage the Classroom
So That Character Matters

Thoughtful teachers build character through academics by managing their classrooms in ways that foster both intellectual and ethical responsibility.

For example, Scott Tiley, a former computer lab instructor and now middle school head at Michigan's Grosse Pointe Academy, used a "computer pledge" to teach computer ethics. After discussing the pledge with his students, he asked them to sign it as an expression of their commitment to the moral code of the classroom:

GROSS POINTE ACADEMY'S
COMPUTER PLEDGE

- **I pledge that I will respect copyright laws.**
  No copying of software is permitted. Please respect
  what others have created and use only legal copies
  of software.
- **I pledge that I will be careful with hardware.**
  Please treat each computer, keyboard, and mouse
  with respect. Report anything that's not working.
- **I pledge that I will respect "electronic privacy."**
  You may open only three kinds of folders on the
  GPA network: your own, the class folder, and the
  lost and found folder.
- **I pledge that I will leave the computers as I
  found them.** Please do not install software or alter
  the control panel, clock, colors, patterns, desktop
  settings, fonts, etc.
- **I pledge that I will do what I can to be helpful
  in the GPA Computer Lab.** Everyone needs help
  with something at some point.

  *I have read the above pledge and give my
  word as a student or faculty member to follow
  it. I am part of a community of computer
  users, and I know that whatever I do has an
  effect on someone else.*

Some teachers give students meaningful responsibility for the
academic life of the classroom by regularly seeking their input on
how to approach an upcoming unit. One teacher asks, for example,
"What's the most exciting way we could study the Civil War? If we
can't do that, what's the second most exciting way we could study
it?" When students see their ideas being used by the teacher, they
feel respected as thinkers and become more committed to their
learning.

8. Teach Curriculum Content as if Character Matters

To teach character and academics simultaneously is to view the curriculum through a character lens. What are the natural opportunities for highlighting character that can be found in virtually any academic subject?

We must first of all see character development as a fundamental purpose of the academic curriculum. As Kevin Ryan and Karen Bohlin point out in *Building Character in Schools,* the curriculum should carry the intellectual and moral heritage of our culture. At its best, the curriculum is a source of moral wisdom and examples of how to live a life of purpose. In any academic discipline, biographical and autobiographical material can introduce students to men and women of distinguished achievement and raise such questions as: What strengths of character enabled them to achieve what they did? What obstacles did they have to overcome?

A science teacher can promote respect for the environment and the virtues—care in collecting data, truthfulness in reporting it, cooperation in the pursuit of knowledge—needed to do science. Math teachers can emphasize the importance of perseverance, model empathy for students by teaching in a way that accommodates individual differences, and foster the skills of cooperation through cooperative learning. Social studies teachers can foster appreciation of cultural diversity, examine the struggle for justice throughout human history, and study individuals whose moral actions—good or evil—have changed the course of history. A foreign language teacher can use the Internet to find the latest news (about war and peace, world hunger, political developments) reported in the language under study and use that information to foster a global perspective. Art and music teachers can help students appreciate the power of aesthetic endeavors to lift the human spirit and the self-discipline required for sustained creative work.

History and literature are rich in moral meaning. In these subjects, do we take care to choose value-laden curriculum content and draw out its character dimension? In an essay on moral literacy,

William Bennett asks, Do we want our children to know what courage means? Then we should teach them about Joan of Arc and Horatius at the bridge. Do we want them to know about kindness and compassion and their opposites? Then they should read *A Christmas Carol* and *The Diary of Anne Frank* and later on, *King Lear*. Do we want them to know that hard work pays off? Then we should teach them about the Wright brothers at Kitty Hawk and Booker T. Washington's learning to read. Do we want them to understand the dangers of unreasoning conformity? Then we should read and discuss *The Emperor's New Clothes*. And if we want them to respect the rights of others, they should study the Declaration of Independence, the Bill of Rights, the Gettysburg Address, and Martin Luther King, Jr.'s "Letter from Birmingham Jail."[5]

Once teachers learn to see the character connections in their academic area, it's a short step to teaching state learning standards and character at the same time. *Making Character Education a "Standard" Part of Education,* written by Linda McKay and Kristin Fink for the Character Education Partnership (www.character.org), gives examples of how to integrate character education and learning standards.

9. Use a Schoolwide Curriculum That Teaches Moral and Intellectual Virtues

Core Virtues (www.linkinstitute.org) is a schoolwide K–6 interdisciplinary character education curriculum that makes strong use of fiction and nonfiction, integrated with American history, world civilization, and fine arts. Each grade studies a different set of virtues, with some virtues treated at more than one level. This curriculum was developed and tested by Mary Beth Klee and colleagues at the Crossroads Academy, an independent school in Lyme, New Hampshire.

In January of the fourth-grade curriculum, for example, students focus on courage and study Maya Angelou's *Life Doesn't Frighten Me;* Longfellow's "Paul Revere's Ride"; Patrick Henry's "Give Me Liberty or Give Me Death"; Saint George and the dragon; and Thomas Jefferson, John Adams, and George Washington. In February of the sixth-grade curriculum, they focus on justice and study Judaism's concepts of law and justice; Greek notions of the good citizen; the trial of Socrates; the French Revolution; American labor conditions at the turn of the century; and Samuel Gompers, Ida B. Wells, Susan B. Anthony, and Eugene Debs. In addition to this rich grade-by-grade curriculum, *Core Virtues* has a monthly schoolwide focus on a common virtue, including such qualities as hope, joy, stewardship, gentleness, and mercy. In every classroom, at every level, the day begins with the Morning Gathering, the highlight of which is reading and discussing a story related to the monthly virtue. *Core Virtues* also includes an extensive annotated bibliography of children's literature.

The cultural critic Neil Postman, in his book *Technopoly*, writes, "Modern secular education is failing because it has no moral, social, or intellectual center. The curriculum is not a course of study at all but a meaningless hodgepodge of subjects. It does not even put forth a clear vision of what an educated person is."[6] The *Core Virtues* program offers an example of a coherent curriculum that does have a moral and intellectual center and a vision of what an educated person is, namely, a person of character grounded in the study of moral and intellectual virtue. (See also *Citizenship and Character: Understanding America's Civic Values* for a widely used high school curriculum; www.BillofRightsInstitute.org.)

10. Structure Discussion as if Character Matters

Capitalizing on the character-building potential of the curriculum depends on the teacher's ability to focus students' thinking on the character dimension of the material at hand.

Consider, for example, one of the most memorable moments in Mark Twain's classic *Huckleberry Finn:* The bounty hunters are searching for Jim, the runaway slave and Huck's river raft companion, and ask Huck if he has seen him. Huck decides to lie to protect Jim, even though he knows that the law requires the return of a runaway slave and even though he thinks that he might go to hell for lying.

In *Building Character in Schools*, Ryan and Bohlin observe

that many teachers might ask at this juncture, "Did Huck do the right thing?" This "moral dilemma" approach engages students in discussing the pros and cons of a particular moral decision and, in the hands of a skillful teacher, can develop students' powers of moral reasoning. The downside of the dilemma method, however, is that the discussion often ends with the class still divided and the moral question up in the air. Students are left with the impression that there are reasonable-sounding arguments for and against almost anything and that morality is just a matter of opinion. Questions of character, moreover, are left unexplored.

Instead of "What's the right thing to do?" a teacher can put the focus on character by asking, "What would be a *courageous* thing to do in this situation? What would show unselfishness? Trustworthiness? Wisdom?"

For an example of a teacher who puts the focus on character, Ryan and Bohlin take us into the eleventh-grade English class of Mrs. Ramirez as they reach the point in the novel where Huck lies to save Jim. She asks her students to take twenty minutes to write an in-class reflection: "What does this decision reveal about Huck, about the kind of person he is becoming? Drawing from our previous discussion of virtues, which virtue is he beginning to show in this scene? Or is he simply acting out of enlightened self-interest? Give evidence from the text to support your response."

At the end of the twenty minutes, Mrs. Ramirez engages the class in a discussion (abridged here) of their papers:

Mrs. Ramirez: What kind of person is Huck becoming?

Deborah: I think Huck is really changing. He stands up for what he believes is right, even if he has to lie.

Steve: Yeah, Huck shows a lot of guts. He's changed a lot from the beginning of the novel.

Mrs. Ramirez: How has he changed?

Steve: I'd say he's gained courage.

Danielle: I don't think so. Huck needs Jim, and he doesn't want him taken away. I think he's acting out of his own self-interest.

Norma:	No, for the first time, Huck realizes that Jim is a person, not property. It reminds me of people who hid Jews in their homes during the Holocaust and then lied to the Nazis. Huck shows respect for Jim *and* courage.[7]

Other virtue-centered questions the teacher might pose: What have you learned from this character that might be helpful to you in the development of your own character? Which person(s) in the novel, in your judgment, had the worst character? Why?

11. Teach as if Truth Matters[8]

Did the Holocaust really happen? Who shares the blame? Did Pope Pius XII fail to come to the aid of Jews, as some have claimed, or do much to help them, as others have argued? Is American history a story of commitment to human freedom, a story of discrimination and exploitation, or a combination of the two? Is global warming really happening, and if so, how serious a threat does it pose? Is our planet threatened by overpopulation, or are bad policies and practices (such as corruption and incompetence within nations and exploitation from without), rather than too many people, the real cause of poverty and deprivation?

Questions like these are questions about what's really true. They make it clear that in school and in life, the most important intellectual virtue is the pursuit of truth. That virtue includes a cluster of supporting intellectual virtues: an openness to considering all sides of an issue in the search for the whole truth; a respect for evidence even when it contradicts our bias; a willingness to admit error; a desire to keep learning; and a humility in the face of all that we don't know.[9]

But in order to pursue the truth and to see education as fundamentally about truth seeking, we have to first believe that objective truth exists and can be known. Some current schools of thought—subjectivism and postmodernism, for instance—argue that all "truth" is subjective, that we process experience through our personal "filters" and thus each create our own truths. In the national debate about how to teach history, some historians—as in the book *History on Trial*—argue that it is "preposterous folly" to believe that historical "facts" exist "objectively and independently of the interpretation of the historian."[10]

There is, of course, a partial truth in this line of argument. But acknowledging that historical interpretations are biased should not cause us to give up striving for greater objectivity and completeness in getting the historical record right. When historians of the past have been shown to be wrong, they have been shown to be wrong about *real things;* their claims about the past were different from what really happened.[11]

What, then, is objective truth? As Boston College philosopher Peter Kreeft points out, objective truth—whether it's historical truth, scientific truth, or moral truth—is truth that is independent of the knower. It's true whether or not I know it. To give an obvious example, the fact that Franklin Delano Roosevelt was the U.S. president when Pearl Harbor was bombed is objectively true whether or not I know it to be so.

The notion of objective moral truth has profound implications for character education. If moral truth were purely subjective, there would be no objective right or wrong, no binding moral standards that everyone has to follow. You might think lying, cheating, and stealing are wrong, but I could say, "Hey, that's just your opinion." We'd each be free to follow our private conscience. If, on the other hand, right and wrong do exist, then everyone's first moral duty—as we should point out to our students—is to *discern* the truth and to *form our consciences correctly,* in accord with what's truly right.

Do people sometimes disagree about where the truth lies? They do. As a nation, we once disagreed about slavery and women's right to vote. Today we disagree about issues such as abortion, capital punishment, and how to respond to the threat of terrorism. But the fact that some issues are controversial or complex shouldn't deter us from persevering in trying to know the truth as fully and objectively as we can. In the past, that is how our intellectual and moral mistakes were corrected.

Consider just one example from the historical realm that underscores the importance of seeking the objective truth. Who was responsible for the horrific slave trade that supplied slaves to pre–Civil War America? In one published teachers' guide, teachers and students are told merely that Africans were "kidnapped," "captured," or "abducted" from their homelands in the largest forced migration in recorded history. The guide makes no mention of the role that African royal families and indigenous slave dealers played in supplying European slave merchants. By contrast, as an example of a source that does confront the whole truth, historian Sheldon Stern quotes from the book that accompanied a recent four-part PBS series on "America's journey through slavery":

> The white man did not introduce slavery to Africa. The bowing of one human being to another was an accepted notion from the moment man first sensed frailty on the part of a rival. . . . Long before the arrival of Europeans on West Africa's coast, the two continents shared a common acceptance of slavery. . . . Africans and Europeans stood together as equals, companions in commerce and profit. Tribe stalked tribe, and eventually more than 20 million Africans would be kidnapped in their own homeland.[12]

"Any apology for slavery," Stern says, "should also be joined by Portugal, Britain, France, and especially Brazil, which purchased over six times more African slaves than the United States. America received under 5% of the Africans brought to the New World. In addition, the Moslem Arab states, which imported more African slaves than the entire Western hemisphere, could confront their past by helping to abolish the slavery which persists *today* in Mauritania and Sudan."[13] In learning the whole truth about slavery, students learn not only a lesson about history but also an important lesson about human nature: No nation or race has a monopoly on evil.

12. Teach with a Commitment to Balance

A commitment to truth often translates into a commitment to balance. Harvard scholar Peter Gibbon, author of *A Call to Heroism: Renewing America's Vision of Greatness,* has written about the notable lack of balance in the recent treatment of American history and particular historical figures.

The truth is ill-served if we omit or gloss over our nation's faults and failures, such as the displacement and killing of Native Americans, the enslavement and later segregation of blacks, the internment of Japanese-Americans during World War II, and foreign policies that have supported repressive governments. But the truth is also poorly served if we emphasize the negative and downplay our country's virtues and achievements. Indeed, the virtue of patriotism, defined as the love of what is noble in one's country, requires that we recognize not only our nation's shortcomings but also the democratic ideals that have been the spur for moral progress—at least in some areas—in narrowing the gap between what we profess and what we practice.

Gibbon says that when he travels around the country talking to students about American figures such as George Washington, they tend to be cynical, focusing on faults—on the fact, for example, that Washington owned slaves. (Washington did not, like Benjamin Franklin, go from being a slave owner to being an abolitionist, but he did free his slaves before his death.) He reminds students that Washington was human. His father died when he was eleven. He watched his half brother Lawrence die from tuberculosis and his stepdaughter Patsy succumb to epilepsy. His own face was scarred by smallpox, his body weakened by malaria. When the American Revolution came, he didn't want to be commander. His soldiers were few and untrained, and defeat at the hands of Britain, the eighteenth century's superpower, often seemed certain. But he didn't quit. He learned to dodge and retreat and use the wilderness. He forced himself to appear confident despite frustration and fatigue.

"I tell students," Gibbon says, "that Washington was great because he showed extraordinary courage—not just the courage to face bullets, but the courage to stick to a cause no matter how great the odds, to shake off failure and transcend pain, to take risks and to grow."

When the war was over, Washington wanted to retire to a quiet life tending his garden at Mount Vernon. But the new nation was fragile and wanted him to be its first president. He put his country's welfare before his personal happiness and served for eight years. As president, he was a masterful administrator and prudent statesman, always placing honor above politics. "Washington was not brilliant like Hamilton nor eloquent like Jefferson," Gibbon concludes, "but our first president had character."[14]

13. Model Balance and Fairness in Dealing with Controversial Issues

Balance must also characterize the school's handling of controversial issues, whether the issue is abortion, capital punishment, homosexuality, or war against Iraq. Out of respect for the diversity of views on such moral issues that exists within the school and its surrounding community, public school educators must take great care to treat a controversial matter in a way that's fair to conflicting perspectives or not treat it at all.

For example, prior to the onset of the war against Iraq, a group of students at Chicago's Walter Payton High School asked permission to perform *Lysistrata*, Aristophanes' antiwar play in which women vow to abstain from sex until men abstain from war. Principal Gail Ward consented but insisted that the performance be followed by a panel discussion including persons who supported military action. After the panel, students who had been involved in putting on the play said they had learned the importance of hearing different viewpoints.[15]

Controversy is an important opportunity for adults to model how to think through complex moral issues. What sources of information should a person seek out in order to develop an informed judgment? What point of view are we getting in any given source? How does one remain open to new evidence that might call for changing one's mind? In the matter of war and peace, what have moral philosophers historically put forth as criteria for a "just war"? What are the possible long-range as well as short-range consequences of military intervention versus diplomatic efforts? In order to expose her students to reasoned arguments on both sides of this issue, one Albuquerque high school teacher who strongly opposed war against Iraq organized a debate in her classroom between herself and a colleague who supported military action. In so doing, she not only helped her students gain more knowledge to draw from in making a judgment about the war; she also taught them a memorable lesson in intellectual integrity.

14. Teach as if Justice Matters

Even young children have a rudimentary sense of fairness. One of the most important challenges of character education is to develop that sense into a strong social conscience, a universalized commitment to justice.

What is justice? Treating others as they deserve to be treated. We should help students appreciate that every person has intrinsic dignity and value—sacred value, if one believes that we are each created in the image of God. No person has more or less value than any other. Every human life is unique, precious, and unrepeatable. Every human being has human rights that derive from our dignity as persons. More than thirty of these rights are proclaimed in the 1948 United Nations Universal Declaration of Human Rights. They include the right to a livelihood and living conditions that meet basic human needs and are consistent with human dignity.

The stark reality, however, is that millions of our fellow human beings do not enjoy conditions that support human development and dignity. *Civics in Action* (www.civicsinaction.org), an online source of classroom lessons (grades six through twelve) linking character and current events, carried a lesson on global citizenship that included these statistics:

- 1.3 billion people—one of four—lack safe drinking water.
- Nearly 11 million children—3 million more than the population of New York City—die worldwide each year of diseases such as diarrhea and measles that could be prevented with simple shots and basic sanitation. One of five children dies before the age of five.
- More than 110 million children of school age do not attend school. Worldwide, one of every six persons is illiterate.

Some global problems are approaching the catastrophic stage. On the pediatrics ward of a hospital in Johannesburg, South Africa, half of the newborn babies are HIV-positive. Medicines needed to prevent mother-to-child transmission of the HIV virus reach only a very small percentage of women in sub-Saharan Africa. A visitor to this hospital asked, "How long will these babies live?" A nurse answered, "Less than a year."

Education for justice must also examine the growing disparities between the haves and the have-nots of the world. Just as the gap between rich and poor within the United States has widened in past decades, the gap between rich and poor nations has also steadily widened. Whereas affluent Western countries consume *more* every year, for example, some countries in Africa today consume 25 percent *less* than they did in the 1970s.

Our children have also inherited a world where terrorism and the violence it provokes are new threats to global peace. People may differ regarding when or whether to use force to combat terrorism, but one would hope that all people of conscience would agree with the principle, "If you want peace, work for justice."

Students should read accounts that put a human face on the suffering caused by injustice. Six weeks after the terrorist attacks of September 11, the *New York Times Magazine* carried an article by the journalist Peter Maass depicting the plight of Pakistani youth ripe for terrorism.[16] It described twenty-one-year-old Emroz Kahn, who since he was twelve years old has worked twelve-hour days, six days a week, dismantling car engines with a sledgehammer and chisel. He earns $1.25 a day. Under the skin of his forearm is a piece of pipe he drove into his body by mistake. It has been there for three years. He says he cannot afford to pay a doctor to take it out. "We work like donkeys," he says. "Our life is like the life of animals."

"These young men," the article continues, "live where globalization is not working. They believe, or can be led to believe, that America—or their pro-America government if they live under one—is to blame for their misery."

Kids, of course, can't solve the world's problems. But they should at least know about them and be challenged to take small steps, even while they are still in school, to make the world a more just and caring place. Books such as *Kids Explore Kids Who Make a Difference* and *The Kid's Guide to Service Projects* and websites such as www.kidscanmakeadifference.org offer students ways to be part of the solution instead of part of the problem. And once they are informed about national and international issues, they can e-mail or write the president (White House, Washington, D.C. 20500) and their congressional representatives to express a thoughtful opinion about how their country can use its influence for good. If they do these things now as students, they will be more disposed to do them when they are adult citizens.

Finally, we should challenge students to extend their concept of justice to include living creatures other than humans. Children, in fact, often have for animals a natural empathy that can provide a starting point for developing a broader sense of justice.

A new book worthy of study by secondary students is Matthew Scully's *Dominion: The Power of Man, the Suffering of Animals, and the Call to Mercy.* It takes an unblinking look at our society's growing cruelty to animals. One doesn't have to elevate animals to equality with humans—Scully doesn't—to be disturbed by practices such as those of modern "factory farms" that, for the sake of efficient production, raise animals under conditions so cramped, filthy, and painful that one shudders to read of them. Scully writes, "Kindness to animals is not our most important duty as human beings, nor is it our least important."[17] He asks whether we can foster human dignity and respect for life in a society that treats other sentient beings as production units. His book is a stirring call to conscience.

It should be amply clear that educating for intellect and educating for moral character are equally important goals of character education. The two main ways that students demonstrate character in school are by doing their work diligently and by treating others respectfully. And it should be clear why intellectual development and moral growth are both essential for full human development and the betterment of the world. If we want our students to become competent and creative problem solvers able to improve the human condition, we had better help them hone their intellectual skills. If we want them to use their brains to benefit others and not just themselves, we had better help them develop their moral conscience.

Character education, rightly understood, aims to develop the whole person. Better students, better citizens. It's the foundation that everything else builds on. That's why, in the words of Dr. John Walko, director of Russell Sage College's Academy for Character Education, "Character education isn't something else on your plate. It's the plate."

For research and educational recommendations concerning students' social, moral, and political development, see *Children's Social Consciousness and the Development of Social Responsibility*[18] by Sheldon Berman, whose Hudson, Massachusetts, school district received a 2001 National District of Character award for its programs in ethics and service learning (www.hudson.k12.ma.us). For an example of an academic curriculum used by the Hudson Schools to develop ethical responsibility, see Facing History and Ourselves (www.facinghistory.org). For other helpful resources on academics and character development, see Kathy Beland's *Providing a Meaningful Academic Curriculum,* part of *Eleven Principles Sourcebook* (www.character.org), and Ron Ritchart's *Intellectual Character: What It Is, Why It Matters, and How to Get It* (Jossey-Bass, 2000).

CHAPTER 7

Practice Character-Based Discipline

Discipline is something that has to be developed from the inside, like a backbone, not locked on from the outside, like a pair of handcuffs.

—A TEACHER

Discipline yourself, and others won't need to.

—MAXIM

For a great many schools, discipline is the entry point for character education. If there is not respect for rules, authority, and the rights of others, there is not a good environment for teaching and learning. Many schools turn to character education because they are distressed by the decline they see in student respect and responsibility and hope that character education can reverse that trend.

Character education asserts that discipline, if it's going to work, has to change kids *on the inside*. It has to change their attitude, the way they think and feel. It has to lead them to *want* to behave differently. It has to help them develop the virtues—often respect, empathy, good judgment, and self-control—whose absence led to the discipline problem in the first place. If those absent virtues aren't developed, along with a commitment to putting them into practice, the behavior problem will occur again. In short, effective discipline must be *character-based*; it must strengthen students' character, not simply control their behavior.

Discipline falls into two categories: prevention and correction. Good prevention strategies will greatly reduce the frequency of behavior problems. But some problems will still occur, and character-building strategies will be needed to correct them.

Let's look at eighteen discipline strategies, starting with prevention. What these strategies have in common is faith in every student's capacity for goodness, however deeply it may be buried, if we can find a way to tap into that potential.

1. Share the Agenda

Many classrooms are plagued by the "double agenda problem." The teachers' agenda is to teach the material, but the students' agenda is not to learn it. The challenge is to get students on board with the instructional agenda.

One way to do that is to *explain* to students the objectives of a given lesson, their rationale, and the learning patterns the teacher will use to accomplish those objectives. Preparing this explanation also helps the teacher step back and ask, Are my curriculum content and instructional methods as effective as they might be? Many discipline problems stem from weak content or poor pedagogy.

Ann Jackewenko, who teaches eleventh-grade English in central New York, seeks to engage her students at the beginning of class by addressing three things she has written on the board:

1. What we're going to learn today
2. Why it's important to know this
3. How we're going to learn it (for instance, teacher lecture—10 minutes; cooperative learning— 15 minutes; whole-group discussion—10 minutes; start the homework assignment—5 minutes)

"Students like having the big picture," she points out. "If you *don't* take the time to explain to them why it's important to learn a particular point or skill, they'll often fight you with the attitude, 'Why do we have to know this?'"

2. Hold Students Accountable

Teachers who are effective disciplinarians set high expectations for both academics and behavior and then hold students accountable. They're often known for being "strict."

Deb Halliday, who teaches fourth grade in central New York, is that kind of teacher. She says, "I have a strict homework policy. My students are expected to do their homework each night and hand it in each morning. If homework isn't done, the student must do it during recess. There's no way around it, and the class knows it."

3. Teach Principles of Responsibility

When Natalie Douglass was called in to consult with an Indiana alternative school for 150 difficult adolescents, she began by training the faculty to teach students "The Five Principles of Responsibility." These principles were displayed on large-print posters in every classroom:

1. I am responsible for my behavior. If I behave well, I get the credit. If I mess up, I must accept responsibility and not try to blame somebody else.
2. I am responsible for my learning. No one can learn for me.
3. I am responsible for treating all persons with consideration and respect.
4. I am responsible for contributing to my classroom and my school.
5. I am responsible for the environment—for treating it with care so others may enjoy it.

During the first two weeks of school, all teachers spent time teaching and illustrating these five principles. Thereafter, whenever students acted inappropriately, the principles of responsibility provided a framework for a productive conversation. The teacher would go over to the student and quietly ask, "Which principle of responsibility do you think is involved here?"

Students became more reflective about their behavior. When teachers handled disruptions in this way, discipline referrals to the principal's office dropped from an average of twelve to fifteen a day during the previous school year to only two or three a day.

We live in a society in which taking responsibility for one's actions is becoming less and less common and passing the buck the norm. "It seems as if everybody is a 'victim,'" says a principal. "I have a fifty-year-old friend who blames most of her problems on her alcoholic father. He died when she was two." Teaching kids the principles of responsibility is a step in the right direction, toward getting them to take responsibility for their behavior and their lives.

4. Involve Students in Generating the Rules

When he was an award-winning high school history and psychology teacher, Hal Urban put students in groups of five or six and gave them the following work sheet to complete:

IF WE MADE THE RULES

Students would *not* be allowed to:

1) _____

2) _____

3) _____

4) _____

5) _____

Students would be *encouraged* to:

1) _____

2) _____

3) _____

4) _____

5) _____

The groups then reported out, first the things students would not be allowed to do, then the things they would be encouraged to do. Mr. Urban kept a running list on the board. He proposed a few additions of his own (noted by an asterisk in the final list).

"I did this with each of my classes," he says. "Then I took all the lists home, made a composite list, and brought that in the next day and gave every student a copy. I said, 'You own them, you honor them.'" Here is a typical list produced by this process:

CLASS RULES: DO'S AND DON'TS IN MR. URBAN'S CLASS
(written by the students and the teacher)

You are allowed and encouraged to do the following in this class:	*You are not allowed to do the following in this class:*
Follow the Golden Rule	Discount/ignore other students
Be respectful of teacher	Discount/ignore the teacher
Take good notes	Sit and do nothing
Say "please" and "thank you"	Swear/use bad language
Listen	Interrupt/have side conversations
Have a positive attitude	Complain/act like a "hard ass"
Keep the class clean	Litter
Express your opinion	Dominate conversations
Participate	Sleep/put head down on the desk
Have good manners	Be rude
Be on time	Come late

"People always ask me how I handled consequences," Urban says. "I had a number of signs in the room: Compliments Spoken Here, No Discounts/Everybody Counts, Hard Work, Respect Others, and A Positive Attitude. If a student forgot a rule, I would just knock on one of my signs or go over to that student's desk. I had very few problems."

5. Teach the Golden Rule

Classroom discipline is a golden opportunity to teach the Golden Rule.

Gary Robinson taught fourth and sixth graders in the Skaneateles School District, Skaneateles, New York. On the first day of school, he would ask his students, "How would you like to be treated in this class—by me, the teacher, and by everybody else in the room? Write down two or three ways you'd like to be treated."

Students wrote that they wanted to be treated fairly, with respect, not made fun of or embarrassed, not left out, and so on. Mr. Robinson had them share their lists with a partner and discuss them as a class.

He then asked a second question, "How should you treat everyone else in the room?" Students could see it logically followed that if *they* wanted to be treated with respect and fairness, then that's exactly how they should treat everyone else. Mr. Robinson enlarged upon this point for the class:

> Every right carries a responsibility. If you've got a right to respect, then you've got a responsibility to extend that same respect to other people. You can't claim a right unless you accept the responsibility. They are two sides of the same coin.

He summarized, "We're saying you should treat others as you wish to be treated. Does anybody know what that's called?" Somebody in the class usually knew: "the Golden Rule."

"That's my main classroom rule," Mr. Robinson said. Then he

unfurled a large banner with these words writ large: TREAT OTHERS AS YOU WISH TO BE TREATED. He hung the banner above the blackboard, where it remained for the rest of the year.

Next he asked, "What happens if someone breaks the Golden Rule?" He explained his system of consequences:

> The first time you break the Golden Rule, I'll stop teaching and just give you the "evil eye" [this with a smile]. I want you to ask yourself, "What did I do to break the Golden Rule?"
>
> The second time you break the Golden Rule that day, I'll say your name. Again, I want you to be thinking, "What did I do to break the Golden Rule?"
>
> The third time, I'll ask you to take a seat at the Golden Rule Table in the back of the room and write me a paragraph on "How I Broke the Golden Rule." The first chance I get, I'll come back, and we'll have a conversation about what you wrote.
>
> If this problem has been going on for a couple of days or more, I'll ask you to write me a behavior improvement plan, "How I Plan to Follow the Golden Rule in the Future."
>
> If the problem isn't limited to just one person, I might ask you to help lead a class meeting on how we can work together to solve that problem.

By asking "How would you like to be treated?" and "How should you treat everyone else?" Mr. Robinson guided his students to the Golden Rule and helped them see its moral logic. His system of consequences held them accountable to the Golden Rule and gave them continuing practice in using that standard to evaluate their behavior.

6. Share the Plan with Parents

At the elementary and middle school levels, a copy of the teacher's discipline plan should go home to parents at the beginning of the year. It should let them know the classroom rules and consequences, and at what point parents will be asked to help solve a problem. All this can be communicated in a positive way. Here, for example, is the letter sent home by Amy Conley, a third-grade teacher at Burton Street Elementary School in Cazenovia, New York:

> Dear Parent or Guardian,
>
> I would like to fill you in on my discipline plan for the coming school year. Because I believe that success in life develops through *self*-discipline, I want to give all students every opportunity to manage their own behavior. To achieve that I will be using the following discipline plan.
>
> Expectations
> 1. Be respectful of yourself, others, and our classroom.
> 2. Be responsible for yourself, your belongings, and our classroom materials.
> 3. Participate in our safe and caring classroom.
> 4. Do your best; never give up!
> 5. Follow the Golden Rule.
>
> When expectations are not met (*we rarely have to go beyond consequence 2*)
> 1. Reminder
> 2. Thinking zone—3 minutes
> 3. Thinking zone in another third-grade classroom—3 minutes
> 4. Parent called
> 5. Conference—student, parent/guardian, Mrs. Conley, and Mrs. Gordon (principal)
>
> The children and I have discussed this plan together, but please review it with your child. In my experience, this plan helps to create a very positive climate in the classroom because students know what is expected of them. Thank you very much for your time.

7. Practice Procedures

Many discipline problems occur because teachers and schools don't take the time to teach procedures for behavior in the classroom and other parts of the school building.

Says former high school history teacher Charlie Abourjilie, "Because I wanted my students to know my procedures for handing in papers, coming into class and getting to work, giving me admit slips when they had been absent, and so on, I took about fifteen minutes each period during the first week of school to practice these procedures. I demonstrated the procedures I wanted them to follow when they came into class each day. Then I took them out in the hallway, bookbags and all, and had them go into class following those procedures. We did this three or four times until everybody got it right. This saved a lot of time down the road."

The schools in Florence, South Carolina, teach procedures for proper behavior outside the classroom. Southside Middle School principal Patricia Slice explains:

> Our district has trained a team of lead teachers from each middle school in how to teach procedures. They in turn train all the staff in their building. Then, during homeroom and other designated periods of the first week of school, all teachers—using lesson plans prepared by the lead team— teach desired behaviors for common areas of the school such as the hallways, the cafeteria, the courtyard, the library, the playground, and the buses. We no longer take any of this for granted. As a result of taking the time at the beginning of the year to deliberately teach students appropriate conduct, we're seeing far fewer behavior problems.

8. Use the Language of Virtue

"Language shapes character," writes Linda Popov in *The Virtues Project Educator's Guide* (www.jalmarpress.com). The language of virtue can create a culture of character.

Deb Halliday uses the language of virtue to compliment her fourth-graders. Instead of giving general praise such as "Good job" or "Nice work," she'll say such things as:

I admire the *effort* you put into that project.
I appreciate your *courtesy* in raising your hand instead
    of yelling my name across the room.
Thank you for being *patient*.

Similarly, the language of virtue can be used to correct or redirect behavior:

What would be a *kinder* way to say that?
What would help you discuss this problem in a *more
    peaceful* way?

Ray Tufts uses the language of virtue in his work as assistant principal at an alternative school in Renton, Washington. Many of his students have been previously expelled from other schools, and some have criminal records.

When they're sent to his office for a behavior problem, he begins by saying, "Tell me what happened from your point of view" and listens respectfully to the student's side of the story. Then he points to his Virtues poster (listing fifty-two virtues from Linda Popov's book) and asks, "Which of these virtues might you have forgotten? Which ones might have helped you avoid the problem you had?" Sometimes he'll give students a story or article to read that deals with a virtue they need to develop.

9. Help Students Learn from Mistakes

Says a middle school principal, "Our philosophy is that kids will make mistakes. We teach them that it's how they *respond* to their mistakes, in school and in life, that makes all the difference."

At this principal's school, when students do something wrong, they are usually asked to respond, sometimes in writing, to four questions:

1. What mistake did you make?
2. What did you learn from that mistake?
3. How can you avoid that mistake in the future?
4. Do you need to make a plan?

10. Have Students Make a Behavior Improvement Plan

When a behavior problem persists, students need to make a written plan to improve their behavior. Every school should have a procedure for doing that and a process whereby students evaluate how they're doing with their plan. This procedure shifts responsibility for managing behavior from the adults to the students.

At one elementary school in Minneapolis, students who have recurring discipline problems go to the P/T (planning time) room. There they write out a "Plan for Success" that addresses these questions:

1. What rule did I break?
2. When will I do the work I'm missing because I'm at P/T?
3. What's my plan for getting back to work and improving my school life?
   - I will stop: _____
   - I will start: _____
   - When will I begin? _____

When students present their completed plan to their teacher, they agree on a time (for example, two days later, a week later) for the student to self-assess by answering the following questions about progress in following through with their plan:

- What I wanted to do: _____
- What I did: _____
- How did I do?
  _____ I kept my plan and I feel great.

_____ I like most of what I did, but I'll make my
plan work better next time.

_____ I like a little of what I did. The plan was
better than I was.

_____ I need to make a new plan. This one didn't
work for me.

- What can I do to continue or improve my plan?

---

11. Discuss *Why* a Behavior Was Wrong

Says Emily, an eighth grader: "When a kid does something wrong, don't just punish them, *talk* to them. Explain *why* what they did was wrong. That's what my mother does with me. If you don't explain why it's wrong, they'll just do it again."

All too often, teachers don't take a student aside and explain why a particular behavior was wrong. An important teachable moment is thereby lost. The reasoned moral explanations we give our children are essential for developing their conscience: the inner voice by which they give themselves reasons why something is right or wrong.

Why is it wrong to steal? Because there's a person behind the property, and stealing violates the rights of that person.

Why is it wrong to lie? Because lying violates trust, and trust is the basis of human relationships.

Why is it wrong to cheat? Because cheating is a form of lying. It deceives other people.

Kindergarten teacher Helen Jackson got a call from the mother of Jonathan, a boy from Jamaica. He had told his mother that Brian, a classmate, was calling him "tan man." This upset Jonathan so much that he didn't want to go back to school.

Mrs. Jackson took Brian aside, sat down with him, and spoke to him in a gentle but serious tone:

Brian, there are two kinds of hurts: outside hurts that you can
see, like a cut or a bruise, and inside hurts [pointing to her

heart] that you can't see, like a hurt feeling. But even though you can't see the inside hurts, they are very real. They actually hurt more and last longer than the outside hurts.

When you call Jonathan "tan man," you're causing an inside hurt for him. In fact, it hurts so much he doesn't want to come back to our class. I wouldn't let anyone make that kind of inside hurt for you. And we can't let anyone make that kind of inside hurt for Jonathan. Our classroom has to be a place where everyone feels safe and happy to be here. Do you understand? Tell me what I said.

Psychologists call this method of reasoning *induction*. It induces children to appreciate, at an intellectual and emotional level, the effects of their actions on others.

12. Use Time-out Effectively

At the early childhood and elementary levels, one of the most common disciplinary consequences is time-out. Most teachers, however, have had the unhappy experience of sending students to time-out and having them come back no better, and often worse, than when they left.

Whether time-out works depends very much on how students perceive the *meaning* of time-out. We should explain to them, "The purpose of time-out is to help you gain control of your behavior, so that you can come back and contribute to our classroom community in a positive way."

A sports analogy can help students understand:

How many people have ever watched a basketball game? Why does the coach call time-out? The players are making mistakes, throwing the ball away, and so on. They've lost control of their game.

So, what's the first thing the players have to do in time-out? They have to *settle down and get control*. What's the second thing they have to do in time-out, before they can go back into the game? They have to *make a plan* so that they don't make the same mistakes.

It's the same in the classroom. When you lose control, you have to go to time-out and do two things. First, settle down and get control. Second, make a plan for what you're going to do to avoid making the same mistakes. Then tell me your plan, and you'll be back in the game.[1]

Some children will need this concept explained to them more than once. Even with such explanations, a particular child may still sometimes resist going to time-out. If that happens, it may help to take the child to a quiet spot and ask calmly, "Do you remember the reason for time-out? What should you do there so you can come back and join the group?" If that doesn't work, a hierarchy of consequences should be in place, so that the teacher can matter-of-factly give the student a choice: "Jeff, you can go to time-out, calm down, and make a plan, or you can go to the principal's office and call your parents. You decide."

13. Design Detention That Builds Character

A boy in a North Carolina middle school observed, "Detention is one of the dumbest ideas I've ever seen. You just sit there. It doesn't help."

How can detention be turned into an experience that has the potential to improve a student's attitude and behavior? Buck Lodge Middle School in Adelphi, Maryland, is a highly diverse urban school and a 1998 National School of Character (301-431-6290). A few years ago, it redesigned detention to make it a time for meaningful student reflection. Now, when students go to detention, they're asked to take out three sheets of notebook paper and

1. Write a paragraph on why you are in detention.
2. Write a paragraph about at least three ways you could have handled this situation differently and not be in detention.

3. Tell about your best subject in school. Tell about your worst subject. How can you improve?
4. List 5 positive qualities about yourself.
5. List 3 qualities you need to improve on.
6. Write 3 paragraphs about your life. Discuss when you were younger, your life now, and what you plan to be doing with your life ten years from now.
7. Write a paragraph about how you have helped someone else become a better person.
8. Will you be returning to detention? Write a paragraph explaining your answer.

14. Teach Restitution

One of the most important moral lessons for young people to learn is "When you do something wrong, you should do something right to make up for it." Bad behavior usually creates some kind of damage—to property, feelings, relationships, or the peace and order of a classroom or family. If you've done damage, you have an obligation to try to fix it.

Apologizing is therefore only the first step a child should take when he or she has done something wrong. As an old saying has it, "'Sorry' doesn't get the hay in." The second thing is to ask, "What can I do to make up for it?"

Teachers and schools sometimes use restitution as a disciplinary consequence but make the mistake of dictating the form the restitution will take ("You wrote on the wall, now clean it off") rather than asking the student, with adult help if needed, to come up with an appropriate way to make amends. The problems with the "Here's your restitution" approach are (1) the student may very well resent the imposed restitution and do it grudgingly, without feeling any remorse for the offense; and (2) the student is not required to *think about* his or her misdeed, the problem it caused for someone else, and what would help to fix the problem and make the victim feel better.

The goal of restitution should be to stimulate students' thinking and maximize the character development that occurs as a result of the disciplinary experience. That's why it's better to ask the student, "What do *you* think would be a good way to make up for what you did?"

15. Have Kids Help Each Other

Cheryl Watson, a third-grade teacher in San Ramon, California, devised a way to involve children in helping classmates behave well and do their work well. She puts students in groups of four she calls "peer pods."

Peer pods typically meet once a week. If someone in a particular pod is getting in trouble with the teacher that week because of a certain behavior, podmates make suggestions for how to avoid that problem in the future ("If you're always getting yelled at for talking to Mike, maybe you shouldn't sit next to him"). If a group member is having trouble in a particular academic subject, podmates might suggest things that have worked for them ("Here's how I study for the spelling test").

Says Watson, "The kids come up with things I would not have thought of."

16. Prepare for a "Guest Teacher"

Even classes that are fairly well behaved for their regular teacher often act up for a substitute. Teachers are embarrassed when they return and get the report on how badly their kids behaved.

To avoid that scenario, Hal Urban, when he knows he'll be having a "guest teacher" (a more respectful term than "sub"), asks his students to think about, and sometimes write about, two questions:

1. If you were the guest teacher, how would you like to be treated?
2. If this person were your mother or sister, how would you want students to treat her?

Reflecting on these questions makes a difference in students' behavior. Urban comments, "I've had substitutes leave me notes such as 'These were the most polite kids I've ever had.' I always read the note to the class. They like hearing that their efforts were appreciated."

17. Give a Difficult Child Responsibility

> You have to look at people with two eyes.
> One eye sees what the person is now.
> The other sees what the person can become.
> You have to keep both eyes open all the time.
> — MILES HORTON

On a Tuesday morning in October 1999, at Buell Elementary School in Michigan, a first-grade boy came to school carrying a concealed handgun and a knife. At 10:00 A.M., as students were changing classes, he shot and killed six-year-old Kayla Rolland.

The boy and his brother lived in a crackhouse where guns were traded for drugs. He was kept after school nearly every day for pinching, hitting, fighting, and saying the f-word. Once asked "Why do you fight with other kids?" he answered, "Because I hate them."

Here was a child crying out for help. Disciplining him by keeping him after school clearly was doing nothing to assuage the anger that led him to lash out.

What might have helped to change the tragic trajectory of this boy's life? We can find clues in the story of Billy, described by Richard Curwin in his book *Rediscovering Hope: Our Greatest Teaching Strategy.*[2]

Billy was a fourth-grader in a rural community. He was surly with his teacher, fought constantly, and did little schoolwork. His father was in jail. His mother was an alcoholic. Billy himself had already started to use alcohol in times of stress.

In workshops, I ask teachers, "What could you do to try to get Billy to stop fighting and at the same time build his character, when you're probably not going to be able to change the character of the world he comes from?"

Some teachers suggest that Billy needs a mentor: an adult or older student who would work with him and give him the love and attention that he appears to be lacking at home. What Billy's school did, however, was even more effective: It put *Billy* in the role of mentor. His teacher, the principal, and the counselor got together and presented him with the following plan:

1. He could be the special friend and protector of a first-grade boy in a wheelchair.
2. He could help the boy on and off the school bus, sit with him at lunch, be his guardian on the playground, and visit him daily in his classroom.
3. If he got in any kind of a fight at school, he lost the privilege of further contact with the first-grader for the rest of that day.

By the last stipulation, the school was in effect saying, "If you want to have this special responsibility, you have to control your fighting. We're confident you can do that." Often teachers or schools try to boost the self-esteem of a problem child by giving him a special role, such as classroom helper, but neglect to make having that role contingent on improved behavior ("If you hit somebody, you lose the privilege of that job for a day"). A lever is thereby lost that could have been used to motivate behavioral change.

Billy quickly came to treasure his time with the younger boy. The two children became good friends. One day, when Billy learned that the younger boy was out sick, the teacher saw a tear in his eye. He was learning to care by giving care; as Gandhi said, "The heart learns what the hand does." Billy's fighting became only an occasional occurrence. Though he still struggled academically, his attitude toward himself and toward school was much more positive.

Why did this intervention work? Billy had a new social role and responsibility. Somebody was counting on him. He felt needed and important. He was making a difference in somebody's life.

With students labeled "at risk," Curwin says, we typically do more for them. That doesn't change their feelings of inadequacy or failure. What they really need is an opportunity to do something for someone else. Once they feel competent and helpful, their self-worth goes up. The character education principle here is that if we want kids to develop responsibility, we should give them responsibility.

18. Design a "Tough Love" Program for Difficult Students

High school teachers often ask, "Isn't the character of kids pretty much formed by the time they get to us?"

Fortunately, human nature has a remarkable plasticity, a capacity for growth, if we can find the right intervention. This remains true of teens.

In our own small city of Cortland, New York (population 18,000), a program called S.T.A.R. (Student Transition and Recovery Program), for kids with chronic school behavior problems, is causing people to sit up and take notice.

Breck Aspinwall, a twenty-year veteran Cortland junior high school science teacher, says, "The difference this program has made in three of my eighth graders has been nothing short of miraculous. Their grades have shot up. The discipline issues have dropped to near zero. Most important, they are beginning to understand that self-discipline and structure are positive forces."

Jointly operated and funded by the school district and the county's social services department, S.T.A.R. works with problem students ages ten to sixteen, the sort of kids who exhaust teachers and are frequently given in-school suspension and out-of-school suspension and eventually placed in alternative schools. Students may be referred to S.T.A.R. by a teacher or required to participate by family court. They stay in the program for one day, thirty days, or six months, depending on the severity of their situation and the nature of their referral.

Parents are responsible for getting their child to the National Guard Armory by 5:30 A.M. every school morning. There Stacy Sawyer and another drill instructor lead students in rigorous physical exercises. Says fifteen-year-old Kristy Gower, "I hated the calisthenics at first, but now I love running. It puts me in a good mood for the rest of the day." At the end of the school day, the students are bused back to the armory, where they do their academic homework together.

Captain Terry Vandenberg, a former marine, coordinates the program, which also employs two drill instructors, a psychologist, and two tutors. Many students say they consider the personal tutoring the best part of the program.

On day one, S.T.A.R. students pledge to obey nine basic rules:

1. I will be on time to my appointed place of duty.
2. I will respect and listen to adults.
3. I will present a neat, clean appearance at all times.
4. I will do as I am told by adults.
5. I will not drink alcohol or take drugs.
6. I will not fight.
7. I will not lie, cheat, or steal.
8. I will accept responsibility for all my actions.
9. I will do the best I can to improve myself each day.

S.T.A.R. also includes home visits. Someone on the S.T.A.R. staff is on call, twenty-four hours a day, if a student needs help for any reason. "This program really adopts these kids in a very personal way," says the social service commissioner. "They can't help feeling cared about."

On Fridays there are guest speakers. Every Saturday morning, S.T.A.R. students do some kind of community service. One Saturday, they all gave blood.

Andrea Dowd, a ninth-grader, said she is participating in the six-month, court-ordered version of the program. She had gotten suspended from the junior high school for skipping classes and getting into lots of fights. Before S.T.A.R., things had gotten so bad that she was placed in a foster home. Since joining S.T.A.R., she has brought her grades up to passing and has been able to live at home. She says:

I cried during the first day of the program. The push-ups and

running were really hard. But I don't get in trouble anymore.
I used to have a real attitude. I disagreed with everybody and
thought of myself as a loser. Now I want to graduate.

S.T.A.R. succeeds through a combination of high demand and
high support. Any committed school could reproduce the essence of
S.T.A.R.: character building through tough and creative love.[3]

*   *   *

When surveys ask teens about discipline, they often say they wish
their parents and teachers had disciplined them more and demanded more of them. Kids want the structure that firm, fair, and
reasoned discipline provides. They thrive on it.

That doesn't mean that discipline is easy. As any veteran
teacher will attest, students today are coming to school with more
problems—more stress, more anger, less self-control, less awareness of right and wrong—than they brought in the past. Even the
most resourceful and dedicated teachers are often weighed down
by the increasing number and severity of behavior problems they
have to deal with.

Nevertheless, it remains for us to persevere in finding ways,
even with the most challenging students, to discipline in a manner
that builds character. And we must also invest at least as much energy in creating a moral environment that helps to prevent problems
as we spend in correcting misbehavior. To discipline is to teach.
Properly understood, discipline is not crowd control but character
education, with self-discipline as its ultimate aim. No aspect of
character education is more basic to creating a school of character.

CHAPTER 8

Teach Manners

Manners are of more importance than laws. Upon them, in great measure, the laws depend. Manners are what vex or smooth, corrupt or purify, exalt or debase, barbarize or refine us. . . . According to their quality, they aid morals, or they destroy them.

— EDMUND BURKE, BRITISH STATESMAN

The people who really know your character are waiters and clerks.

— KATHERINE PIPIN

In April 2002, the Public Agenda published a survey that struck a national nerve: *Aggravating Circumstances: A Status Report on Rudeness in America* (www.publicagenda.org). Based on interviews with 2,013 U.S. adults, the report included these findings:

- Nearly 60 percent of Americans say they often encounter reckless and aggressive drivers on the road.
- Almost half say they are often subjected to loud and annoying phone conversations.

- Almost half say bad service has driven them out of a store in the past year.
- Three-quarters say they often see customers treating salespeople rudely.
- 79 percent say that "the lack of respect and courtesy should be regarded as a serious national problem."

As Public Agenda's president, Deborah Wadsworth, saw the results, "Lack of manners for Americans is not about whether you confuse the salad fork with the dinner fork. It's about the daily assault of selfish, inconsiderate behavior on the highways, in the office, in stores, and in myriad other places."

"In the long decline of the civilized West," observes one social historian, "there has been nothing so grating as the gradual disappearance of manners."

Manners are minor morals. They are the everyday ways we respect other people and facilitate social relations. They make up the moral fabric of our shared lives.

Saying please when we'd like something, thanking people (waitresses and clerks, for example) when they do us a service, holding a door for the person behind us, not talking in movie theaters, turning off our cell phone when we're in a group setting, covering our mouth when we yawn or cough, using language that doesn't offend—all these are small but meaningful ways of trying to make life a little more pleasant for the people around us.

If we fail to teach these everyday habits of courtesy and consideration to our children, we will not prepare them to be socially competent and likable people. When society in general fails to teach manners to the young, it coarsens human relations and paves the way for the gross violations of civility that are ever more common. One example of the latter is that funeral directors and police, especially in metropolitan areas, increasingly report blatant disrespect for funeral processions. One Virginia funeral director says that drivers regularly cut off his hearse and often give him an obscene gesture as they go by.

What can we do in our classrooms and schools to restore the habits of civilized conduct known as good manners?

1. Get Kids to Think About Why Manners Matter

One year, Hal Urban put up a sign in his high school classroom: "No one ever went wrong by being polite." He had always enjoyed a good rapport with his students, who were college-bound and typically from affluent families. But he was troubled by what he saw as a decline of basic courtesy. He decided to hit this issue head-on by devoting the first class of the new school year to a discussion of manners.

He began by making two points: "In my experience, most people are capable of courtesy when they know clearly what is expected of them. Moreover, the classroom is a more positive place when everyone treats everyone else with courtesy and consideration."

He then distributed a handout titled, "Whatever Happened to Good Manners?" At the top was a quote from George Bernard Shaw: "Without good manners, human society becomes intolerable." Below that, under the heading "How Things Were Different Not Too Many Years Ago," were ten changes he'd seen in student behavior over his twenty-plus years of high school teaching. He walked his class through these observations, which included:

- Students rarely came late to class. When they did, they apologized. Today many come late. Only rarely does one apologize.
- Students didn't get up, walk across the room, throw something in the wastebasket, then walk back across the room while the teacher was talking. Today this is done often, and nothing is thought about it.
- Students used to listen when the teacher was talking. Today many students feel they have a right to ignore the teacher and have a private conversation with their friends.
- Students didn't swear in classrooms or the hallways. Today some students can't talk without swearing.

- Students used to say "please" and "thank you." Today only a few students use those words.

Under this list of observations were six questions:

- Why is this happening?
- Is society better when people treat each other with respect? If so, why?
- Is a classroom better when both students and teacher show mutual respect?
- Why does Henry Rogers say, "Good manners are one of the most important keys to success in life"?
- What is the "Golden Rule"? If it's so simple, why do more people today have difficulty practicing it?
- Which impresses people more—being "cool" or being courteous?

Urban then instructed the class, "Please take out a sheet of paper and answer the six questions. *Don't* sign your name. I'll collect your papers and read them aloud to the class."

He collected students' written responses, read them aloud, and used them as a springboard for a discussion of manners. This took the rest of the period.

Urban comments, "This activity made a noticeable difference in students' behavior. In the weeks that followed, several told me they wished their other teachers would discuss good manners." An exchange student from Germany told him, "I enjoy your class not just because I'm learning a lot of American history but also because of how polite everyone is." At the end of the semester, a boy said, "That manners page you handed out really made me think. Sometimes we do rude things and aren't even aware that we're being rude."

What were the features of this lesson that made it an effective character education experience for these high school students?

First, Urban took a whole class period to discuss good manners. That sent an unmistakable message: Manners matter.

He exercised directive leadership. He didn't ask students, as a values clarification approach might, "How many people think manners are important?" Rather, he designed the whole structure of the lesson to guide students to the conclusion that manners are important in school and life.

He started positively by stating his belief that most people are capable of courtesy if they know clearly what's expected.

He involved students actively. He recruited and respected them as thinkers by seeking their input.

He succeeded in getting all of his students to think about this issue by posing good questions and having them write anonymously. Anonymity gave them the freedom to be candid. About the importance of writing, Urban says, "If I want quality thinking and quality discussion, I almost always have students write first. Writing gets everyone involved. I get a much richer range of responses than if I simply posed the questions to the whole group, in which case only a few students carry the class."

Finally, he taught this lesson on day one. Students could reflect on manners without feeling defensive, since they hadn't yet had a chance to commit the kinds of lapses he was describing. One of the hallmarks of character education is that it's proactive: It teaches what's right before something goes wrong.

Things will still go wrong, of course. It takes time to change habits:

> By the end of the first month, I'm usually exhausted. It takes me that long to persuade all of my students that I really do expect them to abide by these standards. This past semester I had one kid who thought he could go to sleep in my class because that's what he did in other classes. I just kept walking over to his desk and saying matter-of-factly, "I'm sorry, Dan, but you can't sleep in this class." He eventually got the message.

Character education doesn't eliminate human nature. But by being proactive, the teacher puts a framework of expectations in place. Then the teachable moments—the inevitable times when students fall short of the expectations—are more fruitful, because there's an established standard of behavior to refer to and a shared commitment to honor that standard.

2. Teach the Hello-Good-bye Rule

All across the country, teachers say that many students today do not return adults' greetings. "You say hello to a kid in the hall," says one elementary school teacher, "and they don't say anything back."

Returning a greeting, like all manners, must be learned. Gary Robinson made it a point to teach his fourth- and sixth-grade students the courtesy of greeting another person and of saying good-bye. After establishing the Golden Rule as his "most important classroom rule," Mr. Robinson would tell his students

> My other rule is my hello-good-bye rule. When you come into the classroom, I'd like you to say, "Hello, Mr. Robinson." I will, of course, return your greeting and say hello back to you. And when you leave the classroom, I'd like you to say, "Good-bye, Mr. Robinson."
>
> When you enter somebody's space, it's common courtesy to greet them. You should do the same thing with your parents whenever you come into your house. And when you leave a person's space, you should always say good-bye. That's just the polite thing to do. Besides, when twenty-four of you guys walk through that door and say, "Hello, Mr. Robinson," it makes me feel great.

3. Teach Alphabet Manners

Susan Skinner teaches kindergarten at the Heathwood Episcopal School in Columbia, South Carolina. She has a bulletin board displaying a different manner for each letter of the alphabet. When she teaches a letter of the alphabet during a given week, she teaches the corresponding manner at the same time.

A Accept a compliment graciously.

B Be on time.

C Clean your hands.

D Do chew with your mouth closed.

E Elbows off the table.

F Friendliness to others.

G Good grooming shows self-respect.

H Hang up your clothes.

I Interrupt only for a very important reason.

J Join in and include everybody.

K Kindness to all living things.

L Lend a helping hand.

M Magic words: "please" and "thank you."

N Never point or laugh at others.

O Obey the rules.

P Pleasant tone of voice is a plus.

Q Quiet when others are working or sleeping.

R Remember others on special occasions.

S Sit up straight.

T Thank the host or hostess.

U Use your beautiful smile.

V Visit a friend who is lonely or sick.

W Watch out for little ones.

X "X" out bad habits.

Y Yawn if you must, but cover your mouth.

Z Zip your zipper.

"I've probably gotten more positive parent feedback on my alphabet manners than any other thing I do," Skinner reports. "Parents are very happy that their children are learning these manners in school." And by sending home a copy of the alphabet manners she's teaching in her classroom, she gives parents an unspoken invitation to do the same at home.

4. Implement a Manners Curriculum

Implementing a formal curriculum on manners is a way to ensure that all students in a school, not just those in a particular teacher's classroom, get instruction in basic courtesies.

Jill Rigby is a mother turned educator who got drawn into creating such a curriculum. An interior designer by training, she was asked in 1992 to volunteer at her twin sons' school—Saint James Episcopal Day School in Baton Rouge, Louisiana. She soon found herself in conversations with other parents about students' unruly cafeteria behavior. She said, "Why don't we come into the cafeteria once a week and talk to the children about manners?"

They drafted her for the job. Soon she was doing weekly, often humorous lessons on putting your napkin in your lap, chewing with your mouth closed, and the like.

Other schools began calling to ask, "Where can we get this program?" In response, Rigby developed her lessons into a K–5 curriculum guide titled *Manners of the Heart* (www.mannersoftheheart.com), now used by hundreds of schools around the country. There's also a companion guide for parents, *Manners of the Heart at Home*. The school curriculum has three parts: (1) everyday courtesies (such as smiling, saying please and thank you, playing by the rules, and saying I'm sorry); (2) communication skills (such as introducing someone, telephone manners, and writing thank-you notes); and (3) table manners (such as asking for something to be passed, posture, table talk, and manners for eating out). Rigby explains her approach:

> I define manners as an attitude of the heart that is self-giving, not self-serving. The objective of our curriculum is to teach children that manners come from the heart, not from memorizing a set of rules. If respect is the foundation of how we treat each other, manners and etiquette will come easily.

Rigby has had graduates of her curriculum come back to her with stories of how her lessons in manners helped them in high school and even on dates.

*   *   *

When our children act with good manners, they will elicit a positive response from other people. They will be happier themselves—more secure, confident, and poised—when they know how to behave. They will be more likely to teach manners to their own children someday if they become parents. By their courteous behavior, they can help to create a more considerate, gracious, and well-mannered society. These are all good reasons to make the teaching of manners part of every character education program.

An excellent resource for getting kids to reflect on manners is George Washington's *Rules of Civility and Decent Behaviour in Company and Conversation,* 110 guides to good conduct that he wrote out for himself when he was fourteen years old (available from Applewood Books, Box 365, Bedford, MA 01730).

CHAPTER 9

Prevent Peer Cruelty and Promote Kindness

Children remind me of chickens, seeking out the weak and wounded and pecking them to death. They have discovered that my nine-year-old son, who is autistic, is bothered by loud noises, and they scream and whistle in his ear until he cries.[1]

—A MOTHER

Your children who have ridiculed me, who have chosen not to accept me, who have treated me like I am not worth their time, are dead.

—COLUMBINE SHOOTER ERIC HARRIS'S
E-MAIL SUICIDE NOTE TO THE
LITTLETON COMMUNITY

"The school's most powerful moral influence," observes psychologist and character educator Marvin Berkowitz, "is the way people treat each other." In many schools, most of the adults are making a conscientious effort to treat students with love and respect. But in those same schools, even schools that are ostensibly committed to character education, kids are often devastatingly cruel to each other.

When peer cruelty goes unchecked, it's a very serious problem for many reasons. The school is sending the message that the law of the jungle rules. This threatening atmosphere interferes with learning; students won't be focused on schoolwork if they're worried about getting cut down in their classroom, harassed in the hallway, ostracized at recess, or bullied on the bus. Cruelty at the hands of their schoolmates deprives them of what every child needs: the experience of being accepted and valued by peers. Peer rejection, one study found, is more likely to cause a child to leave school than academic difficulties.[2]

Students who persecute peers are not only hurting others; they are also deforming their own character. By age twenty-four, according to the U.S. Department of Justice, 60 percent of students who bully will have a criminal conviction.

For students who are regularly subjected to abuse by peers, school is a miserable experience. After graduating from his suburban high school, one boy wrote the following letter to his principal:

> Before I came to this school, I went to a school where I was liked and into sports. I thought that joining the soccer team when I came here in eighth grade would be a good way to make friends. Instead, for reasons I never understood, four kids on the team decided to pick on me. They started by calling me names and one day after practice pushed me into the swamp behind the school. When I tried to get out, they kept pushing me back. This went on until I teared up, and then they called me "crybaby." When I finally got out, I told the coach—which was a big mistake because he made them run laps, and then they *really* had a reason not to like me.
>
> One day outside of school, as I was talking to two girls I liked, these guys came up behind me and pulled my pants down. As they walked away, they said, "You can't do anything about it." They kept this up all through high school. I was constantly afraid of being humiliated. These kids were

ruining my life. I thought about what I'd like to do to them, but I didn't have the courage to carry it out.

Some students who are subjected to this kind of tormenting do carry out their desire for revenge. A 2000 study of school shootings by the U.S. Secret Service found that two-thirds of the shooters had felt persecuted, bullied, threatened, attacked, or injured by others.

Other victims of peer cruelty become at risk for suicide. A mother says

My nice, pretty seventh grader has no friends. She eats alone in the cafeteria, she walks alone in the halls. She says it is like she is a ghost. She does not know what she has done wrong. Needless to say, she's depressed and said last night that she would like to kill herself. My husband and I are at a loss as to what to do.[3]

One eighth-grade girl who did kill herself left this note to her parents: "All my life I have been teased. I love you very much, but I just couldn't stand it anymore."

Peer cruelty, of course, has always been with us, but research shows that it's on the rise.[4] In recent years, the problem has been reflected in the proliferation of anti-bullying programs.

Much more pervasive than classical bullying (a stronger child picking on a weaker victim) are the everyday emotional cruelties—teasing, taunts, gossiping, rumor spreading, and exclusion. In a nationwide survey of nearly 70,000 students in grades six through twelve, only 37 percent said "students in my school show respect for one another."[5] The problem facing a great many schools is now a general peer culture where disrespect and meanness have become the norm.

Schools have no higher moral obligation to students and their parents than to do everything in their power to prevent peer cruelty and create a culture of kindness and respect. There is no more important measure of the effectiveness of a character education program than its progress toward this goal.

1. Begin with Character-Based Discipline

The first strategy in preventing peer cruelty is character-based discipline (chapter 7). All of the discipline strategies that help kids develop respect for rules and the rights of others will help to curb bullying.

An essential part of character-based discipline is enforcement that holds students accountable to rules through fair and firm consequences. With bullies, behavior contracts have often proved helpful. For example, a contract could state, "I will not hit or hurt anyone. If I do, I will have to call my parents and report what I did."

2. Create a Caring School Community

The second strategy must be the creation of a caring school community in which all students feel a sense of security and belonging.

It's possible to measure, through a survey, the extent to which a caring school community exists. Students and staff are asked to indicate their agreement or disagreement, on a five-point scale, with such statements as "People in this school care about each other" and "Students in this school help each other, even if they are not friends."[6] Using such an instrument to investigate six diverse school districts in different regions of the country, one study found a clear pattern: The stronger a school's sense of community, the more likely it was that students showed the following positive attitudinal and character outcomes:

1. Greater liking for school
2. Less feeling of loneliness in school
3. Greater empathy toward others' feelings
4. Stronger motivation to be kind and helpful
5. More sophisticated conflict resolution skills

6. More frequent acts of altruistic behavior
7. Higher academic self-esteem
8. Stronger feelings of social competence
9. Fewer delinquent acts
10. Less use of tobacco, alcohol, and marijuana

Schools seeking to strengthen their sense of community should consider using an available survey (see chapter 11) to get baseline data at the beginning of their effort and then repeat the survey later to assess their progress.

3. Implement an Effective Anti-Bullying Program

Many schools have taken the further step of implementing a school-wide anti-bullying program.

Schools pursuing this strategy should take care to select a program that is evidence-based. In 1999, a committee of educational researchers examined more than five hundred programs ostensibly designed to prevent violence and found only four school-based programs with proven effectiveness.[7] In one study, schools that created their own anti-bullying programs rather than using tested approaches experienced a 35 percent *increase* in bullying behavior.[8]

Perhaps the best known of the effective approaches is the *Olweus Bullying Prevention Program* designed by Norway psychologist Dan Olweus. Implemented over the past twenty years in Norway's elementary and junior high schools, this program has (1) reduced bullying by 50 percent or more; (2) significantly reduced general antisocial behavior such as vandalism, fighting, and stealing; and (3) improved classroom climate and students' satisfaction with school life.

Now used in a growing number of U.S. schools, the *Olweus Bullying Prevention Program* has four major components:

1. **General Prerequisite: awareness and involvement of adults**
2. **School Measures**
   - Administration of an anonymous bully/victim questionnaire
   - Formation of a Bullying Prevention Committee
   - Staff training and time for ongoing staff discussion groups
   - Effective supervision during recess and lunch periods
3. **Classroom Measures**
   - Clear classroom and school rules about bullying
   - Regular classroom meetings
   - Meetings with students' parents
4. **Individual Measures**
   - Individual meetings with students who bully
   - Individual meetings with victims
   - Meetings with parents of students involved
   - Development of individual intervention plans

For more information on the *Olweus Bullying Prevention Program* and the three other evidence-based programs identified by Blueprints for Violence Prevention—*Life Skills Training, Promoting Alternative Thinking Strategies (PATHS),* and *The Incredible Years*—visit www. colorado.edu/cspv/blueprints.

4. Get Students to Take Responsibility for Stopping Peer Cruelty

Bullies gain power when there is a tolerance for their behavior. An estimated 85 percent of bullying occurs with other students watching. Bystanders often passively observe or aggravate the problem by cheering the bully on or even joining in.

A Canadian study found that if even one student spoke up to express disapproval of a bullying incident, the bully typically stopped within ten seconds.[9] Our challenge as educators is to create a school culture in which most students hold the belief that they should do something to try to stop any cruelty they observe.

Some schools have had success in promoting peer intervention by recruiting an anti-bullying team of students at each grade level. These teams then work with a teacher or counselor to brainstorm and carry out strategies for reducing peer cruelty. Team members subsequently step in on behalf of victims. Says a high school senior in Clarksburg, West Virginia, "We don't yell at the kids picking on someone. We just say, 'Hey, man, that's not a cool thing to do.'"

In Erie, Pennsylvania, the Ophelia Project (www.opheliapro ject.org) focuses on "relational aggression," including all the behind-the-back ways kids are mean to each other. The project trains high school students as mentors who go into middle and elementary school classrooms and lead discussions: "What do girls do when they want to be mean to each other? Let's make a list. Okay, what do boys do?" Then the high school mentors role-play common scenarios depicting the aggressor, the victim, and the kids in the middle. A sample situation: Someone is mad at Kelly and tries to get all of Kelly's friends mad at her, too.

The goal of the role playing is to demonstrate to students how the kids in the middle have the power to influence the group dynamics in a positive way. "The message we want to get across," says Ophelia Project founder Susan Wellman, "is that what bystanders do makes a significant difference."

5. Build Classroom Community

A central strategy in preventing peer cruelty is to create a strong sense of community in every classroom.

That begins with helping students get to know their classmates. A seat lottery—changing kids' seats on a regular basis—is a simple way to do that. A mother remembers with gratitude how her own sixth-grade teacher used this strategy:

> Halfway through my sixth-grade year, we moved. I dreaded going into my new school in the middle of the year. But every

week, the teacher assigned us a new seat by lottery. I got to know a lot of other kids in a short time and was able to make friends. There was a very comfortable atmosphere in that class.

Marty Kaminsky, a fourth-grade teacher in Ithaca, New York, describes how he uses the ritual of "morning meeting" to create and renew the sense of community in his room:

> The first day of school and every day thereafter, I sit down with my students and conduct a morning meeting. For at least fifteen minutes, we share the birth of kittens, the loss of a tooth, anxiety about an upcoming move. We sing songs. We celebrate individual accomplishments. Through our morning meeting, we are saying to every child, "You are part of us. You are welcome here."

Morning Meetings, a publication of the Responsive Classroom (www.responsiveclassroom.org), is a rich source of greeting rituals and other activities for this start-of-the-day time.

6. Foster Friendship

As psychologist Michael Thompson points out, students can better handle social cruelty if they have one friend. An estimated 20 percent of children, however, are at risk of having no friends.

Wise teachers therefore take deliberate steps to foster friendship in their classrooms. Beverly Oakley, a second-grade teacher at Long Island's Southampton Elementary School, reads several books on friendship at the start of each school year. And every day, for five minutes immediately after recess, she has her students circle up for "Friendship Time."

> At Friendship Time, I'll ask the children, "What is a nice thing that you saw someone do during the morning or while you were at lunch or recess?" It doesn't have to be anything big; someone might say, "I saw Joe pick up the crayons." I

give a sticker to each of the students who is named. We usually do three or four students on a given day. They put their stickers on a laminated card I give them. All the kids get recognized eventually.

Of all the things I do, Friendship Time is the one that means the most to them. At the end of the year, I have them each make a book on second grade—what they liked, what they will remember. They always mention Friendship Time. Several years later, when they're fifth- and sixth-graders, students will stop by, and even if they can't remember anything else about second grade, they remember Friendship Time.

"Since I started Friendship Time," Oakley says, "I almost never get complaints about behavior during recess—'he did this, she said that.' And if someone tells me about a friendship problem they're having—such as a friend who isn't playing with them—I'll say, 'Let's talk about that at Friendship Time.'"

7. Do "Anonymous Compliments"

Mark Twain once said, "I can live for two months on one good compliment." Rick Mansfield, a fifth-grade teacher in Merrick, New York, keeps the compliments flowing in his classroom through his weekly "Anonymous Compliments" activity.

1. Each student draws the name of a classmate from a bowl.
2. Before the end of the week, each student writes a compliment about his or her person on a strip of paper, shows it to the teacher, and, with the teacher's approval, puts it in the compliment box.
3. On Friday, the teacher posts the compliments on the bulletin board next to class members' names.

Mansfield reports, "This activity takes almost no time but does a great deal to create a positive classroom climate. And because a compliment is anonymous—anyone in the classroom could have written it—there's a generalized good feeling toward classmates."

8. Implement Quality Cooperative Learning

Cooperative learning has students work in twos, threes, or fours on a task that requires interdependent learning (each student has a job to do) and individual accountability (each must demonstrate mastery of the material by taking a test or turning in a paper or project). Dozens of studies show that cooperative learning contributes to both academic achievement and character development, including perspective taking, team skills, the appreciation of differences, and the integration of all students into the classroom community.

However, to have these benefits, cooperative learning has to be designed well. Many adults have negative memories of "group work" in which some kids got a free ride, a bossy student took over, and the teacher gave a group grade (not a good idea) that penalized students who had done higher-quality work than their teammates.

Quality cooperative learning requires that the teacher and students identify the behaviors that bring about effective cooperation and continually monitor and assess how effectively pairs or groups are working together. For example, Betty House and her fifth-grade students in Ithaca, New York, developed the following chart to guide their cooperative learning:

WE WORK BEST TOGETHER WHEN . . .

1. We help each other and don't fight.
2. We're all kind to each other—no put-downs.
3. We encourage each other.
4. We communicate and share our ideas.
5. Everyone has a job to do.
6. Everyone contributes and feels included.
7. Someone compliments me.
8. We listen to all ideas and take turns sharing them.

9. People don't complain.
10. I feel respected.

Students are most likely to grow in their cooperative skills if the teacher reviews such a list before every cooperative activity and then asks students after the activity to use the list to evaluate how well they worked together.

9. Teach Empathy through Children's Literature

Peer cruelty—especially toward kids who are "different"—almost always reflects a lack of empathy. Children's literature that depicts cruelty and the suffering it causes is a valuable tool for teaching empathy.

Eleanor Estes's *The Hundred Dresses* (Harcourt Brace, 1944), Lauren Mills's *The Rag Coat,* Margy Knight's *Who Belongs Here?,* and Taro Yashima's *Crow Boy* are four picture books on this theme. Our center's fall 2001 newsletter (www.cortland.edu/c4n5rs) includes an article, "Children's Literature and Character Development," by my colleague Joy Mosher recommending many children's books that can be used to foster perspective-taking, respect, and kindness. The literature lists in Michele Borba's *Building Moral Intelligence,* Mary Beth Klee's *Core Virtues,* and *Character Education Through Story: K–6 Lessons to Build Character Through Multi-Cultural Literature* (www.CharacterEducation.com) are other valuable sources.

I was recently working in an elementary school where children's unkind treatment of each other was the staff's top concern, as it so often is. I read *The Hundred Dresses* to several fourth-, fifth-, and sixth-grade classes and conducted circle discussions with each group.

The book tells the story of Wanda Petronski, a poor, quiet girl who always wears the same faded blue dress to school. She has no friends. The other girls, led by the popular Peggy, constantly tease Wanda about her one dress. Finally, one day Wanda blurts out, "I have a *hundred* dresses at home—all different colors!" After that, the girls' teasing becomes merciless. Maddie—Peggy's best friend—wishes she and the others would stop picking on Wanda but doesn't have the courage to say anything.

The time comes for the annual art contest conducted each spring by their teacher. On the day the winner is to be announced, the children enter their classroom amazed to see one hundred beautiful drawings of dresses—each different—displayed on the walls. They were all drawn by Wanda, the teacher explains, but she is not present to receive the first prize. The teacher then reads a letter from Wanda's father:

> Dear Teacher:
>   My Wanda will not come to your school anymore. Jake also. Now we move away to big city. No more holler Polack. No more ask why funny name. Plenty of funny names in the big city. Yours truly,
>   Jan Petronski

In every class I read this story to, the children listened intently. You could tell it hit home. I asked, "How many of you have ever been left out or made fun of at school?" Most of the hands went up. I asked, "How many of you have ever taken part in making fun of another kid or excluding kids because they're different in some way?" Most students either looked down or slowly raised their hands.

As the discussion progressed, I asked them to think about Maddie, the girl in the story who felt sorry for Wanda but did nothing. After Wanda moved away, Maddie had a sick feeling in the pit of her stomach. She felt like a coward. I said, "What are some ways Maddie could have helped Wanda? Suppose she wanted to be friendly toward Wanda but still stay friends with Peggy. How might she have done that?" In each class, students came up with good ideas.

Then I said, "Suppose you see someone in your class or school being treated badly—made fun of or left out. Maybe that's happening right now to someone you know. What are some things you could do to help?" We made a list on the board. I asked each student to write down one thing they would try to do, and I asked the teacher of each class to make time the next week for the children to write about whether they followed through on their intentions.

10. Have Children with Disabilities Teach Their Peers

In developing empathy, there is no substitute for face-to-face experience. Firsthand experience is especially valuable in helping kids understand and support schoolmates who have disabilities.

Kathleen Scanlon is the school nurse at Frederick Leighton Elementary School in Oswego, New York. She helps disabled children talk to their classmates about their disabilities and how they cope with them:

> With a parent present, I'll meet with the child and ask, "What would you like to share with the class? *How* would you like to share it? What *don't* you want to share?" One fourth-grade boy had spina bifida and didn't want to tell that he had a catheter because of bladder control difficulty. One third-grade girl who had epilepsy was worried that someday kids would see her having a seizure and did want to talk to them about that. Having the child be part of the planning is key. Sometimes they decide to read something to the class about their disability or to tell a personal story. Sometimes they'll do part of the presentation, and I'll do part.
>
> I've had students come back to me when they're in junior high and high school and thank me for the opportunity to do this and for asking them how they wanted to do it.

11. Use the Seven E's to Teach Caring

There are seven E's of teaching any virtue:

1. *Explain it* by defining it, illustrating it, and discussing its importance.

2. *Examine it* in literature, history, or current events.
3. *Exhibit it* through personal example.
4. *Expect it* through codes, rules, contracts, and consequences.
5. *Experience it* in relationships and activities.
6. *Encourage it* through goal setting, practicing the virtue, and self-assessment.
7. *Evaluate it* by giving students feedback on how they're doing.

Jan Gorman, a first-grade teacher at Meachem Elementary School in Syracuse, New York, illustrates how to implement the seven E's. She starts the school year by teaching a virtue a week, beginning with caring. On the board she has a large sign, CARING, along with a photograph of two children working together.

She gathers the students in a circle and elicits their thoughts about the following questions on the board:

- What is caring?
- Who can show caring?
- Where does caring take place?
- How can each of us show caring? In our classroom? In our school? In our families?

She makes a visual web of the children's responses, which remain posted in the front of the room.

She then reads a picture book that illustrates the theme of caring. She often begins with Peter Golenbock's *Teammates,* the story of how Brooklyn Dodgers captain Pee Wee Reese stood by Jackie Robinson when Jackie faced racism, even from some of his teammates, for being the first black man to play major league baseball. After the story, she conducts a discussion, asking, "Who in the story showed caring? Who did not show caring?"

Then she says, "I want you to remember this story and to try to show caring toward each other during the rest of the day." When a child behaves in a caring way, she compliments that child, sometimes calling the class's attention to a thoughtful act. If a child behaves in an inconsiderate or unkind way, she will speak to the student privately: "Did that behavior show caring? Remember our story. Remember our discussion."

On each subsequent day of the week, she reads a different story about caring, followed by another class discussion. She repeats her challenge to children to act in a caring way in their own interactions and again looks for opportunities to comment on their behavior.

"By the end of the week," she says, after five such stories and discussions, "caring has been established as an expectation in my classroom." Her children have been immersed in this virtue. It has become part of the classroom culture. During the following week, she repeats this process with a different virtue.

12. Use the Power of a Pledge

A pledge, especially if it's repeated daily as a classroom ritual, can build classroom community and strengthen students' commitment to doing the right thing.

The "Children's Diversity Pledge" is an example of a pledge that helps students value the differences that enrich human community. The pledge teaches that we should all try to find the good in other people, just as we want them to find the good in us.

CHILDREN'S DIVERSITY PLEDGE
- I believe that all kids are different and special in their own way.
- I believe that all kids deserve to be loved, accepted, and respected for who they are.
- I will work on being a good friend, so that all children feel welcomed around me.
- I will not judge people because of where they live, the color of their skin, how they dress, their abilities, their spiritual beliefs, or whether they are a girl or a boy.

- I can and will find the good in all people.
- I will not tell or listen to jokes that make fun of other people.
- I will be a peacemaker in my family and school.
- I will show pride in my family and heritage.
- I will learn as much as I can about the family traditions of other kids in my school.[10]

13. Have Kids Keep a Good Deeds Journal

One of the best ways to inhibit a negative behavior is to develop a positive habit that is its psychological opposite. It's hard to be mean to other people, for example, if you set out each day to perform acts of kindness.

Acting on that insight, Saint Rocco Catholic School in Providence, Rhode Island, winner of a Blue Ribbon Award from the U.S. Department of Education, has its students keep a daily "good deeds journal." At the start of each day, students write in their journal a good deed they did the day before in school, at home, or in the community.

In all subjects, teachers make a connection to the good deeds theme. In language arts, the teacher might comment on a good deed performed by a character in a story; in social studies, on a good deed performed by someone in the news. Students learn that a good deed can be anything that contributes to another person's happiness, even something as simple as a smile.

"I like the good deeds journal because it helps me to be more aware of helping others, one girl says. "I can even see an improvement in my friends because they are trying to be more courteous and kind to each other." A Saint Rocco's parent says, "My children now readily shovel snow for our elderly neighbor without expecting or accepting money in return. They are also more sensitive about social issues when watching TV."

14. Celebrate Kindness

We celebrate what we value. Classrooms and schools that care about kindness find ways to recognize and honor it.

For example, Donna Funk, a special education teacher in Cortland, New York, gives each of her students a "Look what I did today" page. To recognize positive actions she gives kids stickers (1" x 3" rectangles, each with a graphic, that she makes on her computer and prints out on adhesive label paper). Students put these stickers on their page so they can see at the day's end all the good things they did. Some sample stickers are "I shared with someone," "I gave a compliment," "I listened to someone," "I let someone else go first," "I said excuse me," "I calmed myself down," and "I was a good friend." Funk comments:

> Most of my developmentally delayed students come to me unable to speak positively about themselves. When I would ask them about a particular positive action they had just performed, they would typically respond, "I was good." The stickers give them language they can use to identify their specific accomplishments.

15. Have Peers Recognize Peers

When students recognize each other for acts of character, virtue has a better chance of becoming a peer norm rather than something kids do just to please adults.

One third-grade teacher often ends the day with a two- to three-minute class meeting in which she asks, "Who has a good word for someone today?" On the board she has a list of character words: kind, caring, hardworking, determined, fair, generous, and so on. A student might say, "Sara was kind to me when she gave me some of her paper." Or, "Steve was determined to solve the math problem he got stuck on."

Many schools make a schoolwide effort to involve students in noticing other kids and adults performing "acts of character." Students write the act and the person's name on a printed form (placed everywhere in the building) and drop it in a box. As part of the morning announcements, students take turns drawing three or four forms from the box and reading what those persons did. Forms not drawn are sent to classroom teachers so they can pass them on to the students whose positive actions were reported.

16. Use a Class Meeting to Discuss Bullying

Despite a school's proactive efforts to prevent peer cruelty, some children will still engage in hurtful behavior and will need additional help in learning to act in a prosocial manner. The class meeting—in which the offending child can hear peers say what behaviors they like and dislike—is often more effective than teacher correction alone.

Peter Sullivan, a second-grade teacher in central New York, had a student he believed was in the beginning stages of becoming a bully. Charles came from an unhappy home environment. He showed little respect for others' rights or feelings. He consistently invaded the personal space of other students and often grabbed or pushed to get what he wanted.

Sullivan used a class meeting to address this problem:

Charles was present but not singled out. Our ground rule was, "Give examples of bullying, but no names, please." I asked children to tell how they felt when they were the victims of these behaviors. This discussion got us all on the same page: No one likes to be bullied.

Later that day, I met with Charles to discuss his bullying. I emphasized that I liked him but did not approve of this behavior. I asked him to remember and think about what kids said in our class meeting, how they felt when they're bullied. As we talked, I made a list of "Feelings about Being Bullied" on a piece of paper.

I asked Charles to carry this list in his pocket and read it at least once a day. We agreed to meet in a week to see how he was doing. I wanted Charles to know that I care about him and am serious about wanting him to succeed. His behavior has in fact begun to improve.

17. Build Bonds Through Buddy Classes

Many schools develop a caring community by using "buddy classes" to create nurturing relationships between big kids and little kids. These connections go a long way toward making the school feel like a family.

For example, a fifth-grade class might buddy up with a third-grade class, a third-grade class with a kindergarten, and so on. Older students help their younger buddies with schoolwork and do special projects together. Sometimes the older kids read to their younger buddies and sit with them during assemblies.

Says principal Bob Storrier, who uses buddies extensively at Enders Road Elementary School in Manlius, New York, "These relationships give the older children a sense of responsibility and the younger ones a sense of security."

18. Create "School Families"

Saint Rita's K–8 Catholic School in Dayton, Ohio, has put into practice an idea borrowed from a public school. It groups its students in "families," one child from each grade. A seventh- and eighth-grade boy and girl serve as the "parents" and are actually called "Mom" and "Dad" by the younger children.

At the start of the school year, these family groups spend much of the first three days together in games and other activities that build bonds. During the rest of the year, the family groups come together for regular events (in a public school this might be weekly assemblies) and for special occasions such as holidays.

Principal Mary Ann Eismann describes the results:

At these events, the older students try to be good role models for the younger ones. In general, the older members of a family group look out for the little ones. They help them solve problems. They're glad to see them in the hall and on the playground. They're happy to see them when they return after an absence. There is no craziness at our school, just a very peaceful and loving atmosphere. We think much of that is due to our family groupings.

19. Implement Advisory Groups

At the middle school level, friendship and inclusion are more important than ever. Therefore, it's very important for schools to provide structures that ensure that no student gets left out.

Advisory groups are one good way to make sure every student has a home base. Advisories typically consist of an advisor and eight to twelve students. Some advisories meet every day before school or during lunch; some meet less often. The advisory can address school issues, share good news, plan group activities (for instance, a field trip), discuss an educational TV series they're all watching or a book they're all reading, or talk about current events. An advisory provides every student with two things crucial for young adolescents: a supportive peer group and an adult who knows and cares about the student as an individual.

A middle school advisory group also helps parents stay connected to the school at a time when parents' school involvement typically declines. The advisor usually has several scheduled meetings with the parent during the school year, is available for other meetings as needed, sends the report card home, and generally keeps parents updated about their child's academic progress and any problems.

Some middle schools tried an advisory system but dropped it when staff or students complained it wasn't working. A better solution is to conduct a survey of both staff and students, asking, "What do you like about advisory, and what would you change to make it better?" If middle schools don't have something like advisory that meets every student's need for inclusion, many students will look for intimacy and identity in gangs, drugs, or premature sex. Others will suffer a painful loneliness.

A recent publication with activities for advisory groups is Sarah Sadlow's *Advisor/Advisee Character Education* (www.CharacterEdu cation.com).

20. Create a Safe and Respectful School Bus

How can a school promote respectful and responsible behavior on the school bus, which for many children has become a ride in terror?

Lynn Lisy-Macan describes how she tackled this challenge when she was principal of Brookside Elementary School, a 1998 National School of Character in Binghamton, New York:

> In response to increasing bus problems, we initiated bus meetings three times a year to discuss appropriate bus behavior. We assigned each bus group to a room in the school. The bus driver and three other staff met with each group. At the first meeting, we did icebreaker activities to pair "bus buddies," kids who then sat together on the bus each day. This created a sense of community on the bus.
>
> At the first meeting we brainstormed: "What does a safe and respectful bus ride look like?" "What does a safe and respectful bus ride sound like?" "What does it *not* look like and sound like?" The drivers talked about the rules they have and why those are important. Finally, we discussed "What can each of us do to help create a safe and respectful bus ride?"
>
> We made charts based on these discussions to refer to in later meetings. The second meeting took place before the snow flew, to discuss safety issues related to winter weather and to ask, "How are we doing in creating a safe and respectful ride?" If there were any behavior problems, we addressed those.

A third meeting was held in the spring to head off the end-of-the-year slide. In addition, all of our buses had signs that told students what our character Word of the Month was, plus its definition and a reminder that character is important on the bus, too.

"Bus behavior problems at our school," Macan reports, "declined significantly."

*   *   *

The peer culture is a powerful teacher. If schools do not take proactive steps to shape a positive peer culture, the worst in human nature will often prevail. By contrast, when schools take deliberate steps to create a caring community, students can learn morality by living it. In such a community, virtues are not words on a wall but emotional realities felt in the heart and experienced in relationships. And by placing respect and caring at the center of its moral life, the school meets the deep human need to belong. It becomes what every school ought to be: a place where respect and kindness are normative, where exceptions to that norm are treated as a serious matter, and where every student feels valued, safe, and significant.

Other recommended resources are the March 2003 issue of *Educational Leadership,* devoted to "Creating Caring Schools"; the 2002 report *Safe and Sound: An Educational Leader's Guide to Evidence-Based Social and Emotional Learning Programs* (www.casel.org); and Peace-Builders (www.peacebuilders.com).

CHAPTER 10

Help Kids (and Adults) Take Responsibility for Building Their Own Characters

Make yourself the kind of person you want people to think you are.

—SOCRATES

Parents can only give good advice or put their children on the right path. The final forming of a person's character lies in their own hands.

—ANNE FRANK

Most adults, including most teachers, don't see themselves as engaged in their own moral growth.

—RICK WEISSBOURD

To ensure progressive growth in the moral life, we must first know ourselves. We must know our particular faults and failings, as well as our strengths and the progress we've made in trying to lead a good life. We gain this self-knowledge by continually examining our behavior and reflecting on the kind of person we are and would like to be. "The unexamined life is not worth living," as Socrates said, because only by examining our life can we improve it.

We must also each make a sincere effort to become a better person—more patient, more sensitive to the needs of others, quicker to forgive, more willing to admit when we're wrong. We must persist in this effort even when we fail, as we surely will.

Finally, we must ask, are we carrying out our good intentions? Are we making gains, however small, in practicing the virtues?

These three things, then, are essential for developing our character and becoming the best person we can be: self-awareness, efforts at improvement, and evaluation of our progress.

When students and adults in a school don't think about the kind of character they want to possess and don't work on developing it themselves, a character education program will fall far short of its potential. It will feel like an uphill battle, something you're pushing at people. The behavior of individuals and the ethos of the school won't improve as much as they should.

"We've been doing character education now for seven years," said the headmaster of a K–12 independent school. "I think we need to do more to *personalize* it." He sensed that for most of the students, and probably most of the faculty, character education was something "out there." They hadn't made a personal commitment to trying to improve their own character.

It's true that part of our character is "caught"—absorbed from positive role models and the experience of being treated with love and respect. But beyond that, improving our character is a matter of intention, effort, and often struggle. We don't become wiser, more patient, more self-disciplined, more truthful, more courageous, more forgiving, and more humble persons automatically. We do so by deliberately striving to be that kind of person.

Here are sixteen strategies for helping all learners, adults as well as young people, undertake this vital task.

1. Teach Why Character Matters

Why bother to develop a good character? Why be good?

If we can't answer those questions for students or engage them in reflection that will help them arrive at solid answers, we're going to have trouble getting them to care about character.

When I talk to young people, here's how I make the case:

> Why is character important? Look around. Good character is the key to self-respect, to earning the respect of others, to positive relationships, to a sense of fulfillment, to achievements you can be proud of, to a happy marriage, to success in every area of life. But don't take my word for it. Interview people who have lived most of their lives. Ask them, when they look back, what are they proud of? What gives them fulfillment? What would they do differently if they could live their lives over?

All human beings have a deep desire to be happy. We should invite young persons to consider "What does it mean to be happy? What leads to happiness, and what does not?"

Unless our children are challenged to think seriously about such questions, many will adopt the media culture's definition of happiness: material comforts and pleasure, especially sexual pleasure. And if that becomes their definition of happiness, they won't see the point of developing character qualities such as self-control, sacrifice, and service.

We should share with students what cross-cultural research tells us about human happiness. The book *Cultivating Heart and Character* by Tony Devine and colleagues reports that cultures around the world affirm three life goals as sources of authentic happiness:

> ***maturity of character***—becoming the best person we can be
>
> ***loving relationships,*** such as marriage and family
>
> ***contributing to society***—making a positive difference in
>   the lives of others.[1]

When we pursue these life goals, which all require leading a life of virtue, we are living in harmony with our deepest selves. When we neglect or go against these goals—show bad character, act unlovingly in our relationships, take from others without contributing to their good—we make ourselves unhappy.

Especially when they enter adolescence, our children need to find a purpose for their lives. Many teens, lacking a sense of purpose, seek escape in drugs, alcohol, sex, and endless consumption of electronic media. Growing numbers take their lives. They need help in resisting the seductions of a media culture that tells them that life's purpose is maximizing their pleasure. Even those teens who are working toward worthwhile near-term goals (getting into a good college, getting a good job) need a larger vision that will help to sustain them in the face of life's inevitable disappointments and sufferings. Many people achieve their dreams and find themselves asking, "Is this all there is?"

We can, by holding up the three universally affirmed life goals—maturity of character, loving relationships, and making a difference—offer our children a framework for living that can bring lasting fulfillment. For many of us, this won't be the whole framework—we might add a relationship with God in this life and the next—but the three life goals represent something that all worldviews can embrace and all schools can teach.

2. Teach "Nobody Can Build Your Character for You"

The next step in encouraging young people to take charge of their character is to help them understand that they are, in fact, responsible for the kind of person they become. Here's the message we want to get across:

> Nobody can build your character for you. Parents and teachers can't build your character. They can teach you right from wrong, provide a good example, set and enforce rules, and encourage you to be the best person you can be.
>
> But they can't reach inside you and build your character. *You* have to do that. Character building is an "inside job." It's a personal responsibility, one that lasts a lifetime. Everybody's character, yours and mine, is a work in progress.

3. Teach "We Create Our Character by the Choices We Make"

We create our character by the choices we make. Good choices create good habits and good character. Bad choices create bad habits and bad character. How can we persuade young people that they're making choices all the time—choices that affect the habits they're forming and the kind of person they are becoming?

High school teacher Hal Urban put it this way to his students: "Life is a series of choices you get to make."

> You get to choose how to treat other people. You can put them down or build them up.
>
> You get to choose how much you'll learn. You can loaf your way through school or work hard and make the most of your education.
>
> You get to choose how you'll handle adversity, the inevitable misfortunes of life. You can let adversity crush you or you can look for a source of strength and deal with whatever life hands you.
>
> You get to choose your belief system and purpose in life. You can wander through life aimlessly or you can search for the ultimate meaning of life and then live according to it.
>
> Finally, you get to choose your character. You can become less than you're capable of or all that you're capable of.

If young people see themselves as making choices, they're more likely to take responsibility for their choices. If you own the choice, you own the responsibility.

Kindergarten is not too young to begin teaching kids that we're each responsible for creating our character. Deb Brown taught kindergarten for twenty-one years. In her book *Growing Character*, she says that most of her students came from broken homes, and most qualified for free or reduced lunch. She taught her students "the character message": *Each of us is responsible for creating our character by the daily decisions we make.*

To help them make good decisions, she taught them "wise sayings." She drew these from fables, fairy tales, proverbs, and stories from her own life. She'd capture the moral of each story in a simple saying: Actions speak louder than words. Honesty is the best policy. If you want to have a friend, be a friend.

She had her class repeat these sayings at different times of the day—lining up for recess, washing hands for lunch, packing bookbags to go home. Soon they knew them by heart. "These wise sayings," she told them, "can help you stop and think *before* you make a decision. Use them to make good decisions."

During her last year of teaching kindergarten, she had a boy named "Cody." Cody's dad was in prison for murder. He and his friends tried to steal some stereo equipment, didn't set out to hurt anyone, but ended up killing the clerk. Cody talked to Mrs. Brown about how much he looked forward to visiting his father at Christmas. "It's going to be a 'touching visit' this time," he said. "I won't have to talk through the glass. I can sit on his lap."

The day after the Christmas break, Cody came up to Deb Brown and said, "You know, Mrs. Brown, on the way home in the car, I kept thinking about my dad. I just know if he had your class, he wouldn't be where he is now. He would have made better decisions."

Though only five and a half, Cody had already gotten hold of a very large idea: We shape our character by our decisions, and our character shapes our lives.

4. Study Persons of Character

We can motivate students to think about character—and the sort of character they'd like to possess—by exposing them to persons of character. We can have them read a short biographical sketch, listen to a story, or watch a good video about a historical or contemporary person of widely admired character. As kids get older, a book-length biography or full-length film can serve this purpose well.

One of my favorite character education videos, part of the new *Animated Hero Classics* (www.teachvalues.com), tells the story of Harriet Tubman. Born into slavery on a Maryland plantation, she not only fled to freedom herself in 1849 but returned at great risk to help more than three hundred others escape on the Underground Railroad (a network of secret paths that led slaves to freedom in the North). Among her admirable character qualities were selflessness, courage, a deep sense of her own dignity, determination, loyalty, and faith.

Having a guest speaker who embodies good character can be even more effective. I recently got to hear one such person, Fred Sarkis, a seventy-seven-year-old retired businessman who lectures all over the country to rapt audiences of students of all ages. One of ten children, he grew up in the Great Depression and had to spend nearly all his time, when he wasn't in school, helping his father sell vegetables door-to-door in inner-city Rochester, New York. His talk is full of lessons about life and character—none more important than the value of taking personal responsibility for what you make of your life. (For a free copy of *Yes, Pa*, Fred Sarkis's abridged autobiography, visit www.yespa.org. For the full-length autobiography, visit www.prisonerofthetruck.com. To schedule Fred Sarkis as a speaker, at no cost to the school, e-mail Fred275@aol.com.)

To encourage students to connect personally with an example of good character, we can pose questions for reflection and writing:

- What is one quality this person had that you'd
  like to have as part of your own character?
- What is one thing you could begin to do to
  develop that quality?

There are now many good sources that teachers can turn to for inspiring stories of character: *Portraits of Character* (forty-eight stories for grades three through eight, with thinking questions and writing ideas, www.KaganOnline.com); the *Standing Tall* curriculum (everyday heroes, all grades, www.giraffe.org); *A Study of Heroes* (famous heroes of history, grades five through twelve, www.sopriswest.com); *50 American Heroes Every Kid Should Meet* by Dennis Denenberg (Heroes4US@aol.com); *Uncommon Champions: Fifteen Athletes Who Battled Back* by teacher Mary Kaminsky (grades four and up, www.amazon.com); www.Teach WithMovies.com, a website offering lesson plans for using movies as character development teaching tools, including an annotated list of movies *not* recommended; and Onalee McGraw's *Love and Life at the Movies: Educating for Character through the Film Classics* (Onalee@educationalguidance.org).

5. Have Students Do Character Interviews

A face-to-face conversation with someone who exemplifies good character—or exemplifies a particular virtue such as hard work, kindness, or courage—can make the concept of character come alive. Here is a sample assignment:

1. Interview a person (for example, a member of your family, someone in school, a member of the community, or a well-known person) whose character you admire.
2. Ask the following questions:
   - How does having a good character help a person in life? How did it help you?
   - Who had the most influence on your character? How did they influence you?
   - How did you help yourself develop a good character?
   - What advice would you give to young people today who want to develop good character?
3. Write up your interview (all interviews to be posted on the bulletin board) and be prepared to share in a small group three valuable things you learned from doing this assignment.

6. Have Students Assess Their Own Character

To help students (or staff) assess their own character strengths and areas for growth, we can provide a character traits inventory. Barbara Lewis's book *What Do You Stand For?* offers one such inventory, based on twenty-nine virtues.[2] The instructions are "For each pair of statements, check the one that describes you. Or check *both* sentences if you believe that you already have a particular trait but would like to develop it further." Sample pairs include

1. ____ I have positive attitudes.

   ____ I'd like to have better attitudes.

2. ____ I have clean habits and a clean mind.

   ____ I'd like to have more positive habits, thoughts, and influences.

3. ____ I have the courage to do and become what I want to be.

   ____ I'd like to be more courageous.

4. ____ I'm able to forgive others and myself.

   ____ I want to learn how to forgive more easily.

5. ____ I treat others with respect and courtesy.

   ____ I need to be more respectful and courteous.

6. ____ I'm responsible and hardworking.

   ____ I want to develop my sense of responsibility and my work ethic.

Alternatively, items like these can be presented as five-point scales:

I treat others with respect and courtesy.

Does not describe me   Describes me

1   2   3   4   5

Writing is another good way to engage students in assessing their character strengths and areas for improvement. At Hilltop Elementary School in Lynnwood, Washington, students first write on the general topic "A Person of Character," then write essays reflecting on their own character:

1. My strongest virtues are . . .
2. I need to work on . . .
3. I need to work on these virtues because . . .

At Eagle Rock School in Boulder, Colorado, students are given a sentence completion pair designed to make them aware of their capacity for positive change by having them reflect on ways they have already changed:

I used to be . . .
But now I am . . .
I used to be . . .
But now I am . . .

7. Teach Daily Goal Setting

Once people have assessed their own character, we can encourage them to build on their strengths and plan ways they'd like to improve.

Daily goal setting and self-assessment are an effective approach. We can take a lesson here from the American statesman Benjamin Franklin. He believed there was an "art of virtue" that could be learned by anyone, including children.

Franklin made a list of thirteen virtues he wanted to get better at:

Temperance "Eat not to dullness; drink not to elevation."

Silence "Speak not but what may benefit others or yourself."

Order "Let all your things have their places."

Resolution "Resolve to perform what you ought."

Frugality "Waste nothing."

Sincerity "Use no hurtful deceit."

Justice "Wrong none."

Moderation "Avoid extremes."

Cleanliness "Tolerate no uncleanness in body, clothes, or habitation."

Tranquility "Be not disturbed at trifles."

Chastity "Rarely use venery [sex] but for health or offspring, never to the injury of your own or another's peace or reputation."

Humility "Imitate Jesus and Socrates."

In a notebook, he listed one virtue per page. In his autobiography, he wrote:

> I determined to give a week's strict attention to each of the virtues successively. And like him, who having a garden to weed does not attempt to eradicate all the bad herbs at once but works on one of the beds at a time, I hoped to see in my pages the progress I made.[3]

Each time he failed to practice the week's virtue, he made a mark on the page. At the end of the week, he tallied his offenses. "I was surprised to find myself so much more full of faults than I had imagined. But I had the satisfaction of seeing them diminish."

In the spirit of its namesake, Benjamin Franklin Classical Charter School of Franklin, Massachusetts, a 1998 National School of Character, uses daily goal setting and self-assessment with its elementary school students. Every Franklin student keeps a "character record book." At the end of the day, students take out these books and write entries in response to three questions regarding that week's virtue. For example, if the virtue that week is courtesy, the questions are

1. How have I shown courtesy today?
2. How have I *not* shown courtesy today?
3. How will I show courtesy tomorrow?

8. Teach Kids to Make "Goal Strips"

"Goal strips" can help kids learn to set specific goals they want to accomplish within a specific period of time. Michele Borba, in her book *Parents Do Make a Difference,* instructs

> Cut a 3" x 12" colored paper strip for each goal. Fold the strip into three even sections. On the first section, boldly print the words "I will." In the middle section print *what* you will do, and in the final section print *when* you will do it. Now set a goal using this *will + what + when* formula. For example: "I will clean my room in 45 minutes."[4]

Other examples are "I will get my homework done every night next week," "I will do my chores without being asked for three days in a row," "I will say 'hello' or 'hi' back to everyone who greets me today."

9. Help Kids Connect the Virtues with Life

Patricia Cronin is a Chicago-based clinical psychologist who works with inner-city junior high school girls.[5] "Especially at this age," she says, "we need to help young people see how the virtues relate to real life—how these habits of character will help them in an area that is important to them during this time of their lives."

> Two issues that are very important to girls of this age are friendship and boyfriend-girlfriend relationships. What virtues or character strengths will help them fulfill their hopes and avoid hurtful problems in these areas? We can help them see that in relationships with boys, the virtues of self-respect, confidence, modesty, a strong conscience, and the courage to resist sexual pressures are qualities that will make for fulfilling relationships and protect their heart, their health, and their future.

Similarly, what virtues are needed to make and keep a friend? Here we discuss empathy, listening, mutual respect, loyalty, patience, forgiveness, and a generous spirit. What problems occur in a friendship when these qualities are missing? We find that the virtues become more real and meaningful to students when we organize them around these developmental needs.

Cronin then encourages each girl to select a particular virtue, set small daily goals for improvement in the practice of that virtue, and work on that virtue for a month. At the end of each day, students self-assess and, if they choose, record their progress in a journal.

10. Assess "Levels of Responsibility"

At Hilltop Elementary School, teachers do "reflection time" with their whole class for the last few minutes of the school day and/or at other times through the school day. Kids help each other assess their behavior and hold each other accountable for trying to do better.

From first grade, students at Hilltop have been taught to use a "Levels of Responsibility" chart to reflect on their behavior. This chart is posted in every classroom, the specials rooms (art, music, and physical education), and the principal's office.

Says a third-grade teacher, "I usually start off by asking, 'How did your day go?' Then I'll say, 'Would anyone like to share what level you were on today?'"

Levels of Responsibility

Level 4:
Respectful
Responsible
Helps Others
Characteristics: All the characteristics of Level 3, plus doing what is assigned and more, giving help when the opportunity arises, creativity beyond what's expected.

Level 3:
Respectful
Responsible
Characteristics: Hard work, doing what is expected, respecting the rights and work of others, cleaning up work carefully, using time well, using materials carefully and responsibly, productive conversation, persistence.

Level 2:
Works when reminded
Characteristics: Work accomplished with reminders or questioning done by adult present, not much work seen, conversation unproductive, may be silly, works sometimes and other times not working.

Level 1:
Not working
Characteristics: No work or very little work seen at end of allotted time, wandering, unfocused.

Level 0:
Bothering others
Characteristics: Loud talking, often silly or goofy, work accomplished is minimum or carelessly finished, actions interfere with another's ability to concentrate, abuse of materials.

"Kids are usually very honest," says one Hilltop teacher. "After they self-evaluate, I'll say, 'Okay, so what are you going to do tomorrow to improve?' Sometimes I'll make suggestions, but usually they help each other think of ways they can do better."

11. Use Character Quotes to Help Kids Set Goals

Many teachers like to put up a character quote on the board each day and have students copy it down in a character quotes journal, put the quote in their own words, and respond to a question about it. Suppose the quote were

> Life is 10 percent what happens to me
> and 90 percent how I react to it.
> —CHARLES SWINDOLL

A reflection question on this quote could be "What was a time when keeping a positive attitude helped you overcome a difficult situation?"

Action assignments (perhaps for extra credit) related to this quote could be

- Find and interview a person who shows a positive attitude. Ask, "How do you keep a positive attitude, even when things go wrong?"
- Each day, keep count of the number of times you complain about anything. At the start of each day, set a goal to reduce the number of your complaints.

For 204 character quotes and action assignments organized around weekly virtues, see *Character Quotations* (Lickona and Davidson, www.KaganOnline.com).

12. Do a Goal-Setting Bulletin Board

A San Diego teacher, at the start of every school year, teaches his students the importance of goal setting. One of his first assignments is "Find newspaper or magazine articles about individuals who set and pursued a goal." Students briefly share their articles with the whole class and then hang them on the bulletin board.

"This activity," the teacher says, "convinces students that goal setting helps people succeed in life." During the following week, he teaches students how to set their own goals—for his class, other subjects, extracurricular activities they may be involved in, and life outside school. By the end of the month, this teacher says, "almost all my students are setting daily goals."[6]

13. Have Students Set 100 Goals

One of high school teacher Hal Urban's favorite assignments was called "100 goals." The directions to his students read

1. Write at least 100 goals, more if you wish.
2. Divide them into categories. You can choose your own categories based on your interests. Here are some you might want to consider:

   - education
   - career
   - family
   - things you'd like to own
   - fun/adventure (things you want to do)
   - self-improvement
   - service to others
   - U.S. travel
   - foreign travel
   - reading
   - learning
   - spiritual growth
   - creating/making/building
   - major accomplishments

3. After you write the 100 goals, select the *10 that are the most important to you.* Write them in any order. Then write a paragraph on your #1 goal. Explain why it is so important to you.
4. You have two choices:
   - Treat this as just another stupid school assignment that has to be done; or
   - Treat it as if you're writing a preliminary blueprint for the rest of your life.
5. This will be a significant part of your second quarter grade.

Janelle Hernandez, one of Mr. Urban's former students and now a premed student at U.C. Santa Barbara, says

> I still have my goals posted, and I look at them every day, just like he encouraged us to do. One of my goals was to run the hundred-meter hurdles in eighteen seconds. I really didn't think I could do it, but every day Mr. Urban encouraged me and asked about my progress. And I finally did make my goal.

"I've had students write to me ten or fifteen years after graduation," Hal Urban remarks, "sending me their list of one hundred goals with the ones checked off that they've already achieved. They say, 'If you didn't make us do this assignment, I never would have even dreamed of most of these goals, let alone achieved them.'"

14. Have Students Develop a Portfolio

Schools can help students take responsibility for their personal growth by encouraging them to develop a portfolio that documents their service and achievements. For example, Troup High School in LaGrange, Georgia, offers a Leadership Award to those students who, by the end of high school, have built a portfolio that includes at least fourteen of sixteen listed items. Some sample items are

1. Documentation of ten volunteer hours toward a school improvement project
2. Documentation of twenty volunteer hours toward a community improvement project
3. A current résumé
4. Special awards or recognitions
5. Attendance at, and summary of, a local or state government meeting
6. Photos of samples of your work
7. A career search on two careers of your choosing
8. Participation in an extracurricular activity for at least a year
9. Three letters of recommendation
10. School administrator's letter attesting to exemplary conduct during high school

Says principal Bill Parsons, "I promote the portfolio constantly. I talk to students about how it will help them present themselves when they apply for college or a job. We have samples of previous portfolios on display in the guidance office to help students believe, 'Hey, I can do this.'"

15. Have Students Write
a Mission Statement

In his book *The 7 Habits of Highly Effective Teens,* Sean Covey (son of Stephen Covey) describes a character development activity—"a personal mission statement"—that is now used in some high schools as part of a character development course.

"A personal mission statement," Covey explains, "is like a personal credo or motto that states what your life is about." A high school boy wrote this mission statement:

- Have confidence in yourself and everyone else around you.
- Be kind, courteous, and respectful to all people.
- Set reachable goals; never lose sight of them.
- Never take the simple things in life for granted.
- Appreciate other people's differences.
- Ask questions.
- Remember that before you can change someone else, you must first change yourself.
- Speak with your actions.
- Make time to help the less fortunate and those who are having a bad day.

A senior girl testifies to the difference that writing a mission statement made in her life:

During my junior year, I couldn't concentrate on anything because I had a boyfriend. I wanted to do everything for him to make him happy. Then, naturally, the subject of sex came up. I wasn't at all prepared for it, and it became a nagging, constant thing on my mind. I felt like I wasn't ready and that I didn't want to have sex, but everybody else kept saying, "Just do it."

Then I participated in a character development class at school where they taught me to write a mission statement. I started to write and kept on writing and writing. It gave me a direction and a focus, and I felt like I had a plan and a reason for doing what I was doing. It really helped me stick to my standards and not do something I wasn't ready for.[7]

16. Enable Students to Reflect on Life's Largest Questions

Especially in adolescence, character development cannot be divorced from personal issues and existential questions that are beginning to take center stage for a young person. Here are some questions that teenagers have posed when given the chance to do so anonymously: Who am I? What is the meaning of life? What is the purpose of my life? Am I really doing the things that are going to make me happy, or are they for my mother or the values of our society? Will I ever find true love? How can I let people know what I feel when I hardly trust anyone? Why do people commit suicide? Why is there so much suffering in the world? Do things happen for a reason?[8]

In her book *The Soul of Education,* Rachael Kessler argues that schools can—and must—enable young persons to pose questions like these and begin to share their thoughts in an atmosphere that honors their questions and their struggles to answer them. She quotes Thomas More's *Care of the Soul:* "The soul is interested in eternal issues." The soul of adolescents, she says, has seven needs: (1) a yearning for deep connection; (2) a longing for silence and stillness; (3) the search for meaning and purpose; (4) a hunger for joy; (5) a need to create; (6) an urge for transcendence; and (7) a need for initiation into adulthood.

The opportunity to formulate and discuss questions related to these developmental needs helps a teenager make sense out of life, deal with its difficulties, and draw support from peers and caring adults. In such discussions, Kessler has found, teens often feel secure enough to express faith convictions—something they rarely feel comfortable doing in a public school context.

To be unable to pose and discuss questions of existential import creates a disconnect between school and life. That often leaves a young person looking for answers in the wrong places or simply feeling alone. Asks one tenth grader, "Why this emptiness, in this world and in my heart? How does this emptiness get there, go away, and come back again?" Kessler observes, "The vacuum of spiritual guidance and fulfillment in adolescents' lives often leads to despair and alienation. Only recently are educators and social scientists beginning to see that this absence of meaning is a critical variable in violent and self-destructive behavior in our youth."

Facilitating discussions like these, of course, takes a skilled and sensitive teacher or counselor who can create a climate of safety and trust. See Kessler's book for examples of how she and other educators have done that.

*   *   *

Most schools find that their character education programs work well at the elementary school level but that older kids, middle school and high school, are a tougher challenge. Secondary students will resist character education if it seems like something adults are doing *to* them. That's one reason why it's important, especially with older students, to help them develop the sense of being authors of their own "life story." There's no better way to do that than by engaging them in becoming the architects of their own character.

We must also remember that if we want to nurture young people's growth in character, we must see *ourselves* as engaged in the same humble process of trying to become a better person. New research on adult development indicates that adults' character qualities are not static.[9] Some adults become wiser, more patient, more giving over time; others become more selfish.[10] If we aren't making a serious effort ourselves to increase in virtue, we won't have as much empathy with kids and the difficulties they face in overcoming their faults and developing their character.[11] The challenge for all of us, at every stage of life, is to stay on the moral journey, keeping in mind the words of Eleanor Roosevelt: "Character-building begins in infancy and continues until death."

PART FOUR

Create Schools of Character

CHAPTER 11

Make Your School a School of Character

The school itself must embody good character. It must progress toward becoming a microcosm of the civil, caring, and just society it seeks to create.

— ELEVEN PRINCIPLES OF EFFECTIVE
CHARACTER EDUCATION[1]

Character education is about becoming a school of character, a place that puts character first.

How does a school become a community of virtue, a place where moral and intellectual qualities such as good judgment, best effort, respect, kindness, honesty, service, and citizenship are modeled, upheld, discussed, celebrated, and practiced in every part of the school's life—from the example of adults to the relationships among peers, the handling of discipline, the content of the curriculum, the rigor of academic standards, the ethos of the environment, the conduct of extracurricular activities, and the involvement of parents?

"Over time," says one California principal, "the de facto mission of our school has evolved into helping our students get into Stanford. I'd like us to be asking, Are we developing a better person, a fuller person, a healthier person in every sense? Are we helping students develop the sense that they are *moral agents*—able to create a better character for themselves and a better world for us all?"

"Give me a blueprint," one high school principal said. The truth is, if you study twenty different schools that have achieved National Schools of Character recognition, you'll find twenty different stories, each reflecting the creative ideas of the people who shaped the character effort. But beneath the great diversity of character education success stories are common strategies that can guide any school. Taken together, they provide a game plan for starting, sustaining, assessing, and continually improving a systematic effort to educate for character.

These strategies for becoming a school of character can be summed up as staff involvement, student involvement, and parent involvement. Those are the three groups whose participation is crucial to the success of a school's character education initiative. Strategies for involving parents were described in chapter 3; strategies for involving students will be described in chapter 12. This chapter focuses on where character education necessarily begins, with the school staff.

1. Create a Touchstone

In their implementation manual, *Educating for Character in the Denver Public Schools,* Charles Elbot, David Fulton, and Barbara Evans write, "Many schools that have created deep, sustained character education have done so with the aid of a schoolwide touchstone."[2] The touchstone is a creed or "way" that expresses the shared values and aspirations of all members of the school community. The importance of having a touchstone, the authors note, has been borne out in numerous studies from the business and nonprofit world. "A creed or 'way' has been the glue that has held successful organizations together and kept them focused even during turbulent times."[3] Such a creed creates an "intentional community," one in which members feel strong connections and a shared moral identity because they are joined by commonly held values.

Here, for example, is the touchstone of Slavens School (http://slavens.dpsk12.org), a Denver K–8 school and 2001 National School of Character. Its touchstone was developed over the course of a year with input from staff, students, and parents.

At Slavens we take the high road.

We genuinely care about ourselves, each other,
and our school.

We show respect by using kind words and actions,
listening thoughtfully, standing up for ourselves, and
taking responsibility for our own behavior and learning.

This is who we are even when no one is watching!

As Elbot and colleagues point out, a touchstone can serve as an ever-present reference point ("Is that the Slavens way?") in the life of a school, guiding the daily decisions of students and staff. It is broader and deeper than a mere rule (such as "No pushing in line," "Clear your trays in the cafeteria"); it is meant to inspire critical thinking and ethical judgment about a wide range of situations, including ones for which there may be no specific rule. What does it mean, for example, to "take the high road" in any given circumstance?

Creating a school touchstone can begin by examining the school's mission statement (usually longer, more complex, and harder to remember than a touchstone statement). What ethical and intellectual values are expressed by the mission? What important values are missing or should be made more explicit in a touchstone? A school committee can then write four or five "We" statements, such as those in the Slavens way, to propose as the school's creed or touchstone and circulate this draft among staff, students, and parents for their feedback. (For a copy of *Educating for Character in the Denver Public Schools,* with suggested steps for creating a school touchstone, contact Charles Elbot: charles__elbot@dpsk12.org.)

2. Have a Character-Based Motto

Does the school's creed live in the hearts and minds of staff and students? One way to help that happen is to choose a school motto—ideally, one of the belief statements in the touchstone—that captures the touchstone's essence and then make that motto a vibrant part of school culture. Here are four examples of school mottoes:

We take the high road.
(Slavens School, K–8)

Together, we are the best we can be.
(Sheridan Hills Elementary School)

Whatever hurts my brother hurts me.
(Saint Benedict's Preparatory School, for boys)

Purpose, Pride, and Performance.
(Mountain Pointe High School)

The last of these schools, Mountain Pointe High School of Phoenix, Arizona, was a 1998 National School of Character. The three P's of its motto figure prominently in all of the school's communications, from the parent newsletter to the student handbook. Teachers use the language of purpose, pride, and performance in their classrooms. Students are asked to keep track of how they use their time in the course of a day (how much time they spend watching TV, for example) and to assess their use of time using the standard represented by the school's motto.

3. Seek the Principal's Support for Making Character a Priority

The priorities of the principal are usually the priorities of the staff. During the eight years our Center for the 4th and 5th Rs has conducted Summer Institutes in Character Education, we've found that when the principal or the principal's clearly designated representative attends at least part of our institute as a member of the school's team, there's a much better chance that character education will be implemented in that school.

This doesn't mean that the principal has to be the hands-on leader of implementation. We worked with one elementary school where the principal, nearing retirement, appointed his media center director to head the character education committee. She got special training. She wrote and secured a small grant to provide a series of workshops to train the rest of the staff. When new faculty joined the school, she oriented them to the program and did a demonstration class meeting with their students to help them learn how to conduct such discussions. She developed a character education resource center for the teachers and a resource center for parents. But although she was the in-the-trenches champion of the character education effort, everyone knew that this initiative was one of the principal's top priorities—something he signaled by attending all the staff development workshops and asking teachers to include, in their weekly lesson plans, how they were promoting character development.

What if you can't get active leadership or support from your principal? Then a group of faculty should ask the principal for permission to present the idea of character education for consideration by the staff. One of the stronger character education programs in our area was begun by a group of middle school teachers who, faced with a passive principal, decided to take the initiative to make their school a better place.

4. Form the Leadership Group(s)

Developing a school of character requires a leadership team to plan and sustain implementation. Our experience in working with schools over the past decade leads us to make four recommendations in this area:

1. Make use of the school's existing infrastructure. For example, is there a school improvement committee or other team that could head the character effort or form a subcommittee to do so? At the secondary level, can academic departments take a leadership role?

2. Create several small committees, each with a different task. This divides the labor and gets more people involved. The broader the participation, the broader the ownership. For example, Wasatch High School in Heber City, Utah, maximized staff and student involvement by forming eight different committees, including curricular infusion, building enhancement (character posters), student recognition, community service, and extracurricular activities.

3. Extend an invitation to all, including potential naysayers.
Reach out to recruit influential individuals, including persons who
might be skeptical about or even opposed to the character effort.

4. Make sure all groups are represented. All the key groups that
make up the school community—administrators, teachers, professional support staff (counselors, psychologists, librarians, coaches),
other support staff (secretaries, custodians, and cafeteria and playground aides), students, and parents—should be represented on
one or another of the character education committees.

5. Develop a Knowledge Base

The leadership team needs to become knowledgeable about character
education. There are now dozens of helpful character education websites (students can help to research these). A good place to start is the
Character Education Partnership's website (www. character.org),
which, among many resources, includes the foundational document,
Eleven Principles of Effective Character Education. Our center's website (www.cortland.edu/c4n5rs) offers an overview of a twelve-point
comprehensive approach to character education and links to other
sites. The website of Boston University's Center for the Advancement
of Ethics and Character (www.bu.edu/education/caec) provides lots
of good resources, including a comprehensive bibliography.

Books that provide an introduction to the field are *Character Education in America's Blue Ribbon Schools* (elementary level) by
Madonna Murphy, *Building Character in Schools* (middle and high
school) by Kevin Ryan and Karen Bohlin, and my own *Educating for
Character: How Our Schools Can Teach Respect and Responsibility*
(K–12). To get a common picture of the field, some leadership groups
have all members read the same book. In other cases, committee
members each take different readings and provide a summary for the
rest of the group.

I also strongly recommend visiting other schools that have been
doing character education for a while (ideally for more than two years)
to see firsthand what a working program looks like. A valuable part of

such a visit is sitting down with the character education committee(s) and asking, How did you get started? cover costs? get faculty and other staff on board? get students and parents involved? What's worked, and what hasn't? How have you tried to assess impact?

If possible, the leadership group should also get some formal character education training through a conference, workshop, course, or other professional development opportunity.

6. Introduce the Concept of Character Education to the Entire Staff

I strongly recommend inviting *all* school personnel to an introductory meeting on character education. Inviting everyone makes a statement: We are all important members of the school community. We all have a part to play in modeling good character for our students and making our school the best it can be.

This introductory session should address four basic questions: (1) What are the goals of character education? (2) What will it require of me, in my work? (3) What will this look like if we do it schoolwide? and (4) What will be the benefits if we do this?

Let's look at how to approach each of these questions.

7. Consider "What Sort of Persons Do We Want Our Students to Become?"

The goals of character education are three: persons of good character, schools of character, and a society of character.

That raises the important question, What is "good character"?

Staff can address that question by asking, What qualities do we want our graduates to possess? What moral and intellectual strengths will best equip them to lead fulfilling, purposeful, and productive lives and to build a better world?

In small groups, staff can brainstorm and list these qualities on a sheet of butcher paper and then post their lists around the room for all to view. (Nearly always, different groups list many of the same qualities.)

A next useful step is to compare the character qualities generated by the staff with a preexisting conceptual scheme defining good character, such as the ten essential virtues described earlier and their supporting virtues:

10 ESSENTIAL VIRTUES

1. **Wisdom**
   - Good judgment; ability to make reasoned decisions.
   - Knowing how to put the virtues into practice
   - Discerning what's important in life; ability to set priorities

2. **Justice**
   - Fairness (following the Golden Rule)
   - Respect for others
   - Self-respect
   - Responsibility
   - Honesty
   - Courtesy/civility
   - Tolerance (respect for freedom of conscience, legitimately exercised)

3. **Fortitude**
   - Courage
   - Resilience
   - Patience
   - Perseverance
   - Endurance
   - Self-confidence

4. **Self-Control**
   - Self-discipline
   - Ability to manage one's emotions and impulses
   - Ability to delay gratification
   - Ability to resist temptation
   - Moderation
   - Sexual self-control

5. *Love*
   - Empathy
   - Compassion
   - Kindness
   - Generosity
   - Service
   - Loyalty
   - Patriotism (love of what is noble in one's country)
   - Forgiveness
6. *Positive Attitude*
   - Hope
   - Enthusiasm
   - Flexibility
   - Sense of Humor
7. *Hard Work*
   - Initiative
   - Diligence
   - Goal Setting
   - Resourcefulness
8. *Integrity*
   - Adhering to moral principle
   - Faithfulness to a correctly formed conscience
   - Keeping one's word
   - Ethical consistency
   - Being honest with oneself
9. *Gratitude*
   - The habit of being thankful; appreciating one's blessings
   - Acknowledging one's debt to others
   - Not complaining
10. *Humility*
    - Self-awareness
    - Willingness to admit mistakes and take responsibility for correcting them
    - The desire to become a better person

When staff compare the list they generated with the ten essential virtues, they can ask, What commonalities do we see? Do the ten essential virtues and their supporting virtues provide a general framework that serves our school's needs? How might this scheme be modified to fit our school's culture and the developmental level of our students?

Whatever the list of target virtues a staff settles on, it's important that it be comprehensive, touching on the important virtues in one way or another, and that the staff own it. Separately, a survey should be distributed to parents and older students—middle school and up—so that their input can be incorporated.

Once character is defined, a definition of character education follows naturally: Character education is the deliberate effort to develop the virtues that enable us to lead fulfilling lives and build a better world.

8. Consider "What Will Character Education Mean for Me?"

To address this question, I recommend an easy-to-do activity using the handout "100 Ways to Promote Character Education." (For the complete list, contact our center, c4n5rs@cortland.edu, or see Appendix G of *Building Character in Schools* by Kevin Ryan and Karen Bohlin.) The list includes such items as

1. Lead by example. Pick up the piece of trash in the hall or in the schoolyard.
2. Whenever you witness peer cruelty, intervene to stop it, helping the perpetrator understand why it is wrong.
3. Teach children how to write thank-you notes. As a class, write thank-you notes to people who have done thoughtful things for the students.
4. Regularly use the "language of virtue"—such terms as respect, responsibility, integrity, wisdom, diligence, perseverance, and humility—and teach students to do the same.

5. Share with students one of your personal heroes and why he or she is a hero for you.
6. Help students develop media literacy—the ability to evaluate the truth and worth of what is presented on TV, the Internet, and in other media.

To conduct the activity

- Have staff form pairs.
- Ask people, individually, to spend seven minutes silently reading the list of "100 Ways," with these instructions: "Circle those things you already do. Star those things you haven't done but would be willing to try."
- After the seven-minute time for silent reading, give partners 5 minutes to share one thing they circled and one thing they starred.
- Ask the whole group, "What conclusions can you draw from this exercise?" Three points to draw out are (1) We already do a lot of these things, even if we haven't called them character education, (2) There are a lot of other things we could be doing, and (3) There are many different ways to implement character education; we don't all need to be doing the same thing.

9. Consider "What Will Character Education Look Like If We Do It Schoolwide?"

Once staff begin to feel comfortable with what character education will mean for them in their individual work, they're ready to consider what it might mean for the whole school.

I find that the quickest way to convey what character education means for a school is by looking at case studies—reading and discussing character education success stories from around the country. When a school staff can see how similar schools facing similar problems have improved student learning and behavior and staff morale through character education, they naturally think, "Why couldn't that work for us?" If, in addition, you can arrange for a live presentation by an enthusiastic principal or character education co-ordinator whose school has a reputation for having a strong character program, so much the better.

Here's how I suggest using the case-study approach:

1. Put staff in mixed triads (different grade levels, different subject areas, or different work roles). Give each person a packet of character education success stories, containing at least one story at the elementary level, one at the middle school level, and one at the high school level. The mix of stories is important for showing that character education has been done effectively at all developmental levels and for helping people to see how their efforts can contribute to or build on work at other levels. Three sources of success stories are the Character Education Partnership's annual National Schools of Character publications (www.character.org); Philip Vincent's *Promising Practices in Character Education, Volumes 1 and 2* (www.Character Education.com); and back issues of our center's *Fourth and Fifth Rs* newsletter, available on our website (www.cortland.edu/c4n5rs).

2. Instruct the participants, "Take six minutes to read the first story silently. Star two or three things this school did that you think your school might benefit from doing. At the signal, share what you starred—and why—with the members of your group."

3. After giving triads five minutes to discuss what they selected as promising strategies, ask someone from each group to briefly report which strategies their group chose and why. Keep a running posted list of all the strategies selected and the number of times each is mentioned.

4. Repeat this process with a second success story and again with a third, each time asking the triads to discuss, "What additional strategies do you see being used in this story—ones you'd like to consider for possible use or adaptation in your school?"

5. After considering several such case studies, ask, "Based on the stories you've read, what do you see as the benefits of a good character education program?" List them. Ones named usually include improved student learning, fewer discipline problems, higher staff morale, students taking leadership roles, and greater parent or community involvement.

6. Close by reviewing the composite list of strategies generated by the small group reports and ask, "Which strategies were most often named?"

If the school staff subsequently commit to making their school a school of character, the top five strategies can be taken as the beginning of its character education plan. If a character education program is already in place, these strategies can be used to enhance the existing effort.

To illustrate how I format case studies for ease of identifying effective strategies, here is one I often use: the story of Kennedy Middle School (541-687-3241) in Eugene, Oregon. Kennedy was the only middle school in the nation to win a National School of Character award in the 1999 competition sponsored by the Character Education Partnership.

The Kennedy Middle School Story

A substitute teacher says of Kennedy, "I've been in every school in the district, and I can tell you, when you walk into Kennedy, there's a definite difference. It's a warm and caring place." Just a few years ago, "warm" and "caring" were not words used to describe Kennedy. Finding parents to help monitor lunch was difficult because parents felt uncomfortable and threatened around several groups of students. Here is how Kennedy became a school of character:

1. It tied character education to school improvement. In the fall of 1995, Kennedy teachers who were unhappy with disrespectful student behavior met with the school's Site Council, which included parents, community members, support staff, and students. Together they came up with three school improvement goals, one of which dealt with school climate and character.

2. It adopted a character education curriculum called Second Step (www.cfchildren.org). Says Kay Mehas, then principal of Kennedy: "*Second Step* is a schoolwide curriculum that teaches such skills as how to communicate, problem-solve, and work together in a community. It actually changes students' behavior."

3. It trained the staff. Mehas and a Kennedy counselor attended a "train the trainer" institute to learn how to train the other staff to teach the *Second Step* curriculum. Before the new school year began, Kennedy held a training day for all staff. The staff decided that every Tuesday from 9:45 to 10:25 A.M. would be dedicated to teaching *Second Step* lessons.

4. It involved support staff in teaching the curriculum. Kennedy invited every member of the staff—including secretaries, custodians, cafeteria workers, and playground aides—to take part in teaching the *Second Step* lessons. A secretary would be paired with an eighth-grade math teacher, a custodian with an eighth-grade science teacher, and so on. This inclusion would show students that the entire school was committed to character development.

5. It made a more effective use of the curriculum in year two. Mehas recalls, "After the first year with *Second Step,* some students still weren't coming to school with common expectations about classroom behavior. We wanted to say to them right at the start of the school year, 'This is how we treat each other at Kennedy Middle School.'" So instead of spreading out the *Second Step* lessons—one a week over the whole year—Kennedy decided to concentrate them: a lesson a day for the first three weeks of school. Says Mehas, "We're now able to spend more time teaching the academic curriculum because we have fewer behavior problems."

6. It provided multiple opportunities for student leadership. These included

    Respect Committee. This group, which meets every day, has the mission of ensuring that all students feel comfortable and respected at the school. For example, it organizes assemblies at which students from different backgrounds share their cultural heritages.

Leadership Club. This club meets weekly to discuss ways to improve the school. One year club members worked with a landscape architect to create a design and then plant trees to enhance school grounds.

Teens and Tots. A service learning class, this program involves Kennedy students in working at Relief Nursery, a child care and support facility for abused children and their families.

Jump Start Tutors. Kennedy students work with their at-risk peers, teaching them study skills and helping with assignments in different subject areas.

Student Conveners. Elected representatives from each class function as Kennedy's student government.

7. *Students developed a system for recognizing positive behavior.* Kennedy's student conveners created a schoolwide system, PRIDE (Personal Responsibility in Daily Efforts), for recognizing students on a daily basis for "doing the right thing." Every six weeks, Kennedy students who have all their assignments in on time, no more than one absence, no more than one unexcused lateness, and no behavioral referrals become a member of PRIDE. For each PRIDE celebration, qualifying students participate in special activities such as ice skating, snow skiing, movies, and swimming. Every six weeks, students have a fresh start, so they have many chances to make PRIDE.

8. *It took steps to create closer teacher-student relationships.* In seventh and eighth grades, Kennedy implemented the practice of "looping," whereby students remain with the same teachers for more than one year. Looping allows faculty to develop closer relationships with both students and their parents.

9. *It increased parent involvement.* Kennedy has had so many parent volunteers that one parent now serves almost full-time as the volunteer coordinator. Parent volunteers cover the office and other essential staff functions while the regular staff are teaching the *Second Step* lessons during the first three weeks of school. Parent volunteers also run the school library and help with the many clubs.

10. It evaluated impact. Kennedy looked at academic and behavioral indicators to assess its character education efforts. In 1997, only 59 percent of Kennedy's students met Oregon's state academic standards, and discipline referrals averaged one hundred a month. In 1998, 74 percent of Kennedy's students met state academic standards, and discipline referrals were down to thirty-five a month.

Schools that already have a character effort under way feel affirmed by finding from these case studies that they are using a number of the practices employed by nationally recognized schools. And they also find new ideas that can be used to keep their program fresh and growing.

10. Analyze the Moral and Intellectual Culture of the School

The next step is to take a close look at the strengths and areas for improvement in the school's moral and intellectual culture.

This is an indispensable step in creating a school of character. If this isn't done, a school may end up ignoring the "elephant at the table"—the big problems right under its nose that, unaddressed, will undermine a character education effort. The most powerful character education curriculum consists of the moral and intellectual experiences that make up the day-to-day life of the school. More than anything else can, these lived experiences—the ways adults relate to students, the ways students relate to adults, the ways students treat each other—shape character.

A systematic way to reflect on these experiences is to use the following four-part analysis of the school's moral and intellectual culture. This analysis may be completed individually by staff prior to a staff meeting, with results compiled and presented by the character education leadership group, or it may be completed and discussed in groups of three or four at a staff meeting.

Analysis of the School's Moral and Intellectual Culture

1. *Positive Experiences:* In your judgment, what positive, character-building experiences (for example, requiring students' best work and supporting them in meeting that standard, trying to make every student feel valued, and preventing bullying) do we, as a school, already provide for our students?

2. *Omissions:* What important character-building experiences are we as a school not adequately providing?

3. *Trouble spots:* What undesirable student or adult behaviors (for example, peer cruelty, academic dishonesty, bad language, disrespect for school property, poor sportsmanship, and adult disrespect toward students) are we as a school neglecting to deal with adequately? (Give examples, but no names.)

4. *Inconsistencies/mixed messages:* What institutional practices are at odds with the character qualities we seek to develop as a school? Such practices may include professing one thing by our rhetoric and another by our practice, failing to enforce the school's discipline code evenhandedly, inequities in educational opportunities, overreliance on extrinsic incentives to motivate good behavior, time pressures that keep staff from paying attention to character development, or failure to involve parents.

If the moral and intellectual culture of the school is *not* a matter of rigorous and continuing reflection, then the character of a school—and all its efforts in character education—will be the poorer.

11. Choose Two Priorities for Improving the School Culture

Reflection must be followed by action. The first step in devising an action plan to strengthen the school culture is to focus on just one or two concerns that the above analysis brings to light. A way to choose a focus is to distribute an "Improving the School Culture" survey listing expressed concerns and to ask staff (and separately, students and parents) to indicate which ones they think the school should concentrate on in the coming year. Here is one such survey:

Improving the School Culture

Of the following school issues, which *two* do you think we should focus on, as a school, in the coming year? (Give a 1 to your top choice, a 2 to your second choice, or add other items if your top priorities aren't listed here.)

_____ Increasing students' responsibility toward their academic work

_____ Increasing respect for teachers and other school staff

_____ Increasing the respect that adults show students

_____ Increasing peer kindness and reducing bullying and other peer cruelty

_____ Increasing academic honesty

_____ Increasing respect and responsibility regarding sexual attitudes and behavior

_____ Increasing parental involvement

_____ Improving language in the building

_____ Improving the sportsmanship of students and adults at athletic events

_____ Improving staff morale

_____ Building school pride

_____ Addressing issues of unfairness (example:_____)

_____ Other: _____

_____ Other: _____

For each of your top two issues: What is one thing you think the school could do to bring about improvement in this area?

_____

_____

_____

12. Ask "Should We Commit to Becoming a School of Character?"

The next step is to decide, Should we commit to becoming a school of character? If so, what action steps should we take toward that goal?

If all of the preceding steps have been done well, there's a strong likelihood that a solid majority of the staff will say yes, it makes a lot of sense to commit to becoming a school of character. By this point, staff should be thinking, Character education is basically about helping kids become good students and good people by being the best school we can be in every way.

However, if there's still resistance to making a formal commitment to becoming a school of character, find out why. It may be that staff feel overwhelmed by current pressures and priorities. They may wonder, When are we going to get the time to do this, and do it well? They may be reluctant because past reform initiatives have faded when there wasn't time for follow-through. To encourage frankness about reasons for reluctance, I recommend asking staff to state their reasons in writing, anonymously. Then, at a subsequent meeting, distribute a list of reasons expressed and brainstorm possible ways to address these concerns.

However long it takes to get it, staff commitment is essential. When people feel as if change is being pushed at them, they resist it. But when they feel as if they have a voice in the change, they are much more likely to support it.

13. Plan a Quality Character Education Program

The next task is to plan the substance of the character education program. The challenge here is to design a program that has most, if not all, of the components that constitute quality character education. Here are twenty components—a kind of character education audit—that show up repeatedly in character education success stories.

20 Common Components of Quality Character Education

1. Administrative leadership/support, including, ideally, a character education coordinator
2. Strong staff involvement
3. Strong student involvement
4. Strong parent involvement
5. A school touchstone (creed) and motto that emphasize character
6. Use of the language of character in everyday interactions and in the school's behavior code, routines and rituals, assemblies, extracurricular activities, student handbook, report card, public relations, and communications with parents
7. An agreed-upon set of target virtues, encompassing work-related and interpersonal virtues
8. A schoolwide plan for intentionally promoting and teaching the school's target virtues
9. Behavioral examples generated by staff and students of what these virtues "look like" and "sound like" at

different ages and in different parts of the school
environment

10. An emphasis on the responsibility of *all* staff and
students to model these virtues

11. Ongoing integration of these virtues into instruction
across the curriculum

12. The use, where appropriate, of a published character
education curriculum

13. An approach to discipline that teaches the virtues
and recognizes good character in a way that keeps
the focus on the character reason for doing what's
right

14. A schoolwide effort to develop a caring community
that prevents peer cruelty

15. A character-rich visual environment (using signs,
posters, quotes)

16. Hiring staff who are persons of good character
committed to modeling and teaching character

17. Staff development in the skills and strategies of
character education and accountability for using
them (Are they part of lesson plans? Do the
principal's observations take note of them?
Do staff regularly report and share what they
are doing to promote character development?)

18. Scheduled time for staff planning, sharing, and
reflection on the character program and the school's
moral and intellectual culture

19. At least modest financial support (Character
education doesn't usually require a big budget,
but some funds are needed for in-service workshops,
conferences, release time for planning and program
development, and a resource library of books and
materials; a purchased curriculum will be a larger
expense.)

20. A plan for ongoing assessment of program
impact

14. Choose an Organizing Strategy for Promoting the Virtues

The school staff should also discuss and decide how to organize its character education program. Here are ten options, many of which can be combined:

10 Organizing Strategies

1. *A virtue a month*
2. *A virtue a week,* related to the monthly theme
3. *three- or four-year cycle of virtues* (six one year, six others the next, etc.), thereby avoiding the repetition of the same virtues year after year (The *Core Essentials Curriculum,* www.coreessentials.org, is an example of a three-year program.)
4. *A yearly theme* (such as "The Year of Peace," "The Year of Self-Discipline," "The Year of Courage"), often in combination with a quarterly focus (for instance, "Promoting Peace in Our Classrooms," "Promoting Peace in Our School," "Promoting Peace in Our Families," "Promoting Peace in Our Community and World")
5. *Assigning a developmentally appropriate virtue to each grade level* for study over the entire school year, for example orderliness in kindergarten, effort in first grade, kindness in second grade, responsibility in third, perseverance in fourth grade—thereby affording the opportunity for in-depth study, repeated practice, and habit formation
6. *A common set of character expectations* that all grade levels work on year round, with individual teachers choosing which virtue or virtues to emphasize at any given time through a book, activity, or curriculum unit (Montclair Kimberley Academy, www.montclairkimberley.org, a pre-K–12 independent school and a 2003 National School of Character in

Montclair, New Jersey, uses this approach; the *Six Pillars of Character* promoted by the Character Counts! Coalition, www.charactercounts.org, can also be used in this way.)

7. *A character education curriculum framework,* such as the K–6 *Core Virtues* (www.linkinstitute.org; see chapter 6), that recommends developmentally appropriate virtues and corresponding curricular resources in such areas as literature and history

8. *A published character education curriculum* with sequenced lesson plans (such as *Second Step,* K–12, www.cfchildren.org; *Promoting Alternative Thinking Strategies,* K–6, www.channing-bete.com; and *Positive Action,* K–12, www.posaction.com

9. *A character education "process model,"* such as the *Caring School Community,* elementary, www.devstu.org; *Responsive Classroom,* elementary, www.responsiveclassroom.org; Seattle Social Development Project, elementary, http://depts.washington.edu/ssdp/; and our center's twelve-point comprehensive approach, K–12, www.cortland.edu/c4n5rs; these models are based on classroom and schoolwide strategies such as those described in this book.

10. *A school culture approach* that emphasizes creating an ethos of moral and intellectual excellence and stresses character in all curricular and co-curricular programs but doesn't necessarily name a target set of virtues to which the whole school formally commits; this approach is used by some secondary schools with a long-standing tradition of emphasizing character.

The school's character education leadership team can present a list of these different possibilities to the staff, briefly describe what it sees as their pros and cons, have staff discuss in small groups the options and possible combinations, and then facilitate a staff decision on an organizing strategy to launch (or refocus) the program.

My own view is that a thoughtful combination of compatible strategies, including the process strategies (9) that integrate character deeply into the daily life of the classroom and school, offers the best chance of success. I also strongly recommend that a school staff regularly revisit their decision—at least every two years—to consider whether a modification or different approach might increase the effectiveness of their character-building efforts.

15. Make Assessment Part of the Plan

There are at least three important reasons to assess a character education initiative: (1) What gets measured, matters; staff motivation and accountability for implementing a character education effort will be much greater if there is a plan to assess results; (2) assessment will tell you to what extent your character education program is actually making a difference; and (3) assessment data can then be used to guide decision making about how to increase program effectiveness.

The necessary work of assessment is more likely to get done if the school sets up an assessment committee that has this responsibility. The assessment effort can start modestly and expand over time. Eventually, it should try to answer the following four questions:

1. *To what extent are staff implementing the character education program as intended?* You can reasonably expect program effects only to the extent that staff are competently putting the program into practice. Teacher self-reports and principal observations can serve as data sources on staff implementation.
2. *To what extent do students understand the target virtues being taught at their grade level?* Can they define them? give several behavioral examples? write about a time when they did or didn't display a particular virtue? describe how a particular role model exemplifies a virtue?
3. *To what extent are students progressing in the*

practice of the virtues? Progress can be measured
by school data such as discipline referrals, test
scores, and prosocial conduct such as volunteering
for service or leadership activities; a school climate
survey; and data from a survey focused on a particular aspect of character such as academic honesty.

4. ***To what extent is behavior improving in a
   particular part of the school environment
   or school life?*** Specific areas include corridors,
   cafeteria, playground, buses, assemblies, and
   athletic events.

Assessment requires work, but it's not as complicated as it may
sound. For starters, you'll certainly want to look at data the school already collects on student conduct and academic achievement. To
evaluate the overall character of the school, there are a number of
school climate measures available, including *The School as a Caring
Community Profile (SCCP)* (free from www.cortland.edu/c4n5rs)
that our center developed for elementary school use and the *Character Education Survey* (free from charactersearch@aol.com) designed
by Meg Korpi for grades seven through twelve. (See our center's website above for further information on character education assessment
instruments.) Both of these instruments measure staff and student
perceptions of the school environment. For example, our *SCCP* instructs the respondent, "On a scale of 1 to 5, where 1 means 'almost
never' and 5 means 'almost always,' circle the number that describes
how often you observe the following behaviors in your school." Sample items include "Students treat classmates with respect," "Students
behave respectfully toward all school staff," and "In their interactions
with students, teachers act in ways that demonstrate the character
qualities the school is trying to teach."

On the last of those three items, the teachers in one elementary
school we worked with gave themselves an average rating of 4.5,
whereas on the same item, students (grades four through six) who
completed the survey gave teachers a significantly lower rating, 3.1.
The faculty were brought up short by the discrepancy between their
self-perception and students' perception and, to their credit, made

narrowing that gap their highest priority for the coming year. This is a good example of how assessment data can be helpful in guiding decisions about program improvement.

Suppose you were concerned about bad language, which in some states is now ranked by teachers as the number one behavior problem they have to deal with in the school building. One middle school, following several parental complaints that their children were uncomfortable with the amount of bad language in the building, asked its student council to take the lead on this problem. With guidance from its faculty advisor, the council developed a language survey that defined three kinds of bad language—put-downs, obscene/vulgar language, and swearing/profanity—and asked students grades five through eight to indicate, for each category, whether they considered such language "always wrong in school and deserving a consequence," "wrong in school but deserving just a reminder," or "no big deal."

The results of the survey were shared and discussed schoolwide. Six months after efforts by adults and the student council to get students to improve their language, the council did another survey and found that (a) two-thirds of students agreed that "teachers have spoken to students about bad language more often this year," (b) a third of students said they had heard less bad language that year and that students "apologized more quickly when they used it," but (c) two-thirds said they didn't notice any change. Some progress had been made, but obviously more work remained to be done.

16. Build a Strong Adult Community

In the long run, the quality of a school's character education effort will be a function of the quality of the adult community. To what extent do staff know, respect, and support each other?

Strengthening a staff's sense of community can be as simple as making sure people feel appreciated. A new principal took over a Saint Louis middle school that was suffering from low staff morale. One of the first things she did was to tape a large manila envelope, marked "Appreciation Notes," on the door of every staff member— teachers, counselors, custodians, and administrators. She sent an invitation to all staff, students, and parents: "Whenever the spirit moves you, please write a note expressing appreciation for something a particular staff person has done and put it in the envelope on that person's door. You don't need to sign it."

Gradually, envelopes began to fill up. Parents wrote to thank teachers for ways the teachers had helped their child. Colleagues affirmed each other for things they had always admired or been grateful for but never put into words. Many students also wrote notes. Morale in the building soared. Faculty said, "This is the most important thing we've done in ten years."

17. Make Time for Character

The lack of time is the number one enemy of sustained educational reform. How can time be protected for planning and monitoring a quality character education program?

A school needs to find the time to pursue the character education goals of intellectual and moral excellence. Some schools have cleared the deck in faculty meetings and used them for meaningful sharing and professional growth. Says Pat Floyd-Echols, principal of the K–5 Dr. Martin Luther King Jr. Magnet School in inner-city Syracuse, New York, "We now devote *all* of our faculty meetings to staff development and sharing. The memos that we used to read at meetings we now send out by e-mail or put in mailboxes. Using our faculty meeting more productively has made us a closer staff. It has also enabled us in the past two years to raise our students' math scores by being more consistent in our instructional approach."

Another good staff development activity is a common book project. Staff commit to reading and to discussing as part of a faculty meeting a book that pertains to character development. I recommend starting with ones that are enjoyable to read and that people can apply in their personal and family life as well as in their professional work. Hal Urban's *Life's Greatest Lessons*, Daniel Goleman's *Emotional Intelligence*, Stephen Covey's *The 7 Habits of Highly Effective People*, F. Washington Jarvis's *With Love and Prayers*, William Bennett's *Book of Virtues*, Ernest Boyer's *The Basic School*, Chip

Wood's *Time to Teach, Time to Learn*, Michele Borba's *Building Moral Intelligence*, Richard Curwin's *Rediscovering Hope: Our Greatest Teaching Strategy*, Anne Colby's and William Damon's *Some Do Care*, Viktor Frankl's *Man's Search for Meaning*, Alfie Kohn's *Punished by Rewards* (controversial but worth a look, given the temptation to overrely on extrinsic incentives), and Helen LeGette's *Parents, Kids & Character* are all good candidates.

Support for this kind of adult development is absolutely essential to becoming a school of character. As Rick Weissbourd, author of *The Vulnerable Child*, points out, "We will never greatly improve students' moral development in schools without taking on the complex task of developing adults' maturity and ethical capacities." We cannot give what we do not have.

Most educational change has a short shelf life: here today, gone tomorrow. That's why experienced teachers are often cynical, thinking, "This too shall pass." The business of becoming a school of character must not become a passing fad, because developing good character is at the heart of effective schooling and what it means to be human.

Educational reforms that endure—those with the power to transform school culture—are ones that remain in the forefront of a school's collective consciousness. Over time, they become part of a school's identity, how it defines itself. To have that kind of transformative power, character education must be regularly thought about and talked about by a critical mass of staff, especially by a core of committed teachers who can sustain a school culture when the administrative leadership changes. The challenge for that critical core is to keep the character conversation going.

* * *

Three recommended resources that can help your school become a school of character are *Eleven Principles Sourcebook: How to Achieve Quality Character Education in Your School or District*, by Kathy Beland (www.character.org); *Building Character in Schools: Resource Guide*, by Karen Bohlin, Deborah Farmer, and Kevin Ryan (www.josseybass.com); and *Professional Learning Communities at Work*, by Richard DuFour and Robert Eaker (www.neosonline.com).

CHAPTER 12

Involve Students in Creating a School of Character

The best education is education we do with students.

—A PRINCIPAL

I n the moral life of the school, there is no better opportunity for students to take on authentic responsibility than by helping to create a school of character.

Students must be engaged as essential partners in that task. When students are in visible leadership roles, and when all students have a voice and a stake in the character education effort, adults will be far more effective in promoting good character than they can ever be acting alone. Indeed, character education without this kind of active student involvement will ultimately prove to be a frustrating and disappointing exercise. "We know character education is the right thing to do," said one superintendent, "but we're not getting the results we want. Kids know the right words to say, but it often doesn't translate into behavior."

Here are eight strategies for involving students as indispensable allies in creating a school of character and in developing the kind of commitment to character that's more likely to show up in behavior.

1. Involve Students in Planning and Leading the Character Education Program

At all age levels, students can play a meaningful role in planning and leading the school's character education program.

At Saint Leonard Elementary School in Saint Leonard, Maryland, a 1998 National School of Character, counselor Allyson Sigler oversees a Kids' Character Committee at each grade level (1–6). Every month, three or four students from each classroom rotate onto their grade's committee. Over the course of the school year, every student has a turn to serve.

At the start of every month, the Kids' Character Committee for each grade has two working lunches with counselor Sigler. In that meeting, they

1. Discuss what the character trait of the month looks like and sounds like, and what it feels like to show that trait.
2. Develop, with Sigler's assistance, a presentation and poster that will teach their classmates about the trait.
3. Plan additional ways to involve their class in learning about and practicing the trait over the course of the month.

Strategies for teaching the monthly trait include role playing, creating a song about the trait, playing a game that highlights the trait, and asking the class what they would do in certain situations to show the trait. Students on the Kids' Character Committee are also in charge of making the school's morning announcements, delivering "LEOgrams" recognizing students for acts of good character, and creating and distributing the flyer reminding everyone about the monthly food pantry drive.

"The children receive a trait pin to wear for the month so they can be identified as members of the committee," Sigler explains. "They take a lot of pride in being experts on, and role models for, their character trait."

2. Use Class Meetings to Give Kids a Voice and Responsibility

The class meeting is an interactive discussion in which students share responsibility for making the classroom a good place to be and learn. Conducted in a circle, which enables everyone to see everyone else, class meetings can be used to develop a discipline code, plan special events such as a field trip, solve a classroom problem, or contribute to the solution of a schoolwide problem. In some classrooms, students can request a meeting about a matter they'd like to bring up.

To solicit student input for improving the classroom, some teachers also have a suggestion box. Students can anonymously submit a topic for a class meeting discussion. Many teachers teach their students how to lead the class meeting, following agreed-upon "rules for good talking and listening," and can even step out of the classroom without a disruption in the meeting process.

3. Involve Students in Participatory Schoolwide Student Government

When students learn and practice discussion and decision-making skills in class meetings, they're prepared to participate in a vitally important schoolwide process: student government that shares responsibility for making the school the best that it can be.

When a school does not have this kind of student government in place, it is ill-equipped to address academic dishonesty, vandalism, peer cruelty, sexual harassment, racial tensions, bad language, poor sportsmanship, and other such problems. Because these problems are located in the peer culture, they are difficult or impossible to solve by adults acting on their own. Peers are needed to help shape the norms that influence student behavior.

Unfortunately, student government as practiced in most schools doesn't govern anything. It is typically an isolated group with no constituency. Members don't represent anyone but themselves; they don't seek input from, or report back to, other students. This kind of disconnected student government has little or no power to influence the peer culture.

Schools have a much better chance of solving problems in the school environment if they set up participatory student government. In this approach, student delegates serve as representatives of their classrooms (or homerooms) and report back to them.

Participatory student government also prepares students to be participating citizens in a democratic society. Currently, the youngest voters are the least likely to vote in any election. To value democracy, young people need to *experience* democracy firsthand during their formative years in school.

What follows are various structures for giving students a voice in, and responsibility for, solving a wide range of school problems and for developing the kind of character and citizenship that democracies demand.

The Special-Focus Student Council

The cafeteria in many schools is a war zone. Aides scream at kids, kids yell at each other, food fights are common, and the place is a mess when students leave.

That was the situation in teacher Mary Ann Taylor's Theodore Roosevelt Elementary School in urban Binghamton, New York. "Frankly," she says, "the thought of trying to change this was intimidating." The approach she used illustrates how a special-focus student council can be created to deal with a particular problem.

1. With her principal's support, Taylor formed a Cafeteria Council made up of two elected student delegates from each classroom.

2. In every classroom at every grade level, teachers held class meetings addressing two questions: What are the characteristics of an ideal cafeteria? What should be the rules for cafeteria manners in our school?

3. At the council's weekly lunchtime meetings, delegates were responsible for reporting what their class had said in their meetings. Under the guidance of Taylor and the school's principal, the delegates discussed the various proposals for manners and cafeteria improvements and shaped them into tentative action proposals.

4. Delegates then took these action proposals back to their respective classrooms for further discussion and refinement. This back-and-forth feedback continued for several weeks.

5. The Cafeteria Council simultaneously conducted a survey of all students, staff, and parents, asking, "How can we improve our cafeteria?" It also solicited ideas on an ongoing basis through a suggestion box and sent a monthly newsletter to all families, reporting its progress.

Following all these efforts, cafeteria behavior improved greatly, the noise level dropped dramatically, students were enthusiastic about cafeteria improvements, parent feedback was very positive, and a recycling project emerged as a spin-off. Most important, the school decided to keep its new delegate system of democratic student government as a way to deal with other problems in the school.

Linked Primary and Intermediate Student Councils

One of the objectives of participatory student government is to give as many students as possible a chance to take leadership roles. That participation is a spur for their character development.

Interlocking primary-level and intermediate-level student councils, a system devised by former New York State principal JoAnn Shaheen, is a way to give more students an opportunity to be part of the process. In this approach, "Little SAC" (Student Advisory Council) is formed from delegates elected from each classroom in grades K–3 or one through three. "Big SAC" is made up of delegates elected from grades four through six, plus officers (president, vice-president, secretary, and treasurer) who are elected, after a campaign, by the entire student body. In addition, the teacher selects a third delegate from each classroom, usually a child who might not be elected but who would benefit from the experience.

Here's how Little SAC and Big SAC function:

1. The principal meets separately with Little SAC and Big SAC weekly for thirty minutes, usually over lunch.
2. The vice-president of Big SAC also chairs Little SAC and serves as a link between the two groups.
3. Big SAC and Little SAC can tackle problems separately or jointly.
4. Besides problem-solving, both SACs can and do carry out community service projects and school fund-raising.

For example, in Birch Meadow Elementary School north of Boston, second-grade delegates to Little SAC complained in their weekly meeting that the big kids (intermediate grades) were "hogging the playground equipment" at recess.

The chair of Little SAC, a fifth grader who served as vice-president of Big SAC, reported the second graders' complaints at Big SAC's next meeting. Big SAC delegates then took the issue back to their respective classrooms, where the problem was discussed and suggestions elicited for the equitable use of playground equipment. At its next meeting, Big SAC formulated rules for the fair use of playground equipment. These were taken by its vice-president back to Little SAC for their consent. The playground problem was thereby solved.

The High School Congress

Several years ago, a high school north of New York City instituted a school government they called their "Congress." Here's how it works:

1. Student delegates are elected from "seminars," which meet during the period following lunch every Wednesday.
2. Congress also includes elected representatives of the faculty, administration, and parent body.
3. Congress meets over lunch hour every Wednesday to discuss issues of concern raised or reported by delegates.
4. Delegates carry concerns and recommended action steps into their respective seminars. There they solicit feedback, which they take back to Congress the following week.

When I attended a meeting of the Congress, two years after its inception, I asked the students, "What have you accomplished that you feel good about?" The first two accomplishments they mentioned involved vandalism. The cafeteria phone installed for student use had been ripped out of the wall by someone. After this happened twice, administration refused to reinstall the phone. Some students had also been vandalizing other students' artwork hung in the hallways—writing graffiti on it or cutting a canvas with a knife.

Both kinds of vandalism ended after they were discussed in Congress and in seminars throughout the school. Discussions aired people's feelings about such grossly disrespectful behavior and addressed the responsibility everyone had to try to prevent it and to report any incidents they witnessed. These discussions appeared to work by creating an explicit peer-group norm: It wasn't cool to rip out the phone intended for all students' use or to deface somebody else's artwork.

4. Provide Informal Opportunities for Student Input

Informal structures can complement the work of formal student government and give additional students an opportunity to play a part in improving their school.

For example, two counselors at a Saint Louis middle school established what they called "The Breakfast Club" as a way of giving students a chance to give feedback on their school. They drew twenty students' names from a hat and invited them to meet with them for twenty minutes before classes on Thursday. Milk and donuts were provided.

Seated in a circle, students each responded to two questions: "What is one thing you like about our school? What is one thing that would make it better?"

Before leaving the meeting, students signed their names on the Breakfast Club members list (posted on the back of the door) and drew twenty new names to be invited to the next week's meeting.

Students' comments and suggestions were recorded, typed up, and distributed to the school staff. Many of the suggestions were implemented.

"Word quickly spread," the counselors said. "Even tough kids were asking how you get to go to this Breakfast Club. It was a simple thing, but it created a different atmosphere in the school."

5. Challenge Students to Mount a Schoolwide Campaign

Counselor Debra Hines is the advisor to the student council at Carlisle High School in Carlisle, Pennsylvania. Two years ago, she says, her school administration was on the verge of canceling school dances because increasing numbers of students were drinking before and during dances (in the bathrooms, for example). The drinking was also contributing to a lot of inappropriate behavior on and around the dance floor. Hines describes the school's response:

We gave the problem to our student council. We said, "You guys will have to figure out a way to solve this problem. Otherwise, dances will be history."

Their initial reaction was, "We're just twenty kids; there are four thousand students in this school!" But they took it on. They did morning announcements such as, "Hey, did you know that dances will be canceled if there's drinking?" They put up signs, large and small, all over the building, even in the bathrooms: "Be cool, don't drink at dances" and "Don't drink at dances and ruin it for everybody." They held assemblies and did funny skits sending the same message.

At first, the signs got ripped down, but they just put up more and didn't give up. At the next dance, there wasn't a single incident, even though there were more than a thousand students. And this has had a lasting effect; we haven't had to do it again.

Even without the broader participatory process that a delegate student government system provides, the Carlisle council showed that a creative and persistent student campaign can be effective in changing peer behavior.

6. Establish a Mentoring System

A well-designed mentoring system helps to establish an important school norm: Older students have a responsibility to be supportive role models for younger ones.

For example, at McLean High School in McLean, Virginia, freshmen with identified needs are paired with senior mentors who are leaders in the school. The senior mentors receive specialized training in character development and mentoring. The student pairs meet individually and as a group throughout the school year. Seniors help their freshmen charges learn the ropes of their new school and develop good study habits.

Some high schools have done action research to evaluate the

impact of a senior-freshman mentoring program and found that freshman students who receive this guidance get better grades and are less likely to be referred for discipline problems.

When seniors take on this kind of formal mentoring role, they're also more likely to socialize younger students in informal ways. At Maryland's Eleanor Roosevelt High School, a 2002 National School of Character with three thousand students, older students will often "call out" younger ones who skip class, use bad language, put down a peer, or speak disrespectfully to a teacher. A senior girl told me, "We look at the freshmen as the babies of the school. It's up to us to teach them how to act. If they're doing something wrong, we just tell them, 'That's not the Roosevelt way.'" In such a school, students are a powerful force for upholding the school's moral norms.

7. Establish a Character Club or Committee

Students can also make a difference in the character of their school through a club or committee that has a schoolwide responsibility.

At Franklin High School in Portland, Oregon, students started a World Affairs Club. Its mission is to promote awareness of cultural diversity through school displays, information supplied to the school's daily bulletin about the cultures represented in the school, periodic cultural assemblies, and materials that teachers can use to lead classroom discussions.

Other students at Franklin are in charge of the Student Mediation Program. Its mission is to mediate conflicts between students and between teachers and students. Students who have had their conflicts mediated by a peer say that they have learned skills that they can use in everyday life. Since the institution of the Student Mediation Program, Franklin's suspension rate has dropped significantly.

Mount Rainier Elementary School, a 2001 National School of Character, is an urban school located on the border of Washington, D.C. Fighting had been a problem there. "A lot of our students were coming to school angry," says principal Phil Catania. "They had been hurt, and they wanted to hurt somebody."

Mount Rainier decided to make the virtue of peace an explicit focus in its character education program. It also instituted a "Peace Promise," which all classes now recite every Monday and Friday morning: "I promise to show respect, I promise to act responsibly, I promise to be peaceful."

At the end of each day, a student Peace Committee, made up of fifth and sixth graders, splits up and travels to every classroom, asking whether, in the judgment of class members, they all kept the Peace Promise. If at least fourteen of the school's sixteen classrooms report that they kept the Promise, the Peace Committee records it as a "Peace Day" for the school. At the beginning of the year, Mount Rainier sets a goal for the number of Peace Days it hopes to have that year, and the Peace Committee keeps a large running tally posted in the front of the school and in every classroom. In 2000–01, Mount Rainier set the goal of 160 Peace Days and achieved it.

8. Recognize Student Leadership

If we want students to take a leadership role in improving their school, we should recognize them when they do.

Some districts, at their annual spring awards assembly, give awards to individual students or groups of students who have made significant contributions to improving their school. Other districts arrange for media coverage of the good things students are doing. Some regional and state character education conferences now include a special recognition ceremony that presents awards to students who have made a positive difference in their school environments.

*   *   *

I've been in schools where both staff and student leaders complain about the apathy of the student body. Participatory school structures go a long way toward solving that problem by giving students broad responsibility for the life of the school. Especially when these strategies are used in combination, they have the power to mobilize the peer culture on the side of virtue. Over time, the peer-group attitude comes to be "This is our school. If there's a problem, we should help to fix it." Problems in such schools become opportunities for students' growth in leadership, citizenship, and virtue. In the process, students become full partners with adults in creating a school of character.

For ways to involve students in the creation of honor codes, see David Gould's *A Handbook for Developing and Sustaining Honor Codes* (Council for Spiritual and Ethical Education, www.csee.org). For an assessment instrument, "Academic Integrity Survey," that has been widely used to study academic honesty, contact Professor Don McCabe (dmccabe@andromeda.rutgers.edu).

For additional examples of democratic governance in high schools, contact Mary McCarthy, character education coordinator for Massachusetts's Hudson Public School District, a 2001 National District of Character (mmcarthy@hudson.k12.ma.us) and Bill Parsons, principal of Georgia's Troup High School (parsonswr @troup.org). For further examples of student leadership in high school character education, see *Smart and Good: Developing Performance Character and Moral Character in America's High Schools* by Thomas Lickona and Matthew Davidson (available September 2004, www.cortland.edu/c4n5rs).

PART FIVE

Create
Communities
of Character

CHAPTER 13

Involve the Whole
Community in Building
Good Character

A community consensus on values is a strong predictor of healthy adolescent adjustment, far stronger than variables such as affluence or ethnicity.

— CONCLUSION OF A TEN-YEAR STUDY
OF TEN AMERICAN COMMUNITIES[1]

For the young to become moral, they must be in the presence of people who take morality seriously.

— MARY WARNOCK

Schools and families working together are a powerful alliance for character. But in a culture that often undermines good character, schools and families need support from the wider community.

A recent Associated Press story profiled Cameron, a seventh-grade boy in a conservative southern community. Although Cameron's middle school is safe and orderly, he says he and his friends are repeatedly approached by schoolmates pushing acid, marijuana, and other drugs. Cameron is active in his church youth group, and his parents see to it that the whole family eats breakfast and dinner together each day. TV is allowed only on weekends. Neither Cameron nor his younger sister is allowed to take the bus to school; their mother drives them. She's home every day when the kids get in from school; she gave up her teacher's salary to stay home and raise her children. "He's never unsupervised," she says of Cameron, "so he doesn't have the opportunity to get into a gang or do drugs."

The story of Cameron's family illustrates the high degree of vigilance that many parents now feel they must exercise to protect their children from the pressures, temptations, and bad examples they will encounter outside the home. The reality, however, is that most parents can't or won't exercise this level of vigilance. We need to create a world in which it is easier to raise a moral child. We need to create *communities of character,* ones that surround children with models and messages that support schools and parents in their character-building efforts.

Raising children of character, in short, must be the shared work of all those groups that educate, care for, and influence the young. The proverb "It takes a village to raise a child" has become a cliché of American public life. But as the educator Chip Wood points out, there is a prior question: "What does it take to raise a village?"

The process of "raising the village"—taking deliberate steps to create a community of character—is under way in at least some cities, towns, and villages. Let's look at fifteen strategies that communities large and small have used to try to create an environment that builds good character in citizens young and old.

1. Strengthen the School-Community Partnership

Creating a community of character should begin with strengthening the existing institutions responsible for the education and moral development of the young. Education of the next generation is the primary way society renews itself. Anything the community can do to improve the character of its schools and the effectiveness with which they serve all students will help to build a community and society of character.

For starters, the community should do everything it can to support strong K–12 character education in the schools. All segments of the community—government, police, business, and ordinary citizens—stand to gain when the school does a good job of teaching honesty, respect, hard work, and other virtues. If schools are educating for character effectively, young people will become more responsible community members now and more responsible citizens as adults.

The community can also help schools deal with particular problems. In chapter 7, I described a successful school-community partnership in our city of Cortland, New York, that has helped kids who were chronic discipline problems become successful students.

School attendance has been the focus of other school-community partnerships. An estimated 30 percent of students do not show up regularly for school. Schools typically send letters home when a student has been chronically absent, but such efforts often fail with the "hard cases." Says Tom Jarczynski, a school pupil personnel worker in Saint Mary's County, Maryland, "We've had instances of kids who, over five years of elementary school, missed a total of a full year of school. Schools were constantly sending home letters to the parents but to no avail."

In response, Saint Mary's County has come up with a whole new approach that has the school and several community agencies hold a conference with parents of chronically absent students. The child is also invited. "We had a little girl who had missed more than fifty days of school in first grade," Jarczynski recalls. "Then during the first two weeks of second grade, she missed six days. We contacted the mother and called her in for a conference."

Chaired by the director of Social Services, the meeting includes Jarczynski as the school representative, the sheriff's deputy, someone from the Health Department, and a representative of Juvenile Services. "Parents are usually surprised to see all the agencies that are there," Jarczynski says. "They think, 'Oh, it's not just the school that's telling me this.'

"In the case of the second grader, the mother started out by claiming that her daughter had been sick a lot. But as we talked, it came out that if the little girl said she didn't want to go to school on any given day, for whatever reason, the mother just let her stay home. We made it clear to the mother that she had a responsibility to make sure her daughter got to school unless there was a good reason for not attending."

Since implementing this approach, Saint Mary's County has had a much higher success rate with chronically absent students. Getting several community agencies involved in addressing school absence has also increased school-community cooperation in becoming aware of a particular family's situation and responding to its other needs.

2. Strengthen Families

Strong communities require strong families. For that reason, any effort to create a community of character must make strengthening families a high priority. Chapter 3 detailed the many ways schools can partner with parents in mutually beneficial relationships.

Chattanooga, Tennessee, population 156,000, is a city that has worked hard to strengthen families. Its efforts to do so and its community-wide character initiative are described in *A Gift of Character: The Chattanooga Story* by Dr. Phil Vincent, Nancy Reed, and Jesse Register.[2] Family Resource Centers, located in several parts of the city, offer parenting classes, GED (general equivalency diploma) programs, and an afterschool "Lights On" program. Through the Lights On program, students can take music and ballet lessons along with enrichment in reading, math, and science. Parents can learn about improving family life, stress management, and healthy living.

Concurrently, Chattanooga Neighborhood Enterprise, a nonprofit corporation, has invested more than $200 million to build or rehabilitate over six thousand units of affordable housing for low- to moderate-income families. This is another example of Chattanooga's trying to make sure its community improvement effort benefits all segments of the community. By contrast, a social worker in another city comments, "A lot of people don't like to admit it, but there's a big split in our community between the haves and the have-nots. It's the well-off kids who turn out for the youth activities, not the low-income kids."

Families also need time together—an increasingly scarce commodity in an age of overscheduled children. William Doherty, author of *Take Back Your Kids,* tells of a soccer coach for a traveling soccer team who told the parents of the student players that families could take vacations only during the second and third weeks in August. "We have become like sheep," says Doherty, "led by the people who schedule our children's lives." Along with other parents and local community leaders, he has helped to found Family Life First in a Minneapolis suburb to empower parents to become confident leaders in family life and strike a balance between children's individual activities and family life. The problem of lost family time, as Doherty observes, is too big to be addressed by individual families alone; they need community support.[3]

3. Commit to Becoming a Community of Character

Just as families and schools benefit when they intentionally model and teach good character, communities also benefit from making a conscious commitment to character. In many communities, this commitment has taken the form of a resolution by the town or city council calling upon all community groups to join in the character effort.

Canandaigua, New York, population 11,000, called its resolution a "Character Education Partnership Agreement" (www.canandaigua schools.org/community.cfm). Focused on five character traits—respect, responsibility, caring, honesty, and healthy lifestyles—the agreement reads in part, "As partners in the development of the character of our youth, we promise to promote these character traits in our interactions with others and accept the responsibility of modeling behavior which reflects these traits."

Mayor Ellen Polimeni, also the middle school principal, led the school district's Character Education Council in the effort to recruit community partners. In just two months, they got more than thirty-six community groups to sign on.

4. Create a Leadership Group

A successful community-wide character initiative needs a leadership group that coordinates the effort and sustains implementation.

In the town of Hamburg, population 56,000, outside Buffalo, New York, a nine-member board of directors oversees its "Character First in Hamburg" initiative. The board has recruited volunteers to serve on five committees—Education, Government, Faith-Based Organizations, Community, and Business/Public Relations—each of which is responsible for promoting good character within its sphere of influence.

In Roswell, New Mexico, population 45,000, former mayor Tom Jennings observes, "Everything depends on your leadership group. You want everyone in the community to feel represented. We got good leaders by handpicking persons of character from all parts of our community. Our forty-member Character Commission is co-chaired by a judge and a lawyer—a man and a woman."

5. Give Everyone a Chance for Input

To maximize ownership, all community stakeholders should have an opportunity for input into developing the vision of a community-wide character initiative.

Hamburg, New York, used a "Character-Building Summit" as its vehicle for community input. The summit's planning committee invited representatives of more than a dozen groups, including public and private schools, the school board, the district's Youth at Risk Program, the Teachers' Center, the business community, the religious community, volunteer organizations, senior citizens groups, civic organizations, the town recreation departments, the public library, the Boy Scouts and Girl Scouts and other youth groups, the medical community, the youth bureau, the police department, the YMCA, the Red Cross, the town council, and students. On the day of the summit, nearly four hundred people representing these various groups filled the town hall to capacity.

The morning agenda placed participants in mixed groups of ten, each with a facilitator, for ninety minutes. Each group's charge was to: "brainstorm any and all ideas that could result in improving character in the Town of Hamburg." After lunch, participants were put in homogeneous groups for ninety minutes (students together, parents together, and so on) with the instruction, "Take the morning's ideas that pertain to your group and turn them into action proposals."

Students proposed a teen center for recreation and tutoring, more media coverage of positive actions by youth, and commercials by kids promoting character. Parents proposed required community service for all youth, monthly character messages from the schools to parents, and a commitment by families to do less outside the home and spend more time together. Community and business representatives recommended a monthly character trait to be promoted in all the schools and showcased throughout the community, as well as greater involvement of senior citizens in the lives of youth. Educators suggested highlighting character through the academic curriculum and more character-building work with at-risk students. Members of the religious community proposed publicizing the character effort with their memberships and integrating the target character traits into sermons, religious instruction, and youth activities.

Hamburg's five Character First subcommittees are now responsible for following through on the proposals.

6. Identify the Target Virtues

Different communities have used different processes for arriving at the character traits they wish to promote. In some, the community's character education leadership group has chosen monthly or bimonthly traits, which were then adopted by the schools.

Other communities have used a broader participatory process. In Toppenish, Washington, population 9,000, students from grades four through twelve were trained to go to meetings of community organizations and ask, "What character qualities do you think most important to promote in Toppenish?" More than one hundred traits were nominated by forty-seven organizations. At an October 1997 community forum, the high school gym walls were lined with colorful signs made by students and each displaying a nominated trait and its definition. Every community member present was given ten stick-on dots with the direction, "Place your dots on the ten traits you find most admirable—and would like to see taught in our schools and upheld by all area residents." The eight traits receiving the most votes became the basis for the school-community character education effort.

7. Provide Leadership Training

For many communities, the next step has been to provide formal training for the leadership group. Three organizations that provide such training are the North Carolina–based Character Development Group (www.CharacterEducation.com), the Illinois-based International Association of Character Cities (www.charactercities.org), and the California-based Character Counts! Coalition (www.character counts.org).

8. Get Business Involved

Businesses have a big stake in character education. Character education that fosters honesty, dependability, pride in work, and the ability to cooperate will create a stronger workforce. For this reason, businesses have often been willing to help underwrite character education in the schools and to be partners in a community-wide effort.

In Saint Louis, Sanford McDonnell, former CEO of the Mc-Donnell Douglas Corporation, approached the area's Cooperating School Districts in 1987 about how business and the schools could work together to promote character throughout the community. What resulted was Character*plus,* which now involves eighty-seven public school districts and 300,000 students in what is the nation's largest character education effort (http://csd.org/staffdev/chared/characterplus.html).

McDonnell comments, "We don't promote one set of values. Instead, we give schools a process that lets them and their local community identify their own core values." That decentralized process is clearly well suited to large-scale metropolitan efforts like the Saint Louis initiative.

Businesses can also support a character initiative by emphasizing character in the workplace. In Saint Louis, for example, McDonnell was a catalyst for getting corporations to provide ethics training for employees at every level.

9. Promote Community Awareness of Character

Part of the challenge in creating a community of character is keeping character in the public eye.

In some communities, the computers in all city and county offices display the monthly character trait and a related quote when employees log on (for example, "Deal with the faults of others as gently as with your own" —Chinese proverb). In La Palma, California, population 15,000, the *City Newsletter,* mailed to every resident, includes a character insert with quotes pertinent to La Palma's monthly character theme.

Local media can also help. In Chattanooga, radio talk shows have been an effective venue for raising awareness of the character effort. The *Chattanooga Times/Free Press* has sponsored an eight-page monthly newspaper insert on the monthly virtue—and printed 175,000 copies, including 45,000 for direct distribution to all of the county's students.

Keeping character in the public consciousness also means creating a visual culture that surrounds people with the character message. In many communities, local printers have donated printing of storefront signs, refrigerator posters for parents, and school cafeteria place mats—all highlighting the virtue of the month. When Ed Bohrer was mayor of Gaithersburg, Maryland, he noted, "We've got our character logo on our public works trucks, buses, trash cans, and new park pavilion. Of course, the most important exhibit is our own behavior. In our local elections, I challenged all the candidates to model the character qualities. We had fewer negative allegations and more civility."

10. Integrate Character into All Community Programs

An effective community character initiative integrates intentional character building into a wide range of community programs.

In Maryland's Talbot County, for example, the county's summer camps have infused the target virtues into year-round youth activities and daily summer camp lessons. In Easton, Maryland, Coach Everett Warren describes the community's effort to emphasize character in all of its youth sports programs: "We stress making a dedicated effort, being disciplined in one's behavior, and showing respect for both teammates and opponents. No trash talk is allowed. No cutting corners to win is acceptable."

11. Create a Special Role for Police

The police also have an important role to play. In La Palma, the police department has used the Six Pillars of Character (trustworthiness, respect, responsibility, caring, fairness, and citizenship) as "performance expectations." All members of the department take an oath pledging to exhibit good character in accord with the Six Pillars. The police chief is in the schools often, meeting with principals to exchange information about problem youth behavior, reduce response time, and head off trouble before it happens.

In Canandaigua, the police department has organized an after-school program of tutoring, field trips, and other activities between

2:30 and 6:00 P.M. in the Salvation Army Building. "During that afternoon time," says Police Chief Patrick McCarthy, "there had been
a high incidence of shoplifting and criminal mischief. Since we instituted the afterschool program, those problems have decreased
significantly."

12. Give Kids a Leadership Role

Just as schools have more success with character education when students are in leadership roles, community initiatives are more effective
when young people are contributors rather than just recipients.

"As part of our character initiative," says Roswell's former mayor
Tom Jennings, "we created a teen council that meets monthly with
the city council. We wanted their input. We also established a Town
Meeting for Teens. At one of their first meetings, they pointed out
that we had no teen center. So we worked with them to get a grant
to turn an old airport terminal into a youth center where teens can
now go to dance, play Ping-Pong or pool, watch videos, or just hang
out. We've given them the responsibility of providing their own security. If somebody is out of line, they throw them out."

13. Recognize Good Character

Communities, like schools, should recognize and celebrate good
character.

Says Rita Mullins, former mayor of Palatine, Illinois, population
65,000, "Our city council has youth and community groups come to
city hall each month to receive Certificates of Service for the community service they do."

Every month, the City Council of Gaithersburg, Maryland,
gives a Character Award to a young person or adult in the community. Any citizen can submit a nomination.

In Saint Louis, the *Post-Dispatch* newspaper ran a series examining nine character traits through the lives of exemplary young people
in the community and the persons who influenced their development.

14. Have Community Volunteers Teach Character in the Schools

"Walk tall with a smile."

"Shake hands with a firm grip."

"Learn to forgive."

Once a week for fifteen minutes, "character coaches," community volunteers, teach lessons like these to students in elementary and middle school classrooms in five counties (Dorchester, Talbot, Caroline, Queen Anne's, and Kent) on the Eastern Shore of Maryland. The program is called "Winners Walk Tall" (www.winnerswalktall.org), in the belief that learning and acting on these messages will help children become winners in life.

Originally designed by Cincinnati businessman Bob Mauk (513-763-3021), the Winners Walk Tall program was brought to Maryland by retired businessman Dick Allen. A volunteer character coach visits the same elementary or middle school classroom once a week for every week of the school year. (A Winners Walk Tall manual, introductory video, and on-site assistance for starting the program and training volunteers are all provided free to any interested school.)

During each character lesson, students are asked to participate actively and practice the character skills. For example, in the lesson on "Shake hands with a firm grip, look the person in the eye, and smile!" each student walks to the front of the room, stands tall with a smile, and firmly shakes the hand of the character coach.

I spoke with Don Carson, a retired businessman in his seventies who does two stints a week as a character coach. "It makes my day," he said. "I grew up in this town. I learned respect, responsibility, and courtesy from my parents and teachers. I'm now a grandfather of nine. I'd like to pass on some of what's helped me in life to young people today."

Says Dick Allen, "Winners Walk Tall is citizen-initiated, citizen-financed, and citizen-managed. Everybody loves it. It's broken down the school-community barriers." Allen's initiative shows the potential of a community-driven model of character education.

15. Assess the Impact of a Community Character Initiative

A community's leadership committee has the job of assessing whether the character initiative is making a difference. Assessment starts with examining readily available data. Canandaigua's Mayor Polimeni notes that "since launching our community-wide initiative, we've seen a substantial drop in juvenile offenses and school suspensions."

A research-based approach to assessing a community character-building initiative comes from the *Healthy Communities, Healthy Youth* program created by the Search Institute (www.search institute.org) of Minneapolis, Minnesota. In its three decades of research on over 100,000 sixth to twelfth graders from more than two hundred U.S. towns and cities, Search has identified forty "developmental assets" in young people that promote positive attitudes and behaviors and protect them from high-risk behaviors. Search divides the assets into eight categories:

1. *Support* (including family love, other supportive adult relationships, and a caring school climate)
2. *Empowerment* (being given useful roles in the community)
3. *Boundaries and expectations* (for instance, family rules, adult role models, positive peer influence)
4. *Constructive use of time* (including involvement in creative activities, youth programs, and a religious community)
5. *Commitment to learning* (school engagement, achievement motivation)
6. *Positive values* (for example, caring, integrity, social justice, and the belief that it is important not to be sexually active or to use alcohol or other drugs)
7. *Social competencies* (including decision-making and conflict resolution skills)
8. *Positive identity* (including a sense of purpose and a positive view of one's own future)

In its research, Search finds that

- Fewer than half of the young people studied possess twenty-five or more of the forty assets; the average young person has only eighteen.
- Youth with the most assets are the least likely to engage in the high-risk behaviors of problem alcohol use, illicit drug use, sexual activity, and violence.
- Youth with the most assets are the most likely to demonstrate four patterns of positive attitudes and behaviors: school success, valuing cultural and racial diversity, maintaining good health, and delaying gratification.

Search has helped hundreds of communities across the nation to determine the extent to which a community's young people possess the forty assets and then to plan a community intervention that will help develop the assets. (For another instrument that is being used to assess a community-wide character initiative in DuPage County, Illinois, www.healthydupage.org, see *Global Portraits of Social and Moral Health*, available from Matthew Davidson, davidsonm@cortland.edu).

The challenge with community-based character initiatives, as with school-based character education, is sustaining it. A program can't depend on a charismatic mayor or a particular city council; those come and go. It can't be mostly bells and whistles, logos and billboards. Those get old. For a community of character to develop and endure, an abiding concern for character must become part of the community's culture—its ordinary infrastructure and everyday conversation. A concern for character must define a community's sense of "how we do things" and "who we are." Strong character education programs in the schools will play a key part in maintaining this focus on character.

Those cautions notwithstanding, the effort to expand character education beyond families and schools is one of the most promising developments in the national character education movement. Parents and schools need help. The moral development of our children is influenced by the ethical level of the adults they witness and interact with in many situations. As the child moves into the wider world, sociologist David Popenoe observes in *Seedbeds of Virtue,* the moral lessons taught by parents and teachers must be sustained by others.[4] To raise children of character, we really do need communities of character.

EPILOGUE

*I expect to pass through this life but once. If, therefore,
there is any kindness I can show, or any good thing I can
do, let me do it now and not defer or neglect it, for I
shall not pass this way again.*

—WILLIAM PENN

In his book *With Love and Prayers*, F. Washington Jarvis, an Episcopal priest and headmaster for nearly three decades of Boston's prestigious Roxbury Latin School, tells the story of Billy McDonald.[1] Billy was captain-elect of the school's football team and a young man for whom a golden future seemed to be waiting. Then, at seventeen, at the end of his junior year, he was diagnosed with leukemia.

Chemotherapy that summer reduced his two-hundred-pound body by almost a hundred pounds. All of his hair fell out. At first, he was filled with self-pity. Up until this point, everything in his life had gone well for him. Now he was dying.

Then one day Billy visited the hospital's cancer ward for children. There he saw kids two, four, and six years old who, like him, were facing almost certain death from cancer. That night he said to Father Jarvis, "I guess I'm really lucky." "Why is that?" Father Jarvis asked. "At least I've had seventeen years," he said. His eyes filled with tears as he told of an eight-year-old boy who asked him, "Billy, do you think I'll ever play football like you?"

From that point on, Father Jarvis says, Billy was no longer a "victim." He couldn't change his lot in life, but he could choose how he would respond to it. He died the following March, two months before he would have graduated, but he faced his death positively and with dignity.

Life is difficult, full of sufferings large and small—including the final suffering of death. The purpose of life, it has been said, is a life of purpose. What enables us to find a noble purpose for our lives in the midst of life's inevitable trials and disappointments?

Of all the virtues that are part of strong character, the one most essential for a life of purpose is love. Mother Teresa said, "We are created to love and be loved." "We are not called to do great things," she said, "but to do small things with great love."

We don't know from Father Jarvis's account if Billy ever returned to the cancer ward for children. It seems likely that he would have. But even the one visit of which we're told was enough to take him out of himself.

When people came to the great psychiatrist Alfred Adler suffering from depression and feelings of worthlessness, he would ask them, "Do you wish to be cured?"

They would answer, "Yes, certainly."

He would reply, "Then I will prescribe for you a therapy guaranteed to bring results. For two weeks, every day, do something to bring happiness to another person."

If we want happiness for our children, we will try to teach them this wisdom: that to live a meaningful life is to develop their gifts—which requires making the most of their education—and then to use them in whatever way they can to contribute to the lives of others.

Our ability to contribute does not depend on our circumstances. It can be done in times of good health and good fortune; it can be done from a sickbed or a wheelchair. When my wife's mother was dying of cancer, she always brought joy to the hospice workers who came to care for her—by smiling, being glad to see them, and inquiring about their lives. When my friend Jack, at age forty, was suddenly left blind and unable to walk by a virulent attack of meningitis, he overcame a suicidal depression—through what he experienced as a great grace—and subsequently dedicated his life to praying for the needs of others and using his spiritual sight to serve God.

In his 1959 classic *Man's Search for Meaning*, the Jewish psychiatrist Viktor Frankl recounts the horrors of Auschwitz and how, though the Nazis could strip him of everything else, they could not control his mind or spirit. Human beings, Frankl says, within the limits of endowment and environment, become what they make of themselves. "In the concentration camps we witnessed some of our comrades behave like swine while others behaved like saints. Man has both potentialities within himself; which one is actualized depends on decisions, not conditions." Frankl concludes, "After all, man is that being who has invented the gas chambers of Auschwitz; however, he is also that being who has entered those gas chambers upright, with the Lord's prayer or the *Shema Yisrael* on his lips."[2]

As we enter a new millennium, we live in a hurting world, one of great inequities and moral challenges. The richest 20 percent of the planet's population consume 80 percent of its resources. Of the nearly 5 billion people who live in developing countries, three-fifths have no access to basic sanitation. Every day, 24,000 people die of hunger and related causes. Each year, 600,000–700,000 persons contract leprosy. More than 20 million people in the world live as refugees.

We can teach our children—in our homes, in our schools, and in our communities—that they can make a difference for good, starting with what is close at hand. We can bring to the fore what is often hidden: how many ways there are to do good and how much happiness comes to those who extend help as well as to those who receive it. In a culture that increasingly devalues life, we can teach our children to respect and protect the dignity of every life at every stage of development.

Not that it will be easy for them—or us—to overcome, especially in today's hedonistic culture, what Walker Percy called "the suck of self." The darker angels of our nature are ever with us; the quest for character will always be a struggle. But it is a struggle worthy of our best efforts. As we know now, perhaps more keenly than in the recent past, the most important measure of a nation is not its economic wealth, its technological genius, or its military might. It is the character of its people.

THE HILLTOP ELEMENTARY SCHOOL STORY
Lynnwood, Washington
1999 National School of Character
425-670-7604

In the early '90s, Hilltop Elementary School, located in a suburb of Seattle, faced a trend that schools across the country were seeing: growing student disrespect for both adults and peers.

Geri Branch, principal at the time, recalls, "The pressure was on me to be tougher and meaner. But we began to realize that this was a far deeper issue than discipline. We needed to change the idea of what students considered 'cool'—from disrespectful to respectful."

Then Branch read a book on educating for character and offered copies to every interested teacher to read over the summer break. When the faculty returned in September, they decided to pursue character education as the best way to change the culture of their school.

Six years later, in 1999, Hilltop was one of seven elementary schools in the country to be named a National School of Character. Branch and her staff described eleven components as central to their work.

1. *Strong parent involvement.* Parents were invited to evening meetings to get their response to the idea of becoming "a school of character" and were enthusiastic about this focus. Hilltop subsequently invited each family to volunteer in a classroom for two hours per week (75 percent now do). Parents have received weekly letters from the principal and classroom teachers, including suggestions on how to foster a particular virtue with their children at home. When Hilltop teachers retire, both students and their parents are now invited to the farewell appreciation ceremony. Parents say they are grateful to be included.

2. Building a caring school community. Hilltop's motto is: "We are here to learn, to love, to care, to share, and to grow—together." Branch explained:

> We want all of our students to feel valued and connected. As part of that, we try to make sure that every child has a friend in our school. We work on the goal of building community in every classroom. As a school, we now begin each academic year with what we call our New Year's Day Assembly. We introduce new staff and new students. We celebrate being back together as a family. We review school-wide rules regarding respect and responsibility and safety. We ask the children to think about and write down the goals they will work on during the coming school year.

Hilltop nurtures cross-age caring relationships through its buddy system, which pairs an older class with a younger one. The principal also makes an effort to get to know every child personally through her Friday "lunch with the principal." On that day, she eats lunch in her office with thirty-six students, two from each classroom, twelve at a time in three different groups. She says, "I use this time to talk with children about their accomplishments, their interests inside and outside school, and also about the virtues."

3. Class meetings. A Hilltop teacher says, "The class meeting is the backbone of our program." Branch elaborated:

> Our teachers use the class meeting to help children get

to know each other. We do community-building activities throughout the year to help students discover their similarities and differences, likes and dislikes. We use class meetings for paying each other compliments. We use them to discuss how we live together and set up rules. We use them to teach conversation skills such as active listening and looking at the person who's speaking. And we use them to empower children to be problem solvers. If there's a problem with cliques on the playground, or if people are leaving a mess in the classroom after doing projects, those are issues for a class meeting. We ask, "How can we work together to solve this problem?"

Hilltop considered class meetings such an important part of its program that all teachers attended training sessions on how to conduct them. Teachers vary in the meeting format they use and in how often they hold them; some do them daily, others as the need arises. But the expectation is that all staff will use them to intentionally teach the virtues and to give students the experience of democratic participation.

4. *Reflection.* Teachers typically do "reflection time" for the last few minutes of the school day, during which time students use a "levels of responsibility" chart to evaluate their behavior. (See chapter 10 for the details of this process.) Teachers say this time helps children hold themselves and each other accountable to high standards.

Faculty meetings are conducted in a circle to promote a sense of community and good participation. In these meetings, faculty continually reflect on Hilltop's programs, especially the character education effort. Counselor Linda Babin observed, "Reflection at our school has been transformational for both kids and adults. For kids, it helps them to really internalize the virtues. For adults, it enables us to ask, 'What's working? Where are the problem spots?'"

5. *A social skills approach to discipline.* "We now focus on discipline as something we do with our students, not to them," Branch said. "When it comes to discipline, you have to look past what kids are doing and find out *why* they're doing it. We want them to understand why they should behave in a certain way. When they understand that, behavior is much more likely to change."

About 75 percent of Hilltop's approach to discipline is now proactive, teaching social skills.

> We practice manners—saying "please" and "thank you," holding the door for someone coming behind you—all of the time, everywhere in the building. Manners are the glue of our relationships. Visitors always comment on the good manners of our students.
>
> We teach children to make "I statements," for example, "I didn't like it when you did that because . . . ," so that they are able to express their anger in a safe way.
>
> We teach a strategy for solving conflicts: *Stop, think,* and *plan*. Ask, what is the problem? What are some possible solutions? Would a particular solution be fair? Would it work? How would people feel about it? After you try the solution, ask yourself, Is it working? If not, what else could I try? We also do a lot of mediation, helping kids work things out.

6. *The Window Room*. A unique part of Hilltop's approach to discipline is its multipurpose Window Room, a bright, sunny room staffed by two educational assistants with involvement and supervision by the school counselor. Initially, students were referred to the Window Room just for negative behavior, but now they come for a variety of reasons:

> *Cool-down time.* When a staff member is upset with a student's behavior, or when a student is upset about something, the Window Room can be a place for cooling off and getting back to appropriate choices and behavior. Depending on the circumstances, the supervising adult may ask the student to write about what occurred, perhaps offering an apology.
>
> *Interpersonal problem solving.* Students may come alone

or with another person to discuss a conflict they're having. Sometimes an adult guides the student(s) in working out a solution; sometimes they work it out on their own.

Emotional support. Some students come to seek emotional support from an adult regarding a problem they might be having at school or home. Some students are scheduled for weekly one-on-one time with an adult.

Quiet work space. Some students come to the Window Room to find a quiet place to work, away from all distractions.

Alternative to recess. Rather than outdoor recess, many students choose to come to the Window Room to play games, read, do artwork, or just talk to each other.

Positive reinforcement. Staff sometimes send students to the Window Room in appreciation of especially positive behavior or commendable performance in the classroom.

In-school suspension. Occasionally, a misbehaving student is sent to the Window Room as a place to complete assigned work away from the classroom.

7. The Justice Committee. Hilltop's Justice Committee, like the class meeting, teaches students the democratic process. This committee has the job of dealing with school problems that haven't been solved through other school procedures. The principal oversees the committee; students in grades four through six are eligible to serve. Service is considered a responsibility of school citizenship, similar to jury duty. Teachers randomly choose a different student from their classroom every three weeks to take a turn. A student or staff member can present a problem for consideration, and the Justice Committee brainstorms possible solutions. Recommended solutions are then presented to the principal for approval.

For example, Hilltop students typically take a portion of their lunch outside for recess. Litter on the school grounds was making a lot of extra work for the custodian. He took his concern to the Justice Committee, which recommended that all classrooms discuss this problem. The outcome was a schoolwide renewal of the commitment to keeping the grounds clean.

8. A *monthly focus*. "For the first three years of our program," Branch said, "we focused only on respect and responsibility. After a while, it began to sound too routine. We tried doing three virtues a year. That still didn't give us enough momentum. So we went to nine virtues, one a month, with building respect and responsibility as the integrating theme."

September:	Perseverance/hard work
October:	Cooperation/sportsmanship
November:	Service/citizenship
December:	Kindness/caring
January:	Tolerance
February:	Fairness/justice
March:	Courage
April:	Trustworthiness/honesty
May:	Self-discipline

9. *Curricular integration*. Hilltop's faculty regularly integrates character education into reading, writing, social studies, and physical education. One common approach is teaching the virtues through discussing stories, both fictional and those found in the daily newspaper. (Sample assignment: "Be looking for examples in the paper of kindness or cruelty; bring those in to share with the class.") Picture books like *The Empty Pot* (about a boy who had the courage to appear before the emperor with the empty truth) have proved to be a good source of character lessons, and so have chapter books such as *The Witch of Blackbird Pond* and *Roll of Thunder, Hear My Cry*.

Many teachers have students write about the qualities they admire in famous historical and contemporary figures ("I admire Sally Ride because . . ."). One teacher explains, "I move from the study of famous figures to having kids write about their own talents and character strengths. We also bring in multiple intelligences: Are they strong in musical intelligence? Artistic intelligence? Social intelligence? And so on."

Hilltop teachers say that integrating character education has made academic subject matter more meaningful and motivating for children.

10. Recognition. "Many schools rely on extrinsic rewards to motivate good behavior," Branch says, "but we think that can be counterproductive. As a society, we suffer from a preoccupation with 'What will I get for doing this?'" Hilltop stresses social recognition rather than material rewards. Branch commented:

> We are constantly paying attention to positive behavior. If a student holds a door, I'll say, "Thank you for holding the door. That was a very thoughtful thing to do." They're not doing it so much to please you but because they are connected to you. They value the relationship. That's why taking the time to build caring relationships is so important.

Hilltop also has Celebration Assemblies. These recognize students by giving them the opportunity to perform—to do musical recitals, skits, plays, and readings of poems and stories, many of which highlight the virtue of the month. Student performances are then repeated at community events, other schools, and nursing homes.

At the close of the school year, Hilltop has hosted its own Character Education Conference, often with a nationally known presenter. Other schools in the district, and sometimes beyond, are invited to attend. The afternoon includes recognition and appreciation of all the things Hilltop staff do to make the character education program a success.

11. Nurturing transitions. In the past few years, because of retirements and moves, Hilltop has experienced a turnover in approximately half its staff, including bringing on a new principal, Penny Smith. In some schools, staff turnover and especially the departure of a strong principal have spelled the undoing of a character education program. But Hilltop has stayed the course. Counselor Linda Babin says, "In order to support new staff coming on board, we have held monthly meetings to discuss character education strategies and the foundational philosophy underlying our approach to character education. Our new staff have told us that they feel warmly welcomed and supported and that they can see the high level of teamwork and cooperation that goes on among all our staff."

Since Hilltop began its character education program, it has seen not only improvement in students' behavior but also a slow, steady rise in their standardized test scores. Moreover, on a district School Climate Survey, Hilltop ranked above the average in thirty-eight of the forty indicators.

What stands out in the Hilltop story? Two things, both stemming from the principal's thoughtful leadership: the emphasis on community and the emphasis on reflection. No character education program I know of makes the quality of human relationships more central. The priority attached to developing a caring school community pervades everything Hilltop does. When I visited Hilltop a few years ago, the warmth and caring of the school were something you could almost reach out and touch.

No school recognized for character education excellence spends more time on reflection. Hilltop's motto could be, "The unexamined life is not worth living." Class meetings examine the quality of collective life. End-of-the-day "reflection time" examines the level of respect and responsibility exhibited by class members during that day. Academic instruction examines the virtues as they appear in literature, history, current events, and other subjects. The handling of discipline, including the Window Room, gets children to reflect on the reasons underlying a behavior problem they're having and how to solve it. Faculty devote half of their regular meetings to sharing what they're doing in character education and how they can do it better.

These days, time for reflection is an increasingly scarce commodity in schools, especially with mounting pressures from the standards and testing movements. But without reflection time for both students and staff, quality character education is impossible to achieve. Creating a culture of character requires that all school members continually think and talk about how to make the virtues a living matter. Hilltop exemplifies how to do that.

NOTES

INTRODUCTION

1. Robert D. Putnam, *Bowling Alone: The Collapse and Revival of American Community* (New York: Simon & Schuster, 2000).
2. Kristin Anderson Moore and Jonathan Zaff, *Building a Better Teenager: A Summary of "What Works" in Adolescent Development.* Child Trends Research Brief (November 2002), www.childtrends.org.

CHAPTER 1: WHY CHARACTER MATTERS

1. Daniel Goleman, *Emotional Intelligence* (New York: Bantam Books, 1995).
2. Stephen Covey, *The 7 Habits of Highly Effective People* (New York: Simon & Schuster, 1989).
3. William J. Bennett, *The Book of Virtues* (New York: Simon & Schuster, 1993).
4. *101 Giraffe Heroes: Ready-to-Read Scripts About People Sticking Their Necks Out for the Common Good* (Langley, WA: The Giraffe Project, 2001), pp. 7, 37.
5. Dennis Wholey, *Are You Happy?* (Boston: Houghton Mifflin, 1986).
6. Coach John Wooden with Steve Jamison, *Wooden: A Lifetime of Observations and Reflections On and Off the Court* (Chicago: Contemporary Books, 1997), p. 177.
7. Thanks to Spencer Johnson for this felicitous phrase.
8. Louis A. Tartaglia, *Flawless! The Ten Most Common Character Flaws and What You Can Do About Them* (New York: Eagle Brook, 2000), p. 13.
9. William Bennett, *The Index of Leading Cultural Indicators: Facts and Figures on the State of American Society* (New York: Simon & Schuster, 1994).
10. See, for example, David Blankenhorn, *Fatherless America* (New York: Harper Perennial, 1995), and Urie Bronfenbrenner, "Discovering What Families Do," in David Blankenhorn, ed., *Rebuilding the Nest* (Milwaukee: Family Service America, 1990).

11. Center for Academic Integrity, www.academicintegrity.org.

12. "The Wallet Test," *Reader's Digest* (December 1995), pp. 17–18.

13. J. Wechsberg, ed., *The Murderers Among Us* (New York: McGraw-Hill, 1967).

14. B. C. Andrus, *The Infamous of Nuremberg* (London: Fravin, 1969).

15. Eve Fogelman, *Conscience and Courage: Rescuers of Jews During the Holocaust* (New York: Doubleday, 1994), p. 68.

16. Samuel P. Oliner and Pearl M. Oliner, *The Altruistic Personality: Rescuers of Jews in Nazi Europe* (New York: Free Press, 1988).

17. Anne Colby and William Damon, *Some Do Care: Contemporary Lives of Moral Commitment* (New York: Free Press, 1992).

18. Kevin Phillips, *Wealth and Democracy* (New York: Broadway Books, 2002).

19. A 2001 survey conducted for *Seventeen* magazine and the Kaiser Family Foundation reported that 55 percent of high school students said they had engaged in oral sex, compared to 40 percent reporting sexual intercourse.

20. A. Jarrell, "The Face of Teenage Sex Grows Younger," *New York Times* (April 2, 2000).

21. Kathleen Parker, "Even Children Corrupted by Society's Sex Obsession," *Orlando Sentinel* (April 1, 1999).

22. Benedict J. Groeschel, *The Cross at Ground Zero* (Huntington, IN: Our Sunday Visitor, 2001), pp. 60–61.

23. Quoted in John A. Howard, *Detoxifying the Culture* (Baltimore: AmErica House, 2001), p. 180.

24. David Reardon, *Making Abortion Rare: A Healing Strategy for a Divided Nation* (Springfield, IL: Acorn Books, 1996).

CHAPTER 2: RAISE CHILDREN OF CHARACTER

1. Theodore R. Sizer, *Horace's Hope: What Works for the American High School* (Boston: Houghton Mifflin, 1996), p. 25.

2. Cited in Robert Evans, "Family Matters: The Real Crisis in Education," *Education Week* (May 22, 2002), p. 48.

3. Evans.

4. Evans.

5. James Stenson, *Compass: A Handbook on Parent Leadership* (New York: Scepter, 2003).

6. Diana Baumrind, "Early Socialization and Adolescent Competence," in S. E. Dragastin and G. H. Elder, eds., *Adolescence in the Life Cycle* (New York: Wiley, 1975), p. 130.

7. Baumrind.

8. Laurence Steinberg, B. Brown, and S. M. Dornbusch, *Beyond the Classroom: Why School Reform Has Failed and What Parents Need to Do* (New York: Simon & Schuster, 1996).

9. See, for example, Moore and Zaff, *Building a Better Teenager.*

10. Johann Christoph Arnold, *Endangered: Your Child in a Hostile World* (Robertsbridge: East Sussex, UK, 2000; U.S. publisher: Plough, 800-521-8011), pp. 81–83.

11. Gary Ezzo and Robert Bucknam, *On Becoming Childwise: Parenting Your Child from Three to Seven Years* (Sisters, OR: Multnomah Publishers, 1999).

12. Dolores Curran, *Stress and the Healthy Family* (Minneapolis: Winston Press, 1985).

13. Amy Welborn, "Since When Does Indecent Exposure Not Harm Kids?" *Our Sunday Visitor* (June 23, 2002).

14. *America's Youth: Measuring the Risk* (Washington, DC: Institute for Youth Development, 2002).

15. Wooden, pp. 6–7.

16. Originally published by the Christian Action Council but no longer in print.

17. Thanks to Bess Koval for providing the full text of this story and to Lynn White for first recording it as Helena told it to her.

18. Sheila Stanley, "The Family as Moral Educator," in R. Mosher, ed., *Moral Education: A First Generation of Theory and Research* (New York: Praeger, 1980), pp. 341–55.

19. J. M. Wallace and D. R. Williams, "Religion and Adolescent Health-Compromising Behavior," in J. Schulenberg et al., eds., *Health Risks and Developmental Transitions During Adolescence* (New York: Cambridge University Press, 1997), pp. 444–68.

20. Martin E. P. Seligman, *Authentic Happiness* (New York: Free Press, 2002), pp. 59–60.

21. Quoted in William Kilpatrick, *Why Johnny Can't Tell Right from Wrong* (New York: Simon & Schuster, 1992), p. 262.

CHAPTER 3: BUILD A STRONG HOME-SCHOOL PARTNERSHIP

1. For research on the benefits of parent involvement, visit the website of the North Central Regional Educational Laboratory, www.ncrel.org/sdrs/areas/pa0cont.htm.

2. *1999 National Schools of Character* (Washington, DC: Character Education Partnership, 1999).

3. "Benjamin Franklin Classical Charter School," *Schools of Character* (Washington, DC: Character Education Partnership, 1998).

4. Thanks to James Stenson for several of these parent support group suggestions.

5. Rick Allen, "Forging home-school links," *Education Update* (November 2000).

6. Thanks to Peggy Alexander for this idea.

7. For more information about the LAMO program, contact George Keator, LAMO, Box 693, Lenox, MA 02140, 413-637-0468.

8. Cindy Christopher, *Building Parent-Teacher Communication* (Lancaster, PA: Technomics, 1996).

CHAPTER 4: TALK TO KIDS ABOUT SEX, LOVE, AND CHARACTER
1. Bob Bartlett, "Going All the Way," *Momentum* (April/May 1993), p. 36.
2. Abridged from *Choosing the Best* (Marietta, GA: Choosing the Best, Inc., 1998).
3. National Institutes of Health, *Scientific Evidence on Condom Effectiveness for Sexually Transmitted Disease Prevention,* 2000, www.niaid.nih.gov/dmid/stds/condomreport.pdf.
4. *Sex, Condoms, and STDs: What We Now Know* (Austin: Medical Institute for Sexual Health, 2002), www.medinstitute.org.
5. Guenter Lewy, "Religiousness and Social Conduct," paper presented at "Beyond Relativism" conference, George Washington University, June 1999.
6. John R. Williams, "Ethical Sexuality," in T. Devine et al., eds., *Cultivating Heart and Character* (Chapel Hill, NC: Character Development Publishing, 2000), pp. 317–64.
7. Kim Painter, "The Sexual Revolution Hits Junior High," *USA Today* (March 15, 2002).
8. To access data on sexual activity among high school students, visit the Centers for Disease Control website, www.cdc.gov/nccdphp/dash/yrbs/2001/index.htm.
9. Centers for Disease Control, *Youth Risk Behavior Surveillance, Morbidity and Morality Weekly Report* 49, no. SS-5 (June 2000).
10. For poll data, see Tom and Judy Lickona, with William Boudreau, M.D., *Sex, Love & You: Making the Right Decision* (Notre Dame, IN: Ave Maria Press, 1994).
11. Brent C. Miller, J. Kelly McCoy, and Terrence D. Olson, "Dating Age and Stage as Correlates of Adolescent Sexual Attitudes and Behavior," *Journal of Adolescent Research* 1, no. 3 (1986), pp. 361–71.
12. Stan Weed, *Predicting and Changing Teenage Sexual Activity Rates* (Salt Lake City: Institute for Research and Evaluation, 1992).
13. George Eager, *Love, Dating, and Sex* (Valdosta, GA: Mailbox Club Books, 1992).
14. Lorraine Ali and Julie Scelfo, "Choosing Virginity," *Newsweek* (December 9, 2002).
15. Susan A. Walders, "Mourning Life Lost to Hasty Decision," *The American Feminist,* 9 (www.feministsforlife.org).
16. *Sex, Condoms, and STDs.*
17. J. Kikuchi, "Rhode Island Develops Successful Intervention Program for Adolescents," *National Coalition Against Sexual Assault Newsletter* (Fall 1988).
18. D. Orr, M. Beiter, and G. Ingersoll, "Premature Sexual Activity as an Indicator of Psychosocial Risk," *Pediatrics* 87, 1991, pp. 141–47.

19. Josh McDowell and Dick Day, *Why Wait* (San Bernadino: CA: Here's Life Publishers, 1987).

20. David G. Myers, *The Pursuit of Happiness* (New York: Avon, 1993).

21. I'm indebted for the first seven of these "rewards of waiting" to Kristine Napier's *The Power of Abstinence* (New York: Avon, 1996).

22. Thanks to Janet Smith for this point.

23. Statistics taken from *"The NetValue Report on Minors Online,"* Business Wire, December 19, 2000.

24. Sean Covey, *The 7 Habits of Highly Effective Teens* (New York: Fireside, 1998).

25. William Byne and Bruce Parsons, "Human Sexual Orientation: The Biological Theories Reappraised," in *Archives of General Psychiatry* 50, no. 3, 1993, pp. 228–39.

26. Robert Michael et al., *Sex in America* (University of Chicago Press, 1994).

27. Gary Remafedi, "Risk Factors for Attempted Suicide in Gay and Bisexual Youth," *Pediatrics* 87, no. 6 (1991), pp. 869–75.

28. Theo Sandfort et al., "Same-Sex Sexual Behavior and Psychiatric Disorders," *Archives of General Psychiatry* 58, no. 1, p. 89.

29. For reviews of the research literature on the physical and psychological risks associated with same-sex sexual activity, see *The Health Risks of Gay Sex*, by John R. Diggs, Jr., M.D. (available from diggsthis@aol.com), *Health Implications Associated with Homosexuality* (1999) by the Medical Institute for Sexual Health (1-800-892-9484), and, from a Catholic perspective, *Homosexuality and Hope* (2000) by the Catholic Medical Association, P.O. Box 757, Pewaukee, WI 53072.

30. Thanks to Robert Kittel for this point.

31. Scott Phelps and Libby Gray, *A. C. Green's Game Plan Abstinence Program* (Golf, IL: Project Reality, 2001).

32. Mary-Louise Kurey, *Standing with Courage* (Huntington, IN: Our Sunday Visitor, 2002), p. 179.

33. Lance Morrow, "Fifteen Cheers for Abstinence," *Time* (October 2, 1995).

CHAPTER 5: BUILD BONDS AND MODEL CHARACTER

1. Leslie Laud, "The Heart of Character Education," *The Fourth and Fifth Rs* 7, no. 3 (www.cortland.edu/c4n5rs), 6.

2. M. D. Resnick et al., "Protecting Adolescents from Harm: Findings from the National Longitudinal Study of Adolescent Health," *Journal of the American Medical Association* 278, no. 10, 1997 pp. 823–32.

3. Bonnie Benard, "Fostering Resiliency in Kids," *Educational Leadership* 51 (November 1993), pp. 44–48.

CHAPTER 6: TEACH ACADEMICS AND CHARACTER AT THE SAME TIME

1. Theodore Sizer and Nancy Sizer, *The Students Are Watching: Schools and*

the Moral Contract (Boston: Beacon Press, 1999), p. 10.

2. Julea Posey and Matthew Davidson, *Character Education Evaluation Toolkit* (Washington, DC: Character Education Partnership, 2000).

3. Daniel Solomon et al., "A Six-District Study of Educational Change," *Social Psychology of Education* 4, pp. 3–51. See www.devstu.org for a summary of this research.

4. *2000 National Schools of Character and Promising Practices Citations* (Washington, DC: Character Education Partnership, 2000), www.character.org.

5. William J. Bennett, "Moral Literacy and the Formation of Character," in Jacques Benninga, ed., *Moral, Character, and Civic Education in the Elementary School* (New York: Teacher's College Press, 1991).

6. Neil Postman, *Technopoly: The Surrender of Culture to Technology* (Westminster, MD: Vintage Books, 1993), p. 186.

7. Kevin Ryan and Karen Bohlin, *Building Character in Schools: Practical Ways to Bring Moral Instruction to Life* (San Francisco: Jossey-Bass, 1999), pp. 30–31.

8. I am grateful to James B. Murphy for this phrase.

9. Thanks to Mary Beth Klee for her authorship of *The Portsmouth Declaration: A Call for Intellectual and Moral Excellence in School* (Link Institute, www.linkinstitute.org, 2000).

10. Gary Nash et al., *History on Trial: Culture Wars and the Teaching of the Past* (Westminster, MD: Vintage Books, 2000).

11. Keith Windschuttle, *The Killing of History* (Paddington, Australia: Macleay Press, 1966).

12. Charles Johnson et al., *Africans in America: America's Journey Through Slavery* (New York: Harcourt Brace, 1998).

13. Sheldon Stern, "Beyond the Rhetoric: An Historian's View of the Proposed 'National' Standards for United States History," *Journal of Education* (fall 1994), pp. 61–73.

14. Peter Gibbon, *A Call to Heroism: Renewing America's Vision of Greatness* (New York: Atlantic Monthly Press, 2002).

15. Sam Dillon, "Schools Seek Right Balance as Students Join War Debate," *New York Times* (March 7, 2003).

16. Peter Maass, "Emroz Khan Is Having a Bad Day," *New York Times Magazine* (October 21, 2001).

17. Matthew Scully, *Dominion: The Power of Man, the Suffering of Animals, and the Call to Mercy* (New York: St. Martin's Press, 2002), p. 398.

18. Sheldon Berman, *Children's Social Consciousness and the Development of Social Responsibility* (New York: State University of New York Press, 1997).

CHAPTER 7: PRACTICE CHARACTER-BASED DISCIPLINE

1. Thanks to Chip Wood for this sports analogy.

2. For a summary of this story, see Richard Curwin, "The Healing Power of

Altruism," *Educational Leadership* 51 (November 1993), pp. 36–39.

3. For more information about S.T.A.R., contact Dr. John Lutz, Superintendent, Cortland City Schools, Valley View Road, Cortland, NY 13045, 607-758-4100.

CHAPTER 9: PREVENT PEER CRUELTY AND PROMOTE KINDNESS

1. Eli Newberger, *The Men They Will Become* (New York: Perseus Books, 1999), p. 183.

2. Michael Thompson, *Best Friends, Worst Enemies* (New York: Ballantine Books, 2001).

3. Charlene Giannetti and Margaret Sagarese, *Cliques: 8 Steps to Help Your Child Survive the Social Jungle* (New York: Broadway Books, 2001).

4. Dan Olweus, "A Profile of Bullying at School," *Educational Leadership* (March 2003), pp. 12–17.

5. Darcia Bowman, "At School, a Cruel Culture," *Education Week* 60 (March 21, 2001), pp. 1, 16.

6. Eric Schaps, Marilyn Watson, and Catherine Lewis, "A Sense of Community Is Key to Effectiveness in Character Education," *Journal of Staff Development* 17 (Spring 1996), pp. 42–46.

7. Olweus.

8. Olweus.

9. Cited in an ABC television special on bullying, February 2001.

10. Cultural Exchange Entertainment Corporation, 1994.

CHAPTER 10: HELP KIDS (AND ADULTS) TAKE RESPONSIBILITY FOR BUILDING THEIR OWN CHARACTERS

1. Tony Devine, Joon Ho Seuk, and Andrew Wilson, eds., *Cultivating Heart and Character: Educating for Life's Most Essential Goals* (Chapel Hill, NC: Character Development Publishing, 2000).

2. Barbara Lewis, *What Do You Stand For?* (Minneapolis, MN: Free Spirit Publishing, 1998).

3. Ben Franklin quoted in "Benjamin Franklin Classical Charter School," *Schools of Character* (Washington, DC: Character Education Partnership, 1998).

4. Michele Borba, *Parents Do Make a Difference* (San Francisco: Jossey-Bass, 1998).

5. Patricia Cronin, Ph.D., 220 E. Walton, Chicago, IL 60611, 312-337-5836.

6. Borba.

7. Sean Covey.

8. Rachael Kessler, *The Soul of Education* (Arlington, VA: Association for Supervision and Curriculum Development, 2000).

9. Gil Noam, "Reconceptualizing Maturity," in G. Noam and K. Fischer, eds., *Development and Vulnerability in Close Relationships* (Hillsdale, NJ: Erlbaum, 1995).

10. Thanks to Rick Weissbourd's fine article, "Moral Teachers, Moral Students," *Educational Leadership* 60 (March 2003), pp. 6–11 for this point.

11. Thanks to James Coughlin for this point.

CHAPTER 11: MAKE YOUR SCHOOL A SCHOOL OF CHARACTER

1. For the full document, *Eleven Principles of Effective Character Education*, see the Character Education Partnership's website, www.character.org.

2. Charles Elbot, David Fulton, and Barbara Evans, *Educating for Character in the Denver Public Schools: An Implementation Manual* (Denver: Denver Public Schools, 2003), p. 44.

3. Elbot, Fulton, and Evans.

CHAPTER 13: INVOLVE THE WHOLE COMMUNITY IN BUILDING GOOD CHARACTER

1. F. A. Ianni, *The Search for Structure: A Report on American Youth Today* (New York: Free Press, 1989).

2. Phil Vincent, Nancy Reed, and Jesse Register, *A Gift of Character: The Chattanooga Story* (Chapel Hill, NC: Character Development Publishing, 2001).

3. William J. Doherty, *Take Back Your Kids: Confident Parenting in Turbulent Times* (Notre Dame, IN: Sorin Books, 2000).

4. David Popenoe, "The Roots of Declining Social Virtue: Family, Community, and the Need for a 'Natural Communities Policy,'" in Mary Ann Glendon and David Blankenhorn, eds., *Seedbeds of Virtue* (Lanham, NY: Madison Books, 1995), pp. 71–104.

EPILOGUE

1. F. Washington Jarvis, *With Love and Prayers: A Headmaster Speaks to the Next Generation* (Boston: David R. Godine, 2000).

2. Viktor E. Frankl, *Man's Search for Meaning* (Boston: Beacon Press, 1959), pp. 136–37.

INDEX

Contents

Acknowledgments

With the completion of each new book project (this is number twenty), I am made increasingly aware of how much book writing requires team participation. Norma, my wife, is indispensable as editor, rewriter, computer operator, copy editor and encourager, and I thank her for her love and partnership. I would also like to thank CREDO, my publisher, and their staff.

To those in Wycliffe Bible Translators (WBT) and Wycliffe Associates who write advertising copy and handle the important but often unsung task of orders and mailings—thank you!

I wish to thank Dr. Dale W. Kietzmen, Manuel's longtime friend (since 1948) and President of World Literature Crusade, for his valuable insights and suggestions both before and after the completion of the manuscript. Also to Bob Goerz, Mexico's Summer Institute of Linguistics (SIL) Branch Associate Director for reading the final manuscript and his sensitivity to details.

A special word of appreciation must go to Manuel's host of worldwide friends and his American board for their faithful prayers, financial support, direction and encouragement both to Manuel and the Totonac Cultural Center.

Finally, I thank our Heavenly Father for his faithfulness in every area of the Totonac Cultural Center ministry. And I thank Him for Manuel's fidelity to the Gospel and the mandate of the Great Commission. I pray that we who are team members will remain "steadfast, unmovable, always abounding in the work of the Lord."

Prologue

Manuel Arenas, An Instrument For God

What can I do to help my fellow countrymen, my fellow Totonacs? Everything I have done in the past and everything I want to do in the future is designed to help them. The most important thing I can do is to give them God's Word and have them come to faith in Jesus Christ. But I realize that most of my people are poor. They have great physical needs. I cannot make them rich, but I can at least help them in a number of different ways.

Manuel Arenas first spoke these words in 1968 at the beginning of his lifelong dream—a school where young Totonac students could be taught a series of practical skills coupled with an academic and Bible school curriculum. All this to equip Totonacs to minister spiritually and practically among their own people.

This statement of purpose was articulated out of Manuel's personal journey from superstition and fear to spiritual freedom that began in his highland Totonac village of Zapotitlán de Mendez, Puebla, Mexico. Bonded to his culture through his native Totonac language and the demands of his surroundings, Manuel was destined to perpetuate a way of life that had gone unchanged for millenia. But then one day in 1941, two strangers entered his village. Newly married Herman and Bessie Aschmann had responded to what they believed was God's will for their lives and had come to live and work among the highland Totonac people as Wycliffe Bible translators. Their task was to learn the difficult, long-worded Totonac language, reduce it to writing, prepare an alphabet and reading materials and translate the New Testament into the Totonac language.

For this formidable task, the Aschmanns needed help—someone, or several people, who would be predisposed to teach them the language and be willing to struggle with them in couching the meaning of the New Testament words and concepts into meaningful Totonac words and concepts.

Manuel, then only a lad of ten or twelve, was one of these.

Possessed of a winsome personality and quick, inquiring mind, Manuel knew he wanted something more for his life than he was experiencing. Already he had become disillusioned by the great disparity between himself, his people and the wealthy mestizo landowners. The landowners' children always had more food to eat and money to buy trinkets at the general store. And they had warm clothing, particularly warm pants and jackets to ward off the dank, bone-chilling winter winds that swept down the high mountains into the valley.

There was also the disparity between houses. The mestizos' houses, with their several rooms and tile roofs, had windows and doors that opened and closed. His windowless house, always dark and smoky, had bamboo walls and a palm-thatched roof.

But the chief disparity that pained Manuel was language. Mestizo children spoke Spanish; he spoke Totonac, and when he entered the one-room school house in Zapotitlán, he was ridiculed and humiliated for failing to understand the Spanish word for "sit down." Out of that painful humiliation, however, was born a resolve—a resolve to work for justice.

In the book titled *Manuel*, published in 1970, I wrote about the forces that shaped Manuel's early life and ministry, his encounter with Wycliffe translators Herman and Bessie Aschmann, his crisis of faith and confrontation with his father and about a whole new world of friends and ministry that opened to him. This included his schooling, involvement with Wycliffe, the acquisition of land and the beginning of what is now called the Totonac Cultural Center. In the providence of God, *Manuel* is currently in its sixth printing and has been translated into fourteen different languages, including Icelandic and Bahasa Indonesian. Therefore, in the interest of giving you a more in-depth understanding of Manuel—the man and his unique ministry—I invite you to read the book *Manuel* (available through the Book Room, Wycliffe Bible Translators, Inc., Huntington Beach, CA 92647, USA) in conjunction with this, its sequel.

In the spring of 1985, at a special Wycliffe Associates presentation in which Manuel was the featured speaker, Manuel asked me if I would consider writing an update or sequel. "So much has happened since you ended the first book," he said. "God has given me many more special privileges. I have traveled all over the world, including the Soviet Union. I have friends in every country I visited. I would like people to know the results of the works that have been started—of the four dreams the Lord put into my heart: to establish churches, a Bible school, a radio ministry and a ministry to the sick through our clinic. I want people to know because it will strengthen their faith.

"Sometimes when people see a president or a famous doctor or an astronaut they say, 'Look at what he has done!' I don't want that. I am not the one who does the work. I am just an instrument for God. I want people to see the miracles God has done and is still doing among the Totonacs.

"There is another reason I would like the book. Sometimes people have wanted to help my people. They come with plans that are good, but not for Totonacs. I have to say to them, 'These are good plans in your country, but they will not work in the Totonac culture.' And sometimes they don't understand. In this book I want to thank everyone who has wanted to help and everyone who has helped with and prayed for the Totonac people and the Totonac Cultural Center.

"It would be my hope that this sequel to the book *Manuel* will help people everywhere understand all Indian peoples better. All of us have much the same story to tell. All of us share the same hope for the future. And even though Indian peoples were here in the Americas first, I know God has put us all here together. It is my hope that we can all learn to live together in harmony and love."

I shook Manuel's hand and said it would be a pleasure and privilege to once again walk into his life.

In October 1985, I returned to Mexico to visit Manuel and the Totonac Cultural Center. It was immediately obvious that profound changes had taken place since my last visit in 1969, most noticeably the roads. The journey of 160 miles from Mexico City to La Union, the small mestizo town where Manuel's school is located is now reached (part way) over an express tollway. Old landmarks have given way to new cloverleaf systems and access roads. On what had been open grazing land, new towns with unfamiliar names have sprung up. And, of course, the appearance of the school itself has changed.

A new cement driveway leads up to a double garage

and large wrought-iron gate. Students can now play volleyball and basketball on a spacious asphalt court. Lawns were deeper, thicker and greener than I remembered and there were flower beds—Manuel's special preserve—with an abundance of dahlias, camellias, red hibiscus and more. Some trees were struggling to make a comeback after having been frozen in a snowstorm several years before. Solid brick and stone retaining walls looked as if they had always been there, particularly those festooned with flamboyant bougainvillea. And citrus, banana trees and coffee bushes were thriving, providing a modest income for the school.

What began with two small ranch-style buildings has grown to nine buildings which include a large dormitory complex, guest rooms, classrooms and dining rooms for students and staff.

The Bible school, now coeducational, has graduated about sixty students. Of these, thirty-five are pastor-teachers in outlying villages. Three students have gone on for advanced seminary training and the remainder have full-time employment in larger towns. All are in some way actively involved in Totonac churches. When I arrived, eighteen students from five different ethnic minority language groups were enrolled in the program.

A free medical clinic is staffed by a permanent doctor, nurse, many short-term specialists and public-health workers. The week I was there, two dentists from Minneapolis came to conduct a dental clinic. They were replaced several weeks later by a group of doctors from France and the United States.

The school conducts training programs for health workers and maintains a model agricultural farm with a trained staff to assist and encourage Totonac farmers in animal husbandry and crop development. A radio ministry is heard twice weekly by a population in excess of 250,000. A positive adjunct to this ministry has been the sale of Totonac literature and the Totonac New Testament. Manuel, co-translator with Wycliffe's Herman Aschmann, reports sales of the Totonac New Testament to be over 1,000 copies annually.

To implement his vision of establishing churches, Manuel provides funds for the new church buildings in rural areas. To date, there are over 40,000 Totonac believers and forty-six organized congregations. In a style much like his mentor and friend, the late William Cameron Townsend, founder of Wycliffe Bible Translators, Manuel has a genius for starting programs and then delegating leadership and authority to others. It is important to him that the evangelism, Christian education and agricultural programs be continued without his day-to-day supervision.

He is also deeply concerned that Indian leadership be developed from among the Totonac and all Mexico's Indian communities. For this reason, he has encouraged a number of Indian evangelical leaders, pastors, teachers, doctors and lawyers to form an all-Indian fellowship to deal with the many social and economic issues unique to ethnic peoples. He is now this group's elected president. In 1985, seventy Christian Indian leaders from such diverse groups as Zapotec, Mixtec, Amuzgo, Aztec and Totonac met together to plan their strategy on how best to serve their churches and communities.

In June 1985, the John Calvin Theological Seminary in Mexico City recognized Manuel's outstanding leadership, his contribution to Bible translation and the Totonac people by conferring on him the honorary degree of Doctor of Theology.

While I was photographing Manuel holding his newly awarded diploma (beside his beloved flowers), I noticed a young Totonac boy, perhaps twelve or thirteen, picking coffee on a nearby hillside. He was barefoot and dressed in typical Totonac fashion—white wrap-around pants. I couldn't help comparing that young Totonac boy with the man standing before me. A mere forty-plus years earlier, Manuel was a young boy doing the same task and destined by culture and custom to follow the prescribed ways of his people. But then, through Herman and Bessie Aschmann's obedience to God's call to give a nation the New Testament, Manuel was introduced to the Light of the Word. What has emerged from that quiet act is a man who stands out in the midst of his people as a living symbol and example of what God can do with one who chooses to follow and obey Him.

In any summary of a personal history, there is a certain danger of overlooking the important stepping stones, circumstances and interactions with people and events that effect change and growth. I would like to begin this second volume of Manuel's history with an incident that happened late one afternoon in 1972, four years after the school opened. A drama unfolded that would profoundly influence Manuel and his original purpose for the school.

Chapter 1

Conscious Of The Difference

Her clothing was vintage Totonac—a wide, white tubular muslin skirt, the fullness gathered on one side and secured with a red, woven belt that had been given as part of her stipulated dowry. Her blouse was also white muslin and over all this she tied a multi-colored, flowered apron.

Most of her day had been spent grinding corn, patting out tortillas, weeding her small garden, washing clothes in the river and looking after her three-month-old daughter. Yet she had still taken time to weave bright-colored ribbons through her thick, black braids.

This may have been precisely what angered her husband—spending too much time on herself when he thought she should be spending more time gathering wood for the cooking fire.

"You are thoughtless," said the wife to her husband when he returned home from the cornfield without a load of sticks for the cooking fire. "And you are drunk with too much corn alcohol."

"And you spend too much time braiding your hair."

"If you were like other husbands, you would help me more."

It was then the neighbors heard the inevitable—the sharp slap of cold, hard metal against bare skin as the husband struck his wife with the flat side of his machete. There was a terrible, piercing scream. In fact, two. One from the woman and the other from her baby who was strapped to her back. She had been kneeling beside the open cooking fire preparing the evening meal when the argument began. As she started to get up off her knees, her husband struck her across her upper arm, knocking both her and the child into the fire.

One day the woman came to the Totonac Center. It was a hot April day with no breeze, and when Manuel greeted the woman, he was forced to step back, so terrible was the stench.

"When did this happen?" asked Manuel.

"Three weeks ago," said the woman.

"Oh, why didn't you come to see me on the first day? Or even the second? I could have given you some medicine for this wound. Now I can't help you. Not even a doctor can help you. I think you will have to have your arm amputated."

"Oh, no!" cried the woman. "I can't live with only one arm. Who will care for my children? Who will do the work? I am too poor to go to a hospital."

Carefully Manuel explained that there was a government hospital two hours away and they would not charge her for the treatment. "I want to help you," said Manuel. "Here are 300 pesos. Now, please, just forget all about your work and your husband and go immediately to the hospital."

The woman promised she would go in the morning.

About a month later, the sister of this woman came to see Manuel. She told him that when her sister returned home after she had talked with Manuel, her husband asked her where she had been.

"I went to see Mr. Arenas," she said. "He was kind to me and gave me 300 pesos to help me get to the doctors and the hospital."

"Give me the money," said the drunken husband. "You won't need all this. I haven't eaten meat in a month and this will buy me all the meat and liquor I need."

The woman explained that her sister was so ashamed, she couldn't come back to tell Manuel how the money had been spent. "I have come to tell you that both the baby and my sister died two weeks ago."

* * * * *

Manuel related this story to a half-dozen international students from Sweden, Germany and Great Britain who had been attending an international YMCA conference in Mexico City and, at Manuel's invitation, were spending a week at the Center.

"I felt so badly about this woman and her child," Manuel told the students, "it haunted me for a long time. Then I began to think about the possibility of a small clinic at the Center to help people. And although I don't know how it will be done, I am praying and asking my friends to pray that the Lord will help me start a clinic."

With one voice the students said they would pray with Manuel for a doctor or nurse and a supply of medicines. One of the German students, Ernest Engelbert, was particularly moved by Manuel's story and said he would "spread the word" about Manuel's need for a doctor and medicines around his university when he returned to Germany. In the meantime, the students wanted to know more about Manuel, his work and how he felt about being a Totonac Indian.

Manuel exudes a magnetic charisma that is especially evident when he tells his personal story. One is quickly captivated by his intensity, sometimes warm and humorous, sometimes sad and heart-rending, but always positive and confident in the Lord he loves and serves. Manuel continually demonstrates that in all matters of life and faith, Jesus Christ is his Authority, Guide, Friend and Savior; that no matter what occurs—sickness (at that very moment he was struggling with constant pain in his back from a deteriorating disc) or disappointment (he has had several disappointments with friends breaking confidences)—he trusts God and is willing to accept whatever He gives.

With this fundamental premise clearly understood by the students, Manuel began to speak.

"You ask me how I feel about my Indianness. I want to tell you that today, as I speak to you, I am proud of my Totonac Indian heritage. When I go to a government office in Mexico City, or visit the governor of this State of Puebla, or other people in high places, I say, 'My name is Manuel Arenas. I am a Totonac Indian.' Sometimes I will say, 'I am proud of my heritage.' God has given this to me and I also encourage my Totonac friends to be proud of their heritage."

"And are they?" asked a student.

"Some may be, but most are self-conscious about the way they look and dress, and about their language. It is not always possible to be proud and have dignity when you have no shoes or only sandals on your feet, or when everyone else is dressed in Western clothing and speaks a language you don't understand.

"Let me tell you how most of my Totonac friends think. Suppose a Totonac has to go to a government office with a land problem. Or maybe someone has cheated him out of his coffee or falsely accused him. Whatever the problem, I encourage him by offering to go with him to stand beside him or be his spokesman. But when we get to the office, my Totonac friend might say, 'Oh no, I can't go inside. Look at the floor! It is beautiful—all shiny. I have no shoes. I might make it dirty. I might slip.' I say, 'It's all right. Everyone is going inside. Look at the way the people wipe their feet. And you can do the same.'

"On one occasion, a Totonac friend said,'Oh, I can't go to the office, I can't speak Spanish.' I told him it was all right as I would be right beside him and speak for him. But my friend said, 'Even if you stand beside me, how can I tell you what to say? I don't have the words. I don't know how to say what I would like to say. And I am shy and self-conscious about the way I look. Everyone is dressed in nice clothes. I would have to work for years in the cornfields to save enough money to buy nice clothes. No, no, I cannot go. Besides, who in the government will care about me? I am only an Indian. No one cares for Indians.'

"You see," continued Manuel, most of the Totonacs are self-conscious about their Indianness. And even if I promise to go with them to see that justice is done, many still will not go. But I am trying to change this."

"Were you always proud of being a Totonac?" a student asked.

"Oh, no," said Manuel. "When I was a child, I hated my Indianness. My earliest memories include going to the river with my mother and grandmother to wash clothes. In many ways, these were happy times. I could always play my favorite game—marbles, made from guava fruit pits—with other children. To protect me from the sun, my mother would make me a small shelter using the tall grasses and bushes that bordered the riverbank. Here I would sleep and rest when I grew tired. It was here, too, that my grandmother would tell me wonderful stories.

" 'Your great-grandfather told me our ancestors crossed a wide ocean in big canoes from the other side of the world,' she would say.

"This was always a mystery to me. I lived in the mountains and had never seen an ocean or a canoe. Then Grandmother would tell me about the beautiful temples and pyramids my ancestors built. I also had never seen a pyramid but imagined they were like the big Catholic church in town. Only much later, when I saw the great Totonac pyramid complex of El Tajín near the town of Poza Rica, did I understand what my grandmother had told me.

"Grandmother would also stir my imagination with stories about the Spaniards landing at Vera Cruz. 'They built a big city there,' she said 'but they took the best land away from the Totonacs and forced them back to work as slaves. Those who wouldn't work fled into the mountains.' Then lowering her voice and looking from side to side as if checking for eavesdroppers, she would tell me about the wars between the Spaniards and Totonacs. 'Our people had to live in caves and ate only the wild animals they could hunt,' she said. 'And even then, our people only made a cooking fire at night so the enemies could not see the smoke and find them. That was a time of great pain.'

"I never questioned the accuracy of my grandmother's stories. But as I grew older, I began to experience firsthand the reality of her words. I, too, suffered the pain and humiliation associated with a clash of cultures.

"My introduction to this conflict came when I accompanied my mother to pick up laundry from the home of a wealthy mestizo family. Although I was young, I recognized that their polished tile floors, tables and the smell of good things to eat separated me from a way of life different from my own. But the real shock of being different came on the first day of school.

"It was a long walk to the wooden school building from my bamboo house where smoke from Mother's

cooking fire seeped up through the thick, thatched roof
It was a walk that led from rutted, muddy trails to a
wide, cobblestone road lined with stores and shops; a
walk that led to a world where people made fun of the
way Totonacs dressed and spoke.

"The mestizo boys all wore pants and had shoes or
sandals. I was barefoot and wore pajama-like trousers.
They all spoke Spanish and when I spoke, they all
laughed at me.

"Your words sound like animals fighting," they said.

'I knew my Totonac language was different but it was
sweet to my ears and I felt comfortable and relaxed with
it. Why didn't anyone understand this? I walked into
the schoolroom and, not knowing where to sit, stood to
one side facing the teacher.

" '*Sientese* (sit down),' said the teacher.

"I stood where I was and again the teacher spoke to
me. I knew the teacher must want me to do something
because he seemed annoyed and spoke louder. But
unable to understand Spanish, I remained still. Then in
a lowered voice, the teacher repeated the command.
When I still failed to respond, the teacher yelled at me.
And when all the children began to laugh, I was so
ashamed that I ran out of the room and back to my
home. In anguish I explained to my mother that I didn't
understand the language. 'And I want to be dressed like
all the other boys,' I said. 'I want you to buy me some
pants and shoes.' "

Manuel paused in his narrative and said to the
students, "I never realized it before, but I think my
mother felt as much pain as I did that day."

"Did she buy you Western pants?" asked a student.

Manuel gave a faint, reflective smile. "How could
she? Where would she get the money? No, when I told
her I wanted pants like all the other boys, she said, 'It

makes no difference if they laugh. We are Indians. We cannot change our clothes. We have to remain the way your father and all the others dress—like Totonacs.' Even then I continued to ask her for a pair of pants, but my mother just looked sad and said, 'I do not have money to buy you pants. Only the ones who speak Spanish can wear pants.'

When she said this I knew she was right. All the children of those who owned coffee plantations or ran the stores in town spoke Spanish and they all wore pants. And when winter came, all the boys who spoke Spanish had warm jackets while all I had was an old thin blanket."

As painful as this discrimination was for Manuel, he felt he could have endured it if the school teacher hadn't continually made him and others who spoke Totonac feel foolish. Manuel recalls that whenever he had difficulty pronouncing a Spanish word, the teacher made him stand in front of the class and repeat it out loud. If he mispronounced it, the teacher spanked him with a long, wooden stick. And if the teacher caught him speaking Totonac to a friend outside, he did the same thing.* He would stand Manuel in front of the class and make him repeat the Totonac word in Spanish. And again, if Manuel mispronounced it, he was spanked. The teacher did not, or would not, understand that because he only spoke Totonac in the home, he would have extreme difficulty gaining the proficiency demanded.

As Manuel grew older, he observed that many of

---

* Many innovations in Mexico's public education have taken place since Manuel's early school days. The government now has over 25,000 trained bilingual school teachers to serve the rural communities.

those who spoke Spanish not only dressed better, ate better food and had more money, but also had greater privileges and rights. He began to notice that many of his Totonac friends were cheated out of what little money or land they had because they didn't know how to read, or keep accounts, or know the value of money. And if a Totonac happened to protest, the Spanish-speaking person would laugh, shrug and say, "What does it matter? You're only an Indian."

When Manuel was only eight or nine, his father also felt the sting of this injustice. His father owned several acres of prize farmland close to town and many of the mestizos had long coveted it. But his father always refused to sell. One morning as Manuel got ready for school, he was surprised to see his father doing something he had never seen him do before. He was crying. It seems the day before his father had been summoned to town by one of the wealthy landowners. The rich man had given instructions to his workers to get Manuel's father drunk. Manuel's father often sold the family's bananas and eggs to buy liquor, thus when he was offered free drinks, the temptation was too much. When he was drunk, the men brought out a bill of sale for his land, and without his realizing what was happening, they made him put his fingerprint on the paper. As far as Manuel knew, his father was never paid anything for his land.

This picture of his illiterate father crying because he had been cheated out of his land prompted Manuel to begin to think about how he would learn to read and write and help his people. For a long time, however, he thought his dream would never come true. He was thoroughly discouraged by the teacher's continual harassment. Further, his father was not in favor of his schooling and would often say, "Manuel, you will not find what you eat and wear at the school. You will find it only in the cornfield." And so like generations of Totonacs before him, Manuel dropped out of school without learning to read or write and went back to work in the cornfields, because as his father had said, That is what Totonacs do.

Manuel's decision to quit school was a disturbing time for him. At first he didn't or couldn't understand his own feelings. All he knew was that he was ashamed of his Indianness, his Totonac culture and his language. By this time he had picked up some Spanish from playing with other children, but he saw no reason to learn any more. He agreed with his father. The only way to earn money was to work in the cornfields.

It was only after several years of long, hard, toilsome work hoeing corn in the hot sun that Manuel began to wonder what it would be like to go to school at night after his work was done. But there was no night school in his town of Zapotitlán. As he pondered his bleak future—the hoe, the hot sun and his father's increasing anger from too much alcohol—his hopes dwindled. But then something extraordinary happened.

Chapter 2

It's Beautiful To Be An Indian

An early spring morning at the Totonac Cultural Center is a joyous renewal of spirit. It's a kind of mini-celebration of the way life was meant to be experienced. No din of big-city freeways—just the sounds of jungle songbirds that chirp and trill and herald the dawn with unabashed enthusiasm. Beside a gentle brook, an unseen woman adds rhythm by hand-patting tortillas for the morning meal.

Like a sweet elixir, the air around the Center smells clean and fresh, free of the hydrocarbons and nitrogen oxides of heavy traffic. Massive mountains reach tall to the skyline. Above all are giant-pillow white clouds set in a sapphire sky. Finally the warm morning sun creeps gently over the mountain to spill its liquid light into the green valleys. The long, dark shadows of night are gone. A new day has begun.

The five YMCA students had experienced Manuel's gracious hospitality, infectious enthusiasm and winsome storytelling ability the night before. Now, on this their second day at the Center, they were captivated almost seductively by nature in harmony with its eternal purpose—to exhibit beauty and joy for its own sake. The students inhaled the fresh, sweet morning air and walked toward the dining room for the first meal of the day. From behind a screened kitchen door adjoining the dining room, Manuel greeted them with a cheery good morning. Unknown to the students, Manuel was exercising one of his several gifts—cooking. He had prepared their breakfast.

Visitors to the Center who are impressed with the natural, rugged beauty of the countryside, are often equally impressed with the high standards Manuel has set for himself, his staff and students. These standards are immediately evidenced by the immaculate condition of the grounds. One soon learns that Manuel considers it an important tenet of Christian faith to be clean and orderly. Thus, the students give their instructors proper respect and attention. This no-nonsense attitude is further reflected in the dispatch with which the students perform their afternoon work projects. All students help defray their tuition by doing some practical work in the garden or laundry. Some, including the present students, helped prepare the foundations for the new buildings. While all the buildings Manuel envisioned were not yet built in 1972 when the YMCA students made their visit, there was adequate accommodation for staff, students and guests. All this gave the Center the look and feel of a well-established institution of learning.

Adding to this ambience of learning was Manuel's staff, one of whom was, and still is, Felipe Ramos, a handsome, fine-featured, self-effacing, but highly competent Totonac man about ten years Manuel's junior. Like Manuel, Felipe had come to faith in Christ under the influence of Wycliffe translators Herman and Bessie Aschmann. And like Manuel, Felipe had yearned for an education. But while Manuel had obtained most of his education abroad, Felipe had his training in Mexico under the auspices of the long-established school run by the then Mexican Indian Mission, now part of Unevangelized Fields Mission.

Except for a year when Felipe returned to his own village to encourage the struggling believers, he has been Manuel's chief confidant and school administrator. He is as emotionally committed to the school as Manuel and heavily involved in its spiritual leadership and that of the surrounding community. Whenever Manuel leaves the Center for one of his many speaking engagements, or as he likes to call it, "to do my public relations," the responsibility for the Center falls to Felipe. (Felipe is also the pastor of a large church in the town of La Union, and the radio voice of the Totonac radio ministry. More about this later.)

Another staff member who joined Manuel in 1972 is Heinz Steinlein, a burly six-foot-two all-around handyman, master carpenter and electrician. Manuel has many longtime German friends and supporters stemming from his student days at the University of Erlangen. On one of his several trips to Germany, after he had explained his vision of returning to his own people and developing the Totonac Cultural Center, Heinz responded to the challenge of serving the Lord through his practical skills. The bed frames the YMCA students slept on, plus the chairs they sat on in the dining room, were fashioned by Heinz's skillful hands. Heinz would later become Manuel's finance administrator.

Later that morning, after Manuel had finished teaching his class and before he resumed discussion with the students, Manuel said he wanted to explain his teaching methodology.

"I heard some of you say how everything is beautiful here," he began. "How the corridors and rooms have nicely polished tile and how there is no garbage on the floors or in the courtyard. Sometimes when visitors come, they question how anything this clean can be run by Indians. 'Just look at the way some of the Indians live in their villages,' they say. 'There's no sanitation and they live with their animals, including pigs, inside their houses!'

"Now I want to tell you that a pig is a big financial investment. So are the chickens and turkeys. These animals are the Totonacs' bank account. It is the only way they can get any cash. The reason they bring the pigs inside at night is to protect their investment from vampire bats who can transmit rabies. Many times bats suck the blood from sleeping pigs and turkeys—even humans. This causes paralysis and we have had many cases where animals have died.

"I know it is unhealthy for people to live in the same house with their animals. But that is what this school is all about. We want to help our people learn a better way to live. We want to show them how to better protect their investment. And it starts with the knowledge students take back to their villages.

"Another thing I saw adults do when I was a boy in the village was spit on the floor. Everyone spat all over the floor, and I did the same thing. I know this will happen when students first arrive here, but I try to teach them differently. I say, 'If you want to spit, go outside. And if you don't want to go outside, take a piece of paper and spit into it, then put it in a wastebasket so it can be burned.'

"After the first week when I notice the students' unmade beds and messy rooms, I have a little lesson on housekeeping. I go to their rooms and say, 'I am here to make your bed.' When I make it, I say, 'Now doesn't that look better?' Next I take a broom and say, 'This is a broom. I am going to sweep your floor.' After it is clean I say, 'Now, doesn't that look better than before? From now on I want you to do this for yourself. I have taught you to make your bed and sweep the floor so that your house can look like mine.' "

One of Manuel's goals is to have the students adopt a new awareness of their dignity as persons and as young men and women made in the image of God. To them, this is a profound, almost incomprehensible theological concept. Yet a person who has identified himself with Jesus Christ as Savior and Lord should exemplify a lifestyle markedly different from those who are living their lives independently of God. Manuel describes this dignity as having a good testimony before the Lord and a watching community and sets an example by his personal hygiene and cleanliness. He is also willing to pick up a discarded banana skin or any other unsightly trash that would mar the testimony of the school.

Generally, Manuel concludes his practical lecture on housekeeping by reminding the students that cleanliness and good hygiene should be a natural, normal part of their everyday lives at school and at home in their villages. "Remember, when you go home, I want you to be clean there just as much as you are here. Some people think only a mansion should be clean. No. If you only live in a bamboo house, it should be clean and orderly, too."

"I told you yesterday," said Manuel as he continued talking to the YMCA students, "I am now proud of my Indian heritage. At every opportunity I try to encourage the students and other Totonacs to be proud of their country and their distinction as Totonacs. For example, if a man comes to me and says, 'I am just an Indian. Who will care about what happens to me?' or if I sense this man is ashamed of himself for being an Indian, I say to him, 'You are a Christian (even if he isn't, I say the same thing). Isn't it wonderful you know the Lord and He can help you with your problems? It is God's design that you were born Indian. He is the One Who allowed you to be born into this world as an Indian. Therefore, in the eyes of God, it is a beautiful thing that you are an Indian. Now don't be ashamed.' "

Another way Manuel builds self-esteem among the Totonacs is to remind them of the wonderful Totonac pyramids of El Tajín. (These are different from the Aztec pyramids in the valley of Mexico.) He tries to take his students on field trips and suggests that all Totonacs go there if they can. "I want to remind them their ancestors were skillful artisans. They carved beautiful designs and hieroglyphs into great blocks of stone. These stones weighing many tons were quarried and cut with amazing precision. I tell the students the Totonacs were marvelous engineers. They cut these stone blocks with only small hand tools like a hammer and chisel. And then they rolled these huge stone blocks many miles to the building site at El Tajín. When I tell them this they always feel better about being Indians."

"Now I must tell you again," said Manuel to the YMCA students, "I did not always feel this way. Once when I was in Mexico City as a young man going to school, someone asked me if I was an Indian. I was indignant! 'I am not an Indian,' I said. 'I am a Mexican just like everyone else born in this country!'

"Of course, I was right. I am Mexican, but I am also Indian. I wish now I could meet that person and apologize to him. But I am getting ahead of myself. Let me go back in my story when I was about age ten. That was the time when an American came to live in my town of Zapotitlán. His name was Herman Aschmann. We all called him Don Pedro. He told us he had come to learn our language. At first I didn't understand what he meant by translating our language and putting it into the New Testament—God's Book.

"But that didn't matter. It was exciting just to have this man and his wife Bessie come to live in our village. I came as often as I could to stand outside his window or sit in the doorway to observe how they lived. To my disappointment, Don Pedro asked my friend Fulgencio to help him learn our language. But that didn't stop me from visiting and watching. As the months passed, I found a great desire awakening in me as I saw them work together. The books on Don Pedro's desk fascinated me. When no one was around I would sometimes touch them and look closely at them. I would think, If only I could learn to speak and read Spanish, I could understand them. I thought of going back to school, but I knew that was impossible.

"Then a series of events took place that changed my life. One day Fulgencio was hoeing corn on a steep mountain patch. Suddenly he lost his footing. In one terrible moment, he slipped and tumbled down the mountain and landed on some rocks. The people of the village carried him home. But there was no doctor. No one knew how to help him. A few days later Fulgencio died. I know now it was from internal injuries.

"Perhaps a week went by and one morning when I happened to visit Don Pedro, he asked me if I would like to take Fulgencio's place and help him continue to learn our language. 'I need someone to help me translate the New Testament,' he said. I was thrilled with this unexpected opportunity. It was hard work and I was sometimes discouraged. But Don Pedro was always patient and encouraged me when I didn't understand.

"As the months passed, I began to realize these words we translated together were wonderful and powerful words. These words that had come from God were challenging me to obey them. Don Pedro also spoke to me about how God had sent his Son, Jesus Christ, into the world to make all people—even Totonacs—right with God. He told me if I believed in Jesus Christ, God would come to live in my heart.

"The only problem I had with this was that in our home my mother had eighteen dusty gods. They were neatly arranged on a shelf over an open fire pit and were very black from smoke. Don Pedro had told me there was only one true God and, as I pondered this, a great conflict began to arise in my mind. Who was right? Don Pedro or my mother with her eighteen gods?

"One day I determined to discover the truth. Choosing the largest of my mother's sewing needles, I plunged the needle into the foot of the biggest god. I expected something to happen, but nothing did—other than breaking the needle into several pieces. All I could see was a gouge in the wooden foot. There was no blood, no cry of pain. I knew the god wasn't alive.

"At that moment my mother came in and when I told her what I had done, she was visibly shaken. 'Manuel,' she said, 'You will surely die. This is a wrong thing you have done.' Even though I had proven to myself that the gods weren't alive, I was frightened by her words and ran all the way to Don Pedro's house.

"Don Pedro had some visitors and when I told him what I had done and how frightened I was, he shared this with them. Then Don Pedro translated while one of the visitors, Jack Wyrtzen, sat with me and explained more about what it meant to be a Christian.

"That was a wonderful day! The Scriptures that Don Pedro and I had been translating suddenly became clear to me, and I accepted Jesus Christ as my Savior.

"I returned home to find my father very angry with me. He told me I was foolish for spending so much of my time with Don Pedro. 'I was pleased when you gave up the foolish notion of going to school,' he said. 'I told you before, you will not find what you grow or eat there. You will find it only with me in the cornfield. Look at me! I am not starving. Look at my clothing! Look at my house! I do not know how to read or write, yet I have all these things.'

"He blamed Don Pedro for the abnormal amount of rain we had that season. 'His presence in our village has disturbed and angered the ancient gods,' he said. Then my father told me I had also disturbed the gods by believing in a new way, and I would be punished.

"I tried to reason with my father, but it was no use. For more than a week we argued. Finally my father's patience was exhausted. 'The whole village talks and laughs about my son who has chosen to follow a new way,' he said. 'Now I give you thirty minutes to make up your mind. Give up this foolishness. Come back and worship the master gods with your mother, and come to work with me in the cornfields. If you do not, you must leave this house and take nothing with you.'

"I knew it would be impossible to say anything more. Reasoning was pointless. I did as my father commanded and walked out of the house. The Aschmanns took me in. I must tell you I did go back to my house every day to see my mother. I would hide in the bushes and wait until my father left for the cornfields. Then, when I knew he was well on his way and no one else was around, not even my sister or brother, I would go and talk to my mother.

"She was upset with me and urged me to apologize to my father and come back home. I knew I could not do that. Little by little I told my mother about my new faith.

As the months passed, she began to believe. Don Pedro's wife, Bessie, also talked to my mother and eventually my mother became a Christian, too.

"At first I wondered what she would say to my father and what she would do with the old gods. My mother was a wise woman. She felt it was important not to anger my father and left the gods as they were, but didn't worship them. At the same time she was eager to learn all she could about her new faith and no longer urged me to give in to my father and return home. She accepted my decision to break, not just with the old religion, but with the old family ways that might hold me back from doing what God wanted me to do. And what I felt He would have me do was go to Mexico City and get an education.

* * * * *

Within a year of the bold stroke with his mother's darning needle, a stroke that challenged the walls of custom and tradition, Manuel made another life-changing decision. With the help and encouragement of the Aschmanns, he enrolled in a school in Mexico City. His dream of getting an education had begun. Four years later, after learning Spanish and taking a series of special courses and examinations, Manuel completed his requirements for primary and secondary school. He was now ready to pursue higher education. The year was 1950.

When he was not quite twenty-one, and after spending two years at a Mexico City business college, Manuel was given the opportunity to attend Prairie Bible Institute in Three Hills, Alberta, Canada. Manuel remembers that experience as one in which he spent most of his time learning to speak English.

Curiously, when Manuel applied for a Mexican passport to travel to Canada, he had difficultly pinpointing his precise birthdate. With the help of the Aschmanns, he pieced together stories and events and fixed his birthday as June 17, 1932, realizing that he was probably named after a patron saint. (Every day on a Mexican calendar is marked with the name of a different saint.) While this is Manuel's "official" birthdate, he feels he probably was born a year or two earlier.

After an academic year at Prairie, Manuel enrolled in Dallas Bible College in Dallas, Texas, and graduated in 1957. "I began to understand who I was," said Manuel. "I was a true believer in Jesus Christ. He was my Lord. This meant I was equal in his sight with all other believers, no matter what language they spoke, or what country they came from or what color their skin. They knew the Lord, and so did I. When I understood this, I was freed from my inferiority complex and self-loathing. It no longer mattered what people said to me or how they treated me. I was free because I was bound forever to the truth of Jesus Christ."

It was also at Dallas that the vision for a Totonac Bible school began to form in Manuel's mind. The first inkling came one day when he was listening to a sermon in Spanish. How good it would be, he thought, if the Totonacs could hear such a message in their own language! But, of course, that was impossible. Any Totonac who left his village for training in a Spanish seminary or Bible school would naturally minister to a Spanish-speaking congregation in a Spanish-speaking village or town.

Manuel kept that thought to himself for several years. And then one day while he was hiking through his home mountain area during a break from his studies, he realized the Totonacs themselves were the logical ones to minister to other Totonacs. They, after all, knew the countryside, culture and language better than any outsider. And they were conditioned from childhood to the steep mountain trails that left most outsiders breathless before they had spent thirty minutes on the trails.

Thus Manuel reasoned that he himself should be part of the solution and that he should multiply himself by starting a Bible school where young men could be trained as preachers and evangelists to minister to outlying villages. All this Manuel vowed before the Lord that day. But part of the vow included a petition that God would continue to help him get a higher education. At last Manuel had a clear picture of God's purpose for him and his talents.

For the next three years, including summer school, Manuel studied at the University of Chicago. To pay his way, he worked as a cook at the Hilton Hotel. These were happy and enriching days for Manuel, but then an accident almost ended his dreams.

One cold, winter Sunday night, Manuel and several of his friends were returning to Chicago on motorbikes after spending a weekend at a Wisconsin Christian retreat center. By his own admission, Manuel lacks athletic dexterity. Nonetheless, his friends had taught him to ride and he had learned well, without mishap, until that Sunday night.

Shortly after entering the Chicago city limits, Manuel rounded a sharp curve and suddenly came upon a patch of ice. In one frightening moment, he lost control of his bike and was flung sixty feet down the road. Badly bruised, with a serious back injury, he was taken unconscious to a nearby hospital.

This was the second time Manuel had injured his back. The first was years before in Mexico while he was painting the newly constructed SIL linguistic workshop and translation center at Ixmiquilpan. On that occasion, Manuel stood on a stool to paint a ceiling, overreached and fell. The result was a broken back that confined him to a body cast for six months.

Fortunately, Manuel's back wasn't broken in this second accident although he did spend three weeks in the hospital in yet another body cast.

The accident, however, did not keep Manuel from receiving an accredited Bachelor of Education degree from the University of Chicago. And because he had excelled in his German language studies, he received a scholarship to do graduate study at the University of Erlangen in Germany. It was there he fell a third time, ice skating.

Chapter 3

I Am Ready To Go With You

The letter with a German postmark wasn't unusual. Manuel regularly receives mail from Germany—and from France, the USA, Canada and from literally all over the world. Its significance was that it was a direct answer to prayer from a completely unexpected source. In part, the letter read:

> Dear Professor Manuel Arenas:
> My name is Karl Heinz Schmalenbach. I recently graduated as a medical doctor. For some time I have been burdened to obey our Lord's command to "go into all the world and preach the Gospel."
> Several weeks ago I saw my friend, Ernest Engelbert. He told me of his visit with you while he attended the YMCA conference in Mexico City and how you have been praying for a medical doctor who would come to your school and help start a clinic. I am very interested. What would be the requirements?

The principal requirement, above competence and a desire to help people, would be for the doctor to provide his own financial support. Manuel had long understood the place of faith in mission outreach. He had seen the Lord provide month by month, year by year for so many of his Wycliffe friends and colleagues, and indeed for his school and personal needs. Although there were moments in this walk of faith where there was barely enough to meet current expenses, God had always proved faithful and provided. Usually monetary gifts came from friends who had caught his vision for the Totonacs.* Manuel knew it would be difficult to explain this in a letter to someone who was perhaps unfamiliar with the notion of living by faith and who might be expecting a salary. Since he was scheduled to speak at several youth clubs in Europe, he wrote the following reply to Dr. Schmalenbach:

> I am happy the Lord has burdened you to go into all the world with the Gospel. I am happy also that you have an interest in helping the Totonac people. There are many details about the clinic I would like to talk over with you, but I think it would be best to meet you in person.
>
> Since I have been invited this summer to speak at a multinational youth conference in Paris, Switzerland and Holland, it would be easy to meet you at your home in Germany. Then I will be able to answer all your questions.

"The difference between a man age forty and one half that age," said a wise sage, "is mostly experience." In the summer of 1974, at age forty-two, Manuel went to Europe bubbling with energetic enthusiasm. Admittedly, not with the same kind of physical vigor reserved for a

* In 1972, four years after the Totonac Cultural Center began, longtime friends Wallace McGehee and Bill Butler (now chairman of Manuel's board), encouraged Manuel to form a nonprofit corporation in the U.S. To channel funds, Manuel now has a legal board in the United States made up of missionaries and businessmen. Gifts for the Center are tax-deductible and may be sent to: Totonac Center, P.O. Box 2050, Orange, CA 92669.

person half his age. He had, after all, suffered three
serious back injuries—one in Mexico, one in Chicago
and another while ice skating in Germany where he
had spent several weeks in a hospital. Yet even with
these and other assorted ailments and mishaps, Manuel's
enthusiasm was in no way diminished. He was caught
up with the grand sweep of an idea—the idea that
through his Center, Totonac men and women could be
trained to handle the translated Totonac Scriptures
and thereby effect a positive change among his people.

Manuel had gained further experience as a world
traveler and speaker in his capacity as a kind of
ambassador-at-large for Wycliffe Bible Translators
and Wycliffe Associates (a lay service arm for Wycliffe).
In 1964-1965, he served at the "Pavilion of 2,000 Tribes"
during the New York World's Fair. Additionally, he,
with Dr. George Cowan (then Wycliffe's president) and
other Wycliffe personnel, traveled throughout the
United States and Canada speaking in colleges, universities, Bible schools and churches. (In March 1986, he
was presented, along with Elaine Townsend—wife of
Wycliffe's founder—to the mayor of Winnipeg, Mani-
toba and that province's lieutenant governor in special
ceremonies to inaugurate an annual Bible Translation
Day. In July 1986, he was a delegate to "Amsterdam
'86.") Such repeated exposure to men and women at all
levels of commerce and government has given Manuel
a beguiling presence—a presence that combines child-
like wonder with astute tough-mindedness. Such
mental acumen often surprises those who view him as
an interesting curiosity or "just an Indian from Mexico."

In attendance on the evening Manuel spoke to the
youth club in Switzerland, was a young man who had
come to the rally at his fiancée's invitation. When the
meeting ended, he held back and waited until most of

the well-wishers had spoken to Manuel. At an appropriate lull he and his fiancée introduced themselves. The young woman expressed her happiness that the Totonacs had the New Testament in their own language. "How wonderful there are so many believers in Jesus Christ," she said.

But when her fiancé spoke to Manuel, he expressed no such appreciation. Instead, he said, "Can I ask you a question?"

"Certainly," said Manuel.

"In your talk you said you were glad this Bible translator had come to your village; that if he hadn't come, you probably would never have heard about Jesus Christ."

"Yes, that's true," said Manuel. "The man's name is Mr. Aschmann and—"

"That's very nice," interrupted the young man, 'but what I would like to know is why you gave up your religion in favor of this Western religion. Why is it so important for the Totonac people to know about Jesus Christ and Christianity? It's my opinion that if Western man wants to believe this sort of thing, it's okay. But the Totonac people have their own religion. It's just as good as Christianity—maybe even better. Why do you want your Totonac friends to believe like you? I'm sorry, but I just can't believe Christianity is better than your Totonac religion."

"Tell me," said Manuel, "do you know what Totonacs believe? Have you lived in a Totonac house to see how our household gods are worshiped?"

"Well, no, not exactly. But I have read some books—"

"And I have also read books," said Manuel. "Books that describe what our people look like and what they wear, how we build our houses and how weddings and funerals are conducted. These books also tell others what we believe, but what these books can never tell is how we feel down deep inside. We may look happy on the outside and we may laugh, but inside we are a people who have deep churnings, and nervousness and mistrust of others. And many have a great fear of the gods and spirits that live in special trees and rocks and streams."

"But that's just harmless superstition," said the young man.

"Let me give you an example of what it is like to live with what you call 'harmless superstition,'" said Manuel. "When you are thirsty, you take a drink of water whenever you want. But in my village, if you are thirsty at high noon, you must wait. You must wait because the people believe the lords of the water and the nearby stream take away the spirit of the person who drinks water at high noon. If they do happen to take a drink of water at that time, the person becomes sick. The witch doctors are called, candles are lit and special flowers and spices are spread around the sick person. A chicken is sacrificed and the blood poured out on the ground. Maybe the witch doctor will come four or five times and, after about a week, he will tell the sick person that his spirit has returned and he is better. All this is paid for by the sick person's family.

"I grew up fearing the many evil spirits of the forest, of the stream, the earth and trees. I saw how strong they were and how they bullied those who sacrificed to them. But when the New Testament Scriptures were translated into our language and Totonacs began to believe and accept Jesus Christ into their lives, I saw those fears gradually disappear. This is why I want all Totonacs and everyone to become true believers in Jesus Christ. Only He can take away fear and give hope and peace, for this life and for the true life to come."

And so Manuel and the young man talked. Manuel carefully and enthusiastically explained the personal benefits he had received since accepting Jesus Christ into his life. But beyond the personal enrichment of spirit, the maturity and growth and an enlarged world view, Manuel emphasized that authentic Christianity had little to do with religion, traditions or moralizing. Rather, he stressed that Christianity had to do with truth, compassion and love—love of God and his Son, Jesus Christ. A love so strong and full of integrity that it allows the true Christian to treat his neighbor as he himself would like to be treated.

Manuel has been involved in hundreds of similar conversations, from humble Totonacs to sophisticated doctors and lawyers, to students, scholars, businessmen and young children. Most listen attentively. If there is a debate, it is conducted with respect and an honest attempt to understand Manuel's flow of logic and reasoning. While this particular young man treated Manuel with respect, he was nonetheless skeptical and, for the most part, argumentative. Finally at 2:00 a.m., when Manuel realized the conversation had broken down, he signaled his need to retire. "Because we are arguing," said Manuel, "I don't think we should continue talking. I am interested in logical debate, but nothing is achieved by arguing. If you don't want to believe, I can't make you believe. Besides, I don't want to damage my friendship or trust with you. I am tired and must go to bed. Before I go, I would like to know why you came here tonight. And also, I would like to know your decision. Is it yes or no? Are you ready to accept Jesus Christ into your life and heart?"

"I am sorry if you think I have been arguing with you just for the fun of arguing," said the young man. "Perhaps this is a European trait to argue when we are trying to understand something new. It helps to clarify one's thinking. I came tonight because I heard an Indian would be speaking and I was curious. I wanted to see what you looked like and hear what you had to say."

"You have heard me speak and you now know what I look like," said Manuel, "but you haven't told me your decision. Is it yes or no? Would you like to become a Christian like your fiancée?"

The young man paused, turned and looked at his fiancée, then looked at Manuel. "Of one thing I'm certain," he said, "My fiancée is different from any other young woman I have ever known. You ask me to make a decision—yes or no. My decison is yes. Yes, I would like to become a Christian like my fiancée."

"Wonderful," said Manuel. "I will guide you in a little prayer and you can ask the Lord Jesus to come into your heart."

The meeting in Wochum, Germany with Dr. Karl Heinz Schmalenbach and Manuel was warm and cordial. Manuel was impressed with the doctor's zeal to participate in the "Great Commission" and his record of past service. He was active with Campus Crusade, Navigators and other Christian organizations. "Jesus Christ is the way to God," said the young doctor, "and out of love and obedience to Him, I find it imperative to be a part of world mission."

Manuel explained what the doctor should expect if he decided to come. "We have only a small room," said Manuel. "It is a new room built by students from Le Tourneau College in the United States, but we don't even have a desk for you to write on or an examination table. There is no x-ray equipment or special equipment for maternity care. We do have some medicines and can get more. In time, however, we will grow as others learn about our needs."

Then Manuel explained about finances. Did he fully understand the need for friends and a home church who would be willing to participate as his support team and underwrite his personal financial expenses month by month? Dr. Schmalenbach smiled and said matter-of-factly, "Yes, and I am ready to go with you to Mexico when you return."

Clearly the doctor was a man who wanted to explore new avenues of service for his Lord. But there was one obstacle—his mother. She was upset at the thought of her son going to a faraway land to live among people she knew nothing about. The doctor was of age and could easily have overruled her objections, but he was a sensitive son and wanted his mother's approval.

Ever the diplomat, Manuel assured the mother that her son would be perfectly safe at the Totonac Cultural Center. He explained the area was not unlike some areas of Austria with meadows, deep valleys and mountains. "I have a book written about me," said Manuel. "It has been translated into German and it will help you understand how God has called me to minister to my own people."

After reading the book *Manuel*, the doctor's mother thanked Manuel for helping her understand what her son would be experiencing. She promised to pray daily for both Manuel and her son. "That will be wonderful," said Manuel, "And in six months, the Lord willing, your son will return to you."

And that's exactly what happened. In one of his 1974 newsletters, Manuel hinted at the impact Dr. Schmalenbach was having on the Totonacs and they on him.

A few days ago, Dr. Karl Schmalenbach left for Germany. He had worked at the Totonac Cultural

Center for six months as a medical doctor. Three days before he left, the Christians brought chickens, eggs and all kinds of fruit. They were grateful for the many ways he had helped them and wanted him to take these gifts back to Germany.

It was hard to say good-bye to all the Christians the doctor had grown to love. He helped them not only physically, but spiritually as well. Before he left, Dr. Karl made sure that another doctor would come and take his place.

Dr. Schmalenbach was innovative in his ministry. When he noticed orange trees and chickens in the area, he suggested the children should eat more fresh fruit, eggs and poultry to help alleviate their rickets-like problems. He soon discovered, however, that he had placed the parents in a difficult position. Money from the sale of these goods bought staples and clothing. Many Totonacs thought his notion of using their cash crops for food was foolish. With time, however, many began to understand the doctor was right. They wanted the children to be strong and healthy and began to make this sacrifice for them.

Dr. Schmalenbach went further in his medical innovation and suggested to some Totonac men that to have ten, twelve or fourteen children caused economic strain. He also pointed out how much stronger their wives would be, and would indeed live longer, without the heavy burden of repeated pregnancies and the care of so many children.

The Totonac men listened to this well-intentioned young man, but inwardly they knew, because he was from the outside, he didn't understand the social dynamics involved in the need for large families. A Totonac's manhood was linked to the size of his family.

A man with a small family was often ridiculed by his peers for being an inadequate man.

On the other hand, as the doctor said, a large family did strain the food supply. Often children in a large family had nothing to eat for days but black coffee and a few tortillas. This usually occurred just before the new crop of corn was mature enough for harvest.

It was also true many children died. As many as half the children born alive died within the first few weeks of birth. Those who survived the trauma were again at risk when they were weaned, usually directly from mother's milk to diluted coffee and perhaps a softened tortilla. The preteen years offered yet another threat—childhood diseases. These so-called simple diseases—mumps, measles and chicken pox—became disastrous. Particularly was this true where there were complications from malaria, typhoid, worm infestations and vitamin deficiencies. Manuel understood this well. Of his eight brothers and sisters, half died. Yet the people insisted that many children, besides establishing one's manhood, also guaranteed that some would survive to care for them in their old age and continue the honor of the family name.

Dr. Schmalenbach didn't know it then, but he had planted a seed, an idea that would take about ten years to grow and become strong enough to challenge and break through this age-old notion and tradition that a large family signified a *macho* man.

Meanwhile, word was spreading about the dramatic results of clinic treatment. Doses of piperazine medicine, for example, eliminated the worm infestation that sapped strength from so many people. Other medicines eliminated the serious hookworm infestation. And while many people were nervous about receiving injections, those who did bare their arms for the prick of an antibiotic injection and then began to supplement their diets with vitamins and iron pills, claimed remarkable results. Many testified that after a few short weeks they were stronger than ever and could hike over steep trails with an energy they had long forgotten.

Sometimes both the doctor and patient were puzzled over each other's medical procedures. One of the first times Dr. Schmalenbach asked a Totonac man to disrobe for a physical examination, he found little bunches of wild greens tied by a cloth to the man's stomach, hips and small of his back. Puzzled, Dr. Schmalenbach asked Manuel to investigate. "I don't need to ask why he has done this," said Manuel. "This is the way many Totonacs treat a fever."

And so it went. The doctor built confidences and trust as he treated cuts, fevers, typhoid, malaria, administered worm medicine, gave injections and encouraged the people in personal hygiene and sanitary food preparation. After several months, the trickle of nervous patients who visited the clinic swelled into over a hundred patients per day. At one point Manuel became alarmed when he observed the doctor's repeated procedure of starting early in the morning and working almost non-stop into the evening to make sure everyone was helped.

"I didn't invite Dr. Schmalenbach here to become sick," Manuel would say to the people. "I invited him here to help me help you. To do this he must be in good health. So please come back another day."

Manuel's dream and response to human need has developed into a well-established and well-equipped public health center. After Dr. Schmalenbach, a series of doctors, nurses, lab technicians and dentists came from Germany, the U.S., Canada and many other countries. Annually, the Christian Medical Association, headquartered in La Mirada, California, sends a team of specialists (heart, lung, bone, etc.). Rotary International, with headquarters in Evanston, Illinois, through its Rotary Club of Ventura, California, and others, have also played an important role in the ongoing medical ministry to the Totonac community.

The week I spent at the Totonac Cultural Center gathering material for this second book, two highly-qualified dentists from Minneapolis, Dr. Bill Johnson and Dr. Ralph Swenby, did what Dr. Schmalenbach had done—worked nonstop throughout the day. Using two dental chairs, they worked smoothly and with good humor extracting, filling and repairing chipped and broken teeth. Repairs were made with the latest light-cured bonding compounds. Two young female students from the Center acted as dental assistants.

Along with this free medical treatment, the patient receives a simple word of testimony, either from the doctor or dentist (if he knows Spanish) or from one of the school's attending students. Manuel himself frequently stands outside the clinic and greets those who have been treated. "A doctor is good," he will say. "Medicines are good, and if you have health, that is good. If you have land or money and equipment and livestock, all that is good. But what is more important, and best of all, is for you to know the Lord Jesus Christ. He is the Creator and Savior of the world and He loves you very much."

After this straightforward, unadorned statement of fact, many Totonacs ask him to tell them more. They know about Mary and the church saints, but don't understand about Jesus being Lord and the Creator of the universe.

When Manuel asks if they would like God to make Himself known in their hearts and lives by believing in Jesus Christ, many say yes, they would. As is his practice, Manuel follows this invitation by saying, "If you want to become a Christian, you must ask the Lord into your life by a prayer."

The standard reply to this instruction is usually, "What should we say? We don't know any such prayer." To which Manuel replies, "Yes, I know, but now I will teach you how to pray. You don't have to pray long prayers for God to hear you. All you have to do is repeat the words I am going to say. 'Lord, I never heard about You before. But now I understand and believe You died for my sin on the cross so that I can have eternal life. I now accept you into my life as Lord and Savior.' "

On one occasion after the clinic had been established for several years, Manuel related to a group of visitors how he shares his faith with those who come for treatment. One man cynically responded by saying he thought the whole procedure was a bit simplistic. "If indeed such people truly become born-again Christians," he said, "how do they grow spiritually? What kind of follow-up do you have?"

"I am glad you asked that question," said Manuel, "because now I can explain about the church and the Totonac radio ministry."

Chapter Four

If You Give Me The Walls, I'll Give You The Roof

Except for fragments of uncertain accuracy taught to him by his grandmother, Manuel had little sense of history to guide him. Not until he began his formal education did he discover the biographies of great Mexican heroes. These were to provide the insight he needed to understand something of his own place and responsibility in the stream of Mexican history.

For Manuel, one of the most significant actors on the complex stage of Mexican history was the late President Benito Juarez. Perhaps because they share many commonalities, including looks. Like Juarez, Manuel has a stocky body, a round face with black hair and the same look of determination and purpose. Both were born in the rugged mountain chain that runs down Mexico's eastern flank—Manuel in the State of Puebla, Juarez in the adjoining State of Oaxaca. Manuel, of course, is Totonac and Juarez was born of pure Zapotec stock. Like Manuel, Juarez didn't learn to speak Spanish until he was twelve. And each was propelled by a passion to help not only their own people, but other ethnic minorities become participants in the general culture of Mexico without relinquishing their distinctiveness and Indianness.

A contemporary of Abraham Lincoln's, Juarez shared the same ideals of justice and commitment to democratic government. As a leader of his liberal party, Juarez envisioned a peaceful, authentically democratic Mexico and fought to abolish the special powers and privileges granted to the church and men of position and influence who were holdovers from Mexico's colonial days. After a civil war that rivaled America's, Juarez emerged to establish his famous reform laws. Two of these— separation of church and state and freedom of worship—became issues Manuel was forced to deal with in 1972.

In the early seventies, Manuel had three concerns. First, the development of the Totonac Cultural Center. Buildings needed to be built to house the students yet to be recruited. Lessons and curriculum had to be translated from Spanish (or English) by Manuel into Totonac—a monumental task in itself. No Totonac textbooks existed apart from the New Testament, a dictionary, a few primers and supplementary reading material. No history, science or math books; nothing in animal husbandry, tailoring or theology. Everything taught came via Manuel's translation skills.

His second concern was the clinic. Except for coordination of volunteer help, the clinic functioned almost independently. Within the first six months, the clinic was a well-established fixture, writing its own unique history and contribution to the Totonac community.

Manuel's third and most important concern was the development and encouragement of the Totonac church. The Center's whole purpose was to train pastors and laymen to return to their villages where there were clusters of believers without regular spiritual nourishment from the Scriptures.

From the beginning, Manuel realized the school must never grow into a quasi-church. He knew Mexican law disallowed schools to function in an ecclesiastical role. His school and church development must be kept separate. At the same time, he felt no compunction in gathering his eight or nine students and staff members on a Sunday afternoon for a private, informal devotional service. The service was conducted in Totonac with perhaps a student reading a Scripture portion or sharing, hymn singing and a short devotional message from Manuel, and that was it—an informal devotional service conducted on his own premises for members of his "family."

That's what Manuel wanted, and for several years that's the way it was. But little by little, others in the village of La Union and the surrounding community began to appear at these informal Sunday services. Some were Spanish-speaking people from La Union who were curious to see what was rumored to be happening each Sunday afternoon. Others were local believers who desired personal fellowship and inspiration from the Scriptures. It didn't seem to matter for most of those who came that they couldn't understand or speak Totonac. Many were Aztec-speaking people from an Aztec village that bordered the Totonac area.

Wisely, Manuel followed a fundamental public relations principle he had learned from Wycliffe founder, William Cameron Townsend. Namely, present yourself immediately to the mayor or his representative in whatever town or village you are planning to live or do business. Manuel had done this in 1967 and was accepted as one who was bringing a certain prestige to the community. The school was becoming a showplace with well-kept gardens and grounds. Something always seemed to be happening with people coming and going from all over the world. The clinic became known for its exceptional health care and humane treatment of

Indian patients. Local teachers were genuinely pleased to have Manuel and several students accept their invitations to parties and official functions even though they didn't fully understand why their guests abstained from drinking alcohol, smoking and dancing. Clearly the community was learning that the school and those who came and went represented something unique. But then in early 1973, Manuel had to face two difficult problems that severely clashed with his purposes for the Totonac Cultural Center.

The first was that the small private devotional meeting had now developed into a large public meeting. "This was not what I had planned," said Manuel, "but what could I do? Aztec-speaking people, Totonacs and Spanish-speaking people from La Union all came to the afternoon service to hear the Gospel and have fellowship. I could not tell them to go away."

To accommodate these three language groups, Manuel began to address each in their own language. First he gave his devotional in Totonac, then he repeated the same address to those who spoke Aztec (one of the eight languages Manuel speaks), and then he spoke a third time in Spanish for the Spanish-speakers. As taxing as this was, it was not to be compared with the challenge of his second problem—a new mayor!

The mayor with whom Manuel had made friends when he first arrived in La Union was friendly and cooperative. Not so the new mayor. Openly antagonistic toward Manuel and what he represented, he was particularly upset with the large group of people "worshiping on property designed for educational purposes only."

"Don't you know you could have your property confiscated by the government?" said the mayor. "In

fact, I intend to report you to the governor of the state."
And he did.

The first citation from the governor's office notified
Manuel in precise, unambiguous language that he was
in violation of Mexican law. "Religious services that are
reported to be occurring on your school property must
cease. If such reported services continue, your property
will be confiscated by the government in accordance
with its right to do so."

Clearly Manuel faced a serious dilemma. Through
his lawyers he requested and, to his surprise, received
an extension of six months in which to find a suitable
building or piece of property on which to erect a church
building.

At first, six months seemed like an adequate length of
time to find an appropriate site, but it wasn't. Several
months of active searching proved fruitless, and Manuel
asked his lawyers once again to petition for an extension
of another six months.

In May 1975, after a third request for an extension,
Manuel wrote the following letter to his friends and
supporters:

Dear Friend:

This is a matter of urgency! A great problem
confronts the Totonac Cultural Center. The Mexican government is enforcing a law which states
that all "religious" meetings must be held in
churches only. The penalty for violation is confis-
cation of property.

One hundred and twenty adult believers and
thirty children who meet reguarly on Sunday
afternoons at the Totonac Cultural Center to
worship our Lord Jesus Christ will be deprived of
this privilege. We are registered as a school and

cannot endanger the property.

God tells us in I Peter 2:13, 14 to "obey those in authority over you." This we will do, with his help.

In the light of this problem, my Board authorized me to investigate property for sale in La Union, the village one mile from the school. There is one property which has a concrete building adequate for 150 to 200 people and other buildings that can be used as Sunday School rooms. The ground is level and covers three-quarters of an acre. The asking price is $16,000.00 U.S.

The nearest church is twenty miles away. The present interest in God's Word will be stimulated as "you of like precious faith" help us secure a place of worship that there be obedience to the command of Hebrews 10:25.

The Lord bless you as you seek his will as to what He would have you do on behalf of these who are your Totonac brothers.

> Your brother in Christ,
> (Signed) Manuel Arenas

In just over a year, Manuel received enough money from his multiple national friends (American, German, Mexican and others) to purchase a choice piece of land (not the building he described in the letter) that fronted the main road through La Union. Then the process of building a church edifice began.

While reluctantly conceding Manuel's church would become a reality, the mayor nevertheless harassed the builders with inspection demands and minute regulations that hindered the smooth flow of construction. Patiently, Manuel met every demand, demands that often required him to make repeated and unnecessary trips to Mexico City for special permits.

Today there is a new mayor in La Union and a handsome brick church that seats over 400 people. There is a belfry with two big bells, a cement patio and a modest cement house that can serve as a parsonage. The church is now called "Alpha and Omega." Its pastor, Felipe Ramos, is Manuel's right-hand man and chief school administrator. Manuel's expanded travel schedule and other duties preclude him from assuming regular church leadership. He does, however, speak on special occasions. He particularly likes to take part in the church's baptismal services.

But the church in La Union wasn't the only body of believers that occupied Manuel's attention. As a result of the clinic and radio ministries, there were new believers in four different villages without a central place to worship. With new believers being added to the church weekly, Manuel faced two significant challenges. The first was to encourage groups of local believers to meet at least once a week for Bible study, corporate prayer and fellowship. The second was to encourage these local groups to build their own church building.

It pleased Manuel that these groups were meeting, but he wasn't at all pleased they were still meeting in private homes, particularly when some grew to 100 or 150 people. "It makes it difficult for the owner when you meet in homes," said Manuel. "What if the people want to sing until ten or eleven and the owner of the house wants to go to bed early? Then there is the question of who will pay for the kerosene and who will maintain the building. But beyond these practical questions is the question of the law. Just like the school, the home must be separate from the church. The owner of a house-church can get into trouble with the local authorities and invite persecution from other groups of people. It is important to have your own church building and have it registered according to the law. It doesn't have to be made with stone or brick. No, just out of inexpensive materials like bamboo. In this way everyone can help and no one will suffer a financial burden."

Manuel was then and is today particularly sensitive about urging people to give money to church-related projects. On the one hand, he is guided by what he considers a basic New Testament tenet: return to the Lord a tenth of your income, no matter how meager. This desire to live "Christianly" grew out of his dramatic choice to renounce his familial gods. Manuel has learned that the dynamics of true Christianity involve obedience to a loving God who is sovereign over one's life. For him, verbal assent alone is not a vital demonstration of loving faith. The new texture of life with God is a life that demonstrates a faith in action—hospitality, good deeds, kindness and, above all, total and continuing obedience to the will of God in Christ. Yet, Manuel wisely remembers that it took him time to grow into this understanding. His insight, therefore, is not necessarily shared by new believers.

"When a Totonac first comes to the Lord," Manuel said, "I am careful not too push him too hard. I don't want to say, 'Now that you are a Christian you should make a contribution every Sunday.' No, I believe it would be wrong for me to do this. A new believer would say, 'Aha, so this is the reason you want me to become a believer in God, just so you can get my money.' It is much better that I just live before them. In this way these new believers can come to their own conclusions about how best to please God. Those who cannot give a tithe of money during the offering might bring bananas or a squash or some other fruit or vegetable down to the altar. At the end of the service, those who have money buy this produce with cash. The money is given to the treasurer and is used for building maintenance, kerosene for the lamps used in the evening service and for the pastor's salary. And there is one more thing I do. When believers from other areas see how we do things at the church in La Union, they become excited and convinced that they too could have their own church building. When they come to talk to me about it, I say, 'Give me the walls, and I will give you the roof.' (You build the walls and I'll pay for the roof.) In this way I hope to encourage them."

As of this writing, Manuel had "encouraged" forty-three different congregations to construct their own church buildings. Many believers who have observed Manuel's willingness to give have also sacrificed. One believer, a former witch doctor, happily gave a choice piece of property on which to build a church for his local area.

From the beginning of the Totonac Cultural Center, Manuel has understood what mission strategists call the "indigenous principle." Simply stated, "Work, when possible, should be done by the same people being evangelized and whatever is done for them should be done within their own cultural context. Ideally, it should be on a level they can eventually afford to continue." Yet some criticized him for starting another school. Some suggested he send his students to existing schools. But few, if any, of these schools offered what Manuel knew the Totonacs needed. Namely, on-the-spot training in a simple, straightforward, non-threatening institution. A university-level institution would not work. Most educational institutions familiar to Manuel had a philosophy of education that did not meet the unique social and educational needs of Totonac students.

The Totonac Cultural Center, however, provided a place for students with limited or, in most cases, no funds to receive an education specifically designed to equip them for serving their own people. The school was also a place where Totonacs could fellowship as Totonacs, all within their own cultural setting. Those who graduated and returned to their own villages and communities, returned with two prongs of the "indigenous principle" firmly in place. The first was that the church buildings Manuel suggested they build be made from local materials (and thus reasonably affordable). In this way, the church was not imposed from the outside, but blended into the community. With the Christian Gospel acting as "leaven," many communities of new believers assumed their corporate responsibility and experienced profound social changes, all without the direct aid of an expatriate mission worker.

The second prong of the "indigenous principle" Manuel intuitively acted out was that of a catalyst, an attribute he had learned from his friend and mentor, "Uncle Cam." The genius of Cameron Townsend was that he unobtrusively encouraged from the sidelines, and when you accomplished a task, he made you feel as if it was your idea all along!

At the opening of this chapter, I said Manuel had as his chief concern the development of the school, clinic and church. I should have included another concern—the implementation of a radio ministry.

The idea for a radio outreach ministry among the Totonacs came to Manuel in 1972 on one of his frequent speaking assignments for Wycliffe, this time in Kansas City. Some friends suggested to Manuel that a "good way to reach people for the Lord is through radio. After all," they said, "everyone is cashing in on space-age technology that has produced the transistor radio, making it affordable even for Totonacs."

Manuel agreed with his friends. It would most certainly be a "good way" to minister to Totonacs, particularly those who lived in remote mountain villages. But in a conversation with Mr. and Mrs. Wallace McGehee (Mr. McGehee was then president of Manuel's newly formed board), Manuel pointed out some practical reasons why he thought it would be difficult for him to consider such a notion.

"I have the responsibility for running the whole school," said Manuel. "This involves writing letters, speaking, traveling and keeping the needs of the school before all those who are supporters of this ministry. This means I must confer with Felipe and the other teachers. I must handle difficult student problems and speak to and entertain everyone who comes to visit me at the school. And I must attend to the many Totonacs who come at all hours of the day and night to seek my advice on everything from family to cattle and other farming problems.

"In a way I am like Paul, the apostle who had the care of all the churches. I have not just one church in La Union, but many in the outlying areas. I also have the responsibility for the clinic. I must coordinate all the doctors and nurses and dentists and other groups who want to come and help."

Manuel continued to outline the impracticality of introducing a new outreach radio ministry. His reasons included lack of personnel, although he did mention that Felipe might be able to handle such a responsibility. But what about money? Where would it come from?

In his early days, Manuel probably never would have entertained these negative realities. This was truly an out-of-character response. Perhaps the overriding reason for this was his growing back pain. Sometime during the early seventies, Manuel began to experience increasing pain and discomfort in his back and wondered if the reason was stress from his heavy administrative load. Sometimes the pain radiated down his thighs to his calves and burned into his heels. At these moments, Manuel was unable to walk and confined himself to bed rest until the spasms subsided. While he seldom complained about his increasing discomfort, he knew instinctively that one day he would have to face an operation, an operation that had a fifty-fifty chance of leaving him paralyzed.

Meanwhile, the ground swell for the idea of a radio ministry for the Totonacs grew and many of Manuel's friends, including the McGehees, began to pray for its realization. About this same time, Manuel received a letter from a young man of seventeen who said he was enclosing a check to be used for the establishment of a radio outreach ministry among the Totonacs. Apart from the leading of the Holy Spirit, Manuel had no idea why he would have written and sent this money. Thus as he did with the four deutsche marks he received from a young German girl to help start the Bible school, he opened a special bank account labeled, "Radio Ministry."

In April 1975, Manuel's prayer partners received the following newsletter that would introduce them to the Totonac Cultural Radio Program.

Dear Friend:
"Hua' yu' ma' cultura' Totonac hua' ntun kin camasiyuniyan ntuxatian. . . ." (This is the Totonac Cultural Program that gives better understanding.)

With this introduction each Sunday, the Totonac Cultural broadcast is on the air. Potentially it reaches every Totonac village, where transistor radios are becoming more common. Do you know the history of this program?

In 1972, a 17-year-old boy in Kansas City, Missouri, who wants no publicity (Matthew 6:1), sent a gift to start a Totonac broadcast. This was an answer to prayer for many friends of the Totonac people. The young man had received Jesus Christ as Savior through the witness of the "Jesus People" and was eager to get the Word of God to others who had not heard. Through high school, he had worked on Saturdays and after school for a lumber company, saving his money to invest in the Lord's work.

Many hindrances prevented the broadcast from becoming a reality until God's appointed time, October 1974. After the first few broadcasts, letters began coming to Felipe Ramos, the young preacher-teacher from our Totonac Bible Center School, who is the broadcast voice.

As of last month, people from 60 villages have written for the Totonac New Testament and dictionary being offered at low cost, receiving also a free booklet, "The Life of Christ," in Totonac. Many are accepting Jesus Christ as Savior.

Please continue to pray for and help the broadcast ministry that "hearers" may become "believers" as they listen and trust the Lord Jesus.

Thank you for your interest in and love for my people.

The Lord bless you,
(Signed) Manuel Arenas

P.S. You may want to help support this radio ministry. Air time costs $25 each week. Every letter coming in costs $1.00 for the free booklet, letter, subsidized copy of the New Testament and postage. But what unbelievable results!

The response to the radio program was indeed overwhelming. Felipe, who had taken six weeks of special voice training at a large radio station in Poza Rica, conducted the first program. Manuel stayed home to listen and pronounced it a success partly because Felipe sounded "so professional."

Manuel's assessment of that inaugural fifteen-minute radio program must have been accurate because the following day a woman came to visit Manuel at the Center and said, "I am not a Christian, but I enjoyed the program on the radio because it was in my language. Also I now know I need a Savior."

During the next four months, Manuel received an amazing amount of mail. In the month of February 1975, Felipe had ninety-six letters to answer. Manuel assigned one of the students to assist him with this extra work. Wrote one person:

> I cannot read or write but my wife and I work hard every day and we bought a radio. We now listen to the Totonac radio program. During Christmas, the whole family became Christians. The lady who helped me write this letter is a school teacher and a fine Christian, too. We have a Bible study twice a week in her home. Please tell us if anyone can come to our village from the Cultural Center to baptize the whole family and the school teacher.

In some cases, people who were encouraged by the radio program wanted to show their appreciation personally. One day three young men came with gifts of ten eggs, a bunch of bananas and some wild greens. "We have never met you before," they said, "and you do not know us, but through the Totonac radio program we have come to know you very well. We started to hear the program about three months ago and we like it very much because it is in our own language. We have come to tell you that all three of us have accepted the Lord and our lives have changed. We do not have money because we are very poor, but in love we have brought you these gifts to show our appreciation for the Totonac radio program. We also want to tell you that for the last two weeks we have been meeting in our house and after we hear the message, we share with one another."

Many letters to the school came without the aid of a school teacher or paid village scribe. In these cases, it took Felipe and his helper considerable effort to decipher exactly what it was the person wanted. Most seemed to be requesting the Totonac New Testament and dictionary. By June 1975, Manuel wrote his constituents to tell them that the response to the radio program had been "so good that we have run out of New Testaments."

By the end of the first year of broadcasting, the Totonac Cultural Program was reaching over 200,000 Totonacs. As part of his July 1975 summer outreach ministry, Manuel organized his students two-by-two to go to sixty-five villages to visit people who had responded to the broadcast. Said Manuel, "The radio program has given the students in each village an open door for witness and follow-up. And what is really remarkable is that no foreign missionary is involved!"

Thus began a unique ministry among the Totonacs. Unique because for the first time the Totonac language was being used, accepted and celebrated publicly. The Totonacs had always believed their language was inferior to Spanish and, if that were true, it must also hold true that they as persons were inferior. Now this had changed. Twice a week the "whole world" could tune in and hear their beautiful language spoken by a professional announcer. This alone gave many a new sense of self-worth and acceptance.

For several years the radio program flourished without incident. Response from the number of villages grew from sixty-four in the first years to over a hundred. Little did Manuel know that one day the radio ministry would cause him to face a severe political storm. Nor did he know he was about to face a storm of a different origin. Her name was Fifi.

Chapter 5

Storms And Miracles

It started as an embryonic thunderstorm somewhere off the coast of West Africa—just a tropical depression, but as the storm fed on warm air and tropical waters, it matured. In turn, the storm began to ride the heavy shower-laden trades. And when the pressure dropped and the earth's rotation propelled the thunderstorm into a spiral pattern, Hurricane Fifi was born.

Boiling out of the Caribbean, Fifi struck the northern section of Honduras with a maelstrom of wind and rain. Before the hurricane's terrible fury moved into southeastern Mexico, 100,000 people were homeless and 8,000 died. The date was September 20, 1974.

Less than twenty-four hours later, Fifi howled her way across southeastern Mexico toward La Union and the Totonac Cultural Center. Cut off from her source of ocean power and after a collision with the rugged Eastern Sierras, Fifi was on her way to dissipation, but was still a hurricane bringing a sky filled with leaden rain and wild winds gusting from sixty to seventy miles per hour.

The only abnormality Manuel noticed the night before the hurricane hit was that it seemed unseasonably cool. The sky was black without moon or stars, but many nights were like that. About ten, Manuel opened the door to his room just off the main courtyard and breathed in a generous gulp of fresh air. The coffee and citrus trees were rattling in a wind that, only in retrospect did Manuel realize, was stronger than usual.

Manuel's concentration was on his trees. How he loved them! But besides aesthetics, they also served a useful purpose. They were providing a modest income for the school and fresh fruit for the students.

To get him started with his orchard, German friends in Mexico City had given Manuel two hundred orange and lemon trees. These were specially grafted dwarfs designed to bear fruit two years after planting. Likewise, the five hundred coffee trees Manuel planted were imported from Brazil and were designed to mature and produce a crop within the first or second year of planting instead of the customary four years for locally-produced coffee trees.

From the beginning, the dwarf trees were a celebrated novelty among the Totonacs. Most had never seen such trees and expected them to develop in the customary way. When the trees began producing, the Indians noticed how convenient it was for them to harvest the fruit without the trouble of cumbersome ladders.

"Would you please tell us what kind of orange trees you have?" they said. "Did you use an injection on them? Or did you use some tablets? If you did, we would like to buy the same medicine to make our orange trees small."

Seizing the opportunity to widen the Totonacs' understanding of new agricultural husbandry, Manuel explained that the trees' small stature had nothing to do with injections. He explained how they could secure the same kind of trees for their villages by buying them from a special place called a nursery.

It was about 1:00 a.m. when Fifi reached La Union and the Totonac Cultural Center. As the wind began to gust, then blow, howl an tear around the edges of the asbestos roof sheeting that covered the room in which he slept, Manuel knew that all was not well. He quickly dressed but not fast enough to escape what happened next. Before he finished tying his shoes, the wind had torn off a large corner of the roof and the heavy, swirling rain began pouring into his bedroom. His mind occupied with the safety of the students, staff and livestock, Manuel gave little thought to the rain soaking important papers on his desk. Only afterward did he realize that the rain had damaged his important list of addresses and phone numbers of his many worldwide friends.

After determining that everyone was safe, Manuel, his voice barely audible over the roar of the wind and pouring, pelting rain, summoned three students to check the pigs and chickens on the lower piece of property about a quarter mile down the road from the main Totonac Center. During construction of the Center, several friends had encouraged him to build the school on this more accessible flat land. Wisely, Manuel resisted and built the school on "higher" ground for just such a moment as this.

When the students returned, they reported that the normally small creek alongside the property was overflowing its banks and flooding the farm. Manuel didn't need to ask about the pigs and chickens. From the students' description of how deep and swift the water was at the lower end of the property, he knew all they could do was sit out the night and wait until Fifi had belched out her last hurrah.

With the first light of dawn, Manuel inspected the model farm and discovered his worst fears were realized. Months later in one of his newsletters, he shared with his friends and constituents the devastation of that dark night.

Dear Friend,

The damage caused by Hurricane Fifi last September at the Bible school was real sad. For several weeks after losing twenty pigs, four hundred chickens and the water tank, I tried not to visit the area. If I had to pass through and see all the workers repairing the damage, I would just close my eyes.

But now I can tell you that the damage is almost repaired. This time we are using better and stronger material—steel reinforcement and cement blocks for the pigpens and concrete walls for the chicken houses. The old wooden walls did not withstand the great flooding.

We are slowly replacing our pigs; we have several rabbits and soon hope to have chickens again. The banana and orange trees were not too badly damaged. But the coffee trees—the cash crop for the school—and the beans and corn that provide the basic diet for the students were all damaged. We will have to buy these until a new crop can be harvested. Thank you for your gifts and prayers.

> God bless you all,
> (Signed) Manuel Arenas

* * * * *

During the seventies, North American culture was still in the eye of another storm that, like Fifi, boiled out of a distant depression and with hurricane force, forever imprinted its face on American life. It was the age of the counterculture; an age caught up with popular neo-romanticism that in turn fathered a generation of young people trying to transcend reality through drugs, sex, transcendental meditation or Thoreau's example of living an aesthetic lifestyle. We called these young people hippies. One ritual of this counterculture involved traveling to exotic locations in search of gurus, drugs and a simple lifestyle. During the seventies, there seemed to be as many hippies in Katmandu as there were in Kansas City—perhaps more!

Thus it happened one Sunday morning that three young Totonac students from the Totonac Cultural Center met three American hippies—one from Michigan, one from Illinois and one from Arkansas. As part of their practical training, the Totonac students had been sent out to minister and preach in a small evangelical church near the bustling oil port city of Poza Rica. All in their late teens, they wore casual Western shirts, pants and shoes. Their hair was neatly trimmed around their necks and ears, and they walked with purpose along the edge of the warm asphalt road leading into Poza Rica.

As the three students rounded a curve, they suddenly encountered the three American hippies dressed in their full flamboyant "tribal" costumes. For centuries ethnic peoples around the world have made statements about themselves by elaborate tattoos, body painting, scarring and the wearing of adornments. The hippies' attire performed the same function. It distinguished them from other members of their society and made a public statement about their identity and worldview.

The three Totonac students understood the significance of tribal identification, but these three men presented a kind of non sequitur. The Americans or expatriates they had met before were reasonably conservative in their dress. All wore shoes. These three didn't. To their knowledge, none wore elaborate rows of colored beads. These did. They had never seen any with hair the length of a woman's. These three were clearly not average Americans.

With a smile, one of the hippies said in a halting, but understandable Spanish, "We have a problem. We have run out of money. We need food—something to eat. Do you have food you could share with us?"

"Yes, we have food," said Juan, one of the students, "and we will be happy to share it with you. But first I want to tell you about the Lord Jesus Christ."

"Oh, no, you don't," said one of the hippies. "I went to Sunday School until I was twelve and that stuff is for kids and old ladies."

"Are you hungry?" asked Juan.

"Yes, of course, we're hungry," they said.

"Then please listen and afterward we will share our food with you."

For the next thirty minutes, the three Totonac students spoke about Totonacs, Americans, Mexicans and all mankind who were basically sinful and indifferent toward God. "Therefore," said the students, "such people do not deserve anything from a holy and righteous God. But God in his great love for all people gave them his Son, Jesus Christ. And when individual people begin to believe and trust and invite Jesus to come into their lives, He forgives their sins. In this way they are being made ready for heaven and will live forever with God. When we three received this Jesus into our hearts, we began to understand we had been given a treasure no amount of money on earth could ever buy."

No mystical or ecstatic words came from these three young Bible school students. Just plain straightforward words about a just, holy, righteous God and sinful, estranged man who, through Christ's death on their behalf, could be brought back into fellowship with the eternal Creator.

It is impossible to know what precise word, or indeed if it was any word at all that effected the response of one hippie. Perhaps after years of aimless wandering, or alienation from himself and his family, he found something in the loving words and attitudes of these Totonac students that satisfied his spiritual hunger. When they were asked if any of them wanted to accept Jesus Christ into their hearts, one of the hippies said yes.

It was an awkward moment when two of the hippies saw their companion bow his head and in a simple prayer ask Jesus Christ to take over the direction of his life. And then true to their word, the students shared their simple lunch with the three hippies. As they ate together, the young man who had made a profession of faith began urging his companions to do the same. All through lunch they talked, and to the amazement of the Totonac students, the remaining two students finally said, "Yes. If you can, so can we."

"Okay," said the newly born-again hippie, "what's next? What can we do now?"

"Come with us to where we are going to preach. Then afterward we will talk."

The congregation, tightly packed into the small church, with women and girls on one side of the main aisle and men and boys on the other, stirred audibly as the three students made their way to the front followed by the Americans. Few, if any, in the Indian congregation had ever seen hippies before and they were justifiably apprehensive.

"Brothers and sisters in our Lord," said Juan, "rejoice with us today because here you see three men—American men—who have just this morning been born into the Kingdom of God."

And the congregation responded. They rejoiced and made the three young men feel welcome and accepted. After the students concluded the service, the three hippies repeated their roadside question. "What next? What happens now?"

Boldly Juan said, "You need to have your hair cut. No Christian man down here wears his hair as long as a woman's." Seemingly from out of nowhere came a pair of old-fashioned hair clippers. One by one the three men submitted to the barber's skill.

After their hair was cut, the men again asked, "What next?"

"Come with us to our Bible school," said Juan. "You can rest and eat there, then meet the principal of the school, Professor Manuel Arenas."

Captivated, Manuel sat and listened as the students related their story. They likened it to Philip's encounter with the Ethiopian eunuch in Acts, chapter eight. Anxious to determine if the hippies' professions of faith were authentic, Manuel invited each one into his office for a private conversation.

After asking about their backgrounds and reasons for coming to Mexico, Manuel asked each a single question. "Why did you accept Christ into your life?" The response from each was similar. "I invited Jesus Christ into my life because for the first time I saw myself as God sees me. I decided to trust Him because He loves me."

Convinced that they had come into a living relationship with God, Manuel urged the young men to return to their homes and be reunited with their families. Each had told Manuel they hadn't spoken with their families for over a year. "They have no idea if we're dead or alive," they said.

At Manuel's invitation, the men stayed at the school

for several days, then each left for his respective home. Manuel thought it would be the close of yet another chapter in a long series of encounters with people the Lord had brought across his path. But the men began to correspond with him and as time passed, Manuel learned that two of them found jobs and the third enrolled at Gordon College, graduating in 1979.

For all his social action, for all his drive to help the Totonacs better themselves economically, for all his encouragement of better health and nutrition, Manuel stresses that the primary purpose of his ministry is to make known the Gospel of Christ. He always balances the activities of the clinic, the model farm and the school with its opportunity for students to learn a variety of practical skills with an aggressive, but winsome, Christian witness. Those who are sometimes too shy to articulate their personal faith look with awe at someone like Manuel who seems to respond naturally and spontaneously to personal-evangelism opportunities. From the beginning, Manuel has been captivated by the Gospel. To him, it is the best news anyone, of whatever nationality or ethnic background, could hear.

Although more by example than explicit instruction, Manuel expects those who come under his charge to take their faith seriously. When he encounters those students whose convictions aren't as deeply rooted as his and they suddenly decide to change from their original course, he often feels betrayed.

This sense of betrayal and pain is not only for himself, but also for his prayer and financial supporters. And in a certain way, too, he feels he has betrayed the student for allowing him to quit before realizing his potential.

His first experience with this came when six third-year students (who were studying tailoring) decided to give up their original goal of returning to help their own people in favor of permanent employment in Mexico City.

It began innocently enough. One young man decided to visit his sister in Mexico City who worked as a domestic in the home of a Jewish clothing manufacturer. At the suggestion of his sister, the young man asked the clothing manufacturer for a job in his factory. "If you are as good at making shirts as your sister says, I'll hire you," said the man. Within the first three days, he realized he had found a talented young tailor and gave him a permanent job. Later, when he learned the young man had five other friends who had studied to become tailors at the same school and were equally skilled, he hired them as well.

All six intended this job to be summer employment only. They wanted to make enough money to return to school in the fall and complete their fourth year. But as fall drew near, the manufacturer reminded the young men about all the money and freedom they had and how fortunate they were in these "difficult times" to find permanent employment.

"Just think how hard it would be to find such work again if you leave," he said, and the six young men agreed. They had never had so much money. Thus money became more important than further schooling and returning to an obscure Totonac mountain village to teach tailoring.

News of their decision devastated Manuel. He felt everything he had worked for was lost—his world had suddenly collapsed around him. Six of his brightest and most promising students failed to fulfill their commitments. Perhaps he could have handled one or even two leaving, but six? Besides his deep sense of personal failure, how could he explain this to his supporting friends? "I was so ashamed," said Manuel, "that I couldn't tell anyone."

Actually, he did tell one man. When he finally accepted the reality of the young men's resolve to remain in Mexico City as tailors in a clothing factory, he visited an old friend—the pastor of a Baptist church in the same neighborhood where the young men worked and lived.

"I know you share my vision for the Totonac people," said Manuel to the pastor. "You know the great responsibility I feel before the Lord that the young men who have been trained at the Bible school should return to their villages to help and share what they have learned with their own people. I know you feel as I do, because you yourself have obeyed the Lord to preach and minister to this congregation. And you know also how one can be tempted to forget such a calling in favor of a higher paying job." The preacher gave Manuel an enthusiastic nod.

"Now I have a problem and need your help," continued Manuel. "Would you personally invite these six young men to your church? They don't handle Spanish well enough to preach from the pulpit, but they can give a testimony or teach a Sunday School class or work with the church young people. My prayer is they will be salvaged for the Lord. And perhaps with time they will return to the school, complete their education and go back to their people."

This was a bold, creative solution that came from a tender man who understood that the Christian's responsibility before God is to love his neighbor, to serve him and seek his highest good. Manuel had done this and now all he could do was wait and pray. The pastor did as Manuel asked and personally invited all six young

men to his church, and they came. As the years passed,
the young men became personal friends of the pastor
and took an active part in the fellowship and ministry
of the congregation.

Meanwhile, Manuel decided to re-evaluate his practical skills program. To his assembled staff, he said, "We
began this school to train young people to understand
and teach the Bible so that they in turn could go out to
encourage and help their own people. We wanted the
young people to become preachers of the Word. The
practical skills of carpentry, tailoring and good farming
methods were all designed so the student could pass his
skills on to fellow villagers. But because the six who
were taught tailoring have not returned, I am suspending
tailoring and carpentry from our curriculum."

Manuel waited two full years, then made a special
trip to Mexico City to ask the six former students to
reconsider, return to the school and complete their
schooling. "I have prayed for you and continue to
pray," said Manuel. "I pray that God will lead you to
think about your commitment to help and serve your
Totonac people."

But none was interested. The clothing manufacturer
was right. Money did bring its own kind of freedom and
security. Returning to school would mean an uncertain
future. Manuel said he understood and that he would
continue to pray for them.

For the next three years Manuel heard only intermittent reports from his Baptist friend about the six former
students. Then one day, three years after Manuel's
special visit, he received an astonishing letter from
three of the six students. "The Lord has been speaking to us
three. We would like to return to the Totonac Cultural
Center to complete our schooling and if the Lord leads,
to return to our villages and help serve our people."

Years later, Manuel said of that incident, "The Lord taught me a valuable lesson from these students. I came to realize that we can never know how God is going to work or what circumstances He will use to bring people back to Himself. I thought it was a terrible catastrophe when these young men decided not to return, but God turned it around for good. The three did return to complete their courses and went on to serve in the villages. And just recently I learned that the other three students who stayed on in Mexico City were using their money to sponsor another student eight years after they left. How wonderful to realize that, after all, my dreams are being fulfilled."*

Manuel had delegated responsibility for the Bible school to Felipe and other staff members, but urgent and cataclysmic events were always his special preserve. The cataclysm to top all cataclysms occurred one evening shortly after the school supper hour. Manuel, his longtime friends the Wallace McGehees and translation colleague Herman Aschmann (who happened to be staying at the school for several days to work on translation materials) were lingering around the dining room table. All were enjoying relaxed after-dinner conversation when Heinz, who earlier had been a part of the group but had excused himself to work on a carpentry project, suddenly appeared crying, his right hand hidden behind his back.

Immediately, Manuel jumped from his chair. "Heinz, Heinz, what happened? What's the matter?"

In a voice that seemed to come from another dimension, Heinz ignored Manuel's direct questions, drew

---

* As of this writing, Manuel has once again added tailoring and carpentry to the school's curriculum.

his hand into view and said, "What will my mother say when she sees me? What will my mother say?"

"Oh, Heinz," said Manuel, "we've got to get you to the hospital immediately." (The regular clinic doctors were absent.)

What Heinz showed Manuel and his friends was a right hand full of blood and all five fingers dangling by shreds of skin, the result of a series of bizarre circumstances. The table saw he was using had been left out in a tropical downpour. This in turn made the particleboard top soggy. When Heinz turned on the motor, the vibration worked loose the motor mounts and the saw, free of its moorings, traveled across the table top to strike Heinz's hand.

No stranger to severe machete cuts, Herman quickly grabbed a kitchen cloth and bandaged the hand as best he could. "Manuel," said Herman, "help Heinz hold his hand above his heart. That will slow down the bleeding. If we can get him to the hospital in an hour, there just might be a chance."

"An hour?" said Manuel. "It's two hours to the hospital from here."

"We must make it within the hour," said Herman. "It's our only hope of saving the hand."

Under ideal conditions, it takes forty-five minutes to one hour to navigate the tortuously narrow, steep, partly paved, pot-holed artery that links the main highway to La Union. And yet another forty-five minutes to an hour to drive the equally narrow, hairpin mountain road to the town of Huauchinango and the hospital. Herman, who has been driving these mountain roads for more than forty years and who, incidentally, had the only car at the Center, drove, said Manuel, "like an airplane." He covered the one-and-a-half to two-hour distance in exactly forty-five minutes! How they did it is still a mystery.

But getting to the hospital in record time was only the first obstacle in this mountain drama. As soon as they entered the emergency entrance, the doctors began working on Heinz. Within minutes, however, a doctor returned to tell Manuel it was impossible to save Heinz's fingers. "The hand is dead. It's just dead," he said.

Undaunted, Manuel looked straight into the doctor's eyes and said, "Please, you must try. I invited this man to come and help me at my school. I am the one responsible. He must have those fingers to work at his trade. How can I send him back to his mother without his fingers?"

The doctor shook his head. "The saw went through everything," he said, "through muscle, tendons, cartilage, blood vessels and bone. Only the skin is holding them. There is no possible way to save them."

"Please," said Manuel again, "please try to save them."

With a faint smile, a shrug and a sigh, the doctor said, "One of the doctors is an expert in sewing machete cuts. We'll try. Every second counts if this man's fingers are to remain functional."

The hospital had no sophisticated equipment that would allow the doctors to perform microsurgery to tie the blood vessels. Nevertheless, when the head doctor finally returned, he reported to Manuel and Herman, "We have tied the tendons, sutured the tissues and splinted the fingers. All we can do now is wait and see if the blood vessels will connect on their own."

"When will we know if the operation is successful?" asked Manuel.

"In about two days. Let's hope no infection sets in."

"We will pray that none does," said Manuel.

"Ah, yes," said the doctor, "pray. That would be good to do."

More than ten years after his accident, Heinz Steinlein works out of his small office off the main courtyard at the Center and is married to a Mexican woman named Evangeline who works as Manuels's efficient, competent bookkeeper, besides cooking for the many special guests who visit the school. When anyone asks Heinz about his hand, he proudly invites the person to examine it. Amazingly, one has difficulty finding the scar tissue that is just a faint white line across his fingers.

"My index finger is a little stiff," says Heinz, "but it in no way hinders my ability to do carpentry or make furniture."

Often the person responds with, "What a miracle!"

"Yes," says Heinz, "it is a true miracle of the Lord. I still wonder how we made it to the hospital in forty-five minutes. It just can't be done."

There have been a number of other amazing incidents at the Center that could also be classified as miracles. Of course, the existence of the school itself is a miracle of God's power working his will through the lives of ordinary people. But one incident that bears special mention began on a morning early in 1975 when Manuel awoke to discover he couldn't move. His legs were paralyzed.

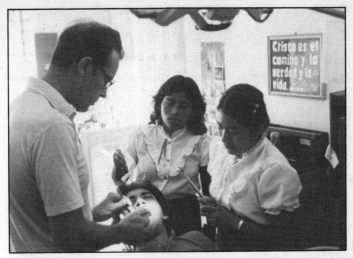

Dr. Bill Johnson and his colleague Dr. Ralph Swenby (not shown) are among several dentists, doctors and other health professionals from the U.S., Canada and Europe who offer their services free of charge to the Totonac clinic. The text above the heads of the two Totonac dental assistants reads, "Christ is the way, the truth and the life."

The Totonac Cultural Center has grown from two small ranch-style buildings to nine. These include classrooms, dormitories for male and female students, dining rooms, offices and guest rooms. The hill above the Center has been cleared and planted with neat rows of coffee bushes.

The Totonac Bible School is now coeducational and offers a full Bible school curriculum to students from a variety of ethnic minorities.

While these Totonac students may lack a certain basketball form, there is nothing lacking in their enthusiasm and intensity of team spirit and competition.

Heinz Steinlein, the school's carpenter, electrician, bookkeeper (he took this over from his wife), supervisor of workers and general handyman, explains how the table saw broke its mountings and traveled across the table to rip through his hand. Amazingly, Heinz's only reminder of that terrible accident is a stiff index finger.

Felipe Ramos is school principal, teacher, pastor, Manuel's administrative right-hand and the voice of the Totonac Cultural Hour. This radio ministry is heard each Sunday and reaches in excess of 250,000 Totonacs in their own language.

Manuel pauses for a moment of relaxation with two of his several German shepherds, Solzhenitsyn and Golda Meir.

Like the young church in Acts, the new community of Totonac believers acknowledge their acceptance of the message of God's redemptive love by obeying their Lord in the act of public baptism. A visiting pastor officiates.

Manuel encourages Totonac congregations by providing funds to pay for roofs of newly constructed churches in rural areas. This is the large Totonac church in La Union.

In recognition of his outstanding leadership, both as a world citizen and among his own Totonac people, and for his role as an educator and co-translator of the Totonac New Testament, the John Calvin Theological Seminary in Mexico City conferred on Manuel Arenas the honorary degree of Doctor of Theology.

Chapter 6

In Between Ten

For more than two months, Manuel slept on a hard board virtually paralyzed from the hips down. Resigned to living the life of an invalid, he began to make himself "useful" by teaching English from his bed to a group of male students from the nearby town of Xicotepec de Juárez. As payment for lessons, the students, particularly one who was taking pre-med, took turns helping Manuel to the bathroom, the shower and staying with him at night to move and make him comfortable.

Shortly after Manuel awoke that September morning to discover he couldn't move, Heinz drove him to see several specialists in Mexico City. None would guarantee that an operation would restore movement in his legs. "Back operations are very complicated," they said, "and this operation could be life-threatening."

During the weeks that followed, Manuel became convinced his death was imminent. He called in Heinz's wife, Evangeline, and instructed her to get his files and government papers in order. "Whoever comes after me must understand how the school is run," he said.

Because he thought the Lord was going to call him home, Manuel severed a serious romantic relationship. The young American woman worked at the SIL headquarters in Mexico City. Whenever Manuel came to town they usually spent a pleasant evening dining at Sanborn's, one of Mexico City's restaurants. "I don't want you to be a widow," said Manuel. "I have no guarantee that a year from now I will be alive."

Letters came, but Manuel, heartsick and in continual pain, could not bring himself to answer them. Eventually the letters stopped and the young woman did as Manuel suggested. She married the young man standing in the wings.

Then one day in late November 1975, a longtime friend, Dr. Wendell Searer from Ventura, California came to visit Manuel. He had heard about Manuel's back problem and offered his help. Distressed over his increasing pain and discomfort, Dr. Searer said simply, "Manuel, I don't want to see you like this. You need surgery, and I believe you will be all right."

"But I am in between ten," said Manuel.

"In between ten? I don't understand," said Dr. Searer.

"Five doctors who have examined me said if I had an operation I would die, or at best be confined to a wheelchair. And five other doctors said my only chance to walk again is to have an operation. All these weeks and months I have been in between these two opinions. Now as the eleventh doctor, you have tipped the balance. You have given me positive hope. By faith I will go to the States and have this operation. But if I should die or be confined to a wheelchair, I will not blame anyone. If this is the way the Lord has chosen to end my life, I will accept whatever He wills for me."

Manuel's trip from Mexico City to Los Angeles via Dallas, was filled with mishap, delay, plane changes and pain—lots of pain. Aboard the flight from Mexico City to Dallas, the pain became so intense he asked the flight attendants if he could lie on the floor. Instead they provided him with three unoccupied seats. When he changed planes in Dallas, he was carried off on a stretcher.

When he arrived in Los Angeles at 2:00 a.m., he asked a policeman to help him find a taxi that would take him to Santa Ana and his hotel. "The man charged me too much," said Manuel later, "but what could I do? I paid him, but he cheated me."

Other complications included a last-minute change in doctors. Longtime friends, Bill and Bettie Butler and Harold and Juanita Leasure, stepped in the gap and offered their logistical and emotional support. After three consultations with Dr. Ward Wiseman, the new doctor, it was determined that Manuel would need a laminectomy (removal of the spongy tissue between the vertebrae) and a possible spinal fusion. The operation was performed January 23, 1976 and for a month after his release from the hospital, Harold and Juanita Leasure nursed Manuel back to health and strength.

By the mid-seventies, the Bible school had an established rhythm and pattern to its evangelistic outreach. On weekends, students fanned out to more than forty villages in groups of two or three to preach, minister and encourage the larger Totonac community. Each time, the students conducted themselves with exemplary courtesy and decorum. Each time, that is, except once. The breach came when some students had to be restrained from physically lashing out at their host who in all kindness fed them a delicious but, in their minds, unacceptable dinner.

The incident actually occurred a couple of years before Manuel's back operation. Because it has gained a reputation all its own, particularly among the third-year students who sometimes instruct the freshmen on what to expect on their evangelistic outreach, it is worthy of being chronicled.

The story began when Manuel visited a Spanish-speaking farmer in a remote area of Totonac country who had been cheated out of his land. Remembering his own parent's pain at being unjustly treated by unscrupulous landowners, Manuel fought and won a legal settlement for the man. Before Manuel returned to the Center, he spent a couple of days with the farmer to teach him some simple arithmetic and geography. When the man tried to repay him, Manuel said, "Thank you, but you don't owe me anything. I did this because I wanted to." Before he left, he presented the man with a Spanish New Testament and encouraged him to read it. The man thanked Manuel with a promise that he would.

Several months later, Manuel took a group of twenty Bible school students on a tour of some new Totonac churches that had sprung up from the clinic and radio ministry. Since they were in the "neighborhood," Manuel decided to visit the farmer he had helped with the land problem.

Almost with the same breath he used to greet Manuel, the man said, "Oh, Senor Arenas, I am happy to see you and I am going to tell you right away I have not been reading the New Testament you gave me. I tell you immediately in case you decide to ask me about it. And if you ask me why, I must tell you there is no time. I get up early in the morning before it is light and go to the cornfields to work. And when I come home in the late afternoon, I am tired from a long day's work. And right after supper I am so sleepy I go to bed. And if you ask me why I don't read it on Sunday, I will have to tell you that Sunday is the day I must go to the market. So you see, there is just no time for me to read the Bible."

"Well," said Manuel with a gentle smile working at the edge of his mouth, "that is the best excuse I have ever heard. I have just one suggestion."

"Yes," said the man, "what is that?"

"Take your Bible with you when you go to the cornfield," said Manuel. "When you stop to eat your lunch, see if you can't find time to read a few verses."

"That is a good idea," said the man. "I never had such a thought before. Now, you have come a long way. Can you eat lunch with me? I will make a banquet for you and the students."

"Thank you," said Manuel, "but we are unable to stay today. Perhaps we could come another day."

When the prearranged date arrived, the man welcomed Manuel and the students with a large cup of *atole* (a favorite fiesta drink made from finely-ground, twice-cooked cornmeal, often flavored with unrefined cane sugar, pineapple or other fruit). After a time of casual conversation, the man announced the main meal would begin. The students sat on homemade pine benches and chairs. Manuel sat with his host at a small table. Just as the meal was about to be served by the farmer's domestic help, Manuel said, "Before we at the school eat, we always pause to pray and thank God for the food. May we do that here?"

"By all means, please do," said the man. "No one has ever done such a thing before."

Manuel's prayer was short and simple. He thanked God for the man's warm hospitality, for the special times of fellowship with friends and for the food they were about to enjoy. "That was beautiful," said the man. "I wish I could pray like that."

"It is very easy," said Manuel. "All that is required is for you to become a true Christian. This means coming to know and trust God and his Son, Jesus Christ. Then when you know God, you can pray and talk to Him.

Otherwise, if you are not a true Christian, to whom
would you pray?"

True to his word, the man had indeed prepared a
banquet—copious amounts of warm tortillas, a large
tureen of black bean soup that had simmered long and
tenderly in the company of garlic, onions, tomatoes and
a variety of special herbs, and a platter of mysterious
white meat. The students, as well as Manuel, expressed
appropriate remarks about its "sweet, toothsome taste."
They were, however, unable to agree as to exactly what
kind of meat it was. Some thought it must be chicken;
others said it was turkey. Manuel thought it was fish the
man had caught in the nearby stream or purchased in
Poza Rica for the occasion. While Manuel was curious
about the meat and tried a couple of times to make
discreet inquiries as to its identity, the main topic of
conversation centered around how one might have
faith in Jesus Christ.

"I believe in God," said the man. "Isn't that enough?"

"It is a wonderful beginning," said Manuel, "but true
faith in God and in his Son, Jesus Christ, means that a
person does more than just say he believes. A person of
faith trusts God as a Person. He trusts Him and makes a
habit of getting to know God through what He has said
about Himself in the Bible. A person of faith acts out in
his life and in his thoughts the things God teaches him
from Scripture. And a person of faith talks to God in
prayer.

"Listen to the words of God from the Bible in John
5:24 that tell us what happens when a person trusts and
acts on what the Bible says: 'I tell you the truth, whoever
hears my word and believes Him (God) who sent me
has eternal life and will not be condemned; he has
crossed over from death to life.'

"Now," said Manuel, "would you like to become a

person of true faith in God and his Son, Jesus Christ?"

"I would," said the man, "yes, I would like that."

"Then bow your head and repeat this prayer after me," said Manuel. "Lord Jesus, I confess I haven't known You before. I now understand that without You I cannot live eternally with You in heaven. I confess I need your salvation in my life and to have this salvation I have to accept You as my own personal Savior. I now by faith accept You into my heart. I pray this in Jesus' name. Amen."

"Now," said Manuel, "how do you feel?"

"Well, I believe what I just said," said the man. "And I know God doesn't lie. If He says I have passed from death to life because I believe in his Son, then I am happy. But there is one question I have. Do I have to repeat this same prayer every day?"

"No," said Manuel, "not at all. Let me teach you a prayer I pray every morning when I wake up and a prayer I pray at night before I go to sleep." And this he did. Manuel also instructed the man to pray for others and to pray for his farm and business and whatever else was on his heart. "Just speak to the Lord from your heart and God will hear you. Also it would be good to attend services at the church. There you will find friends and have fellowship with other Christians and this will give you strength and encouragement."

It was a splendid moment, a moment that far exceeded anyone's expectations. The students warmly welcomed the man into the household of faith and thanked him for the fine meal he had given them. As they were about to leave, Manuel said, "There is just one more thing. Could you tell us what kind of delicious meat we ate for our meal today? Was it fish you caught in the river?"

"No," said the man with a proud smile, "it wasn't fish. It was snake!"

Now it may be true that snake meat and such may be eaten by ethnic groups in Africa, Asia and some parts of the United States—and by this non-Totonac man. But such a thought is absolutely abhorrent to a Totonac. Thus, when one of the students realized what he had eaten, he immediately became ill and began to vomit.

Even with this admission from his host, Manuel thought he was joking. "It is true," said the man. "What you ate was snake. Come, I'll show you." And sure enough, as Manuel and the students rounded the corner of the house, there stretched out was a spotted snakeskin about six inches wide and over six feet long.

Manuel recognized the snakeskin. It was the same poisonous species that had been killed on his own property when the land was being cleared. The students likewise recognized the snake as poisonous, and they were angry—angry enough to strike the man for deceiving them! Here was a man whom Manuel had just won to the Lord and now the students wanted to harm him.

"What folly this is," said Manuel, speaking to the students in Totonac. "I understand your feelings. I, too, am surprised. But we are Christians and are to be different from those who don't know Christ." It took Manuel over an hour to calm the students and allay their fears that the poisonous snake's meat would not harm them. A postscript yet remains to this story: Several years later, the man sold his farm and entered a seminary to become a preacher.

This rhythm for evangelistic outreach has by no means been confined to the Totonac students. Various visiting doctors, dentists, nurses and other guests have all, in one way or another, had an impact as they have shared their faith.

One set of visiting regulars is a father and son medical team—Drs. Houston and Randy Byrd from Port Neches, Texas. Dr. Houston Byrd has been coming to the school ever since the early days of the clinic. On one occasion, after removing a severe growth from a woman's knee, he cautioned her and her husband to make sure she didn't kneel to wash clothes or grind corn. The woman's husband nodded his willingness to do this, then asked the doctor for the growth he had cut off his wife's knee. "I will bury this to appease the evil spirits," he said.

With this straightforward request, Dr. Byrd came face-to-face with the centuries-old Totonac belief in the "Owners of the Underworld." A Totonac who holds onto his or her ancestor's worldview believes in a pantheon of evil beings. Some of these are the "Owners of the Underworld" who are concerned with the forces of nature—soil, seed and harvest, and the "Owners of the Dead" who are responsible for illness and other health-related problems. With each "Owner," ceremonies and rituals must be performed. Totonacs know these spirits are malevolent and must always be appeased through offerings and sacrifices.

Dr. Byrd wasn't aware of the gripping emotional fear associated with this particular worldview. Anyone who has never been bullied by these cosmic forces cannot fully understand such fear. But Dr. Byrd was aware of a supernatural battleground and thus tried to share a wonderful secret with the man and woman—namely God Himself, the Creator of the universe, provided the one and only sacrifice for all time, Jesus Christ. Through an interpreter, he explained that since Christ had paid the debt in full, appeasement and sacrifices amount to cosmic blackmail.

Later, in conversation with Manuel, Dr. Byrd learned

that many Totonacs came to the clinic only as a last resort. Belief in the witch doctor's or shaman's power is strong and the people will try anything before coming to an outsider—even to a free clinic. "In my childhood," explained Manuel, "I remember when someone was sick, we put oil and water in a glass and set it before the household gods. This burned like a candle. I have seen people try to push rice or a ground-up tortilla into the mouth of an idol. Sometimes two or three families get together to sacrifice a chicken or turkey. Then the meat sacrificed to the idol is eaten. They believe that if you eat the meat sacrificed to an idol, you will become holy."

"Totonacs believe that if a person is very sick," continued Manuel, "sacrificing or burning a candle or praying to the household gods is not enough. A witch doctor is called but (most witch doctors or shamans are women and are often the best-dressed people in the village) will not come unless she is paid a certain amount of money. If you don't have money, then she will accept a pig, cow or even a dog. (Dogs are scarce among Totonacs and are highly prized. Most people use them to scare away raccoons from the cornfields. A dog, therefore, can bring a high price in the market.)

"We in the clinic have sometimes conflicted with the witch doctors who say they can cure sickness by reading the smoke of burning incense. When people tell me they want to go to the witch doctor, I ask them, 'Can the witch doctor help you with your toothache? They do not pull teeth. Can they help you with your tuberculosis, typhoid or eyesight? Witch doctors can't make you a pair of eyeglasses.' We also try to teach the people who come to the clinic that sickness and infections are caused by dirt and germs, not evil spirits. And when we talk about evil spirits, we tell them we understand how frightening these are, but then we say, 'Let us tell you about the Lord Jesus. When you trust Him, the devil and all his evil spirits can never touch you.' "

A few days later, Dr. Randy Byrd walked to the woman's village to remove the stitches from her knee. As he did, the students at the school, understanding how difficult it had been for some of them to change from animism to a belief in the one true God, prayed for the woman and her husband and for their entrance into the Kingdom of God. Randy's visit was routine and when he returned, he had nothing extraordinary to report. He did say the man was very grateful for his wife's treatment and when she was completely better, he said he would work a day at the school to show his appreciation and help pay for his wife's treatment. And this the man did.

But the man also did something else. About a month or so after this incident, he returned to the school and asked Manuel to hold in safekeeping the title to a piece of land that had been deeded to him by the government. Manuel said he would be happy to help him. (Manuel frequently encourages Totonacs to save their money by accompanying them to the bank where he teaches them how to open bank accounts and deposit their money.)

For over a year, Manuel heard nothing more from the man. Then one day the man's wife came to visit him. She told him a sad story of how her husband had worked hard in the cornfields, saved two thousand pesos, and buried it in their house for safekeeping. (Manuel remembered how his mother had done the same thing.) "But, alas," said the woman, "Someone came when we were away. They dug up the money and stole it."

Manuel was ready to console the woman when she

continued. "My husband saved yet another thousand pesos and the same thing happened. It was stolen. And then one day an enemy shot and killed my husband while he worked in the cornfield. Now I have nothing, no money, no land, no husband. I am alone with just my children. I don't know where to go or what to do."

"I grieve with you over the death of your husband," said Manuel, "but I do have some news that will comfort you." He then explained how her husband had asked him to keep the title to the piece of property. "This land is now yours," he said.

It was difficult at first for the woman to grasp what Manuel was telling her. Finally, when she understood the astonishing news, she expressed her profound appreciation to Manuel and began to speak about her husband.

"My husband was a hard, difficult man to live with. He was often cross with me. Sometimes he beat me. He did this when he was drunk or when I burned the tortillas. But once when he came to visit you at the school, he bought a Book. It was a Book that spoke our Totonac language. He loved that Book. He read it whenever he could. He even took it with him to the cornfield. I do not understand what was in that Book, but I do know my husband began to change after he read it. He was kinder toward me, he didn't drink as much and he said the Book helped him feel good inside. I don't know what it was my husband found in that Book, but whatever it was, I would like to have it. Can you tell me what was in that Book he got from you?"

"Oh, yes," said Manuel warmly, "I can tell you all about the Book your husband got from us." And when he did, the prayers of the students, who prayed that day a year earlier when Dr. Randy Byrd walked to her village to remove her stitches, were answered. By faith in Jesus Christ as her Savior, she entered into the Kingdom of God.

Of course, not all prayers for the Totonac school and its ministry have been answered as expected. There have been some bitter disappointments and some amazing contradictions. Some students the staff thought weren't qualified for the pastorate have surprised everyone. What some of them lacked in scholarship, they made up in desire, courage, dedication, spiritual warmth and sensitivity. Often these students displayed the ability to encourage people and respond to their needs, In many cases, these students had the more "successful" pastorates.

Thus it was that Manuel, Felipe and other staff members began to look for these added qualities in the students they accepted. And of all who came to the school, none showed more promise than Vicente.*

He came from the same Totonac town as Felipe and bore his same handsome, fine features and mental agility. Felipe became acquainted with Vicente in the church he pastored during his sabbatical year from the Bible school. When Vicente first came to the school, it was only to look for work. On Felipe's recommendation, Heinz hired him to do odd jobs.

It wasn't too many weeks before Manuel recognized that Vicente was a bright, intelligent young man and seemed to display a maturity beyond his fifteen years.

"What do you think about Vicente?" said Manuel to Felipe one day. "Would he make a good student?"

"Yes," said Felipe, "I think he would. I have known him ever since he came to know the Lord when he was

---

* Name changed.

eight. I remember him as one who liked to memorize Scripture and tell others about the Lord. He also has a nice singing voice."

On Felipe's recommendation, Vicente was accepted as a student, but not immediately. Like many Totonacs who live in damp, unheated, drafty highland houses, Vicente had contracted tuberculosis. Manuel, Heinz, Felipe and others spent much time, energy and money on his treatment, and at the end of three long years, he was pronounced cured and released.

Eager to show his appreciation for the help he received, Vicente threw himself into his studies. For the first and second years he was an "A" student. He displayed a willing openness to accept whatever extra-curricular duties were assigned him. He and Felipe collaborated on answering the many letters that came to the Center through its radio ministry. And then in his third year, a black-haired, brown-eyed girl with a ready smile and charming wit came to the school, and everything in Vicente's life changed.

Chapter 7

Something Might Happen If You Stay Too Long

She had come for the summer to assist in the clinic as an interpreter for the English-speaking doctors. Vicente, who was assigned to work in the clinic, worked with her as interpreter for the patients. She, with her Mexican-American heritage, spoke fluent Spanish and English. Vicente spoke Spanish and Totonac. Thus, she transmitted the doctor's English instructions or information into Spanish; Vicente in turn relayed it to the patient in Totonac. While one part of her culture was Mexican, another part was American, and she brought to their teamwork her normal American uninhibited platonic boy-girl relationship model. Vicente, on the other hand, was Totonac. He had never before been involved with a young woman in such an intimate work situation. And although he had heard how American girls were different from Totonac girls, he nonetheless interpreted her smiles, laughter and friendship as aggressive flirtation.

This "eagerness" (as interpreted by Vicente) quickly smote him and he fell hopelessly in love. When the young woman returned to her home at the end of the summer, Vicente's mind was filled only with thoughts of this vivacious girl who, in his mind, wanted to marry him. Nothing else mattered—not his studies, his failing grades, his proposed career or even that he had only one more year to complete his training. He was totally consumed by his love for this wonderful young woman.

Manuel observed all this from the sidelines and decided he needed to write her a letter:

Dear _____:

As you know, Vicente is very much in love with you. He no longer cares to study. If you are also in love with him as he thinks you are, that is fine. But you should know I am urging him to complete his schooling as he has only one more year. Also we do not have accommodations for married students. It is for this reason I am urging him to finish school before he marries.

Almost by return mail, Manuel received a reply telling him that she was sorry about Vicente's infatuation. "He has written me two to three times a week," she wrote, "but I haven't opened any of them. Please tell him that I think he is a nice person, but marriage is completely out of the question."

Like an elder statesman and father figure, Manuel had the unpleasant duty of informing Vicente that he had misread the young girl's intentions. She was not interested in maintaining a relationship.

Vicente's reaction was predictable. It was hard to watch him suffer. But after several weeks, Vicente's attitude toward his studies changed for the better. And then it happened again.

A Totonac student nurse had come to help in the clinic. This time the girl fell in love with Vicente. "I didn't notice it until it was too late," said Manuel. "They had been dating secretly. My problem then was to remind them of their responsibility as Totonacs. None of their friends or families would approve of secret dating. I told them their families expected them to observe proper Totonac custom and expected me to see that such cultural traditions were maintained."

The young woman said she understood and would abide by the school rules and her parents' expectations.

Vicente also agreed, but disobeyed behind Manuel's back. After several weeks, Manuel again called in Vicente, this time with the faculty present. He rebuked Vicente for violating school rules, his culture and his integrity.

"If you want to marry this girl," said Manuel, "that is fine. But please wait until you have finished your schooling. If you marry, this girl will not be able to finish her schooling and become a nurse. If you wait just a year, I will give you a big wedding at the school with a banquet just like we do in the villages. We can invite all your friends, but just wait one year."

Unfortunately, Vicente did not listen. He continued to see the girl, and Manuel finally had to dismiss him. "This hurt me deeply," said Manuel, "but for the sake of the other students and school discipline, I had to do this hard thing.

"It was at this time I began to realize that the American culture portrayed on TV was beginning to affect our Totonac culture. Vicente had spent a lot of time watching TV when he was in the hospital recuperating from tuberculosis and was obviously captivated by the more open boy-girl relationships."

Manuel has never been one to lose faith in the future. All his ministries—the school, clinic, radio program and more—were born in response to rapid and dramatic cultural changes. He knew more changes would come and wanted the Totonacs prepared to meet them when they did. At the same time, he wanted them to remain Totonac with a deep sense of pride and dignity in themselves and their language and culture.

While Manuel represents a more conservative evangelical position, by the 1980s he knew some of the school's policies must change. Not only did the school become coeducational, but Totonac instruction shifted to include Spanish for students who were now attending the school from several different ethnic groups that included Aztec,* Zapotec, Mixtec and Amuzgo.

Happily, the social changes among the Totonacs in the seventies were subtle and carried little of the community alienation that characterized the North American social environment.

One reason for this social restraint was undoubtedly the absence of television. But by 1980, TV sets began appearing in La Union and surrounding areas. The Mexican government had spent millions of pesos to provide electricity in isolated areas, as well as in villages without roads. Large helicopter crews flew in with cement power poles to connect villages to outside electricity. In many communities without electricity, one or two people operated gas generators for small light plants.

Manuel said he noticed TV's cultural effects when he saw the young girls beginning to discard their beautifully hand-embroidered blouses and Totonac skirts for store-bought dresses. "It was the Miss America Pageant that seemed to have the biggest impact," said Manuel. "After such a program it seemed every girl in town wanted money to buy the special shampoos, creams, soaps and dresses they saw on the program. Sometimes they would go without food to buy these things."

On one occasion, Manuel passed a group of Totonac men intently watching an American football game.

---

* Manuel hopes to begin a school particularly suited for Aztec-speaking students.

Manuel knew that like himself these men had little or no understanding of how the game should be played. Yet, as the men watched, they laughed at what seemed to be the appropriate places. Manuel approached one of the men and asked why they were all laughing. "I don't know," said the man. "We were laughing only because everyone else in the television crowd is laughing."

While the advent of TV brought a new turbulence to the Totonacs in and around La Union, one area of Totonac culture was impervious to any outside influence. Even Manuel, beloved and respected as he was, failed to move this rock-hard fact of Totonac life. That steadfast bastion was nothing less than the Totonac diet.

During his years as a student in the States, and from his frequent visits to American homes for meals, Manuel was exposed to many new fruits and vegetables and learned about their importance for maintaining a balanced diet. On one occasion after eating a rhubarb pie, he wouldn't rest until he had imported the thick tart stalks to his own garden at the Center.

But while Manuel was enthralled with beets, carrots, radishes, lettuce, eggplant and cabbage, the students at the school were not. It was Manuel's intention to introduce these and other dishes through the school's dining room. He hoped the students would begin to appreciate these new foods and take them back to their respective villages and into the mainstream of Totonac life. He thought this would be a way to stretch the food supply beyond the normal shortfall of planting-to-harvest cycle. But Manuel should have remembered his own student days and how students universally complain about institutional food. The first time he introduced carrots, he had to explain how they were to be eaten. Most preferred them raw. On one occasion when several American guests were visiting, he served up heaping plates of spaghetti. The students were not amused. Most refused to even try this strange dish. It looked too much like worms! It was, however, a kudo for Manuel when at least they tried rabbit meat.

It took several months, but at last the students prevailed. They were happy for Manuel to feed his guests all the carrots, beets, radishes, cabbages and spaghetti he wanted, just as long as they had their daily ration of traditional tortillas, beans, rice and some kind of meat.

Manuel had no shortage of guests on which to try his newly acquired tastes. One of them was a tall bearded man in rumpled clothes who arrived one day just as Manuel was preparing to leave on a special Wycliffe Associates speaking tour in Florida.

"You must be Manuel Arenas," said the man, when Manuel opened the door.

"Yes," said Manuel, "I am."

"I'm pleased to meet you," said the man. "My name is Anatole Breidenthal. I'm an anthropologist."

Always the consummate host, Manuel laid aside his packing, invited his new guest to the dining room for some refreshment, and gave his full attention to answering Anatole's questions. He soon learned Anatole was a Lithuanian Jew from Tel Aviv who was fluent in English, Spanish and Russian and interested in learning all he could about Totonac culture.

One of Manuel's most engaging personality traits is his exuberance for life and his ability to make instant friends. And when he discovers a person with common interests, particularly a love for culture, languages, travel and geography, he fairly explodes with enthusiasm. Such was the case with Anatole.

As they continued in lively conversation, Manuel

spoke about his great admiration for the Jewish people. "I admire all small countries whose people cooperate and work together to make life better for each other. When I read about how Jewish farmers take barren desert land and make wonderful gardens and orchards, it inspires me to work harder for the Totonacs. By the way, Anatole, how did you learn about the Center?"

"I read the book *Manuel,*" said Anatole. "I have a sister in London, England who read the book, then sent it to me. When I read it, I wanted to know more about you and the Totonacs. And I have come hoping you might be able to in some way help me or advise me in my anthropological study of Totonac culture."

"I will be happy to help you," said Manuel, "My problem is that I must be in the United States in three days. But I will return in a month. In the meantime, I would like you to be my guest at the school. And when you are ready, I will provide a student from the school who will answer all your questions and guide you where you want to go among the Totonacs. But I should warn you. If you stay around too long, something might happen!"

Before Anatole had a chance to question him further, Manuel, aware that anthropologists like to hear about cultural folk tales, said, "I would like to tell you a story my grandmother told me when I was a little boy. It is connected with the story in the Bible about Noah and the flood."

"I would like that very much," said Anatole.

"When you go on your hikes to the Totonac villages and see the beautiful orchids in the trees," said Manuel, "you will remember this story because it tells how we Totonacs came to have such beautiful flowers. This is the story my grandmother told me:

Once there was a beautiful young Totonac girl

with shiny black hair. Her eyes were big and black, her skin was soft, and she smiled beautifully at all the people. But this girl was more than just beautiful. She was also very kind, especially to old people. Whenever this girl saw an old woman standing at the edge of the river bending over the rocks to wash her clothes, she would wash them for her. If there was an old woman in the village too old to grind her corn or make her tortillas, this girl would cook for her so she wouldn't starve.

Not only did this beautiful girl wash and cook, she also made dresses and blouses as beautiful as she was and then she would give them away to the poor women of the village. Children loved this girl because she played with them and watched over them to see that no harm came to them.

So this was the way this beautiful girl lived. But she had a terrible fear. She was afraid to die. She wanted to live a long life so she could help people in need.

One day it began to rain. It rained harder and longer than anyone ever remembered. The water filled the valleys and this girl climbed into a tree to escape from the rising water. But the water came up to the tree where she was. To escape, the girl went to the mountain, but the water from the rain began to cover even the tallest mountain. And then just as this girl thought she was going to die, she heard a voice. It came out of the sky and said, 'Beautiful girl, I know you don't want to die. Because you have been so kind and because you have helped so may people, you will never die. You will be forever in the hearts of all the women in the world. I want to change you. You will become an orchid."

"Each time my grandmother told me this story," continued Manuel, "she would say, 'And so it was that this beautiful girl became an orchid. And when you see orchids in the trees or ladies with orchids or flowers on their dresses, you will know they wear this in memory of the beautiful girl with the shiny black hair and beautiful smile who was kind to everyone. And that is the way you should live, being kind and nice and helping everyone.'"

During the next several hours, Anatole learned that Manuel is not only a great storyteller, but that he enjoys flowers and pets of all kinds. And he learned Manuel enjoys naming his pets after famous people. His frisky German shepherds are named "Golda Meir" and "Aleksandr Solzhenitsyn." Another he calls "Dr. Zhivago." Besides four or five dogs, Manuel has two large parrots and a strutting peacock.

For the next month, Anatole, in the company of a Totonac student, made his way over the steep mountain trails to visit and observe Totonac village life and customs. And as promised, Manuel returned from his speaking tour in time to spend three days with Anatole showing him around Mexico City.

The tour of Mexico City was typical. The only thing atypical for Anatole was the way Manuel prayed and thanked God before each meal they had together in the restaurants. He had never heard anyone pray so spontaneously. Manuel's authentic piety and obvious intimacy with God impressed him.

On the day Anatole was to leave, Manuel took him to the airport. As he was about to depart, Anatole said, "Manuel, I just want to tell you how very much I have appreciated your kindness and friendship to me. I have the deepest admiration for your secular studies and the work you have done and are doing for the Totonacs. And I'm so grateful for the young man you provided to go with me to the village. He was a wonderful help to me.

"I want to tell you that after what I have seen, I am deeply impressed with how the people live their lives. I've noticed that most of them are poor yet they display a peace and contentment I haven't seen in other peoples I've studied and examined. Whatever it is they have, it sure works!"

Anatole ended his kind remarks by inviting Manuel to come and visit him in Tel Aviv. Partly, he said, because he had so many unanswered questions about what it was that caused the people he had visited to respond to life with such positive joy.

"I'm happy for our friendship," said Manuel. "I would like you to write me and I hope one day I can come to visit you. I would also like to meet your sister who gave you the book *Manuel.* Before you go, I have one question I would like to ask you. You said your sister is a Christian. Can you tell me why you are not?"

"That's a straightforward question!" sputtered Anatole. "I don't know if I can fully answer that. I have to tell you that I do enjoy going to church once in a while with my sister whenever I happen to be in London. And as I have said, I am interested in knowing how God has helped you in your work—"

"That is all very nice," interrupted Manuel, "but God doesn't want you to just admire another person or the work he does. He wants you to be awakened to Him and to enjoy Him and the life He has given to you. You have to go now, but would you mind if I prayed for you before you leave?"

Before Anatole could respond, Manuel bowed his head and began to pray: "God, I ask that You will give life to Anatole and that he in turn will give his life to you. And in return, would You give him peace and joy in this life and success in his work? Amen."

Manuel opened his eyes and was about to give Anatole a traditional Mexican farewell *abrazo* (bear hug), when he noticed tears rolling down Anatole's cheeks into his beard. "Manuel," said Anatole softly, "you warned me that something might happen if I stayed too long with you and the Totonacs. I have to tell you something has happened. I am now your spiritual brother. I accepted Jesus into my heart and life while you were praying."

The New Testament pattern for those who newly profess faith in Christ is given to us by Peter and Paul who remained to strengthen and encourage new believers. Manuel could not spend even a day with Anatole, but he could spend another hour if he could get special permission to go through immigration with Anatole.

Graciously, the Mexican immigration official allowed Manuel to accompany Anatole into the waiting area and for the next hour, Manuel encouraged him and suggested that for his own spiritual development and maturity, Anatole begin regular Scripture reading and prayer and be bold to share with others, as he had opportunity, what he had discovered in Christ. Manuel also suggested that as soon as possible he meet with others of like faith for mutual encouragement. Then it was time for Anatole to board his plane for Tel Aviv.

Several years later, Manuel made a special trip to Tel Aviv to see Anatole. To his great delight he discovered Anatole had taken his suggestion and had become established in his faith. Said Manuel, "Anatole has become a special witness to his own people. How glad I am that I never argued with Anatole about my faith. I was just a friend and God worked in his heart!"

Manuel has an innate God-given ability to continually

look for ways he can meet people's needs. Often these
are met through authentic friendships. Sometimes,
however, these needs are met through abrasive circumstances. Such was the case one morning when he
boarded a bus and began to read out loud to the
particular annoyance of two bus passengers.

Chapter Eight

Comings And Goings

While Manuel clearly understands his mandate from God is to minister specifically to his own Totonac people, he is aware of his responsibility to minister to all people. A close examination of his life, practices and responses to people bears a remarkable similarity to that of Paul as recorded in the New Testament Book of Acts.

In his early ministry, Paul traveled from city to city persuading men and women to become disciples of Jesus. Acts 14:22 reveals that Paul and his companion Barnabas spent considerable time encouraging and strengthening the new believers. Manuel, on his visits to hundreds of cities throughout the world, has also been a source of strength and encouragement to others.

On several of his journeys, the Apostle Paul encountered a number of people he had to reprove, as in the case of Elymas the sorcerer in Acts 13:8. He also had numerous encounters where he was required to debate and, by force of intellect and wit, challenge the status quo as he presented the good news concerning Jesus Christ. If you've read thus far, you know that God has also gifted Manuel with considerable wit, charm and ability to persuade and teach.

Paul's biographer historian and physician, Luke, pointed out that in all these comings and goings, Paul was conscious of the Holy Spirit's guidance even when it sometimes seemed contrary to human logic. What was true for Paul has also been true for Manuel.

The big El Norte diesel bus pulled into its accustomed spot in the town of Xicotepec de Juárez the morning Manuel arrived, fresh from spending the night at the Steinlein home. (Many Totonacs who come to visit Manuel are not bound by the "tyranny of the clock." Without such a fine-tuned conception of time, some, in perfect innocence, will knock on Manuel's door just as eagerly at 2:00 a.m. as 2:00 p.m.! For this reason, Heinz, Evangeline and their son Werner have made their home available to Manuel. It's often the only place he can get an uninterrupted night's sleep.)

The bus had come from Tampico on the coast and was almost full when Manuel boarded. Making his way toward the back, he found a middle seat between two professional men in their early thirties, who, although not sitting beside each other, seemed to be friends.

When the bus was finally loaded and roared out of the terminal, Manuel settled back to have a devotional time. He opened his Bible and began reading the Twenty-third Psalm. "As I read," Manuel recalls, "I suddenly thought I should read this beautiful psalm out loud. But then I said to myself, No, if I do this, these men will think I am crazy. Nobody reads out loud on a bus."

Manuel continued to read the psalm to himself but its sheer beauty and the inner nudging that he should read out loud persisted. Reluctantly he obeyed this force that was stronger than logic. About half way through the psalm, the man by the window looked quizzically at Manuel and said, "Do you always read like this? Would you read your private letters or newspaper out loud?"

"No," said Manuel innocently, "I have never before read out loud on a public bus. But this morning as I was reading this psalm, it seemed so beautiful I wanted to share it with someone. I though others might enjoy listening to it because this passage speaks to everyone no matter what their religion. After reading such a passage, it is hard to deny the existence of God and our need of Him. I believe that in spite of what a person says, down deep he is looking for God but is afraid to admit it."

Now fully attentive, the man on the aisle seat interrupted Manuel with, "What do you mean, everyone is looking for God but is afraid to admit it?"

"I'm sure you follow world news from *Time, Newsweek* or *Tiempo,*" said Manuel. "Do you remember when Eisenhower was president of the United States and Russia's Nikita Kruschchev wanted to humiliate him with the Gary Powers U-2 spy-plane incident?"

The two men said they vaguely remembered something about it but had forgotten the details.

"Well," said Manuel, "the news media reported Krushchev as a person who had no religion. Yet, when he was trying to convince the world that the U.S. had sent a U-2 plane to spy on Russia, he said 'As God is my witness.' Now I ask you, how can a man like Krushchev even mention God in such a context if he doesn't believe down deep in his soul there is a God?"

Surprisingly, the two men agreed with Manuel. As they continued to talk, Manuel learned they were lawyers who had spent time in the United States. In turn, Manuel told them about his work and admiration for his own lawyer friends who were helping him develop a Totonac advocacy program.

When the bus finally arrived in Mexico City, the men invited Manuel for lunch at their favorite restaurant.

He happily accepted and when the meal arrived, he asked his new friends if he might pray and thank God for the food. "It's my normal custom," said Manuel. The two men said, "Yes, of course."

Manuel prayed a simple prayer of thanks for the food and then included a request that God reveal Himself to these men in the Person of Jesus Christ as their own Savior and Lord. The men were genuinely touched and thanked Manuel for his prayer.

As they ate, Manuel picked up the conversation where they had left off. "I believe everyone at some time in his life is concerned with the meaning of life and death," said Manuel. "I don't believe the person who tells me he doesn't believe in God. If a person makes such a statement, perhaps he means he can't understand some aspect of God or some idea he has heard about God that may be wrong. I come from a tribe of people who make certain stones into gods. Other people make their work or money their god—" In the middle of his conversation, Manuel was interrupted by three of the lawyers' friends who unexpectably joined them at the table. With the conversation redirected, Manuel finished his meal and then excused himself, but not before the two lawyers arranged another lunch with Manuel the following week to continue their conversation.

The lunch meeting took place two weeks later at the same restaurant. Warm and cordial, the lawyers asked it they could speak in English since they didn't have many opportunities to practice it.

"Perhaps you would like me to read something in English from my New Testament," said Manuel. The lawyers nodded their approval and Manuel read several passages, including John 3:16. Afterward, the conversation fell to the lawyers who spoke of their work and some problems they were facing both professionally and personally.

"When you have such problems," said Manuel, "how do you solve them? Do you go to the mosque? Do you go to a priest for advice and have him say a special mass? Or do you do nothing at all but just wait for whatever happens?"

"We are Catholics," said the lawyers, "but with shame we have to admit we are Catholics in name only. What are you?"

"I am a Christian," said Manuel.

"We are, too," said the two men.

"Wonderful!" said Manuel. "You say you are Christians but are you following Jesus Christ? To be a Christian means to be one who follows Jesus Christ. That's how we get the name. Can you tell me who Christ is, what He taught and what He expects of his followers?"

After a few moments of stammering, the men said they thought Jesus was a great hero for his people and a wonderful man.

"Jesus was more than that," said Manuel. "He is the Savior of the world." At that moment, Manuel reached into his briefcase and pulled out a pocket dictionary. Flipping to the word "Christian," he said, "It says here a Christian is the one who professes and affirms the Scriptures and practices of Christianity. All this is based upon the teaching and practices of Jesus Christ."

Almost immediately after he read, Manuel spotted an American missionary friend entering the restaurant. Beckoning to him, Manuel said, "We are all here practicing our English. Since you are an American, won't you join us? These men would like to hear English spoken the proper way."

"And that," said Manuel, "is how both these men came to know the Lord. For several hours we spoke about the things of God and Christ's redemptive work on the cross. Finally my American missionary friend and I were able, by God's grace, to point them to the way of salvation, and by simple trust, they obtained God's forgiveness for their sins.

"I have never before or since read out loud on a bus, but I am so happy I obeyed the voice of God nudging me to do something that was completely abnormal!"

Manuel may not have read out loud on a crowded bus again, but he has responded to other bizarre situations with the same aplomb and charming naivete. Those who may interpret this deference and humility as "innocence abroad," however, are incorrect in assessing him an easy mark.

In any major airport and even those not so major, seasoned travelers encounter the ubiquitous Japanese businessman. His dark blue business suit, white shirt, black tie and briefcase help identify him. Curiously, when Manuel travels, he is often mistaken for a Japanese businessman. (He has also been mistaken for a Mongolian or Thai.)

Returning from one trip, Manuel asked a Mexican taxi driver to take him to a certain downtown hotel.

"Where are you going?" asked the driver, as he took Manuel's suitcase and stowed it in the taxi trunk.

"To the Hotel La Riviera," said Manuel. (With Manuel's frequent business trips and stopovers, the entire staff at this modest hotel have come to know and love him. Prior arrangements, therefore, have never been necessary. They always find him a room.)

"Do you have a reservation?" asked the taxi driver.

"No, I haven't," said Manuel.

"Oh, I am sorry," said the taxi driver. "This is tourist season. Almost all the hotels are full. Without a reservation you will not be able to find a room."

"It is all right," said Manuel. "I am known at this hotel. I am sure they will have a room for me."

"If you are sure, I will take you. But if La Riviera doesn't have a room, don't worry. I know where to find just the right hotel for you."

Manuel smiled. He had heard such feigned concern before. The driver would receive a certain percentage from the hotel if he brought in a paying customer.

After the usual taxi driver-to-fare chatter, Manuel arrived at his hotel and reached for his wallet. "How much do I owe you?" he asked.

"Twenty dollars," said the taxi driver.

"You must mean twenty pesos," said Manuel.

"No, no," said the taxi driver. "My price is twenty dollars."

"That's too high for such a short trip," said Manuel. "That's much higher than the price listed at the airport."

"All Japanese businessmen pay this amount," said the taxi driver. "You can afford it. You have industries everywhere in the world. And if you don't pay me twenty dollars, I will call a policeman and he will force you to pay me what I asked for."

"Where did you get the idea I am Japanese?" asked Manuel. "I am more Mexican than you."

"How can you be more Mexican than me? I won't force you to pay me the twenty dollars, but just tell me why you don't want to be identified as Japanese. You are dressed like all the other Japanese businessmen and your accent is heavy."

"My Spanish accent is heavy because Spanish is not my first language," said Manuel. "My first language is Totonac."

Visibly surprised, the taxi driver said, "Are you a priest or professor? You look like a respectable person. I want to tell you I am sorry I tried to take advantage of you."

"I am glad you think I look like a respectable person," said Manuel, "because God made me look like this when I became a Christian."

"What do you think I am, an animal?" said the taxi driver. "I am a Christian, too."

"The definition of a Christian is one who follows the teachings of Jesus Christ," said Manuel.

"I have never thought too much about the definition of what a Christian is," said the driver. "I thought everyone who believes in God is a Christian. I would like to know more."

Anxious to get settled in his room, Manuel invited the taxi driver into the hotel lobby. "I have a tract in my suitcase. It will help you understand," said Manuel.

Once inside the lobby, the hotel staff greeted Manuel with enthusiastic Mexican hugs, vigorous handshakes and exclamations of how good it was to see him again. After Manuel paid the taxi driver the correct fee, he gave him a tract that explained the way of salvation. Then he excused himself saying he was quite tired and needed to get his sleep.

About 11:00 p.m., just after Manuel had fallen asleep, his telephone rang.

"Senor Manuel," said the voice, "this is your taxi driver. The tract you gave me? I have been reading it. It is very interesting. I thought you wouldn't mind if I disturbed you. I am in the lobby downstairs. I would like to invite you to have a beer or something and we can talk about this tract."

"I am already in bed and very tired," said Manuel, "I will be happy to talk with you tomorrow."

"Tomorrow I will be busy. I would greatly appreciate it if you could just give me five or ten minutes of your time."

"I will be down in five minutes," said Manuel.

Mexico City is one of those great metropolitan cities that has a reputation as "the city that never sleeps." With the average dinner party beginning about 8:00 or 9:00 p.m., the festivities are often just nicely underway by 11:00 p.m. The two men easily found a small restaurant. Because Manuel has an ulcer problem, he ordered a glass of milk. The driver ordered a tall glass of beer.

After taking a generous gulp, the driver wiped away the foam from his lips with the back of his hand. Then swirling the glass around on top of the condensation that had formed on the table, he said, "I am troubled by a sentence in the tract you gave me. I have read it over and over, but I don't understand it."

"What sentence is that?" asked Manuel.

"It's the sentence that says, 'I am the way, the truth and the life; no man cometh to the Father but by Me.' "

"Just what is it that troubles you about this statement by Jesus?" asked Manuel.

"I believe in St. Peter and St. John and in the Virgin Mary," said the man. "In fact, I believe in all the saints. So what difference does it make if I don't believe just like this tract says?"

"The difference," said Manuel, "is that all the saints were human. They died like all humans do and have no power beyond what they left us as an example to follow or avoid. Some of the saints made mistakes. Peter denied his Lord. Others wanted power. But when Jesus said, 'I am the way, the truth and the life,' He was saying He is the only Savior of the world, that He alone is the way to God the Father. And He proved this by the miracles He did on earth and when He rose from the dead. No other person, no other saint has ever overcome death and risen from the grave, only Jesus Christ."

For the next hour, the two men talked and interacted

with the profound concepts of life and death and life's ultimate meaning. At last the restaurant manager indicated he wanted to close for the night. The taxi driver thanked Manuel for getting out of bed to talk to him and asked when he could talk with him again.

"I'll be back in exactly two weeks," said Manuel. "We can talk again then."

When Manuel returned to Mexico City, he found a note waiting for him at the hotel. The taxi driver wanted to meet him at 4:00 p.m. "After taking care of my business," said Manuel, "I returned to the hotel and to my amazement and joy, found my new friend and new brother. He told me he had become a Christian since I last saw him and for the first time he understood that Jesus Christ was truly the way, truth and life."

Occasionally Manuel sees his taxi-driver friend at the airport. When he does, the man who has become an active witness among his fellow taxi drivers and an active lay preacher in his church, greets Manuel with, "How's my Japanese friend?" Not to be outdone, Manuel responds, "Do you still want the twenty dollars?"

My first introduction to Manuel was in 1958 at the Mexico City SIL headquarters building affectionately known as the "Kettle." He reminded me of a cocker spaniel—eager, all smiles, enthusiastic, serious and attentive when you spoke directly to him, but only able to stand still for a few moments before he was off, seemingly caught up in some inescapable duty that had to be acted upon immediately.

When we met together at the Totonac Cultural Center to research this sequel, I found little had changed in thirty years. He didn't move quite as fast, but still retained that same eager intensity and looked at me squarely to answer any question, no matter how trivial. Also, he still seemed caught up in the pressure of duty. There was little time for small talk. In fact, there was a certain March Hare quality to his intensity. Repeatedly he said, "I must be doing my public relations. I must be doing my public relations."

This drive to do "public relations" is not the Madison Avenue hype. While he is conscious of the need to keep his friends and supporters informed of the school's progress through letters and public-speaking tours, his drive to do public relations has little to do with the Western concept of promoting an individual or organization or particular enterprise such as the Totonac Cultural Center.

Manuel is a member of a tribe, a clan, a larger family group—the Totonacs—but at the same time, he has been able to transcend his tribalness to embrace and understand a Western point of view and culture. He is truly at home in both worlds. When Manuel, therefore, speaks about his "public relations," he is really speaking about his role as an advocate and arbitrator, as well as, of course, his role as teacher and encourager. Since the advent of TV, he increasingly mediates in the emerging social problem of divorce and breakdown of the nuclear family. But perhaps the greatest challenge for his particular brand of public relations is his role as advocate. Both talents focus sharply when he deals with Totonacs who, after falling under the ideological spell of anti-government agitators, discover too late they have been victimized and turn to him for help.

Most of the agitation among the Totonacs has to do with stirring up dissent against the government and large landowners. Through wild rhetoric, some Totonacs have been duped into illegal action and have tried, by force, to take away land from the large landowner. In every case, the Totonac has lost and either been jailed or dispersed, losing what little he had.

Manuel sharply opposes this element and urges the Totonacs to obey the government and its laws. "I am for change and reforms," he says, "but non-violent, peaceful, orderly legal change. I am interested first of all in a spiritual change, the kind that comes about from the love of God in a person's heart. It is the person with a heart full of love who will work for peaceful change within his community."

Some agitators have opposed Manuel for his evangelical stand, yet seem to appreciate his work in the community. Reports indicate that some have even come under cover of darkness to be treated at the clinic. Others say Manuel is a marked man. For this reason, many of Manuel's friends have a mild apprehension for his safety.

On the other hand, Manuel plays his role as an advocate against local authorities who in his opinion have been unfair or unjust in their treatment of Totonacs. Working with his lawyers, he tries to obtain the best legal defense he can for those jailed or accused of a crime. "I am interested in justice," said Manuel. "I don't want to be a judge and try to decide who is innocent or guilty, but when I see a Totonac in jail, I want to know why he is there, what he has been charged with and what his sentence will be."

Growing out of this advocacy role has come a larger ministry that Manuel has called, "The Indian Congress of Mexico." For several years, Manuel has worked with and now serves as the official Mexico representative on the board of CHIEF (Christian Hope Indian Eskimo Fellowship). Endorsed by Billy Graham and under the able leadership of Tom Claus, president of CHIEF, this Arizona-based organization reaches out to "encourage, strengthen and disciple native American Christian believers, church leaders and pastors." CHIEF does this through the agencies of conferences and fellowship groups that are culturally sensitive to a wide ethnic mix.

"I was encouraged to see what Tom Claus was doing in the United States, Canada and Alaska," said Manuel, "but who would take care of Mexico? As I thought about this, it came into my heart that I should try to have a fellowship group like CHIEF in Mexico and invite as many Indian leaders and pastors as I could to come for a conference at the Center."

In 1981, Manuel held his first Indian Congress. Forty-five Indian leaders came. They represented lay leaders and pastors from among the Tarascan, Zapotec, Mixtec, Tzeltal and, of course, the Totonac. Said Manuel, "It was a wonderful experience. For the first time in history, we began to understand some of the problems our brothers in other parts of the country were having. And we gained strength from one another just to know we were not alone."

The second and third attempt to bring together such a congress was fraught with logistical difficulties. The second location at the Tzeltal Bible School in the State of Chiapas proved to be too isolated and too expensive for most of those invited. At the third Congress, Manuel, by example, demonstrated that one's manhood wasn't lost by cooking or washing dishes. Arrangements for this important detail had been overlooked.

But in spite of these difficulties, the notion of a yearly congress of pastors and Christian leaders from among Mexico's ethnic minorities was an idea whose time had come. CHIEF's 1985 quarterly bulletin had the following report:

MEXICAN INDIANS REJOICE
Manuel Arenas, our Mexican CHIEF representative, tells how the Christian Indians throughout

Mexico have taken a giant step forward in the last year!

In the CHIEF conference in San José del Paraiso, Oaxaca, more than 2,000 Christians gathered from thirteen different tribes. They had tremendous times of fellowship together and were challenged to go back to their tribes to reach the lost for Christ.

They started meetings as early as 6:00 a.m. and continued until 11:30 at night, listening to God's Word. Bible teachers Claudio Iglesias, our Kuna Indian leader, and Pablo Silva of the Mexico office of Open Doors, taught the Word and brought workshops especially helpful to the Indians' needs.

There was a great expression of unity and love. It began with the Mixe Indian Christians who were the hosts. They opened up their homes so all had a place to sleep. They butchered cows for meat and had big pots of beans going all the time. The women made great numbers of tortillas, just about non-stop so they could feed everyone.

It was a blessed experience for the Indian church in Mexico. Pray for Manuel as he leads the CHIEF ministries and Totonac Cultural Center in Mexico.

The beginning of this chapter speaks about Manuel's mandate from God to minister to all people. Sometimes, however, possibilities that occur to a visionary, wrinkle the sensibilities of those in a more conservative or legalistic camp. Such was the case in the early 1980s when the German mission, which provided skillful doctors for the clinic and faithfully supported Manuel, turned against him. "It was," said Manuel, "one of the most difficult, painful and darkest periods in my life."

Chapter 9

The Rotary Project

By all outward appearances, life at the school in 1983 and 1984 couldn't have been better. Manuel's dream of helping the Totonacs in "as many different ways as possible" was being realized. The experimental agricultural farm had recovered from Hurricane Fifi and sported handsome cement pigpens, chicken runs and outbuildings. It had been restocked with over two hundred chickens, plus pigs, rabbits and sheep. A healthy section was allocated for growing corn and other vegetables. All this was under the watchful eyes of two young Mexican graduate students from Poza Rica—an agronomist and a trained veterinarian. While maintaining the farms, they gave classes in animal husbandry, land management, crop rotation, plant nutrition and many other practical skills. And under Manuel's direction, there was a cooperative plan with the Heifer Project, to distribute animals to several different villages.

The clinic was treating as many as seventy to a hundred outpatients a day. The Mexican Department of Health had assigned a doctor to serve his internship at the clinic and Manuel had also arranged for an additional Mexican doctor with his American-born wife to serve the larger community of La Union.

The school had a Volkswagen that Heinz drove. A new dormitory was built to accommodate students coming in from the countryside to take animal hus-

bandry and agricultural courses. All these activities
were sponsored in part by Rotary International and the
Rotary Club of Ventura, California. For Manuel, however, this sponsorship precipitated a severe crisis in his
ministry.

Since the beginning of his work among his own
people, Manuel has always accepted help to realize his
goals. Generally, this comes from individuals who have
visited the Totonac Cultural Center, from churches
who have either heard Manuel speak or heard about
the school indirectly, or from Bible schools or Christian
technical schools like Le Tourneau College and John
Brown University.

Then Dr. Searer, a fine Christian doctor and lifelong
Rotarian from Ventura, California (he had organized
medical teams to visit the Totonacs each year) suggested
a larger training program for village medical workers.
Manuel's goal of unselfish service to his community,
including vocational training and international goodwill, meshed with Rotary International ideals. So with
Manuel's and his American board's backing, Dr. Searer
made a proposal for Rotary sponsorship.

The Rotary began to provide a doctor for La Union
and rotated volunteer doctor and dentist teams at the
clinic. They also provided money for buildings and
sponsored two teachers on the experimental farm.
Manuel thought his dream was coming true. Instead,
however, it turned out to be a nightmare.

Trouble surfaced when some of Manuel's European
supporters, particularly the German mission that had
sponsored many doctors and had given money, equipment and medicines for the clinic, objected to his
working with a secular organization. The German
mission reasoned that, while the Rotary was philan-
thropic, they were not spiritually motivated. "Further-

more," they said, "many of the people who come to help in the clinic are not born-again believers. To identify closely with such individuals would lead Totonac believers astray because they would not see 'separateness' (i.e., separating oneself from the world and being unequally yoked with persons who don't share the same worldview). Here was a complication that neither Manual nor his board had considered when they accepted the Rotary's offer of assistance for practical projects.

At first, letters from Germany expressed dismay with this new relationship. When they saw Manuel had no intention of reversing his decision, they sent delegations. One German doctor asked Manuel for the dates he would be at the school. He came, however, when Manuel was absent and was able to persuade some students and village pastors that it was wrong for a secular organization to help in "God's" work. Their disaffection wounded Manuel.

At a meeting between the leaders of his American board and the German mission in Mexico City, Manuel maintained his right as a Totonac and a Mexican to decide how best to provide this physical help for his own people. In letters to the German mission and in verbal confrontation with those who opposed the Rotary involvement, Manuel defended his fidelity to the Gospel. "In order to practice medicine in Mexico," said Manuel, "foreign doctors have to be certified by the Mexican Department of Health. Because they are invited by this department, they are under their jurisdiction and I have no legal authority to ask them to leave."

Two basic issues were involved in this conflict. The American board believed that a foreign entity was out of order to use its resources as a lever to achieve and maintain control over a national ministry. Obviously their view was not shared by the German group. The second issue had to do with the question of "separation." "Separation," said Manuel, "does not mean withdrawal from the world. The Bible tells us to be salt and light in a dark, tasteless world. Jesus also said he came to heal those who were sick, not those who were well. He came to call the unrighteous, not the righteous." Manuel pointed out that we are willing to work with a non-Christian lawyer to get a case settled or an engineer to get work done so why not a doctor in a clinic or agriculturalists on the farm?

Manuel has always taught his students to live their lives in ways that please God, lives that reflect the character of Jesus Christ. To further define his position, he points to his practice of daily Scripture reading and short devotional and prayer time after breakfast with his guests or volunteers, regardless of their religious or ideological backgrounds.

To illustrate how the Spirit of God can use such a simple ministry in a person's life, Manuel relates the story of the Rotary-sponsored Brazilian dentist who came to work in the clinic.

"The dentist was a good man, a kind and thoughtful man," said Manuel, "but he had never opened his life to God in a personal way. One morning I had to leave the school early on business. That morning there was no Scripture reading or devotional time. When I returned in the afternoon, the dentist greeted me warmly and said he was glad I had returned. We spoke for a few moments and then he asked me why we didn't have devotions that morning.

"I explained I had left on urgent business before dawn to get a bus. Then he asked if it was possible to have devotions later that day. I told him it was but I couldn't call everyone back from their work, so I suggested that just he and I have a devotional time together.

"After I read the Scripture and made a little comment, I prayed and then asked the dentist why he had requested this special devotional time. 'I think my soul needs some spiritual food,' he said. 'Wonderful!' I said, and then I asked him if he had ever heard about God and the Lord before coming to the clinic. 'No,' he said, 'but two things have happened to me since coming here. The first is that it seems to me that God is in this place. And the second is that since coming, my grandmother's words keep coming back to me. I think she had the same kind of mind and faith in God as you.'"

Manuel said the conversation then drifted to another subject and he asked the dentist how much longer he would be at the clinic before returning to Brazil.

"I leave in two weeks," said the dentist.

"Fine," said Manuel. "Before you leave, I would like to take you to the famous ancient Totonac pyramids and afterward we will go to a seafood restaurant in Poza Rica."

"I will look forward to that," said the dentist.

When Manuel and the dentist were at the restaurant a few days later, Manuel did as he had done countless times before—he prayed. He thanked God for the time they were enjoying together and then asked God to be with the dentist as he returned to his home. When Manuel concluded his prayer, the dentist questioned him about his faith, then asked specifically how he could become a Christian like Manuel.

"You or anyone can become a true Christian when you are willing to take Jesus into your heart."

"I don't understand," said the dentist. "How exactly can I do this?"

"You must be willing to believe God loves you and died for you, and then just like we did in our devotions, you pray to Him and tell Him you want to follow Him and be his child."

"Is that all?" asked the dentist. "Don't I have to make a longer prayer?"

"No," said Manuel, "you don't have to make a long prayer, or do penance, or give money to a church or in any way do any outward thing. Everything you do is inward. Just believe and trust in God with all your heart like a little child."

And before he left the restaurant that night, the dentist, like many people before him, was born into the Kingdom of God.

Manuel carefully documented this story and others like it as examples of the school's ministry in the lives of those the Rotarians sponsored, but some still believed that he had somehow compromised his faith. "You are mixing believers with unbelievers in your work," they said. If you ask them to leave, we will continue to commit ourselves to the Totonac ministry. If not, we have no choice but to withdraw all financial aid and cease to fellowship with you in any way."

Manuel refers to this rejection as a time of great personal pain and bewilderment. Bewilderment because some were not content to simply stop their own financial and prayer support for the Totonac Center, but encouraged many of Manuel's friends to follow suit.

In an effort to set the record straight and maintain his own identity and the identity and dignity of the Totonac work, Manuel wrote a definitive letter to his German friends, who were still confused over the German mission's attitude and action toward him, the school and the clinic work. In the letter, Manuel emphasized his long-standing practice of extending love and hospitality to all people regardless of ideological background.

"Why did God send his Son Jesus Christ into the world?" wrote Manuel. "Because He loves everyone. And you know He came to his own people, the Jews, but they rejected Him. God then gave us the privilege of telling all kinds of people the wonderful story of God's love, no matter who they are—Rotarians, Jews, Gentiles, whoever."

Manuel admitted that the delegation visiting when he was not at the school had caused serious divisions among several lay pastors. The division centered around who was to be recognized as their leader. "These pastors were acting just like the early Christians in First Corinthians 1:12," wrote Manuel. "In that story, some wanted to follow Apollos; others wanted to follow Cephas or Paul and so on. For the delegation to pit the clinic workers against me was a terrible wrong against the authority of Scripture. The Bible tells us we are to encourage one another and avoid division and those things that divide the church. I want the allegiance of all students to belong to the Lord Jesus Christ, not to me or any other person, foreign or otherwise. If you believe the letters and words against me that have come from the delegation, then I urge you to discontinue supporting me or the Totonac work. But if you have doubt, think of what you know about me and how God has worked among the Totonacs, and let your conscience be your guide."

Manuel concluded his letter by explaining how grateful he was to God for the Rotarians' help. "Because they came, I am happy to tell you two important things have happened. The first is that modern agricultural methods have been introduced to the people. The students are returning to their villages with new techniques and practical ways to care for their livestock, improve their soil and upgrade their crops.

"The second thing is that many of my long-term goals are being realized. One of the most important goals was that the people would have improved diets by adding meat protein and vegetables to their diet. It used to make me sad to see the people eating their seed corn because they didn't have enough food to last between harvest and planting and harvesting again. Now, because the Rotary came and provided money to hire a veterinarian and an agronomist, the people are not suffering from lack of food. They are stronger and can resist disease and sickness."

The letter helped Manuel solidify his position but the misunderstanding between himself and his German friends continued. After receiving this letter, many friends expressed sadness over this rupture but promised they would continue to support and pray for him and the Totonac work. As for the German mission, all was not forgiven and restored even after offical Rotary support ceased. Manuel occasionally still receives critical letters and inquiries from people who have heard from "somewhere" that he is involved with a secular organization. Although it was a regrettable circumstance, Manuel did not let it deter him from his ministry of serving God by serving the Totonac people. He always has more projects and ideas than he has time or energy to accomplish. In fact, two of them were in process when Manuel wrote his letter. One had to do with the way a small Totonac community had been redesigned.

When Dr. Schmalenbach, the clinic's first doctor returned to Germany, he was replaced by Dr. Hans Mammele. Young and eager to do more than merely prescribe pills for the Totonac's many ailments, Dr.

Mammele began to attack one of their most endemic and chronic problems—diarrhea.

He began by taping a practical lecture in Totonac on how to build a latrine from the bamboo that grew in abundance along the riverbanks. Played over loudspeakers to the waiting area, patients could both listen to it and follow the step-by-step explanation from a series of twenty drawings mounted on the wall. Yet in spite of his valiant effort, the high incidents of diarrhea continued. Sometimes, in the case of young children, they were fatal.

"We must attack this problem at the grass roots," said Dr. Mammele to Manuel one day. "I would like to visit one of the villages and speak directly to the Christians. Perhaps the community could be persuaded to build latrines if they saw how this reduces disease."

In the company of a Totonac student, Dr. Mammele spent a week in the town of Mecatlan where he succeeded in persuading several believers to build latrines. He then returned to his clinic duties much encouraged.

Weeks and months passed, however, without any appreciable reduction of the diarrhea problem. Nonetheless, Dr. Mammele was pleased that he had been able to initiate a community health trend that he hoped would grow into full-scale acceptance.

Just before Dr. Mammele was scheduled to leave for Germany, he returned to Mecatlan to check on his project. With pride, several families showed him the latrines they had built. One curious fact, however, puzzled the young doctor. The latrines were almost as clean as when they were first built. When Dr. Mammele asked why, the believers answered, "Oh, we only use them for visitors." Dr. Mammele left Totonac country convinced his project had failed. But it hadn't!

Antonio Morales, a young Totonac man who had dropped out of school in his third year to support his growing family, returned to his village captivated by the idea of town planning and encouraged everyone to build and use latrines. So convinced was he that this important value be adopted, he went from house to house urging every family to consider this innovation.

Furthermore, working in conjuction with the village mayor (a believer along with most of the community), Antonio spearheaded a redevelopment project that proposed a public park in the center of town with symmetrical streets and sidewalks extending from its center. It took about ten years to accomplish, but little by little the people began to build their houses along the street front with latrines out back. Proud of this accomplishment, the villagers now refer to Antonio affectionately as "Engineer Antonio Morales."

Another goal not mentioned in Manuel's letter was to help Totonac men understand that their manhood wasn't validated by the size of their families. With the advent of TV, greater exposure to the outside world and shifts within the culture, Manuel and the clinic staff were being asked unprecedented questions. "I am concerned about having too many children. Is there something my wife and I can do?"

For a Totonac man to even consider such things when the clinic began was unthinkable. Now men were willing to accept responsibility for having only three or four children instead of ten or twelve. When Manuel first learned that men were indeed contemplating smaller family sizes, he instituted a series of special lectures that ran concurrent with clinic hours.

Still another project that occupied Manuel in the mid-eighties was the radio ministry. Under Felipe's able administration, the program was exceeding everyone's expectations. Weekly, Manuel heard of new groups of Totonac believers meeting together and listening to the radio ministry. But then, in October 1983, he received an official letter from the mayor of Poza Rica asking him to answer charges that his radio program was broadcasting religious propaganda in violation of Mexican law.

The meeting between Manuel and the mayor was cordial, but frank and straightforward. "The station manager tells me your Totonac radio program is heard on Sundays," said the mayor. "Is that correct?"

"Yes," said Manuel. "It goes out to over a hundred villages."

"That is why I have asked you to come to see me," said the mayor. "The station manager likes your program as well as Felipe, the one who does the broadcasting. I suppose the radio program is good business for the radio station, but I am told you broadcast religious messages. If you continue to do this, you will be liable for a five-year prison sentence. You know the law. There is to be no religious radio or television broadcasting."

"Yes," said Manuel, "I know the law very well, and we obey the law. Our program features common everyday things the Totonacs are interested in. We talk about the importance of hygiene and how to avoid getting sick by washing our hands and building a fire table to raise our food off the ground. We tell people how to treat malaria and typhoid, and we talk about the Totonac New Testament. This is a book of a high moral value and the government appreciates the good influence that comes from the Bible. We also tell our listeners about the Totonac dictionary and other books that have been translated into their language. At the end of the program we say that life is better if you will invite God into your life. Now, if you like, find a Totonac man who has been offended by our radio program. Bring him here and I will gladly answer all his questions."

The mayor threw up his hands in exasperation. "I have done what has been required of me. The Mexican government is taking a hard look at all radio broadcasting that might be considered religious. I suggest you work out any problems with the station manager."

"The mayor is right," said the station manager when Manuel told him what the mayor had said. "All religious programming was taken off the air in Mexico City. Now we must do the same. I would like to help you and I think we can work out the problems if we do a few things."

The station manager suggested that all Gospel music be discontinued and asked to be given a copy of Felipe's messages translated from Totonac to Spanish. Lastly, he told Manuel that they were going to suspend the broadcast for several months until the situation cooled.

Manuel accepted the station manager's recommendation. "It's part of our Christian responsiblity to obey the government and let them know what we are doing," said Manuel to Felipe. "We don't want anyone to be suspicious of us."

Today, the format remains almost unchanged from before the inquiry. The music is a mixture of Mexican and native Totonac folk tunes. With his fireside-chitchat style, Felipe has achieved almost celebrity status. In one town he visited, the mayor and all the townspeople turned out to welcome the one they had heard on the radio!

Felipe often uses the radio program as a community bulletin board. Sometimes people send in money for a New Testament but do not include their home address.

He then sends out a message over the radio that he has sent a Totonac New Testament to such and such a town for such and such a person. "If this person is listening or is known in the town," says Felipe, "please tell him his New Testament is waiting for him at the place where mail is received." At the end of the program, Felipe, who has talked about most of the things the Totonacs like to hear, invited the listeners to consider God. "Life is much better when God is invited into one's life."

More and more Felipe faces the clash of new and old cultural patterns. Along with the requests for Totonac New Testaments, he often receives letters like one he received from a sixteen-year-old. "I am in love with a girl," wrote the young man, "who has not been chosen by my family. What can I do?" The only thing Felipe can do is respond by suggesting both he and his parents reach an agreement consistent with the old and emerging culture.

While Manuel, his staff and students make every effort to maintain community goodwill and openness, some still choose to oppose Manuel and the school. A few of Manuel's letters indicate that some new believers also face stiff opposition.

> I must go to San Pedro where Christians have been killed. Just now sixteen believers have been brought to the clinic after suffering from smoke inhalation after a leftist mob attacked their church during a prayer meeting. Pray that God will protect me as I go. I want to be a good witness to the town authorities and at the same time protect the believers from further attack.

Yet in spite of the stepped-up persecution against some groups of believers, the Totonac church has continued to grow. About two months after the incident at San Pedro, Manuel reported the following.

We are all rejoicing over a great victory for the Lord. Forty-one new believers were recently baptized in a nearby town as a result of the radio program. These believers were actually from another village where they had been listening to the radio program for a long time. Many wanted to accept the Lord but were afraid of the local witch doctor. For six years he opposed the Gospel, then two months ago he accepted the Lord.

When the people were baptized, the witch doctor gave a banquet for all the believers. For two days they were rejoicing in the Lord! God has again come to our Totonac people. Praise the Lord!

In another letter, Manuel told of eighty-two believers who were baptized. "When I went through this town in 1970," said Manuel, "there were no believers. But through the years the people listened to the Totonac radio program and now without any of us knowing it, scores of people have come to know the Lord."

On these occasions when the Totonac believers were baptized in their rivers and streams, Felipe and others gave a message centered around the liberation and freedom they had found in Christ. "We are new creations in Christ Jesus," they said. "We are liberated from the tyranny of this world and from the old gods and spirits that kept us captive from knowing the true God. All of us will one day die. Some like our brothers and sisters in San Pedro may die sooner than others. But we need not fear. We, as this baptism shows us, have been raised to a new and eternal life in Christ Jesus."

The baptisms and reports of many Totonacs coming to faith in Christ fill Manuel with special joy and satisfaction. He lives for little else. Yet for all his activities, he often experiences the loneliness of leadership. Often the demands from those who believe he has the answers to all their problems become too much for him and he wisely exhorts them to seek God, as he does, for guidance and help.

He seldom complains about his loneliness, nor does he ever speak about another pain—that pain of rejection from his father and siblings years before, when he was ordered out of his father's house because he would not renounce his new-found faith. Sometimes, in quiet moments when he stops to pat his favorite German shepherds, he remembers with sadness the death of his mother and father within a year of each other.

Their deaths occurred when Manuel was studying at Dallas Bible College. It took more than a month for him to learn of his mother's death, and another month to hear about his father's. His mother, of course, had grown in her faith and Manuel had enjoyed special times of fellowship with her when he had visited. But resolution or reconciliation never came between himself and his father or his four older brothers and sisters.

For several years during the Bible school's early development, Manuel would hear pieces of information about his brothers and sisters. Because his hometown was reachable only by steep, rugged mountain trails, he had not been able to return there since his back operation. Then in the early 1980s, Manuel learned from Herman Aschmann that his two brothers and a sister had all died within several months of each other. All that remained of his immediate family was a sister whom he hadn't seen in twenty years.

Manuel learned his sister had a son and that his

nephew had graduated from high school. This was a great surprise to Manuel. He never knew his hometown had a high school. To honor his nephew, Manuel sent him a Bible for his graduation along with an invitation to visit him at the Center. Several months passed and Manuel never heard from him.

Then one morning about 6:00 a.m. as Manuel was drinking a hot cup of tea and preparing to leave for Mexico City, he heard a knock on the dining room door. When he opened it, he saw a young man in his late teens standing before him. "Yes," said Manuel, "who are you?"

"I am Louis Lopez, the son of your sister," said the young man. "I am accepting your invitation."

Chapter 10

A Good Name

Manuel's hometown of Zapotitlán, with its thousand-plus inhabitants, had always been an important trade center for the highland Totonacs. The half-dozen stores made from rough hand-hewn plank boards were bleached charcoal gray by the sun and rain. On the main street fronted by these stores, skinny dogs meandered aimlessly, their rat-like tails perpetually dangling between their legs. Pigs, chickens and turkeys scurried out of the way of mules ladened with heavy sacks of coffee. It was a highland town like many others, but one most resistant to change and the Gospel.

Then, a road came to Zapotitlán and connected it to other towns, particularly to Zongosotla, its neighbor. Zongosotla, about half an hour distant and several hundred feet higher up the mountainside, had always been a town of little significance to the people of Zapotitlán. But the road changed all this. Zongosotla's residents were eager for change and innovation. The Christians even introduced new hymns and songs for their services, songs that had been forbidden by their more conservative counterparts in Zapotitlán.

At first, the changes were almost imperceptible. Slowly people began to move to Zongosotla and make shifts in their life-styles. Instead of hauling coffee sacks and other salable items to market by human carrier or mule train, people began to ride the bus with their goods stashed on top. Those who wanted to visit

Manuel at the Totonac Cultural Center could now reach the lowland in four to five hours instead of the two-and-a-half to three-day hike over slippery, lung-splitting mountain trails.

"Our town is not like it was when you were there," said Louis. "Besides the high school we have many more stores and houses. After the road came, many people moved to Zongosotla. That's where I like to go to church."

"Go to church." This was almost too much for Manuel to comprehend. First, from out of nowhere, his nephew appeared with news of his family and hometown. Now he was telling him he was interested in spiritual things, that he had become a Christian and he regularly attended church!

"How did all this come about?" asked Manuel.

"When your gift of a Bible came, I tried to read it," said Louis, "but I hardly understood a word. Then one day an evangelist passed through Zapotitlán. I showed him the Bible and told him I didn't understand what it was saying. This evangelist was a kind man and he explained over and over what the Gospel meant. Finally, I understood and accepted the Lord. Now that I am a Christian I am telling my whole family about the Lord."

"Have any of them become Christians?" asked Manuel.

"So far none of them are interested," said Louis, "but I am continuing to talk with them and pray for them."

"That is the best thing you can do," said Manuel. "I too will join you and begin to pray more for my sister and six nieces."

Manuel had heard, seen and felt the evidence of God's grace to his nephew. No human could have orchestrated such an event, particularly in a family that had been so fierce and unbending in their resolve to oppose him and his faith. To his further amazement and delight, one day, perhaps a year after his nephew's visit, Manuel received yet another family member at the school. It was Anita, his older sister by eight years.

With tears, Manuel's sister said, "I have come to see you and tell you I am like you. My son Louis is the one who told me about our Lord Jesus Christ and now I have become a believer."

Anita had arrived at the Center in the morning, a time when the sun spilled its pure light across the dark green grass to catch dewdrops and transform them into a carpet of sparkling jewels. A time when sunlight's long shadows skimmed around a field of full-faced sunflowers and through a delicate lace of feathery leaves, ferns and grasses. From Manuel's viewpoint, never was a morning more beautiful or symbolic of this profound moment. Nor was there a time in recent memory when he experienced more joy, pure excitement and grateful praise to God. And he wept.

Full of questions, Manuel first asked why his sister had come to see him after all these years. "I made this long trip to see you because since I became a Christian, I have learned there should be no more barriers between those of us who love the Lord. The more I have grown to love the Lord, the more I have felt the need to see you and make all my past mistakes right."

Still weeping, Anita continued. "I have come to tell you how sorry I am for the way I treated you. When you became a Christian, our father said I was never to see you or speak to you again. He said we must do this to bring you back to the old religion. Now I am so very sorry for all the pain I caused you and the way I spoke against you. I need you to forgive me."

With his own eyes brimming, Manuel reached out to embrace his sister. The next three days Manuel and Anita spoke together and recalled childhood memories.

Manuel wanted to introduce his sister to his larger
work, but Anita had no reference point. She was a
Totonac woman who had lived her life in a tiny
mountain village and could not relate to what her
brother had seen and done. At her age she didn't need
to. Her needs were complete. Her broken relationship
between God and her brother was restored and Anita
Lopez, sister to Manuel Arenas, returned to her mountain village of Zapotitlán a different woman. Her
despair was replaced by rejoicing.

Proverbs 22:1 says that a good name is more desirable
than riches. From personal contacts and hundreds of
letters, Manuel knows that the Center's ministries do
indeed have a good name. Hundreds of satisfied
Totonacs have spread the news that excellent treatment
is available at the clinic. One day Manuel learned the
clinic's good name had even reached a wealthy woman
in Mexico City.

"You have some visitors," said a student to Manuel
one afternoon. "We don't know where they're from but
there are three or four important-looking cars parked
on the outside road. One is a Cadillac!"

"Fine," said Manuel. "They will probably come
inside in a few minutes and ask for me." But Manuel
was wrong. None of the visitors asked for him.

His curiosity aroused, Manuel walked outside to
investigate. Just as the student had reported, four luxury
automobiles were parked alongside the road, and one
was a Cadillac with Mexico City license plates.

Surprised by this prestigious entourage, Manuel
asked the visitors, who were now standing in line
behind several Totonac families waiting their turn to
see the clinic doctors, "Who among you would like to
see me?"

The group of visitors looked blankly at each other and when no one said anything, one woman in the group said, "We really didn't come to see you. We all came to have a consultation with the doctor. We have heard there is a good doctor here and that you have good medicines."

"I am glad you have heard about how good our doctors are," said Manuel, "but I am sorry to tell you these doctors are only for the Totonacs and poor people who have no money and cannot afford a good doctor. You are from the city. There you have fine hospitals, clinics and good doctors and I see by the way you are dressed and the cars you drive that you have money to pay for these medical services in the city."

Three of the four visitors nodded in understanding. They said they were disappointed at not being able to see the doctors, particularly after driving such a long distance. Nevertheless, they thanked Manuel and then drove off in their cars—except for the woman with the Cadillac.

Manuel turned to see why she hadn't left and smiled inwardly. It was gently humorous to see a beautifully manicured, sophisticated woman dressed in an expensive designer dress and white high-heels standing in line behind a group of Totonac women in peasant dresses.

"I am sorry," said Manuel. "You will wait in vain to see the doctor."

"Look," said the woman, "I can pay as much as the doctor will charge me."

"Yes, I know," said Manuel. "I see it is true you can pay. But I must tell you again, the doctor doesn't serve in this clinic to be paid. He came here to help people who cannot pay." With that, the woman turned on her heel and marched toward her car.

A short time later, Manuel began searching for one of his German shepherd dogs. (Unknown to Manuel, the dog had been accidently locked in one of the rooms.) Thinking the dog may have gone outside the grounds, he went out the gate to where the patients were waiting to see the doctor. To his surprise, the woman from Mexico City was standing in line again.

This time Manuel almost laughed out loud. She had wiped off all her makeup, including the green eye-shadow that had outlined her lovely dark eyes. Gone were her shoes, her expensive dress and carefully coiffed hair. Said Manuel, "She had on terrible shoes without heels, no stockings and a dress with holes. I wasn't even sure it was the same woman until I spoke to her and recognized both her voice and gold teeth. Once again I explained the clinic was set up to serve only those who could not afford to pay for medical services and that even though she had changed her clothes, the doctor could not see her. The woman was still persistent. She offered me money and said she could pay the amount the doctor wanted. I told her again the doctor didn't come here to make money, just to serve the poor. Finally she left saying she couldn't understand why I wouldn't take the money she offered. I was sorry to have to do this but also thankful to the Lord that the good name of the Totonac Cultural Center Clinic had reached even the cities!"

The clinic, school and radio ministry are not alone in receiving special recognition. Manuel himself is also recognized as one of Mexico's outstanding evangelical Indian leaders. Under his leadership and encouragement, many of Mexico's ethnic minorities are producing leaders who make decisions and assume responsibility for their own people.

In addition to serving on CHIEF's board and on the

board of the Indian Congress of Mexico, Manuel serves on the board of the Mexican Mission Aviation Fellowship (MAF). In recognition of this and his contribution to the Totonac people, in June 1985, John Calvin Theological Seminary honored Manuel by conferring on him the honorary degree of Doctor of Theology. Unable to attend the special graduation ceremonies where he would be honored, Manuel asked Felipe to receive the degree for him. The seminary graciously accepted Felipe as Manuel's substitute, but they still wanted to hear from him. Thus three months later in September 1985, Manuel, in a special session, addressed John Calvin's faculty and the faculty of a sister seminary in Detroit. Said Manuel:

I am greatly honored by this degree. I know there are many others who are more worthy than I. But in honoring me in this way, you are also honoring the Totonacs and all Indian people. This will encourage them to realize that if this could happen to me, it can also happen to them. And it will encourage students who come to the Totonac Cultural Center to finish the schooling they have begun. Sometimes students come to the school because they think it would be "nice" to have such an experience. And then after several weeks or a couple of months, some get homesick, or they don't like the food, or they think the studies are too hard, or they don't like their teachers. And then they want to drop out and quit.

When they do, I remind them of why they have come. I ask them to remember Jesus' words in the Great Commission and the promise that He will be with them in all their difficulties. I tell them the Gospel was first spread throughout the world by

Christians who were just like them and who suffered great persecutions. I challenge the students to listen carefully to the call of God in their lives, to have a commitment first to Jesus Christ and then to helping their Totonac people. I say, yes, you have problems and life is difficult. But when you know God is calling you and you have a mission and a vision and a dream of what God can do in you and for you, you will continue on in spite of the problems and hardships.

Then I say, when God commanded us to go into all the world with the Gospel, He gave this responsibility to people—people just like you and me. Jesus could have given this job to angels. Instead He gave it to humans who are weak and often want to quit. And this is why I am training students—so they can be instruments God can use. And He can use us even if we are weak.

I want to conclude by saying that all my life I have considered myself to be just an instrument in the hands of God. He can do with me what is best. Also I want the Totonacs, my friends and the public to know all that has happened among the Totonacs—the New Testament translated by Mr. Aschmann and the churches that now number forty-six with more than 40,000 believers in a population of a quarter of a million. All this happened because of God. He allowed me to have a dream, and I dreamed of four things. I dreamed of the Bible school, of the establishment of churches, of the radio ministry and finally the clinic. All these four dreams the Lord has allowed to become a reality. And I say this is a miracle of God.

Now I have yet another dream. I want to see the clinic become a hospital and I am concerned for the rights of Indians who have been cheated out of their land or who are often being jailed wrongfully. When all these things have been accomplished, then I will think of other ways to help the Totonacs and other Indians of Mexico.

I thank you all for this honorary degree. It will be a light of encouragement to all Totonacs. If I can have this happen to me—a boy who grew up in an isolated mountain village—it can also happen to anyone who wants to become an instrument for God.

This concern to be an "instrument for God" and to minister to the Totonacs' spiritual, physical and political needs is a propelling motivation for Manuel and the reason why he has worked long and hard to see his dreams realized. The New Testament law of loving others also motivates his response to the needs of his neighbors. This was evidenced in the lives of nine Totonac students who received tragic injuries during the Great Earthquake in Mexico City.

Three of the nine were young women about age nineteen. The other six were young lay preachers. The women had come to Mexico City to shop for school supplies and other items for the highland schools where they would be teaching. The six young lay preachers had also come to shop and see the sights. On the evening before the earthquake, the nine got together for a reunion at a local restaurant. Afterward, they returned to their respective hotels, planning to return home the next morning. None did.

The earthquake killed over ten thousand, maimed thousands more, including the nine Totonac young people. The men lost arms and hands, two of the girls lost a leg, the other an arm.

When Manuel heard about this tragedy, he immediately contacted several doctor friends in Germany and asked them to help supply the necessary prostheses for the former students. Said Manuel: "The Lord sent the money for these artificial limbs and the young people are undergoing rehabilitation in a Mexico City hospital. In spite of their terrible accidents, they are strong and healthy and the young women have a desire to return to teach school in the highlands. But they have two problems. The village where these girls come from has steep, rough, uneven trails, making walking extremely difficult.* The other problem is marriage. Totonac men never marry women who are maimed. But I am praying that God will work in the hearts of some young men who will be willing to marry these nice girls."

The tragic Mexico City earthquake occurred at 7:19 a.m., Thursday, September 19, 1985. I was to rendezvous with two dentists, Ralph Swenby and Bill Johnson from Minneapolis/St. Paul and Manuel at his Mexico City hotel on the twentieth. The news reaching me in Los Angeles, however, was that the Mexico City airport was closed. Accordingly, I postponed my trip until the following Monday but was unable to notify Manuel. After waiting in vain for me to arrive, Manuel and the two dentists went for dinner at one of Manuel's favorite restaurants. In the middle of their dinner, Mexico City experienced a forceful aftershock. Later, Ralph and Bill told me how Manuel and the people in the restaurant reacted.

"When the people in the restaurant realized they

---

* As this book goes to press, both young women have been fitted with artificial limbs and are teaching school in the lowlands where there is smooth, flat land.

were in the middle of another earthquake, pandemonium broke loose. People tumbled over one another and ran screaming from their tables, abandoning half-eaten meals. Cooks and waiters leaped over the counter and fled the building along with the customers. The only one who seemed calm and unperturbed was Manuel. He stood up and walked toward a thick supporting pillar. Then just as calm as if he had been drinking a cup of coffee said, 'Isn't it great that God is in control?' "

Later that night when the three returned to the hotel, one of the clerks, a friend of Manuel's said, "I don't think it is safe for you to go back up to your room, Manuel. The hotel might collapse. Let me give you a mattress and blanket and you can sleep here in the lobby."

Again perfectly calm, Manuel said, "I am not going to worry. God is in control. When we trust the Lord, He knows his own. Just like we read in the Scriptures, the Lord knows the sheep that are his and He calls each one by name. Since God knows his own children and since we claim to be his children, we can trust Him even unto death. If God chooses, I could die sleeping right beside you here on the floor. I am very tired and tomorrow I have many things to do. Tonight I need my sleep. Now I will say good night and I will see you in the morning."

Ralph and Bill also told me about another guest in the hotel who tried to get a flight out of Mexico City but couldn't. With no other choice but to spend the night in the hotel, the man said, "There is no way I am going back up to one of those rooms. I'm sleeping on the floor next to the front door. At least I'll have a chance to get out quickly if something happens."

As I thought about Manuel standing in that hotel lobby quietly and confidently witnessing to the inner faith and confidence he has in God, it struck me that in this thumbnail drama, the quintessence of his character and mandate was never more perfectly illustrated. Truly his life has been the embodiment of the simple words he spoke in 1968 at the commencement of his dreams for the Totonac people:

Everything I have done in the past and everything I want to do in the future is designed to help people. The most important thing I can do is to give them God's Word and have them come to faith in Jesus Christ.

Afterword

No story about Manuel Arenas would be complete without some word about Herman and Bessie Aschmann. After Herman completed the highland Totonac New Testament in 1952, he immediately set out to encourage a habit of reading among the many beginning Totonac readers. He and Besssie did this by preparing a series of reading helps that included phrase booklets, a Totonac-Spanish dictionary and other reading materials. "I wanted to help the new literates and those interested in learning to read to realize that reading was not an insurmountable task," said Herman.

Besides the highland Totonac New Testament that has had three reprints, Herman, with the efficient help of several intelligent and highly motivated Totonac co-translators, has translated two additional Totonac New Testaments. These are currently serving the lowland Papantla area and two other Totonac dialectical areas. For a team to complete one translation in a lifetime is considered a formidable achievement but three New Testaments in a lifetime is an amazing feat of discipline, skill and dogged determination.

In keeping with Jesus' New Testament practice of discipling, Herman and Bessie have given shape, substance, inspiration and encouragement to a number of Totonac young men who have worked with them on translation projects. Manuel, of course, was one of the first. In his case, as in most discipling relationships, a rich and rewarding friendship has resulted. Felipe was another of those to whom the Aschmanns gave themselves in a discipling-friendship role. And then came a young man named Florencio.

Said Herman: "Florencio was a born writer. He knew instinctively what was needed in the translation. Besides his skill as a translator, he was an active and energetic witness for the Lord. We spent many happy hours going from village to village and town to town selling Gospels and dictionaries."

For several years through newsletters, Herman and Bessie kept their friends informed of what was happening with Florencio and the Papantla translation project. Then one day the Aschmanns' friends received the following newsletter:

"Florencio is dead!"

This is a hard letter to write, but we wanted you to know right away. Our beloved Florencio was attacked and killed on Tuesday evening! He had gone to a nearby village to help a friend. As evening fell on the path he took back to the highway, he was waylaid, savagely beaten and stoned to death.

When I received the news, my mind refused to think for a few seconds, then came overwhelming grief. I wasn't thinking of the New Testament not quite finished, the fun of working with a genius—that enthusiastic young life so full of promise and joy as it grew in Christ. . . . No, I was just completely overcome by my own sense of acute, personal loss. How could we suddenly lose someone who could love us like Florencio! There were still so many intimate feelings to share. When we shared our faith in Christ with him, it was never anything shallow. He could open up his innermost being to us, and this freed us to do the same. Never have we seen anyone drink so deeply and freely of the saving grace of God in Christ as he. The tenderness with which he expressed his appreciation that we were God's instruments in showing him the Way seemed like something God Himself wanted us to know. That he could understand and appreciate that freeing love of God has shown up in the way he has translated God's Word so that others would know it, too. He was so much a part of us, and now he is gone!

At the wake, we found so many who knew and appreciated what Florencio had been doing and yet so many who did not understand. The usual neighbors came and went with food, some to just sit and talk, and still others, who knew how to recite Spanish prayers for the dead, would chant for him. He was already fully enjoying what they so much wanted for him but were trying to get in the wrong way.

While we were on the highway traveling to Papantla, Bessie and I had reworked two of the highland Totonac hymns. It wasn't much, just a few stanzas. When Bessie sang "This World is Not my Home," tears ran down many faces. Later one of the men asked us both to come to the casket and sing together because "these songs are in our language." We sang "When the Roll is Called Up Yonder."

Where do we go from here? Who will help us to finish the remaining work on the New Testament in Lowland Totonac that Florencio left undone? We talked with a few who have been using the five printed books already published as to whether they would like to help. We were encouraged by what they said. Pray for us please, as we feel our way and try to be patient as God works out his plan for this. We're hurting but know much good will come from this!

Appreciating your love and concern,
(Signed) Bessie and Herman Aschmann

In 1983, seven years after that incident, Herman and Bessie moved from Old Mexico to take up residence at a newly constructed Mexico SIL Center in Tucson, Arizona. In a newsletter, they explained the changes in their life-style and residency and also told of a trip Herman made to visit the Totonacs.

While Bessie disposed of our worldly possessions in Mexico City, I took off to the mountains of Totonac land. I found that at age sixty-nine, my legs are no longer as trailworthy as they once were. It was a worthwhile trip. I visited old friends and translation helpers of previous years and learned how the Gospel was spreading and how the translations are being used. I had a wonderful visit with Manuel at the Totonac Cultural Center. And I had an opportunity to visit Felipe and see the good work he is doing with the radio programs. It was into Felipe's and Manuel's dialect of Totonac that we translated the first New Testament. I was encouraged to learn that the third edition of the New Testament as well as other printed materials are selling well.

Next I went to Papantla (the area where Florencio was killed). I visited with Natalio, our principal distributor of the second New Testament. I took with me the last 2,000 copies of the New Testament that were printed.

(When Herman revisited Natalio a year later, all but fifty copies had been sold. Natalio told Herman the New Testament was still much sought-after and that he was holding on to these last copies to sell them to special people who "might be the hungriest and appreciate them the most." Herman thought it was a good idea.)

Herman and Bessie's newsletter also told of the good news that José, the brother of Florencio, had taken up where his brother had left off and he had completed the Papantla New Testament.

Both Herman and Manuel are men of the New Testament. Both have poured their strength and resources into the things that have brought glory to God. And because their service to God has eternal value, both have a continuing story.

For more information concerning the Totonac Cultural Center and Manuel's ministry, write to:

Totonac Center
P.O. Box 2050
Orange, CA 92669